Jeffrey S. Bullington
Beatrice L. Caraway
Beverley Geer
Editors

Head in the Clouds, Feet on the Ground: Serials Vision and Common Sense

Head in the Clouds, Feet on the Ground: Serials Vision and Common Sense has been co-published simultaneously as *The Serials Librarian,* Volume 36, Numbers 1/2 and 3/4 1999.

Pre-publication REVIEWS, COMMENTARIES, EVALUATIONS . . .

"*T*he themes covered in *Head in the Clouds, Feet on the Ground* reflect the interdepartmental impact on a library enterprise of serials in an electronic world. An essential reference guide for libraries embracing electronic resources access, the collection covers every aspect of e-resource management. . . .

This book enables the reader to go to each and every NASIG session and to digest and put to practical use, now and for years to come, the common-sense advice and speculations of renowned serialists–all in the comfort of your office or home!"

Mary Curran, MA, MLS
Coordinator, Bibliographic Standards
University of Ottawa

HEAD IN THE CLOUDS, FEET ON THE GROUND: SERIALS VISION AND COMMON SENSE

Proceedings of the NORTH AMERICAN SERIALS INTEREST GROUP, Inc.

**13th Annual Conference
June 18-21, 1998
University of Colorado
Boulder, Colorado**

Head in the Clouds, Feet on the Ground: Serials Vision and Common Sense has been co-published simultaneously as *The Serials Librarian,* Volume 36, Numbers 1/2 and 3/4 1999.

The Serials Librarian Monographic "Separates"

Below is a list of "separates," which in serials librarianship means a special issue simultaneously published as a special journal issue or double-issue *and* as a "separate" hardbound monograph. (This is a format which we also call a "Docuserial.")

"Separates" are published because specialized libraries or professionals may wish to purchase a specific thematic issue by itself in a format which can be separately cataloged and shelved, as opposed to purchasing the journal on an on-going basis. Faculty members may also more easily consider a "separate" for classroom adoption.

"Separates" are carefully classified separately with the major book jobbers so that the journal tie-in can be noted on new book order slips to avoid duplicate purchasing.

You may wish to visit Haworth's Website at . . .

http://www.haworthpressinc.com

. . . to search our online catalog for complete tables of contents of these separates and related publications.

You may also call 1-800-HAWORTH (outside US/Canada: 607-722-5857), or Fax 1-800-895-0582 (outside US/Canada: 607-771-0012), or e-mail at:

getinfo@haworthpressinc.com

Women's Studies Serials: A Quarter-Century of Development, edited by Kristin H. Gerhard, MA, MLS (Vol. 35, No. 1/2, 1998). *"Candidly explores and analyzes issues which must be addressed to ensure the continued growth and vitality of women's studies. . . . It commands the attention of librarians, scholars, and publishers. (Joan Ariel, MIS, MA, Women's Studies Librarian and Lecturer, University of California at Irvine)*

E-Serials: Publishers, Libraries, Users, and Standards, edited by Wayne Jones, MA, MLS (Vol. 33, No. 1/2/3/4, 1998). *"Libraries and publishers will find this book helpful in developing strategies, policies, and procedures." (Nancy Brodie, National Library of Canada, Ottawa, Ontario)*

Serials Cataloging at the Turn of the Century, edited by Jeanne M. K. Boydston, MSLIS, James W. Williams, MSLS, and Jim Cole, MLS (Vol. 32, No. 1/2, 1997). *Focuses on the currently evolving trends in serials cataloging in order to predict and explore the possibilities for the field in the new millennium.*

Serials Management in the Electronic Era: Papers in Honor of Peter Gellatly, Founding Editor of The Serials Librarian, edited by Jim Cole, MA, and James W. Williams, MLS (Vol. 29, No. 3/4, 1996). *Assesses progress and technical changes in the field of serials management and anticipates future directions and challenges for librarians.*

Special Format Serials and Issues: Annual Review of . . . , Advances in . . . , Symposia on . . . , Methods in . . . , by Tony Stankus, MLS (Vol. 27, No. 2/3, 1996). *A thorough and lively introduction to the nature of these publications types.*

Serials Canada: Aspects of Serials Work in Canadian Libraries, edited by Wayne Jones, MLS (Vol. 26, No. 3/4, 1996). *"An excellent addition to the library literature and is recommended for all library school libraries, scholars, and students of comparative/international librarianship." (Library Times International)*

Serials Cataloging: Modern Perspectives and International!Developments, edited by Jim E. Cole, MA, and James W. Williams, MSLS (Vol. 22, No. 1/2/3/4, 1993). *"A significant contribution to* *understanding the 'big picture' of serials control. . . . A solid presentation of serious issues in a crucial area on librarianship."* (Bimonthly Review of Law Books)

Making Sense of Journals in the Life Sciences: From Specialty Origins to Contemporary Assortment, by Tony Stankus (Supp. #08, 1992, 1996). *"An excellent introduction to scientific periodical literature and the disciplines it serves."* (College & Research Libraries News)

Making Sense of Journals in the Physical Sciences: From Specialty Origins to Contemporary Assortment, by Tony Stankus, MLS (Supp. #07, 1992, 1996). *"A Tour de force . . . It will immeasurably help science serials librarians to select journal titles on a rational and defensible basis, and the methodology used can be extended over time and to other fields and other journals."* (International Journal of Information and Library Research)

The Good Serials Department, edited by Peter Gellatly (Vol. 19, No. 1/2, 1991). *"This is recommended for library educators, students, and serials specialists. It should be useful both to novices and veterans."* (Journal of Academic Librarianship)

Scientific Journals: Improving Library Collections Through Analysis of Publishing Trends, by Tony Stankus, MLS (Supp. #6, 1990). *"Will be of great value to science librarians in academic, industrial, and governmental libraries as well as to scientists and professors facing problems in choosing the most economical and useful journals for library collections."* (American Scientist)

Implementing Online Union Lists of Serials: The Pennsylvania Union List of Serials Experience, edited by Ruth C. Carter, MA, MS, PhD, and James D. Hooks, PhD, MLS (Supp. #05, 1989). *"This practical and very readable book provides not only a useful guide to the development and use of online union lists, but also a fine example of library co-operation and hard work."* (Library Association Record)

Newspapers in the Library: New Approaches to Management and Reference Work, edited by Lois Upham, PhD, MSLS (Supp. #04, 1988). *"Lively varied and written with good sense and enthusiasm. Recommended for those working in or administering newspaper collections for the first time, and also those who, immersed in the problems of this seemingly intractable material, need the inspiration of solutions devised by others."* (Riverina Library Review)

Scientific Journals: Issues in Library Selection and Management, by Tony Stankus, MLS (Supp. #3, 1988). *"This book has significance for those for those who select scientific journals for library collections and for the primary users and producers of the literature as well. More works of this type are needed."* (American Reference Books Annual)

Libraries and Subscription Agencies: Interactions and Innovations, edited by Peter Gellatly (Vol. 14, No. 3/4, 1988). *"Put[s] developments in context and provide[s] useful background information and advice for those contemplating implementation of automation in this area."* (Library Association Record)

Serials Cataloging: The State of the Art, edited by Jim E. Cole, MA, and Jackie Zajanc (Vol. 12, No. 1/2, 1987). *"Really does cover an amazingly broad span of serials cataloging topics . . . Well worth its purchase price."* (Lois N. Upham, PhD, Assistant Professor, College of Library and Information Science, University of South Carolina)

Serial Connections: People, Information, and Communication, edited by Leigh Chatterton, MLS, and Mary Elizabeth Clack, MS (Vol. 11, No. 3/4, 1987). *"The essays are uniformly lively and provide excellent overviews of the aspects of serials control, from acquisition to automation."* (Academic Library Book Review)

Serials Librarianship in Transition: Issues and Development, edited by Peter Gellatly (Vol. 10, No. 1/2, 1986) *"Well-written and tightly edited . . . Specialists in the 'serials chain' and students interested in serials librarianship should give this book top priority in their professional reading lists."* (Library and Information Science Annual)

The Management of Serials Automation: Current Technology and Strategies for Future Planning, edited by Peter Gellatly (Supp. #2, 1984). *"A thoroughly documented review of the* *progress and problems in serials automation strategy and technology." (Information Retrieval & Library Automation)*

Union Catalogues of Serials: Guidelines for Creation and Maintenance, with Recommended Standards for Bibliographic and Holdings Control, by Jean Whiffin, BA, BLS (Vol. 8, No. 1, 1983). *"A clearly written and easily read set of guidelines . . . Recommended for library science collections. Essential where union catalogs are contemplated." (Public Libraries)*

Serials Librarianship as an Art: Essays in Honor of Andrew D. Osborn, edited by Peter Gellatly (Vol. 6, No. 2/3, 1982). *An exploration of the advantages and excellences of the manual check-in operation versus automation.*

Sex Magazines in the Library Collection: A Scholarly Study of Sex in Serials and Periodicals, edited by Peter Gellatly (Supp. #01, 1981). *"Recommended for librarians with collections that include sex periodicals, as well as for those librarians who haven't quite made up their minds and are looking for more background information." (Technicalities)*

The North American Serials Interest Group (NASIG) Series

Head in the Clouds, Feet on the Ground: Serials Vision and Common Sense, edited by Jeffrey S. Bullington, Beatrice L. Caraway, and Beverley Geer (Vol. 36, No. 1/2/3/4, 1999)

Experimentation and Collaboration: Creating Serials for a New Millennium, Charlene N. Simser and Michael A. Somers (Vol. 34, No. 1/2/3/4, 1998). *Gives valuable ideas and practical advice that you can apply or incorporate into your own area of expertise.*

Pioneering New Serials Frontiers: From Petroglyphs to Cyberserials, edited by Christine Christiansen and Cecilia Leathem (Vol. 30, No. 3/4, and Vol. 31, No. 1/2, 1997). *Gives you insight, ideas, and practical skills for dealing with the changing world of serials management.*

Serials to the Tenth Power: Traditions, Technology, and Transformation, edited by Mary Ann Sheble, MLS, and Beth Holley, MLS (Vol. 28, No. 1/2/3/4, 1996). *Provides readers with practical ideas on managing the challenges of the electronic information environment.*

A Kaleidoscope of Choices: Reshaping Roles and Opportunities for Serialists, edited by Beth Holley, MLS, and Mary Ann Sheble, MLS (Vol. 25, No. 3/4, 1995). *"Highly recommended as an excellent source material for all librarians interested in learning more about the Internet; technology and its effect on library organization and operations, and the virtual library." (Library Acquisitions: Practice & Theory)*

New Scholarship: New Serials: Proceedings of the North American Serials Interest Group, Inc., edited by Gail McMillan and Marilyn Norstedt (Vol. 24, No. 3/4, 1994) *"An excellent representation of the ever-changing, complicated, and exciting world of serials." (Library Acquisitions Practice & Theory)*

If We Build It: Scholarly Communications and Networking Technologies: Proceedings of the North American Serials Interest Group, Inc., edited by Suzanne McMahon, MLS, Miriam Palm, MLS, and Pamela Dunn, BA (Vol. 23, No. 3/4, 1993). *"Highly recommended to anyone interested in the academic serials environment as a means of keeping track of the electronic revolution and the new possibilities emerging." (ASL (Australian Special Libraries))*

A Changing World: Proceedings of the North American Serials Interest Group, Inc., edited by Suzanne McMahon, MLS, Miriam Palm, MLS, and Pamela Dunn, BA (Vol. 21, No. 2/3, 1992).

"A worthy publication for anyone interested in the current and future trends of serials control and electronic publishing." (Library Resources & Technical Services)

The Future of Serials: Proceedings of the North American Serials Interest Group, Inc., edited by Patricia Ohl Rice, PHD, MLS, and Jane A. Robillard, MLS *(Vol. 19, No. 3/4, 1991).* *"A worthwhile addition to any library studies collection, or a serials librarian's working library . . . I would recommend separate purchase of the monograph. NASIG plays too important a role in the serials universe to ignore any of its published proceedings." (Library Acquisitions: Practice & Theory)*

The Serials Partnership: Teamwork, Technology, and Trends, edited by Patricia Ohl Rice, PhD, MLS, and Joyce L. Ogburn, MSLS, MA (Vol. 17, No. 3/4. 1990). *In this forum scholars, publishers, vendors, and librarians share in discussing issues of common concern.*

Serials Information from Publisher to User: Practice, Programs, and Progress, edited by Leigh A. Chatterton, MLS, and Mary Elizabeth Clack, MLS (Vol. 15, No. 3/4, 1988) *"[E]xcellent reference tools for years to come." (Gail McMillan, MIS, MA, Serials Team Leader, University Libraries, Virginia Polytechnic Institute and State University)*

The Serials Information Chain: Discussion, Debate, and Dialog, edited by Leigh Chatterton, MLS, and Mary Elizabeth Clack, MLS (Vol. 13, No. 2/3, 1988). *"It contains enlightening information for libraries or businesses in which serials are a major concern." (Library Resources & Technical Services)*

*Head in the Clouds, Feet on the Ground: Serials Vision
and Common Sense* has been co-published simultaneously as *The
Serials Librarian,* Volume 36, Numbers 1/2 and 3/4 1999.

The development, preparation, and publication of this work has been undertaken with great care. However, the publisher, employees, editors, and agents of The Haworth Press and all imprints of The Haworth Press, Inc., including The Haworth Medical Press® and Pharmaceutical Products Press®, are not responsible for any errors contained herein or for consequences that may ensue from use of materials or information contained in this work. Opinions expressed by the author(s) are not necessarily those of The Haworth Press, Inc.

Cover design by Thomas J. Mayshock Jr.

Library of Congress Cataloging-in-Publication Data

North American Serials Interest Group. Conference (13th : 1998 : University of Colorado)
    Head in the clouds, feet on the ground : serials vision and common sense : proceedings of the North American Serials Interest Group, Inc. : 13th Annual Conference, June 18-21, 1998, University of Colorado, Boulder, Colorado / Jeffrey S. Bullington, Beatrice L. Caraway, Beverley Geer, editors.
       p. cm.
    "Has been co-published simultaneously as The Serials Librarian, volume 36, numbers 1/2 and 3/4 1999"–T.p. verso.
    Includes bibliographical references and index.
    ISBN 0-7890-0768-1 (alk. paper).
    1. Serials librarianship–United States Congresses. 2. Serials librarianship–Canada Congresses. I. Bullington, Jeffrey S. II. Caraway, Beatrice L., 1953- . III. Geer, Beverley, 1951- . IV. Serials librarian. V. Title.
Z692.S5N67 1998
025.3′432–dc21
                                         99-25066
                                             CIP

HEAD IN THE CLOUDS,
FEET ON THE GROUND:
SERIALS VISION AND COMMON SENSE

Proceedings of the
NORTH AMERICAN SERIALS
INTEREST GROUP, Inc.

**13th Annual Conference
June 18-21, 1998
University of Colorado
Boulder, Colorado**

Jeffrey S. Bullington
Beatrice L. Caraway
Beverley Geer
Editors

The Haworth Information Press
An Imprint of
The Haworth Press, Inc.
New York • London • Oxford

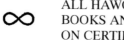

IN MEMORIAM

ELAINE K. RAST
(1933-1999)

These proceedings are dedicated to the memory of Elaine K. Rast, who died of cancer February 12, 1999. Elaine was one of NASIG's staunchest and earliest supporters, having attended every conference (1986-1997) except for the Boulder conference. She served in numerous capacities within NASIG, most recently as our first Archivist. She also served on the Bylaws Committee and as Board Member-At-Large from 1988-1993. She retired as Head of the Cataloging and Automated Records Department at Northern Illinois University in June 1996 after 26 years of service. Elaine was a wonderful mentor to many young librarians who benefited from her experience and personal welcome to the profession. She was always gracious, kind, attentive, and caring, with an incredible energy and enthusiasm for life. Her many friends and colleagues will truly miss her strength of character, her giving spirit and her witty outlook on life. NASIG is very fortunate to have reaped the benefits of her service to the organization.

INDEXING & ABSTRACTING

Contributions to this publication are selectively indexed or abstracted in print, electronic, online, or CD-ROM version(s) of the reference tools and information services listed below. This list is current as of the copyright date of this publication. See the end of this section for additional notes.

- *Academic Abstracts/CD-ROM*

- *Academic Search: database of 2,000 selected academic serials, updated monthly*

- *BUBL Information Service: An Internet-based information service for the UK higher education community.*

- *Cambridge Scientific Abstracts*

- *Chemical Abstracts*

- *CINAHL (Cumulative Index to Nursing & Allied Health Literature), in print, also on CD-ROM from CD PLUS, EBSCO, and Silver-Platter, and online from CDP Online (fomerly BRS), Data-Star, and PaperChase. (Support materials include Subject Heading List, Database Search Guide, and instructional video.)*

- *CNPIEC Reference Guide: Chinese National Directory of Foreign Periodicals*

- *Current Awareness Abstracts of Library & Information Management Literature, ASLIB (UK)*

- *Current Contents: Clinical Medicine/Life Sciences (CC: CM/LS) Weekly Table of Contents Service), and Social Science Citation Index. Articles also searchable through Social SciSearch, ISI's online database and in ISI's Research Alert current awareness service*

- *Current Literature Section: Newsletter of the Health Libraries Group*

- *Hein's Legal Periodical Checklist: Index to Periodical Articles Pertaining to Law*

(continued)

- *IBZ International Bibliography of Periodical Literature*

- *Index to Periodical Articles Related to Law*

- *Information Reports & Bibliographies*

- *Information Science Abstracts*

- *Informed Librarian, The*

- *Journal of Academic Librarianship: Guide to Professional Literature, The*

- *Konyvtari Figyelo-Library Review*

- *Library & Information Science Abstracts (LISA)*

- *Library and Information Science Annual (LISCA)*

- *Library Digest*

- *Library Literature*

- *MasterFILE: updated database from EBSCO Publishing*

- *Newsletter of Library and Information Services*

- *PASCAL, c/o Institute de L' Information Scientifique et Technique*

- *Periodica Islamica*

- *Referativnyi Zhurnal (Abstracts Journal of the All-Russian Institute of Scientific and Technical Information)*

- *Sociological Abstracts (SA)*

(continued)

Special Bibliographic Notes related to special journal issues
(separates) and indexing/abstracting:

- indexing/abstracting services in this list will also cover material in any "separate" that is co-published simultaneously with Haworth's special thematic journal issue or DocuSerial. Indexing/abstracting usually covers material at the article/chapter level.
- monographic co-editions are intended for either non-subscribers or libraries which intend to purchase a second copy for their circulating collections.
- monographic co-editions are reported to all jobbers/wholesalers/approval plans. The source journal is listed as the "series" to assist the prevention of duplicate purchasing in the same manner utilized for books-in-series.
- to facilitate user/access services all indexing/abstracting services are encouraged to utilize the co-indexing entry note indicated at the bottom of the first page of each article/chapter/contribution.
- this is intended to assist a library user of any reference tool (whether print, electronic, online, or CD-ROM) to locate the monographic version if the library has purchased this version but not a subscription to the source journal.
- individual articles/chapters in any Haworth publication are also available through the Haworth Document Delivery Service (HDDS).

NASIG Officers and Executive Board

1997/1998

Officers:

Susan Davis, President, State University of New York at Buffalo
Steve Oberg, Vice-President/President-Elect, University of Chicago
Connie Foster, Secretary, Western Kentucky University
Geraldine Williams, Treasurer, Northern Kentucky University
Beverley Geer, Past President, Trinity University

Executive Board:

Jean Callaghan, Wheaton College
Eleanor Cook, Appalachian State University
Carol Pitts Diedrichs, Ohio State University
Ann Ercelawn, Vanderbilt University
Jim Mouw, University of Chicago
Fran Wilkinson, University of New Mexico

1998 Program Planning Committee

Plenary and Concurrent Sessions:

Ladd Brown, Virginia Tech

Cecilia Leathem, University of Miami

Judy Luther, Co-Chair, Informed Strategies

Michael Markwith, Co-Chair Swets & Zeitlinger

Mary Page, Rutgers University

Bob Persing, University of Pennsylvania

Workshops:

Whitney Alexander, Innovative Interfaces

Jos Anemaet, Oregon State University

Rita Broadway, University of Memphis

Sandy Gurshman, Information Quest

Margaret Mering, University of Nebraska

Marjorie Wilhite, Co-Chair, University of Iowa

Carol Pitts Diedrichs, Board Liaison, Ohio State University

Fritz Schwartz Serials Education Scholarship

Michael A. Brown, University of New Mexico

NASIG
Student Conference Grant Award Recipients

Mariya I. Barash, Wayne State University

Valorie Huynh, University of Maryland, College Park

Carrie McLean, North Carolina Central University

Allan Scherlen, University of North Carolina at Greensboro

Michele Seikel, San Jose State University

Sherry Souliere, Simmons College

Jeffrey A. Steely, University of Texas at Austin

Laura Turner, University of Texas at Austin

Melody Wendland, Emporia State University

Horizon Award Winners

Beth Jedlicka, University of Georgia

Yumin Jiang, Cornell University

Jie Tian, California State University, Fullerton

ABOUT THE EDITORS

Jeffrey S. Bullington, formerly Social Sciences Librarian at Trinity University in San Antonio, Texas, is now Social Sciences Librarian and Bibliographer at the University of Kansas. He is a 1996 graduate of the Graduate School of Library and Information Science at the University of Illinois at Urbana-Champaign. His first publication, co-authored with Priscilla Shontz, is "Tips for New Librarians: What to know in the first year of a tenure-track position," *College and Research Libraries News*, v. 59, no. 2 (February 1998): 85-88.

Beatrice L. Caraway is Serials Cataloger at Coates Library, Trinity University, San Antonio, Texas. Bea is Past-Chair of the NASIG Evaluation and Assessment Committee and helped plan the NASIG conference held at Trinity in 1991. She is active in the Serials Section of the Association for Library Collections and Technical Services. With Beverley Geer, she edits the "Serials Report" column in *The Serials Librarian*. The two recently collaborated to revise *Notes for Serials Cataloging*, second edition.

Beverley Geer is Head Cataloger at Coates Library, Trinity University in San Antonio, Texas. Beverley is a past president of NASIG and is currently Vice-Chair/Chair-Elect of the Serials Section, Association for Library Collections and Technical Services, American Library Association. She is Associate Editor of *Serials Review* and co-editor of the "Serials Report" column in *The Serials Librarian*. Her most recent published work is *Notes for Serials Cataloging*, second edition, which she co-edited with Beatrice L. Caraway.

Head in the Clouds, Feet on the Ground: Serials Vision and Common Sense

CONTENTS

Introduction

The theme for the North American Serials Interest Group's (NA-SIG) thirteenth annual conference was "Head in the Clouds, Feet on the Ground: Serials Vision and Common Sense." The conference was held June 18-21, 1998, at the University of Colorado at Boulder and attracted nearly 700 serialists from the United States, Canada, Mexico, Australia, and Europe.

This year's conference began with two well-attended preconferences, one on developing leadership skills and the other on the various aspects of HTML.

The three plenary sessions provided attendees both vision and common sense. The opening session, an update on Internet publishing, assessed the impact that changes in publishing technology have had on libraries. The second session described how electronic publishing and the changing market have affected intellectual property rights. The final session left attendees with many practical insights on information delivery and use trends that will affect higher education, libraries and publishing.

The concurrent sessions covered the landscape, offering vision as well as common sense advice and practical methods for getting our jobs done. Two of the sessions addressed evaluative criteria, one for online resources and the other for new library services. Consortial acquisitions was addressed, as were archiving and continued access. Also among the topics were age-old but ever pertinent topics such as disaster prepardedness and the pricing of scientific, technical and medical publications. Rounding off the group were sessions on main-

---

[Haworth co-indexing entry note]: "Introduction." Bullington, Jeffrey S., Beatrice L. Caraway, and Beverley Geer. Co-published simultaneously in *The Serials Librarian* (The Haworth Press, Inc.) Vol. 36, No. 1/2, 1999, pp. 1-2; and: *Head in the Clouds, Feet on the Ground: Serials Vision and Common Sense* (ed: Jeffrey S. Bullington, Beatrice L. Caraway, and Beverley Geer) The Haworth Press, Inc., 1999, pp. 1-2. Single or multiple copies of this article are available for a fee from The Haworth Document Delivery Service [1-800-342-9678, 9:00 a.m. - 5:00 p.m. (EST). E-mail address: getinfo@haworthpressinc.com].

taining perspective when approaching processing of electronic and other "different" materials, on building relationships between computer centers and libraries, and on new trends in fulfillment services.

Twenty workshops focused on a variety of issues, including the need for and application of standards, webpage development, the future of holdings, access to government serial information, staff training for system migration, case studies of web-based journals, sharing an automation project among libraries of very different types, and, of course, the ever-changing and developing world of serials cataloging.

This volume includes papers from the plenary and concurrent sessions, as well as summary reports for the preconferences and the conference workshops. Each session, each workshop was practical and informative, and each presented ideas or practical advice that many readers may apply or incorporate into their own areas of expertise. We hope readers will gain vision and common sense from every word.

We, the editors, would like to extend our gratitude to Eleanor Cook and Ann Ercelawn, our NASIG Board liaisons, for guiding us through the editorial process, and to the entire NASIG Board for their wholehearted encouragement. We owe a great debt to the Program Planning and Conference Planning Committees for the superb job they did putting the conference together. Our sincere appreciation goes to all the volunteers who recorded the preconferences and workshops. Lastly, we thank the Coates Library administration for their support.

See you in Pittsburgh!!

Jeffrey S. Bullington
Beatrice L. Caraway
Beverley Geer
Trinity University
September 1998

PRECONFERENCE PROGRAMS

PRECONFERENCE:
LEADING FROM ANY POSITION:
AN ENNEAGRAM WORKSHOP
PREPARING LEADERS
FOR THE 21st CENTURY

Leading from Any Position:
An Enneagram Workshop
Preparing Leaders for the 21st Century

John Shannon
Becky Schreiber

Presenters

Cheryl Riley

Recorder

John Shannon and Becky Schreiber are Organizational Change Consultants, Schreiber Shannon Associates.

Cheryl Riley is Head, Cataloging Services, Central Missouri State University.

[Haworth co-indexing entry note]: "Leading from Any Position: An Enneagram Workshop Preparing Leaders for the 21st Century." Riley, Cheryl. Co-published simultaneously in *The Serials Librarian* (The Haworth Press, Inc.) Vol. 36, No. 1/2, 1999, pp. 5-13; and: *Head in the Clouds, Feet on the Ground: Serials Vision and Common Sense* (ed: Jeffrey S. Bullington, Beatrice L. Caraway, and Beverley Geer) The Haworth Press, Inc., 1999, pp. 5-13. Single or multiple copies of this article are available for a fee from The Haworth Document Delivery Service [1-800-342-9678, 9:00 a.m. - 5:00 p.m. (EST). E-mail address: getinfo@ haworthpressinc.com].

SUMMARY. The Enneagram is a nine-point personality model focused on personal development. Workshop participants took the Riso Hudson Enneagram Type Instrument (RHETI) prior to attending the workshop and brought their scores as a beginning point for working with the model. Among the questions answered during the workshop were: What life experiences (stories) confirm that I am in the correct group? What is our preferred communication style? What leadership attributes are best expressed by our type? What are our leadership challenges? How can we develop our leadership capabilities? *[Article copies available for a fee from The Haworth Document Delivery Service: 1-800-342-9678. E-mail address: getinfo@ haworthpressinc.com]*

The husband-and-wife team of John Shannon and Becky Schreiber have each been providing consulting services for over twenty years, and they have been partners in Schreiber Shannon Associates since 1983. Both are experienced workshop developers and facilitators. John received his M.S. in Applied Behavioral Sciences from Johns Hopkins University and his B.S. from the University of Dayton. Becky has an M.Ed. in Counseling from The American University and a B.S. from Hood College. Both are members of National Training Laboratories and serve as faculty for NTL. John and Becky designed the annual Snowbird and Australian Aurora Leadership Institutes, which they present together. These institutes focus on leadership in large systems change. Both John and Becky are skilled in guiding organizations in change management and leadership development.

John and Becky began by distributing the *Enneagram Workbook* (1997) and then opened the workshop with a brief history of the Enneagram. The Enneagram is a nine-point personality model that is based in oral tradition and has a spiritual and philosophical basis. The Enneagram requires us to relate our life stories and use those stories to discover ourselves. The Enneagram emerged from Sufi tradition and the spiritual belief that an individual lives a life of goodness or sin. It has been used by the Jesuits in retreats for seminarians. In the last ten to fifteen years, the Enneagram has come into popular use, but it is still considered new to the business field. The focus of the Enneagram is on personal development. Unlike the Myers-Briggs, the Enneagram is not an exact science. The Enneagram instrument is approximately 85 percent valid. It is more complex than the Myers-Briggs because it explains not only the type of the individual, but also the differences among people. Individuals using the Enneagram should develop a broader sense of "who I am." According to John, the basic principle of the Enneagram is "know yourself first; fix yourself first." As an individual studies the Enneagram, one can understand how we block ourselves from being good leaders and how we can use the Enneagram to promote our ability to work with others and focus on positive, healthy interactions. According to John and Becky, "to understand others is useful, but to understand yourself is transformative." Although they have been working with the Enneagram for two to three years, John and Becky gain insight into the nine personality types each time they conduct Enneagram training. Workshop participants were requested to spend approximately twenty-five minutes taking the Riso Hudson Enneagram Type Instrument (RHETI) prior to attending the workshop (http://graphics.lcs.mit.edu/~becca/Enneagram/). Participants were requested to bring their scores with them so they would have a beginning number for working with the nine-point model (see Table 1).

After briefly introducing each of the nine types, John and Becky provided more detail about each type.

TYPE 1: REFORMER/PERFECTIONIST/ACHIEVER

Ones are perfectionists and are always striving for improvement. The gift of the one is discernment and a clear sense of right and wrong. The negative for the one is internal anger at others and self; it may be expressed as resentment. The one is almost always harder on self than others. The basic fear of the one is being condemned and the basic desire is to be right. Recommended reading for the one is *Principle Centered Leadership*, by Steven Covey.

TYPE 2: HELPER/GIVER

Twos tend to go out of their way to help others. They are compassionate, caring, very nurturing and generous. The world view of the two is "my love is enough to make the world go around." The gift of the two is sympathy and the negative side is "love has hooks." The basic fear of the two is being unloved and the basic desire is to be loved. Recommended reading for the two is *Servant Leadership*, by Robert Greenleaf.

TYPE 3: MOTIVATOR/PERFORMER/SUCCEEDER

Threes are the cheerleaders of the world. Threes are able to accomplish things. Threes are attractive and competent. The world view of the three is "image is everything." The gift of the three is efficacy and adaptability–they fit! The negative for the three is self-deceit. The basic fear of the three is rejection and the basic desire is to be accepted. Recommended reading for the three is *The Effective Executive*, by Peter Drucker.

TYPE 4: ARTIST/INDIVIDUALIST/TRAGIC ROMANTIC

The four is the emotionally sensitive individual who believes that something essential is missing and completeness can be achieved when the missing part is achieved. The four wants to be unique and celebrates that uniqueness. The positive for the four is being unique; the downside is envy. The basic fear of the four is being inadequate and the basic desire is self-actualization. Recommended reading for the four is *The Heart Aroused: Poetry and the Preservation of Soul in Corporate America*, by David Whyte.

TYPE 5: THINKER/OBSERVER/SAGE

The five is the thinker. The five wants to analyze and research a problem and needs lots of time to understand. The world view of the five is "knowledge will keep me safe." The gift of the five is detachment and the five's vice is avarice. The basic fear of the five is being threatened and the basic desire is to understand the world. Recommended reading for the five is *Crisis in Candyland*, by Jan Pottker.

TYPE 6: LOYALIST/TRADITIONALIST/DEVIL'S ADVOCATE

The six is faithful, committed and loyal. Sixes are able to get behind causes and leaders and have a tendency to take second-in-command types of jobs. They believe the world is a dangerous place and suspect everyone has a hidden agenda. The gift of the six is loyalty and an ability to plan and the negative is fear and doubt. The basic fear of the six is being abandoned and alone while the basic desire is security. Recommended reading for the six is *Managing*, by Andrew Grove.

TYPE 7: GENERALIST/EPICURE/ADVENTURER

The seven is the generalist. Sevens have broad interests and are excited about all the possibilities in the world. Many sevens are known as partyers. To the seven, life is an adventure and there are limitless possibilities. Many sevens have a tendency towards addictions. Their positive attribute is optimism and productivity; the negative tendency is gluttony. The basic fear is being deprived and the basic desire is to be happy and satisfied. Recommended reading for the seven is *Thriving on Chaos*, by Tom Peters.

TYPE 8: LEADER/BOSS/CONFRONTER/ASSENTER

Eights are leaders–those individuals who seem to come to control naturally. The eight is courageous, resourceful and action-oriented. The world view of the eight is "only the strong survive." The positive attribute for the eight is a tremendous strength and the negative is lust and strong appetites. The eight desires to be self-reliant and fears submitting to others. Recommended reading for the eight is *The Power Broker*, by Robert Caro.

TYPE 9: PEACEMAKER/MEDIATOR/PRESERVATIONIST

The nine is the peacemaker who is searching for harmony. The nines are so intuitive about others that sometimes they lose themselves. The world view for the nine is "go with the flow." The gift of the nine is acceptance and the negative side is sloth. The basic desire is to find union with others and the basic fear is separation from others. Recommended reading for the nine is *The Functions of the Executive*, by Chester Barnard.

THE SMALL GROUP ASSIGNMENT

After providing participants with the history of the Enneagram and detailing each of the nine personality types, workshop members were divided into small groups based on the RHETI score. If individuals or group members did not believe someone fit in the group, that person was encouraged to move to the group that represented their second-highest score on the instrument. If the individual felt this move was not correct, participants were instructed to use their intuition to choose a group. John and Becky reminded all participants that the Enneagram is an oral tradition and relies on discussion to further understand individual types. Each individual and each group was given the following questions to answer: What life experiences (stories) confirm that I am in the correct group? What is our preferred communication style? What leadership attributes are best expressed by our type? What are our leadership challenges? How can we develop our leadership capabilities? Both John and Becky joined the group that represented their individual types. After answering the assigned questions, each group was to report back to the entire workshop population.

REPORTS

Each group appointed someone to report the responses the group had agreed on. Each participant had a list of questions included in the workshop materials that John instructed them to complete as they listened to the group reports. Four questions were to be answered about each type: What is the basic motivation of this personality type? What is the leadership gift of this type? Who is someone I know that fits this type? What is the best way to approach an individual with this personality type?

TRANSFORMATION

Enneagram theory incorporates the principle that people visit each personality type in their lifetime. Transformation begins as each type grows into the healthier aspects of our type. The arrows in Figure 1 indicate the positive growth area for each of the nine types. (John cautioned participants about the process of evolving into the negative area for our personality type and indicated that it was inevitable there would be times when each of us would revert, but that the Enneagram could provide goals and directions for us).

TABLE 1. The Nine Personality Types of the Enneagram

The styles are:	What drives them is:
Ones: Reformers	being correct
Twos: Helpers	helping others
Threes: Motivators	working hard and succeeding
Fours: Artists	exploring their true feelings
Fives: Thinkers	objective information
Sixes: Loyalists	worrying about problems and hidden agendas
Sevens: Generalists	excitement, adventure, different experiences
Eights: Leaders	dominating
Nines: Peacemakers	empathizing; seeing all sides of an issue

FIGURE 1

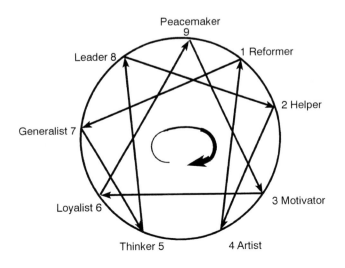

John and Becky recommend the works of Helen Palmer and Richard Riso for those interested in learning more about the Enneagram. Finally, John and Becky discussed the work of Ira Chaloff as an example of how to apply the Enneagram courageously. Chaloff's book *The Courageous Follower* is also recommended for further study. Chaloff identifies five dimensions of courage: the courage to assume responsibility, the courage to serve, the courage to challenge, the courage to participate in transformation, and the courage to leave. John and Becky suggested an individual should determine how to take action instead of complaining about others' faults, that we should do whatever needs to be done, and that we be willing to do anything to get the job done. A challenge of another's idea can only be effective if we have first been supportive, for without trust a challenge will not be considered. Individuals must work to improve organizations and to become a part of deciding what to change and what to keep. Finally, Chaloff suggests that if one cannot support the organization, the question of leaving the organization is appropriate.

RESPONSE TO THE WORKSHOP

Although the workshop ran long, every participant remained. I found this workshop to be a fascinating introduction to a useful personality model. It was interesting that of the approximately fifty participants, we had no fours, one five, and only two sevens. The largest group was the nines. The most helpful portion of the workshop for me occurred when each type identified how best to approach their type. The most difficult part of the workshop for me was trying to identify acquaintances that fit each type. The discussion at the beginning of the session indicated that, for most of us, answering the questions on the RHETI was difficult. Many participants felt they should take the instrument twice and answer once for business relationships and once for personal relationships. No group members were transferred to other groups in this workshop, so it would appear the instrument worked for most participants. Time constraints prevented discussion during the transformation portion of the workshop, but most participants were discussing the types throughout the conference.

BIBLIOGRAPHY

Goldberg, Michael J. *Getting Your Boss's Number.* San Francisco: Harper, 1996.

Palmer, Helen. *The Enneagram: Understanding Yourself and Others in Your Life.* San Francisco: Harper, 1991.

Palmer, Helen. *The Enneagram in Love and Work.* San Francisco: Harper, 1995.

Riso, Don Richard. *Understanding the Enneagram: The Practical Guide to Personality Types.* Boston: Houghton Mifflin, 1990.

Riso, Don Richard, and Russ Hudson. *Personality Types: Using the Enneagram for Self-Discovery.* Boston: Houghton Mifflin, 1996.

Schreiber Shannon Associates. *Enneagram Workbook.* Albuquerque, N.M.: Schreiber Shannon Associates, 1997.

Sheppard, Lynette. *The Essential Enneagram.* Available: http://www.9points.com. 20 September 1998.

PRECONFERENCE:
HTML FROM THE GROUND UP:
SPINNING WEBS IN THE CLOUDS

HTML for Beginners
(Technical Services Emphasis)

Mary I. Wilke

Presenter

Donnice Cochenour

Assistant

Sheila Moran

Recorder

Mary I. Wilke is Head, Acquisitions Department, Center for Research Libraries.
Donnice Cochenour is Serials Librarian, Colorado State University.
Sheila Moran is Serials Librarian, Treadwell Library, Massachusetts General Hospital.

[Haworth co-indexing entry note]: "HTML for Beginners (Technical Services Emphasis)." Moran, Sheila. Co-published simultaneously in *The Serials Librarian* (The Haworth Press, Inc.) Vol. 36, No. 1/2, 1999, pp. 15-21; and: *Head in the Clouds, Feet on the Ground: Serials Vision and Common Sense* (ed: Jeffrey S. Bullington, Beatrice L. Caraway, and Beverley Geer) The Haworth Press, Inc., 1999, pp. 15-21. Single or multiple copies of this article are available for a fee from The Haworth Document Delivery Service [1-800-342-9678, 9:00 a.m. - 5:00 p.m. (EST). E-mail address: getinfo@haworthpressinc.com].

SUMMARY. All participants in the information community use the Web as a tool, and we all need to understand the power of Hypertext Markup Language (HTML) and how it can help us obtain our personal and professional goals. This preconference program offered this opportunity to all those interested in a technical services emphasis. It introduced participants to the basics of HTML with hands-on instruction in standard text formatting and layout conventions. Covering the basic skills of tagging and formatting, creation of links and lists, attendees were able to create a Web document which they could use in their own library technical services departments. *[Article copies available for a fee from The Haworth Document Delivery Service: 1-800-342-9678. E-mail address: getinfo@haworthpressinc.com]*

Hypertext Markup Language (HTML) is a powerful tool for serialists and other information professionals who wish to use the Internet as an information delivery medium. This preconference session was designed for beginners to create a Webpage for staff or departmental use with a technical services emphasis. Participants were introduced to basic Web document creation along with standard text formatting and layout conventions. Mary I. Wilke, head, Acquisitions Department at the Center for Research Libraries, presented this preconference program, and Donnice Cochenour, serials librarian, Colorado State University, assisted.

The goals of this workshop were designed to teach attendees the basics of designing a Webpage document by addressing the following four things:

- Basic HTML tagging
- Basic HTML formatting
- Basic creation of links
- Basic creation of lists

Before going into the details of learning HTML, Wilke instructed us in how to create a Webpage in the simplest way. With your Web browser you could click open the file menu, select "new document," choose either "blank," "template" or "wizard," and then just follow the script for the new document of your choice.

There was a review of the basic requirements for a basic, no-frills gray document with no graphics:

- A text editor that can save in plain (ASCII) text, e.g., Notepad
- A Web browser
- A Web server

Some basic definitions were then reviewed:

- HTML–Hypertext Markup Language, the language/code/instructions used to structure a document.
- Tags–the word, abbreviation or code that labels a part of the document. Tags are always enclosed in angle brackets (< >). They usually, but not always, come in pairs (<tag></tag>). The last tag in a tag pair is always preceded by a forward slash ("/").
- DTD–Document type definition. Good documents begin with something called a document type prolog, which identifies the HTML level used. This is code which alerts the computer via software of document parameters.

Before actually beginning our hands-on experience, Wilke included a visual presentation using containers to help us understand what a Webpage truly is. The largest container, of course, was the entire Webpage, and this container contained many smaller containers or specialized sections for specific information. We were advised that before you actually go to the computer, you should develop an outline of the information you wish to include on your page.

At this point we began to do the basic steps necessary to create a Webpage called "CRL's Acquisitions Department Homepage." It was at this moment that we began to actually write some code. We first opened Notepad and put the feature "word wrap" on and then proceeded to open Netscape Navigator. We learned to toggle between windows by using "Alt" and "Tab" together.

PROLOG

For the prolog we typed the following:
<!DOCTYPE HTML PUBLIC "-//W3C HTML 3.2//EN">
This indicated that the following document was a public document and not a system-dependent one, that it conformed with HTML 3.2 DTD, and that it used English language tag sets.

BUILDING THE LARGEST CONTAINER

We were instructed to begin building our Webpage from the outside in, much like an onion with many layers of skin, and to use the insert key on the keyboard. We did this using tag pairs which were like bookends so that we would not forget end tags. To work properly, there needs to be a beginning tag and an ending tag. So on the next line under the prolog type, we typed "<HTML></HTML>." This is an example of a tag pair. The first tag informs the computer to do something to the information that follows and the matching end tag notifies the computer that the HTML instruction has ended. The end tag always has a slash mark after the first angle and before the tag name. If you type your tag pair together and move the cursor in between the pair, you will never forget to include the end tag.

THE HEAD

The head section of the HTML document contains the title of the document, which displays at the very top of the computer screen. With the cursor in between the HTML tag pair, we were instructed to type the tag pair <HEAD></HEAD>.

THE TITLE

To place a title on the Webpage, we moved the cursor in between <HEAD></HEAD> and typed in our institution name: CRL'S Acquisition's Department Homepage. It was recommended that we always title our document. Otherwise, the Web browser will use the file name as the title of the document. This also completed one of the smaller containers inside the largest HTML container. At this time we were instructed to move the cursor outside of the head tag pair.

THE BODY

With the cursor at the end tag of the head tag pair, type in <BODY></BODY>, then move the cursor between this tag pair.

HEADINGS

In order to have your Webpage look like a traditional document, that is, with a title at the top of the page, you must use header tag pairs.

There are six header tag pairs, <H1></H1>, <H2></H2>, <H3></H3>, etc. These tag pairs instruct the computer to display the text contained in the tag pair in bigger and/or bolder text. <H1></H1> is the largest font size, and <H6></H6> is the smallest font size.

We were instructed to use <H1></H1> for the title, but in order to center this title, we typed in <CENTER><H1></H1></CENTER>. Then we placed the cursor between <H1> and </H1> and typed in our title. It was suggested that headers be used in descending order and only to separate heading text from the rest of the text. We were advised that there were other codes to use for emphasizing text.

LINKS TO A UNIFORM RESOURCE LOCATOR (URL)

To link to another URL from your document, there are codes called anchor tags, <A></A>. The "A" actually stands for anchor. In our example, our text read as follows: "For more information about our library, visit our website at: <AHREF=HTTP://www.crl.uchicago.edu/index.html>CRL HOMEPAGE</A>." HREF stands for "hypertext reference." The address of the hypertext document must follow the equals sign after the HREF. After the address or URL, we were instructed to input text which described the actual link. We were cautioned to consider seeking permission from the Website creator before including the link in your document.

LINE BREAK DESIGNATOR AND HORIZONTAL RULE

We were then shown how to indicate a line break or a full line of empty space. This is done by using the single break tag <BR>. To make a more distinctive break, use the horizontal rule single tag indicator. <HR> is the single tag that displays as a horizontal line across your document.

LISTS

An unordered list is bulleted rather than numbered. To create this type of list, we were instructed to use the unordered list tag pair, <UL></UL>, and the list item single tag, <LI>. To create an ordered list, or a numbered list, you can type in <OL></OL>, again with <LI>

typed in between. A third type of list is a definitions list, and to create this you use <DL></DL>. This is a list where terms are defined.

We were then guided through creating a separate HTML file in the same directory and then linking to that file by placing an anchor tag with a hypertext reference to the file name. Likewise, we were instructed in how to link to a location within the same document.

SAVING

We were shown how to save our document both as a text file and also as an HTML file by adding the .htm extension. We were instructed that saving both text and HTML files often when creating Webpages is a good habit.

SIGNATURE

Finally, all good documents should contain a signature. We were instructed in using the address tag pair, <ADDRESS></ADDRESS>. In between this tag pair, include the following:

- Latest revision date
- Status (e.g., complete or under construction)
- Copyright if applicable
- URL
- Name, address and/or e-mail of the person responsible for the creation of the document

We were reminded to insert a line break after each element of the address.

CONCLUSION

In this preconference session, participants were instructed in the basics of HTML with a technical services emphasis. The goals of this workshop were (1) basic HTML tagging; (2) basic HTML formatting; (3) basic creation of links; and (4) basic creation of lists. The instructor used the metaphors of an onion with many layers of skin or containers within a container to visually orient the participants in creating a Webpage. Attendees were then guided through the various steps necessary to create a Webpage. We started with tips that would prevent us from forgetting end tags for tag pairs. Then we proceeded through an explanation of the six header tag pairs, centering techniques, linking to an URL and various formatting techniques. Lastly we were shown how to do lists. Participants were tremendously impressed that after only a couple of hours of basic HTML instruction, they were able to produce a Web document.

Handouts consisted of a basic manual, an HTML file on disk that served as a template for each person, and an HTML tag "cheat sheet." Participants were encouraged to use the Web resources found at the end of the manual.

HTML for Beginners
(Public Services Emphasis)

Beth Jane Toren

Presenter

Mike Randall
Sean Murphy

Assistants

Marla J. Whitney

Recorder

SUMMARY. Beth Jane Toren presented the basics of Hypertext Mark-up Language (HTML) with a perspective from the public services side of the library. Beth covered document creation, standard text formatting, creation of lists, addition of images, links to other documents, layout conventions and design tips. *[Article copies available for a fee from The Haworth Document Delivery Service: 1-800-342-9678. E-mail address: getinfo@ haworthpressinc.com]*

Beth Jane Toren is the Web Development Librarian at West Virginia University.

Mike Randall is Head of the Serials Department at the University of California at Los Angeles Library.

Sean Murphy is Reference Librarian at the Ruth Ann Musick Library, Fairmont State College.

Marla J. Whitney is Regional Sales and Service Manager, The Faxon Company.

[Haworth co-indexing entry note]: "HTML for Beginners (Public Services Emphasis)." Whitney, Marla J. Co-published simultaneously in *The Serials Librarian* (The Haworth Press, Inc.) Vol. 36, No. 1/2, 1999, pp. 23-25; and: *Head in the Clouds, Feet on the Ground: Serials Vision and Common Sense* (ed: Jeffrey S. Bullington, Beatrice L. Caraway, and Beverley Geer) The Haworth Press, Inc., 1999, pp. 23-25. Single or multiple copies of this article are available for a fee from The Haworth Document Delivery Service [1-800-342-9678, 9:00 a.m. - 5:00 p.m. (EST). E-mail address: getinfo@haworthpressinc.com].

The workshop included both demonstrations and hands-on practice for the topics covered. The handouts included a diskette with sample documents, a glossary of terms, a list of basic HTML tags, and a handout entitled "The Bare Bones Guide to HTML," by Kevin Werbach. The handout is available on the World Wide Web at http://werbach. com/barebones/. The diskette included a document with links to various sources of help for HTML, sources for design tips, and information on special characters that may be used in the creation of a Webpage.

To begin the workshop, the class opened Netscape and Wordpad in side-by-side windows so that the text could be seen in both the HTML form and how it would display on the World Wide Web. Although the class used Wordpad, any word processing software can be used to create a Webpage document. The document must be saved as ASCII or plain text with the file extension name of ".htm." Changes made to the Wordpad document must be saved and will not show in Netscape until the document is reloaded in Netscape. In order to be viewed on the World Wide Web, the document must be loaded onto a server.

The workshop covered the "raw" HTML tags so that we could have more control and understanding of how the HTML tags work. Beth described the format of HTML tags and how they usually come in pairs, one to indicate the beginning of the tag and one to indicate the end. "Greater than" and "less than" brackets (< >) surround each tag. The "end" tag has a backslash in the brackets (</>). Most of the HTML tags are in pairs and are not case sensitive. The ending tag should be added when the beginning tag is created to avoid forgetting to add the ending tag later. The essential HTML tags are <HTML>, <HEAD>, <TITLE>, and <BODY>. Each of these tags requires the end tag </HTML>, </HEAD>, </TITLE>, </BODY>.

The title tag information appears on the Netscape title bar and will appear as the bookmark title. Beth also covered how to change the font size of the HTML document, how to center, how to combine more than one tag, how to create breaks in a line, how to indicate a new paragraph, and how to create hypertext links.

Tips for creating a Webpage:

- Use a hyper-tree format. Try to create an organized hierarchical structure, not a flat structure. Good examples are given in the "The Bare Bones Guide to HTML" document.

- The page display should be fast. Limit the size and number of images since not everyone has access to high-speed lines.
- Content is more important than graphics.
- Name the file for the main page "index.htm" so that it will be searchable on the World Wide Web.
- Name each menu and have links to other menu options at the bottom of each page.
- Make the names of the links clear.
- Use file names that are simple and self-explanatory.
- Use nested lists for outlines.
- If you see a Webpage that you like, use the "View Page Source" option in the "Headers" section of Netscape to see how the page was created. This option shows the raw HTML file for that page.
- Seek critiques of your Webpage. The Web Site Garage (http://www.websitegarage.com/) is one source for critiques. Beth also offered to look over sites created by the class.

The Webpage should also include a phone number and address that corresponds to linked e-mail and a date to show the last time the Webpage was updated.

During the class, the attendees modified an existing HTML file to create their own Webpages. The Webpages included a title, header, links to pictures, animated files, e-mail addresses and links to other Webpages. The body of the document included a variety of font types and sizes and an unordered list.

Beth Jane Toren's workshop on the basics of HTML was well organized and educational. Both Mike Randall and Sean Murphy did a good job of helping individuals in the workshop with problems and questions so that Beth could keep the workshop moving. The diskette and handouts that were given out during the workshop were good ways to help the attendees remember what they had learned during the workshop and can be used also as a starting point for creating a new Webpage.

Web Design–Effective and Aesthetic

Margi Mann

Presenter

Wendy Moore

Assistant

Marit S. MacArthur

Recorder

SUMMARY. Librarians frequently find themselves wanting to put up a Webpage or site but needing guidance in good design principles. This workshop concentrated on two major aspects of design. The first was planning, which is very important and requires considerable time to do well. The second aspect was aesthetics, which is more subjective; some good general guidelines, however, are available. This workshop concentrated on discussing these aspects rather than dealing with the details of Hypertext Markup Language (HTML) coding. Participants were given a planning exercise to do individually, followed by a general discussion of both particular problems and good design principles. Exercise diskettes and a Webliography were provided. Further information is available at the session Website. *[Article copies available for a fee from The Haworth Document Delivery Service: 1-800-342-9678. E-mail address: getinfo@ haworthpressinc.com]*

Margi Mann is Customer Services Representative, WLN, Lacey, WA.

Wendy Moore is Serials Librarian at Furman University.

Marit S. MacArthur is Reference Librarian and Government Publications Serials Cataloger at the Auraria Library, University of Colorado at Denver.

[Haworth co-indexing entry note]: "Web Design–Effective and Aesthetic." MacArthur, Marit S. Co-published simultaneously in *The Serials Librarian* (The Haworth Press, Inc.) Vol. 36, No. 1/2, 1999, pp. 27-32; and: *Head in the Clouds, Feet on the Ground: Serials Vision and Common Sense* (ed: Jeffrey S. Bullington, Beatrice L. Caraway, and Beverley Geer) The Haworth Press, Inc., 1999, pp. 27-32. Single or multiple copies of this article are available for a fee from The Haworth Document Delivery Service [1-800-342-9678, 9:00 a.m. - 5:00 p.m. (EST). E-mail address: getinfo@haworthpressinc.com].

Margi Mann began by explaining that she was presenting the program, with Wendy Moore's assistance, in place of Michelle Flinchbaugh, who was unable to attend due to an emergency. She announced that she would be talking about two aspects of Web design. The first was planning, which is necessary before you actually begin the coding. The second was aesthetics, involving the "touchy-feely" aspects of the site and how people respond to it. There would be only minimal focus on how to actually write HTML (coding tags and attributes). More attention would be paid to how to use the tags and attributes in the HTML standard to produce the desired effects. Mann's presentation used Webpages on "The Process of Creating a Quality Web Page/Site," by Flinchbaugh, to list the important points in the presentation. They are available at http://www-personal.umich.edu/~mflinchb/processm.htm.[1]

The first part of designing a Website is planning. It is important to spend enough time on this step. You should begin by thinking about the purpose and objectives of the site, involving such concerns as what should be covered, how complex the site should be, and how much of the content will be unique and how much will be links to other sites. Identifying the target audience and its characteristics, preferences and technical level is very important. Once goals and objectives have been established, you should summarize them in a paragraph or two and use that summary as a guide when actually creating the site. At this stage you should also decide what maintenance will be necessary, when it should be performed and who will do it. You should be realistic and make sure there is a consensus of all the members of the planning group so as to avoid later problems. You should expect to have to make changes and solve problems once the site is available to the public.

A good way to begin the planning phase is by brainstorming, including as many people as possible. It is important to involve the content providers and those with a vested interest in the site. If there will be multiple pages, you should create a chart of the pages and how they will interact, and then outline the content of each page. You should create a template to provide a consistent "feel" and reassure visitors that they are still in the same site. The template should conform to requirements of the organization. It might contain a logo or signature of responsibility, such as the designer's name, library, or department. Dates of creation and updating should be included. It is important to plan a homepage as a starting point; this will establish a first impression and perhaps determine whether or not a visitor goes on to look deeper into the site. Avoid a tendency to clutter. Keep in mind that people may also come straight into a subordinate page, so you should plan good linking mechanisms. Be flexible and do not get too vested in the original design; chances are it will need to be changed many times. It is a good idea to plan the design in pencil or on a word processor to make changes easier.

At this point the presenters handed out diskettes and assigned the first exercise, which involved each person spending five minutes writing a description of the goals and objectives of a Webpage he/she was thinking of creating. This was followed by a discussion, in which several individuals summarized their plans to the whole group, and the workshop leaders and participants commented on particular problems. One issue discussed was searchability, which is aided by a good table of contents and careful and consistent wording. If the site uses a particular searching tool, you should plan the site based on this tool's characteristics and features, which may require additional research.

A discussion of aesthetics followed. Aesthetics is a very subjective area, and it is important to keep in mind that people will react differently. The basics learned in high school English remain constant–good spelling, composition, page layout, and word processing skills are important. Users process by screen, so you should think about making it pleasing and maintaining a balance between text, white space, and graphics. Hypertext, however, requires new ways of thinking. Whether the page will be one long scroll or broken up into shorter pages is a decision you need to make; people vary in their preferences, and different designs may be better for different purposes. One long scroll may be easier to create but may not be as helpful to users. Most people would rather click than scroll; if the page is long, you should plan for internal links to help the user jump from one place to another. Loading time is another issue. You should plan based on the users' hardware base. If many of them are using older, slower computers, the site might be broken into smaller files that load faster. Thinking through an appropriate page size at this stage is easier than having to go back and break it up later. It is a good idea to design the page on a computer similar to those available to your users. Depending on the target audience, you may need to design the page with partial or total password security.

Once the design is established, you need to evaluate it. Do you have appropriate tools, such as a good HTML authoring program, a scanner, graphics software, and scripts or script-authoring software for forms and other interactive elements? Do you have the necessary skills and resources? Are your decisions well thought out regarding which content to include in the site and which to link to? Does the design take into account the basic principles of user interface design, graphic design, and information design? Flinchbaugh's Webpage, cited above, provides a good listing of principles in these three areas. You should create scenarios of people who will be using the site and what they will be looking for. There are some sites that will do evaluation, but the best evaluators and testers are a subset of future users, or beta-testers. Once the Website is up, you should include an e-mail address so users can provide feedback. A question was raised about guidelines under the ADA (Americans with Disabilities Act). There are some ADA guidelines on the Web.[2] Mann commented that this is really an aesthetic issue, since it affects how those with disabilities experience the site.

A discussion of participants' "pet peeves" about Websites followed, with the purpose of identifying particular problems and how to avoid them. One person brought up beautiful pages that will not print well, such as those with black backgrounds. This is especially important if the page is something people are especially likely to want to print, such as travel directions. Designers should test print their pages. Another complaint was too much "cutesy" animation or graphics that do not go well with the rest of the site. Mann recommended using animation and large graphics sparingly. There was a discussion of problems with frames, especially ones that are too wide. Guidelines on the appropriate use of frames, as well as many other design issues, are available at a number of Websites; a Webliography of such sites was provided for participants.[3] Mann commented that one consideration is the level of your users' technology–some may be using browsers that do not support frames. This led to a discussion of proprietary extensions in Web browsers and whether to use them. Netscape Navigator and Microsoft Internet Explorer each support extensions not supported by the other. You should use these with caution, remembering to design for the lowest common denominator. You should also weigh the real importance of features in relation to content, goals and objectives. If a library's internal technology base changes, it may be necessary to redesign the site based on newly available features; this is a part of maintenance.

It is a good idea to look at the site on various computers so that you can see if all textures and fonts work well on other screen sizes or displays. Moore recommended the *Yale Style Manual* as a general guide at http://info.med.yale.edu/caim/manual/contents.html. It contains guidance on which pixel dimensions work well. Mann recommended using color sparingly.

Mann's final recommendation was to think about what will happen when your page goes down. It may be desirable to provide a paper backup.

This preconference session emphasized the planning and aesthetic aspects of Webpage or site creation. The emphasis was on what you need to think about during the planning phase and some general guidelines on good design principles. An exercise gave the participants some practice in preliminary planning for sites they were considering putting up. There was excellent participation in the discussions, which provided an opportunity for the exchange of information between participants and workshop leaders on both particular problems and general design principles. The workshop did not really attempt to cover the details of HTML coding tags and attributes, but the exercise diskette, handouts, and Webpage for the session provided further information.[4] Handouts included a diskette containing five exercises. Subjects covered included planning the Website, concepts of design, images and image attributes, tables and table attributes and incorporating images and tables into design. A Webliography was provided covering design principles and practical coding issues for Web design. The session Website outlines the points covered in the presentation and also outlines general principles of interface, information, and graphic design. Also included are lists of image and image attributes codes, both required and optional, including syntax, and a similar list for tables and table attributes.

NOTES

1. The Webpages for this workshop are available at: http://www-personal.umich.edu/~mflinchb/processm.htm. September 26, 1998.

2. A good place to start is "Accessible Web Page Design" at the University of Washington at http://weber.u.washington.edu/~doit/Resources/web-design.html.

3. Sites listed include:

- "Hypercontent, Hyperjunk" at http://www.mcs.net/~jorn/html/hyper.html
- "Principles of Web Design" at http://webreview.com/design/talk/sept1/index. html
- "Sucky to Savvy" at http://www.glover.com/ss/ssmain.html
- "The Ten Commandments of Good WWWeb Design" at http://www.mcs.net/~jorn/html/terrorist.html#tencom
- "Top Ten Mistakes in Web Design" at http://www.useit.com/alertbox/9605. html.

The Webliography also includes general style guides, including:

- *Web Design Group Style Guide for Online Hypertext* at http://www. htmlhelp.com/design/style/
- *Sun on the Net Guide to Web Style* at http://www.sun.com/styleguide/
- *Style Guide for Online Hypertext* at http://www.w3.org/Provider/Style/Overview. html
- *Yale C/AIM Style Guide,* which is probably the definitive online text on the subject, at http://info.med.yale.edu/caim/manual/contents.html

4. Some generally helpful sites include "Web Design: More Than Meets the Eye," http://WDVL.Internet.com/Authoring/Design/; *Sizzling HTML Jalfrezi,* http://vzone. virgin.net/sizzling.jalfrezi/; "The Icon Bank-Search Form," http://www.iconbank. com/search.htm; and *Icons 'n Stuff,* http://www.xs4all.nl/~arjenvm/pics/foot.html.

Graphics Animation

Yvonne W. Zhang

Presenter

Sharon Quinn Fitzgerald

Recorder

SUMMARY. This preconference workshop began with a twenty-five-minute PowerPoint overview of the topic. The goals of the session were to (1) convey the notion of an animated graphic; (2) learn how to create one; and (3) have a discussion of pros and cons of employing animated GIFs in Websites. *[Article copies available for a fee from The Haworth Document Delivery Service: 1-800-342-9678. E-mail address: getinfo@haworthpressinc.com]*

The process of building an animated GIF (Graphics Interchange Format) begins with identifying a usable image. An overview of formats commonly employed by computers included (1) GIF; (2) JPEG (Joint Photographic Experts Group); (3) BITMAP; and (4) TIFF (Tagged Image File Format). Only GIF and JPEG image file types are currently supported on the Internet. JPEG supports many more colors and compresses well and does not load much slower than a GIF image.

Four tools available for converting images to animated GIFs were introduced. GifBuilder 0.4.1 is a shareware product for the Macintosh

---

Yvonne W. Zhang is Catalog Librarian, California State Polytechnic University. Sharon Quinn Fitzgerald is Head of Serials, Fogler Library, University of Maine.

[Haworth co-indexing entry note]: "Graphics Animation." Fitzgerald, Sharon Quinn. Co-published simultaneously in *The Serials Librarian* (The Haworth Press, Inc.) Vol. 36, No. 1/2, 1999, pp. 33-35; and: *Head in the Clouds, Feet on the Ground: Serials Vision and Common Sense* (ed: Jeffrey S. Bullington, Beatrice L. Caraway, and Beverley Geer) The Haworth Press, Inc., 1999, pp. 33-35. Single or multiple copies of this article are available for a fee from The Haworth Document Delivery Service [1-800-342-9678, 9:00 a.m. - 5:00 p.m. (EST). E-mail address: getinfo@haworthpressinc.com].

platform and is rather limited compared to some PC tools. GIF Construction Set for the PC environment has many more animated functions. PhotoImpact GIF Animator 1.2 is another animation tool for PCs. Finally, it is possible to build very simple two-frame animated graphics using the HTML tag <LOWSRC>.

A GIF animation tool is capable of combining several individual image files into a single, multi-image GIF file, creating the optical illusion of motion. The tools can be used to adjust the speed at which the frames display as well as the degree of rotation depending on the desired effect. They can also create special effects such as "wipes," "pushes" or a "sandstorm."

The basic steps to create an animated graphic file are (1) create a set of image files using graphics software (e.g., Adobe Photoshop); (2) set options in the GIF animation tool (e.g., palette, size, animation options); (3) check the animation via a Web browser to be certain it functions and displays properly; (4) save the whole set of images as a GIF file; and (5) add the GIF to the Webpage.

GIF animations are used in Websites to provide visual dynamics and to bring the user's attention to a particular function of the page. They are often employed in Web advertisements and Websites designed for children. One should be aware that there are several pitfalls in employing them. They generally have a longer loading time; therefore, the size of an animated GIF should ideally be no more than 36 x 36 pixels. They can also distract the reader from other information on your sight. The presenter recommends using them sparingly to be most effective. In short, keep them simple, fast and relevant.

A number of ready-made animation GIFs are available on the Internet: (1) *The 1st Internet Gallery of GIF Animation* at http://members. aol.com/royalef/galframe.htm; (2) *GIF Animation* at http://www. bendnet.com/users/brianhovis/anime.htm; (3) *Erik's Hot Page* at http:// www.fsap.com/ehi/index2.html.

The remainder of the session was devoted to hands-on exercises using the Macintosh shareware software product, GIFBuilder. Step-by-step instructions were provided in a handout which also included a listing of useful online GIF builder resources. The list included the GIF Animation General Web page and addresses for the animated graphic tools and constructed animated graphic resources, all noted above.

The exercises were organized such that each successive one built on the previous. In this manner, the class was able to build progressively more sophisticated animated GIFs. Each workstation provided the necessary tools including a selection of GIF images to build into an animation GIF so that the class could focus on practice with the latter. Once the animated GIFs had been saved they could be copied into a Webpage template to check their functionality and display.

All members of the class were able to complete at least the simplest exercises and gain some experience in building the animations. Unfortunately, a couple of the workstations locked up and required rebooting in order to resume, and some time was lost in this process. However, the initial presentation and the hands-on instructions were quite clear, enabling all to have an opportunity to try this Web authoring technique. Ample time was allowed for the exercise portion of the workshop, so there was no feeling of being rushed.

During the course of the initial overview, a number of sites on the World Wide Web were visited to illustrate the pros and cons of employing animated graphics. The presenter also visited a number of the recommended resources to familiarize the class with what they had to offer. The syntax for creating two-frame animation graphics with HTML was also provided.

Netscape vs. Internet Explorer

Robb Waltner

Presenter

Everett Allgood

Recorder

SUMMARY. The wonders of the World Wide Web are only beginning to unfold before us. By most accounts, only a fraction of its overall content is currently accessible. In this preconference session, participants were treated to thorough demonstrations of the two dominant Web browsers on the market today. Interestingly, these software programs are not just browsers anymore, and what's more, Web surfers are not the only ones watching! *[Article copies available for a fee from The Haworth Document Delivery Service: 1-800-342-9678. E-mail address: getinfo@haworthpressinc.com]*

In the increasingly prevalent and competitive domain of Internet browsers, the most obvious question centers upon which one to select. Does either the Microsoft Corporation or the Netscape Communications Corporation truly have the better product? These are questions of interest not only to the average Internet user on the Web, but also to those in some of the highest halls of the United States government, as evidenced by a recent lawsuit filed against the Microsoft Corporation by the United States Department of Justice.

Robb Waltner is Periodicals Librarian at the University of Colorado at Denver.
Everett Allgood is Serials Cataloger at New York University.

[Haworth co-indexing entry note]: "Netscape vs. Internet Explorer." Allgood, Everett. Co-published simultaneously in *The Serials Librarian* (The Haworth Press, Inc.) Vol. 36, No. 1/2, 1999, pp. 37-41; and: *Head in the Clouds, Feet on the Ground: Serials Vision and Common Sense* (ed: Jeffrey S. Bullington, Beatrice L. Caraway, and Beverley Geer) The Haworth Press, Inc., 1999, pp. 37-41. Single or multiple copies of this article are available for a fee from The Haworth Document Delivery Service [1-800-342-9678, 9:00 a.m. - 5:00 p.m. (EST). E-mail address: getinfo@haworthpressinc.com].

It was just this type of question and a direct comparison of the two dominant Internet browsers which brought Robb Waltner, periodicals librarian at the University of Colorado at Denver, to Boulder, Colorado, to present a NASIG preconference comparing the prevalent features of the two. He opened the session with an overview of his own Webpage, which serves as an excellent starting point in constructing a comparison of the two browsers.[1] Waltner has many links from his own Webpage to source material useful in making an informed decision.

In the course of navigating through the resources available from his Webpage, Waltner made reference to a few points illustrating the dynamism inherent within the Internet browser world. For example, Waltner's planning for this program began in July of 1997, at which point he began using the two browsers heavily to establish a sense of their features and how the two compared. Within the ensuing months both Microsoft and Netscape upgraded their browsers with new releases. Of course, each new version meant Waltner had to begin anew with much of his comparison, determining which features remained as well as what was new and what was different. These were major upgrades, with each new version moving to Release 4.0. Many new features were introduced, and most remaining features received significant upgrades, which necessitated their re-examination by Waltner. To further compound the issue, less than a month before this preconference session, the United States Department of Justice filed a lawsuit against the Microsoft Corporation, centering upon the Internet Explorer browser software. Obviously this is not an industry in which products and developments sit idle for long periods of time.

Waltner then moved on to a direct comparison of the prevalent features in each browser. One common aspect of the two products immediately apparent to users is that the latest releases no longer simply represent World Wide Web browsers. Each now comes equipped with features ranging from browsers to e-mail to Web authoring/editing programs to security. Because of these multiple applications, Internet Explorer and Netscape Communicator are often referred to as software suites.

Beginning with Microsoft's Internet Explorer, Waltner walked preconference attendees through each of these features, focusing not only on the uses and structure of the application, but also on how users may manipulate, and in some cases enhance, the feature to better benefit personal needs or workflow. One aspect of the Internet Explorer software which became clear time and again centered on how fluid its interfaces are and how easy they are to modify. This idea of offering users several ways to perform any one task within a user-defined interface has always been a controlling theme within the Windows environment.

In examining the features bundled with the Internet Explorer software suite, Waltner introduced one of the latest technologies that both Microsoft and Netscape are pursuing. It is known in the industry as "push technology," and it allows individuals to compile and construct their own personal subscriptions to serially-released information via the Web. These "subscriptions" are known as "channels" and they work like this: Imagine an area of research or interest in which developments happen very quickly. You, an Internet user/informed citizen, are interested in keeping up with these developments in a timely manner with as little effort as possible. Now presume that you discover a site on the Web that is continually updating the information in which you are interested. It would be easy enough to bookmark the site or list it among your favorites so that each time you go on the Web you may easily return to the site to note the latest listings. What if you could somehow tell your computer to check it for you, though?

With channels you can. You set up links to these sites and then enter the information detailing when you want your browser to visit the site and capture the latest data compiled there. For example, if you know the site is updated every evening at 10:00 P.M., you may program your channel to visit the site at 3:00 A.M., when rates and usage are low, capture the data and have it waiting on your desktop when you arrive at work or when you step out of the shower (for users with terminals in their homes) at 7:00 A.M.! This is an amazing feature which is rapidly becoming one of the more widespread of automated applications. Herein we are witnessing computers, desktops and home computers–not mainframes or minicomputers!–taking their first tentative steps towards more proactive behavior. These devices are no longer completely reactive, that is, responding only to a user or programmer interacting directly via a keyboard or voice activator. Granted, this feature is by no means completely proactive. It is still necessary for you, the user, to determine which channels to assemble, how often your browser will visit them, and if or when you wish to remove them from your list. So, the computer is not itself choosing sites of interest to you from which to download information–yet!

But wait, there is more! Internet Explorer's new version, in addition to allowing users to set up channels making use of the new push technology, also offers a feature called the Active Desktop. Waltner feels it may be this feature in particular that led to the United States Department of Justice lawsuit against Microsoft. The reason becomes readily apparent. The Active Desktop allows users to actually capture specific dynamic World Wide Web features–Websites with constantly changing and developing content, such as the *New York Times*–and download a thumbnail image or icon of that site directly onto their desktops. So what is happening with this feature? It is not as proactive or labor intensive (on the part of the computer and browser, that is) as channels, in which the browser actively seeks out and downloads into an existing file. With Active Desktop, the browser is simply providing, directly on the desktop, a real-time, dynamic link to the Internet. The user selects from a choice of Active Desktop items provided by Microsoft's browser software. This list of items, like Microsoft's pre-loaded list of channels referred to above, may be edited by users to add and/or subtract sites of interest. This Active Desktop item then resides on the desktop along with any other icons the user has positioned there for frequent use.

Why all the unrest? One may argue that users presently have a ready connection to the Internet via the Netscape or Internet Explorer icon sitting on their desktop. The primary difference lies in the fact that a click on these icons simply takes one to the browser from which searches may then be launched. The Active Desktop icon, on the other hand, provides a real-time Internet connection to a specific site. One may watch the icon transform as it reflects updates to the site it represents. By clicking on the icon, users are immediately at the site with the latest content. As noted above, Waltner feels this direct linkage of real-time Internet connections residing upon the desktop of an operating system may be one of the critical components in the Department of Justice case against Microsoft.

Waltner led attendees through each of the prevalent features within both software suites. He examined the ability to customize each interface, the mail programs, the browser features, the conference/meeting capabilities and the HTML/DHTML (Hypertext Markup Lanuage/Dynamic HTML) editors.

Most of these comparisons, based on Version 4.0 of both releases, heavily favored Microsoft's Internet Explorer. The one notable exception was in HTML editors, the feature used for creating and editing Web documents. Here Netscape's Composer feature clearly outperformed Microsoft's FrontPage Express. Waltner describes Netscape's Composer as elegant, simple and straightforward, whereas Microsoft's FrontPage Express may be described as nothing but a "dumbed-down" version of its predecessor, FrontPage 98.

Overall, Waltner preferred Microsoft's Internet Explorer because of the program's fluidity and ease of use, though Netscape's HTML editor remains the program of choice between the two. Nonetheless, Microsoft's package has obviously made noteworthy advances in a comparatively short time. A glance back at a preconference presented at the 1995 NASIG conference in Durham, North Carolina did not even mention Microsoft's Internet Explorer as one of the leading browsers.[2] As recently as two years ago, Netscape's Navigator browser enjoyed a 70 percent Internet audience share compared to Microsoft's 30 percent. The most recent surveys reveal usage to be split 50/50 between the two.

This preconference session was informative and timely. With a medium evolving as rapidly as the Internet, it is especially advantageous to see how others working in similar environments and with similar tasks are utilizing the range of resources. The equipment in the room in the Engineering Complex at the University of Colorado at Boulder was less than ideal, and as a result the resolution on some of the screen captures was a bit blurry. The format, though, was lively and well paced, and Waltner's enthusiasm for and knowledge of the topic were evidenced by a number of questions from participants throughout his presentation. When asked how one not quite so knowledgeable may learn more, Waltner quickly replied that the most useful material he has found is typically in journal articles and product reviews. He recommended visiting his Webpage for some valuable initial resources.

NOTES

1. Robb Waltner, *Homepage*. Available July 16, 1998: http://carbon.cudenver.edu/ ~rwaltner

2. Steve Oberg, "Electronic Dream Catchers and Spinning Charlotte's Web: Using and Maintaining World Wide Web Services," in *Serials to the Tenth Power*, eds. Mary Ann Sheble and Beth Holley (New York: The Haworth Press, Inc., 1996): 17-22.

Designing Pages with Frames

Yvonne W. Zhang

Presenter

Kenneth L. Kirkland

Recorder

SUMMARY. Frames are singular features used to structure a Webpage for effective navigation, organization, and appearance. A hands-on computer lab demonstration of the principles of frame use and construction followed a formal slide presentation. Participants needed an intermediate knowledge of HTML. Illustrations and exercises centered on HTML tags that are basic to frames, including relevant attributes, and special tags pertaining to frames. The presentation included resource Webpages with tutorials, design ideas, and links to pages showing effective use of frames, as well as bad examples. *[Article copies available for a fee from The Haworth Document Delivery Service: 1-800-342-9678. E-mail address: getinfo@ haworthpressinc.com]*

Conducted in a computer lab where each participant had the use of a terminal, the workshop consisted of two parts. Part I was a formal spoken presentation accompanied by PowerPoint slides illustrating the uses of frames, defining them, and examining the basic Hypertext

---

Yvonne W. Zhang is Catalog Librarian, California State Polytechnic University.
Kenneth L. Kirkland is Collection Development Coordinator at DePaul University Library.

[Haworth co-indexing entry note]: "Designing Pages with Frames." Kirkland, Kenneth L. Co-published simultaneously in *The Serials Librarian* (The Haworth Press, Inc.) Vol. 36, No. 1/2, 1999, pp. 43-46; and: *Head in the Clouds, Feet on the Ground: Serials Vision and Common Sense* (ed: Jeffrey S. Bullington, Beatrice L. Caraway, and Beverley Geer) The Haworth Press, Inc., 1999, pp. 43-46. Single or multiple copies of this article are available for a fee from The Haworth Document Delivery Service [1-800-342-9678, 9:00 a.m. - 5:00 p.m. (EST). E-mail address: getinfo@haworthpressinc.com].

Markup Language (HTML) tags for frames. Part II was a hands-on session with pre-mounted exercises. The goal of the workshop was to explain how to use frames, to tell us what they are, and to provide a few resources.

Frames divide a Webpage into multiple sections with scrollable or non-scrollable regions as needed. Each region can be independent or related, that is, each region may contain information independent of the other regions. Hot links can be made in different regions to connect to one another.

PART I: FORMAL PRESENTATION WITH SLIDES

- Why should one use frames?
    - To contain stable information such as copyright notice, names of providers, address links, or abstracts.
    - To present Tables of Contents or similar information.
    - To provide easier navigation through the essential links within the hierarchy of the Web documents.
    - To express personal preference in design–some love frames, others hate them.
- What are some potential problems with frames?
    - Excessive or improper use of frames can scatter contents and contexts, which may distract users.
    - Printing problems, such as not clicking on the targeted frame that the user meant to print.
    - Not all browsers have the capability of displaying frames.
    - The HTML syntax is relatively complex and requires advance planning and structuring.
- Examples of good use of frames:
    - JSTOR   http://www.jstor.org/
    - INNOVATIVE WEBPAC http://opac.lib.csupomona.edu/
    - FrameShop   http://www.bagism.com/frameshop/
    - Frames, An Introduction
    - http://www.home.netscape.com/assist/net_sites/frames.html
    - Frames Tutorial
    - http://www.spunwebs.com/frmtutor.html
- Examples of bad use of frames at the time of this presentation (June 18, 1998); by September 26,1998, neither of these was still available:

–File Maker Magazine
http://www.iso-ezine.com/freeissues.issue19/
–I Hate Frames
http://web2.airmail.net/atapaz/www.frames/

It is up to the individual to decide why an example is "bad." Those cited at this session were chosen largely for overcrowding or busyness.

- Basic HTML Tags for Frames
  <FRAMESET></FRAMESET><FRAME   SRC="test1.html">
  <A   HREF="test1.html"   TARGET="masterA"><NOFRAMES>;
  </NOFRAMES>
- Basic HTML Tags for Frame with Attributes
  <FRAMESET ROWS="50,50" COLS="127, *"BORDER=0> ;
  </FRAMESET>
  <FRAME SRC="test1.html" SCROLLING="auto" MARGIN-
  WIDTH="10" MARGINHEIGHT="20" NAME="masterA"
  NORESIZE>
- Special Frame Tags
  <TARGET="_top">
  <TARGET="_blank">

PART II: FRAME-MAKING HANDS-ON EXERCISES

Exercise one called for opening the file "frame**a**.htm" via Netscape, choosing "Page Source" from the "View" menu, copying the file to the clipboard, and pasting it into a Notepad file as frame**1**.htm. This file was then opened from Notepad. Participants edited the new file by substituting two parameters, the Uniform Resource Locator (URL) for one's own institution, and one's own e-mail hotlink, then changing the text of the header. After these simple alterations, participants opened the file in Netscape to see the results.

Exercise two required opening and copying the file "frame**b**.htm" in the same manner, resulting in a new file called "frame**2**.htm." This time the object was to change the dimensions of the frame. This was effected by swapping <FRAMESET ROWs-"80,20"> for <FRAME-SET COL="15,85">, and <FRAMESET COLS="80,20"> for <FRAMESET ROWS="80,20"> as well as moving the tag <FRAME SRC=main_frame2.html" NAME="demo2"> to another location.

Other parts of this exercised reinforced the experience and skill gained in this editing process.

This particular workshop was at the intermediate level, requiring a basic knowledge of HTML coding. Skills covered were frame creation and control. Zhang guided participants through sample exercises she had mounted on the computers beforehand. There were pointers on what to avoid. There were useful tips, such as a reminder to view the source of the files being illustrated to demonstrate how these tags related to the pages when viewed on Netscape. After the clearly presented slides at the beginning of the session, the opportunity to modify some of the tags and text, then to see the resulting effects, worked very well to diminish apprehensions of those previously unaccustomed to wielding Webpage frames. The participants responded avidly to the questions raised, and appreciated the well-chosen animated graphic illustration. The well-designed exercises taught the participants to manipulate frame size and appearance with consistency.[1]

NOTES

1. Recorder's Note: The computer lab sessions, a benchmark of the NASIG 1998 Preconference, illustrate this year's motto, "Head in the Clouds, Feet on the Ground," to which could be added, "and hands on the keyboard, eyes on the screen."

Designing Interactive Forms

Stephanie Schmitt

Presenter

Reeta Sinha

Recorder

SUMMARY. Using interactive forms is a creative and powerful method to enable two-way communication on Websites. This session described some practical applications of interactive forms on library Webpages and the many different features of forms, such as radio buttons, check boxes, pull-down menus, and text areas. After a detailed look at the HTML tagging and structure used to construct forms, the audience was given an opportunity to design and create an all-purpose form that would be loaded to a remote server. *[Article copies available for a fee from The Haworth Document Delivery Service: 1-800-342-9678. E-mail address: getinfo@haworthpressinc.com]*

As one of the sessions held during the preconference on Hypertext Markup Language (HTML), and offered to those already familiar with HTML tags and the basics of Web design, this workshop described one of the more attractive features available on the World Wide Web: interactive forms. Stephanie Schmitt, information technology librarian

Stephanie Schmitt is Information Technology Librarian, Texas Tech University.

Reeta Sinha is Head of Collection Management, Health Sciences Center Library, Emory University.

[Haworth co-indexing entry note]: "Designing Interactive Forms." Sinha, Reeta. Co-published simultaneously in *The Serials Librarian* (The Haworth Press, Inc.) Vol. 36, No. 1/2, 1999, pp. 47-50; and: *Head in the Clouds, Feet on the Ground: Serials Vision and Common Sense* (ed: Jeffrey S. Bullington, Beatrice L. Caraway, and Beverley Geer) The Haworth Press, Inc., 1999, pp. 47-50. Single or multiple copies of this article are available for a fee from The Haworth Document Delivery Service [1-800-342-9678, 9:00 a.m. - 5:00 p.m. (EST). E-mail address: getinfo@haworthpressinc.com].

at Texas Tech University Libraries, presented this workshop, which provided an overview of the various types of forms in use on the Web. Participants were also given a hands-on opportunity to create generic-purpose forms during the workshop. The forms were to be posted to the Texas Tech library server and, after submitting the requested information, attendees would be able to retrieve them from their own e-mail accounts.

The presentation started with a description of interactive forms and how they can be used. Forms on the Web have become popular, since they enable two-way communication between those who host sites and those who visit them. Through interactive forms, one can obtain information from the user, solicit feedback, and place surveys on a Website for completion. One of the simplest types of forms is the pop-up message composer that allows the Website visitor to send an e-mail message directly to someone at the Website. In libraries, interactive forms are being used in all areas for a variety of activities. These include book request forms placed on an acquisitions department or library page, ILL requests that are processed via a Web form, and user surveys conducted by library administration.

The session then moved on to describe the components that make up forms. Forms for the Web have two main parts: the structure and the scripting. The structure of the form is built using HTML tags, while the script is, essentially, coding which takes the information collected by forms and processes it into a format that is easily utilized. Schmitt mentioned Microsoft's FrontPage as an example of software that provides such a script. While Webpages can be constructed and maintained with some degree of independence within an institution, if a form is desired, it is advised that the institution's Web administrator be consulted to assist with the script aspect of the form. There may be a script available already on the server, and correct execution of it will ensure that the data collected via forms can be retrieved and used as intended.

Forms are placed within the <BODY> and </BODY> HTML tags of a Webpage. While pages can have more than one form, a form cannot be placed within a form. The structure of forms consists of the following: a <FORM> tag which references the processing script, fields tags where information is collected from the user, labels that tell the user what information is being sought, and lastly, buttons that submit the data. Fields tags allow data to be collected in three formats:

<INPUT>, <TEXTAREA>, and <SELECT>. The <INPUT> tag can provide space for a single line of text, or radio buttons that a user clicks on to select an option or a value, or check boxes that can be marked. <TEXTAREA> gives the user an area to enter several lines of text, with the length and width of the area defined in rows and columns. The <SELECT> tag lets the user choose from provided options that appear in a scroll box or a pop-up menu. An example of a <SELECT> tag is a scroll box listing the states of the U.S. as place of residence. The user scrolls through the list, clicks on one, and it appears in the box requesting that information. Labels can be placed in a form using any kind of descriptive text that tells the user what kind of information is being requested. In the <SELECT> tag example above, "State of Residence:" could be used as the label. The final elements of the form structure are buttons placed at the end of the form. Generally, buttons submit data or allow the user to clear the form. Buttons can be images that act as buttons, or they can be created by using tags.

The three fields tags each have several attributes. These attributes vary according to the kind of fields tag used, but each tag must have a name, since this defines the name of the information that is being collected. In addition to the name, the <INPUT> tag attributes include TYPE, SIZE and MAXLENGTH (if text is entered), CHECKBOX (if the user enters information using boxes that are checked), and VALUE, which can be used to define a value such as "Submit" for the button used to submit form data. The TYPE attribute indicates how information is being collected–does the form use, for example, a CHECKBOX, or TEXT, or RADIO buttons? SIZE defines the size of the area in which text will be typed. MAXLENGTH limits the number of characters allowed for in the text field. The CHECKED attribute is only relevant if boxes or radio buttons are used on the form.

For <TEXTAREA> (input is obtained by the lines of text typed by the user), the attributes ROWS and COLS define the number of lines and the width of the text area displayed on the form. For example, in a pop-up message composer box, the size of the "box" displayed is defined by the ROWS and COLS attributes.

The fields tag <SELECT> uses the attributes SIZE, MULTIPLE, SELECTED, and VALUE. <SELECT> is the tag that provides the user with choices in a scroll box, for example. SIZE defines how many choices a user sees on a form and whether they are in a drop-down list or in a scroll box. MULTIPLE allows the user to choose more than one of the listed options. SELECTED provides the user one default choice from a list of options. VALUE defines the information that is actually sent back to the server. When using the <SELECT> tag, a companion tag <OPTION> is used. Each choice that can be selected is included as an <OPTION> tag. If a user were asked to select from a list of library types, for example, each type (academic, special, and public) would have a separate <OPTION> tag.

After covering the structure and the tags required to construct a form, the hands-on session began. Participants were asked to write down three questions they would like to ask of users via an interactive form. These questions were used to create a document using the HTML tags for forms. The document was then copied to the Webpage composer software (which included a processing script) available on the Texas Tech library server. Most participants were able to complete the HTML document using the handouts and Schmitt's assistance in a short time.

Unfortunately, the morning hands-on session on designing interactive forms was plagued with technical difficulties. The classroom building had lost Internet connectivity right before the workshop, and this loss of access meant that software was still being installed on individual workstations as the session began. But very soon after starting, participants were able to view Schmitt's projected handouts located at her Website. Print copies of the handouts were distributed, but they are also available at http://www.lib.ttu.edu/nasigecc/. Users were able to create a short form using the word processing software available on each workstation, but, as they attempted to connect to the Texas Tech library server, more problems at the classroom site occurred and many screens froze again. While the audience seemed to experience some general frustration with the technology, Schmitt presented a comprehensive introduction to creating interactive forms for Websites and answered the many, many questions asked by the participants.

HTML Standards–History and Future

Margi Mann

Presenter

Rose Robischon

Recorder

SUMMARY. HTML is being used in libraries as a method of creating Webpages. This workshop provided a historical look at HTML. The other markup languages discussed were SGML, VRML, and XML. Participants followed an HTML timeline to assist with how the different markup languages interact. *[Article copies available for a fee from The Haworth Document Delivery Service: 1-800-342-9678. E-mail address: getinfo@ haworthpressinc.com]*

Hypertext Markup Language (HTML) is used to create Webpages on the Web. HTML is like regular text in that can be stored so that it shares many of the features of regular text, e.g., formatting. There are other features of HTML which are unlike regular text, e.g., connections within the document to other text, documents, items and entities.

These connections not only contain links to other pieces of text, but to other forms of media as well. HTML is nonlinear and cyclic (no beginning and no end).

Margi Mann is Customer Services Representative, WLN, Lacey, WA.
Rose Robischon is Serials Librarian, United States Military Academy, West Point, NY.

[Haworth co-indexing entry note]: "HTML Standards–History and Future." Robischon, Rose. Co-published simultaneously in *The Serials Librarian* (The Haworth Press, Inc.) Vol. 36, No. 1/2, 1999, pp. 51-57; and: *Head in the Clouds, Feet on the Ground: Serials Vision and Common Sense* (ed: Jeffrey S. Bullington, Beatrice L. Caraway, and Beverley Geer) The Haworth Press, Inc., 1999, pp. 51-57. Single or multiple copies of this article are available for a fee from The Haworth Document Delivery Service [1-800-342-9678, 9:00 a.m. - 5:00 p.m. (EST). E-mail address: getinfo@haworthpressinc.com].

Markup language originated in the end of the last century within the publishing industry to guide typesetters with the layout instructions when printing books, documents and newspapers. It is a structure external to texts; thus, the text has two layers (the text and this external structure detailing its layout). Within the text are the embedded codes, which are the instructions. Markup language stores information for the format processor, i.e., font names, boldness, italics, beginnings of paragraphs, shading, background, picture placement, etc.–all the aesthetic aspects that we do not think of when we pick up the page and read it. It is a separate activity from the intellectual content. HTML is not the only markup language in use today; there are also Standard Generalized Markup Language (SGML), Virtual Reality Markup Language (VRML), and Extensible Markup Language (XML).

SGML is the granddaddy of markup languages, and it is making a comeback. It is a formal standard. SGML is officially known as International Standards Organization (ISO) Standard 8879/1986. Most library standards fall under ISO Technical Committee 426. Standards take approximately ten years to get approved, then they are reviewed every five years. SGML is definitely an information standard, and it is in the same family as MARC, SICI, or EDI. Even though approved in 1986, there is still only the original version to date.

SGML characteristics:

- It was the first electronic generalized markup language. There were other generalized markup languages before SGML, but they were not electronic.
- It standardizes ways to specify and define the markup in the documents. A single source file in SGML format can produce multiple formats and outputs, e.g., paper output, video output, etc.
- Any type of document can be marked up in SGML format.

Work in the past ten years has been to align SGML with other ISO standards. The strength of ISO standards is that they are designed to work with each other to minimize incompatibility problems. SGML is aligned with Document Style Semantics and Specification Language (DSSSL) and the Universal Character Set (UNICODE), which includes all known human languages and character symbols. SGML has a very fine degree of granularity in the markup; goes through multiple hierarchies and levels and an infinite number of indentations; is robust; allows exchange of documents between unlike systems; and is ideal for storing documents in a database. One of the major groups behind SGML standards development is the database producers. Data can be put into a database with an SGML front for search engine purposes. SGML is not a predefined set of tags (e.g., HTML tags like <BOLD>, <CENTER>, underline–<U>, etc.) or a standardized template for producing a document. SGML does not impose a structure on the document, which allows the author or a group of authors (e.g., chemists, musicians, etc.) to propose the language, view the description, and create the structure. This means that those in the group that it is meant for can all talk to each other about the document. An SGML document is created using a Document Type Definition (DTD). It says, "Here is my set of tags; here is my structure that I am going to use." DTDs are registered as being part of the SGML standard; they specify the elements, tags, and, more importantly, their relationships to each other. DTDs are created by standards committees, industry groups and others. DTDs can be maintained as a community standard.

SGML has been guided by an international consortium since 1993, a consortium which recently changed its name to Organization for the Advancement of Structured Information Standards (OASIS). It is a very complex standard, not easy to learn, expensive to implement, has a long implementation timeline, is expensive to convert existing documents into, and most importantly, has almost no accompanying software tools on the market to assist with conversion and implementation. SGML requires DTDs between partners, and it can be difficult to get the partners to sit down and hash out the DTDs. SGML led to the first version of HTML, which is an SGML DTD. HTML started its life in the SGML framework. CERN (European Laboratory for Particle Physics) developed this draft SGML DTD in 1991. HTML has created a marriage between SGML and the Internet.

HTML incorporated SGML advantages and eliminated the overhead to convert documents, connecting to the Internet and the exchange problems caused by SGML and DTDs. HTML shares characteristics with SGML: it is a markup language; is directly eye-readable; expresses the document structure; separates the content and the structure; is independent of all hardware and all software tags, elements, and attributes; and is an Internet-based standard.

The first version of HTML had twenty-five elements, was designed to work with other Internet standards (e.g., TCP/IP, HTTP), was under continuous development by the Internet standard community, lacked formatting options, and was never officially named "version 1," which would have defined it as a draft SGML document. Version 2 was developed in 1994. Based on the standards process, this was very quick; standards can easily go five to six years between versions. The responsibility for standards moved to the Internet Engineering Task Force (IETF), the standards body for the Internet community. Within IETF, HTML is overseen by the HTML-WG (Working Group). HTML is officially known as Request for Comment (RFC) 1866. RFCs are always in the public domain and never revised or reissued with the same number. HTML was developed by volunteers on a listserv. Version 2 went to fifty elements; established basic HTML document structure of head, body, and border; introduced basic formatting (e.g., centering, header text, paragraph text, bold, italics, etc.); had basic linking within and between documents; listing (ordered, unordered, and definition lists); insert images; and forms. The characteristics of Version 2 are that it is strictly ASCII; is analytical- and retrieval-oriented; is focused on content providers and database producers; and provides search and retrieval aspects. A problem with Version 2 was that many users had word processing backgrounds and a fair learning curve. Major milestones included an explosive, widespread adoption, the introduction of browsers, and the introduction of HTML editors. HTML Version 3.0 was released in 1995 and represented fundamental shifts in many different regards. Responsibility was turned over to the World Wide Web Consortium (W3C). This version passed into a third and unique standards process. It ceased being a community standard and became instead a worldwide standard. Version 3.0 was released in March 1995, and Version 3.2 was released in January 1996 (time between versions is becoming shorter and shorter). Version 3 had a fundamental shift: it was concerned with appearance and visual appeal and was moving away from content providers and database producers. Features of Version 3 included tables, borders and style sheets. It had ninety elements and introduced proprietary extensions. Browsers did not implement the full suite of HTML elements. HTML is now a commercial standard instead of an Internet standard. There has been an introduction of accessories, e.g., Common Gateway Interface (CGI) scripts and Java. Version 4 was developed in July 1997 and was finalized and announced in December 1997. It introduced "dynamic" HTML. Its features include cascading style sheets, support for multiple scripting languages, in-line frames, object support, and integration with UNICODE. There are three flavors of HTML 4.0: 4.0 straight (used for clean markup and cascading style sheet language), 4.0 transition (used to take care of presentation features and for users of older browser versions), and 4.0 Frameset (used with frames). Version 4 is not backward-compatible with Version 2 nor with the development of other content-orientated SGML DTDs. Tension between commercial needs and standards process is increasing.

Virtual Reality Markup Language (VRML) was proposed in 1994, Version 1.0 came out in the spring of 1995, and Version 2.0 in the summer of 1996. VRML is a content-based, plain ASCII markup language, has unique characteristics of describing 3-D shapes and retroactive environments, and has as its ultimate goals video conferencing and virtual reality. VRML is an offshoot of HTML, but is not compatible with it. Even though the goal is to be dynamic and 3-D, to date it remains static and cannot do movement. Desktop PCs do not have the computing power to support VRML; applications tend to run on supercomputers and are very process intensive. Many developers who work on VRML also worked on developing HTML. Small VRML documents are beginning to show up inside HTML documents as applets or plug-ins.

Extensible Markup Language (XML) made quite a splash this past spring. Discussions for XML began two years ago in July. It is being developed by the XML-WG of the W3C. Version 1.0 was finalized in Spring 1998. XML goals include simplifying SGML, optimizing for contact provision, and optimizing for the Web. XML has a close ongoing relationship with SGML and the SGML working group. It consists of only the markup syntax. It maintains a separation of syntax and semantics–Extended Mark-up Language (XML), Extended Linking Language (XML), and Extended Style Language (XSL). It interoperates with SGML and HTML and has a logical and physical structure. XML is made unique by its linking aspects. XML is far beyond HTML in terms of linking capabilities and is excellent for metadata. Catalogers are beginning to look seriously at XML. (Is XML the next MARC?) It interoperates with other accessory software (CSS [Cascading Style Sheets] Pearl and Java). We are beginning to see documents and publications on XML. XML has a number of applications under development. It allows different communities to define their needs better, e.g., Mathematical markup language (MATHML),

Chemical markup language (CML), etc. XML has its own browser (JUMBO). Netscape and Internet Explorer are looking into ways to incorporate XML.

Each HTML document consists of

- <HTML> tags at the beginning and end of any HTML document (<HEAD> information is not displayed to the user, but it is used by search engines.)
- The <BODY> section (This is where you put all the content. It is what the users will see when they come to the Webpage.)

There are three ways to write HTML documents: with an ASCII editor, with an HTML editor, or with a unique interface. Most word processing packages now have a "save as HTML" option.

General hints for utilizing HTML:

- Choose your HTML tool carefully.
- Know its features.
- Know the standard and proprietary extensions.
- Know your audience (think of your users).
- Learn the tags (so that you know what your editor is doing).
- Check for missing end tags or quotations.
- When structuring, make sure that you have the required attributes.
- Don't forget the title (title tag is what search engines use to display Webpages).
- Break up large documents.
- Use a hierarchy.
- Date your documents.
- Update your Webpages periodically.
- Styling (be consistent, use a template, choose style sheet carefully).
- Think of which browser you are using (think of the version of the browser).

Linking "do's" and one "don't:"

- Do make meaningful links.
- Do think about it before you actually do it.
- Do decide the number of external and internal links on each page.
- Do keep the link content concise.
- Do separate links with regular text or line breaks.

- Do check links on a periodic basis to make sure that they still function.
- Don't try to put too much into the links or make them too wordy.

Final checks:

- View the source code (good for debugging HTML documents).
- View the file as it would appear on the Web.

In this preconference session, each participant was given an "HTML & Standards Glossary," an "HTML Acronym Decoder," an "Historic Timeline for HTML," and an outline of basic HTML document structure.

Imagemaps

Donnice Cochenour

Presenter

Carol Gill

Recorder

SUMMARY. This workshop covered the basics of producing image-maps. An imagemap is a graphic image defined so that a user can click on different areas of the image and be linked to other locations on the Web. It allows the Webpage developer to define areas within an image as buttons, or hotspots, that will link to other Uniform Resource Locators (URLs) in the same way that hypertext links take the user from text in one document to another Web document. The workshop began with a background presentation about the two types of imagemaps in use. Server-side imagemaps have the map definition and coordinates residing on the server along with an interpreting program. Client-side image-maps have the map data and URLs included in the Hypertext Markup Language (HTML) tagging of the Webpage. Mapedit, the popular shareware imagemap editor for Windows, was provided during the workshop so that participants could practice building client-side image-maps. *[Article copies available for a fee from The Haworth Document Delivery Service: 1-800-342-9678. E-mail address: getinfo@haworthpressinc.com]*

Graphical user interfaces like Macintosh OS and Microsoft Windows have become the dominant PC operating systems over the last

---

Donnice Cochenour is Serials Librarian at Colorado State University.
Carol Gill is Science Librarian at Trinity University.

[Haworth co-indexing entry note]: "Imagemaps." Gill, Carol. Co-published simultaneously in *The Serials Librarian* (The Haworth Press, Inc.) Vol. 36, No. 1/2, 1999, pp. 59-62; and: *Head in the Clouds, Feet on the Ground: Serials Vision and Common Sense* (ed: Jeffrey S. Bullington, Beatrice L. Caraway, and Beverley Geer) The Haworth Press, Inc., 1999, pp. 59-62. Single or multiple copies of this article are available for a fee from The Haworth Document Delivery Service [1-800-342-9678, 9:00 a.m. - 5:00 p.m. (EST). E-mail address: getinfo@haworthpressinc.com].

few years. They are considered much easier to use than text-based MS-DOS because they lead the user through a procedure using interactive graphics rather than cryptic MS-DOS commands. Extending this approach into the networked environment, the World Wide Web has stimulated the rapid development of graphical Web browsers such as Netscape Navigator and Internet Explorer. Similarly, the use of imagemaps gives the Webpage developer a way to use a graphical image as a flexible navigation device to provide an intuitive interface to multiple links for related Webpages.

An imagemap is an interactive graphical image that provides links to multiple locations from specified areas or hotspots within the image. Hotspots or links can move users to an anchor on a different part of the same Webpage, open a different Webpage, or run a Common Gateway Interface (CGI) process depending on how the hotspot is defined within the image.

Web browsers available prior to 1996 would only work with server-side imagemaps, which required that the image, a database listing coordinates within the image, and a program to interpret the coordinates all be loaded onto the server. When a user clicks on a server-side imagemap link, the interpreting program looks up the coordinates, determines the corresponding URL for that area, and instructs the browser to open the new URL. A commonly used interpreting program is "imagemap," from the National Center for Supercomputing Applications at the University of Illinois at Urbana-Champaign. Server-side imagemaps tend to run slowly. Each time the user clicks on a hotspot in a server-side imagemap, the map coordinates are transmitted back to the server for the interpreting program to identify the corresponding URL. Then the server sends back a message to open the new URL. Users with slow Internet connections may become impatient waiting for each of these transmissions to take place.

Since early 1996 the major Web browsers have been able to support client-side imagemaps that store the map and link information on the client computer as part of the HTML coding for the Webpage. This significantly reduces traffic over the network since it's not necessary to contact the server before going to the next URL. When the user clicks on a hotspot, the browser can determine the associated URL and open it.

In addition to reducing network traffic, client-side imagemaps make Webpage management and maintenance easier because all of the data is stored in one HTML document and all editing changes can be made in the one document. Client-side imagemaps also make it possible to test a new imagemap on the page developer's computer without loading it onto a Web server, since an interpreting program like imagemap is not required.

When you visit a Webpage that has an imagemap, it is possible to determine which type you are viewing by looking at the status message area at the bottom of the Web browser screen. When the pointer is placed on a hotspot, the URL for that hotspot is displayed in the status message area. If the URL ends with a series of numbers, you're seeing map coordinates from a server-side imagemap that will be transmitted back to the server. If the URL ends in .html or .htm, you're seeing the URL from a client-side imagemap that will be opened when you click on the hotspot of the client-side imagemap.

Since the newer browsers will support client-side imagemaps, the challenge now is to create the HTML code defining the hotspots within an image. Several image editors will create the needed HTML code and insert it in the page the same way that a text editor will insert HTML codes into a new Webpage. Mapedit is a popular shareware WYSIWYG (What You See Is What You Get) image editor that was provided during the workshop for practice in building imagemaps. WebMap is another image editor available for the Macintosh.

Mapedit is not a paint program for creating an image, but it will allow the developer to use an existing image from an HTML document and convert it into an imagemap. The image can be in GIF (Graphic Interchange Format), JPEG (Joint Photographic Experts Group), or PNG (Portable Network Graphics) format and should already be the desired size for display on the Webpage before it's opened in Mapedit. Also, the image should be defined in pixels rather than as a percentage of the screen size. Defining the image in pixels ensures that the coordinates inserted by Mapedit will accurately identify the corresponding URL no matter what size of monitor or screen resolution is used to display the image.

Mapedit provides a familiar drawing toolbar with icons for outlining rectangles, circles and polygons. Clicking on the icon and then on a point within the image will anchor a corner of a rectangle or the center of a circle, then dragging the outline to the needed size and shape and clicking again will finish it. Clicking on the corner points of a polygon and then right clicking on the last corner will outline any polygon. The polygon tool allows flexibility in outlining irregularly shaped areas with the image. After outlining an area, Mapedit will ask for the URL and a text name for the link. Users with no drawing experience can quickly master the basics of drawing in Mapedit.

Imagemap areas that overlap or even surround another area can complicate the construction and use of an imagemap. The software editor will have an order of precedence for displaying links from overlapping areas. For example, with overlapping or surrounded areas, Mapedit will open the link for the area that was defined first. Therefore, any hotspots contained within a larger area must be defined first.

Most of the workshop was devoted to practicing with Mapedit. Cochenour presented several useful exercises for the participants that demonstrated the major features of imagemaps and Mapedit. One exercise produced an imagemap with multiple polygons, a circle and a rectangle all contained within a larger circular hotspot so the participant had to consider which areas to define first. A second exercise linked state outlines on a map of the United States to a list of attendees from those states.

Cochenour also provided a number of helpful suggestions for creating functional imagemaps. Make the message clearer by designing the map to model the information being presented. Large images take longer to load, so the use of smaller images is preferred. Define the image size in pixels rather than as a percentage of the screen size so that the map coordinates can be properly associated with the correct URL. Maintain a balance between the artistic and functional aspects of the image so that neither is overwhelmed by the other. Provide alternate text links on the page for users who may not be able to display images or may not automatically load images. Clearly designate the areas that are hotspots within the image. And limit the number of hotspots on the imagemap so that the number of choices doesn't distract from the information you want to provide.

Web Editors: Means to an End

Robb Waltner

Presenter

Susan Wishnetsky

Recorder

SUMMARY. Creation of Webpages, with their long and complex pages of HTML code for even the simplest of formats, can be greatly facilitated by the use of Web editors. These powerful tools provide shortcuts to change the appearance or arrangement of Webpages, eliminating many keystrokes. Recent Web editors have added many new and sophisticated features to this basic function. This preconference session demonstrated two of the most current products for editing Webpages, Netscape Composer and Microsoft FrontPage 98, covering the capabilities and the limitations of each. *[Article copies available for a fee from The Haworth Document Delivery Service: 1-800-342-9678. E-mail address: getinfo@ haworthpressinc.com]*

Workshops and classes offering instruction in Hypertext Markup Language (HTML) coding, used to format the display of text and images in Webpages, may become less common in the near future. With the rapid advancement of Webpage editors such as Microsoft's

---

Robb Waltner is Periodicals Librarian at the University of Colorado at Denver.

Susan Wishnetsky is Collection Management Librarian, Galter Health Sciences Library, Northwestern University.

[Haworth co-indexing entry note]: "Web Editors: Means to an End." Wishnetsky, Susan. Co-published simultaneously in *The Serials Librarian* (The Haworth Press, Inc.) Vol. 36, No. 1/2, 1999, pp. 63-66; and: *Head in the Clouds, Feet on the Ground: Serials Vision and Common Sense* (ed: Jeffrey S. Bullington, Beatrice L. Caraway, and Beverley Geer) The Haworth Press, Inc., 1999, pp. 63-66. Single or multiple copies of this article are available for a fee from The Haworth Document Delivery Service [1-800-342-9678, 9:00 a.m. - 5:00 p.m. (EST). E-mail address: getinfo@haworthpressinc.com].

FrontPage 98, the site structure, page layout and design, and animation of text and images can all be created and edited in an easy point-and-click medium. Two such Web editors were demonstrated by Robb Waltner in this preconference session.

Web editors simplify text editing in an HTML document by creating an environment similar to word processing programs and allowing the user, while editing text, to view the document just as it would appear in a Web browser. Early Web editors such as HTML Assistant provided relief from the tedium of manual editing of HTML by automating the insertion of basic text formatting tags; later products such as Webber and Netscape Navigator Gold began to support the creation of tables as well. Netscape Composer, the first program demonstrated in the preconference session, has added several valuable enhancements.

Users of Netscape Navigator will feel at home using Netscape Composer, which was designed to have a look similar to that of the browser. Creation of new documents can be performed by choosing "new" in the file menu; the user may also select one of the program's templates or wizards, which have design features already built in. A spell-checking option is also available. In addition to text size, style, justification, and other text formatting elements, a user of Netscape Composer, without any knowledge of HTML code, can quickly and easily

- create, resize, and edit tables
- import and resize graphics
- create hypertext links
- choose from several preset color schemes

Each of these features was demonstrated in a matter of a few seconds. Waltner followed up the demonstrations by taking a look at the HTML source document, which revealed the complexity of the code created by the program for each new feature and the formidable amount of typing required to create the same effects using HTML code alone! However, the creation of frames, online forms, imagemaps, and animation cannot be performed using Netscape Composer; to create such effects, the user must know the HTML codes for the effects and enter them manually into the source document.

Such limitations are far fewer in the second program demonstrated, Microsoft's FrontPage 98, a much more complex and versatile Web editor. The program consists of two parts, a Website "administrative" module called FrontPage Explorer and an editing module called Front-Page Editor. FrontPage Explorer allows the user to create and manage the hierarchy of an entire site, showing all the files contained in the site, the navigation structure within the pages of the site as well as all links to other sites, and the color and design features chosen for each page. A new site may be created in this module, or a preexisting site may be imported and edited within it, by selecting the appropriate command in the drop-down "file" menu. It is also within the Explorer module that a Webpage or site is actually published on the World Wide Web. A hyperlink "status" feature can show whether all the links are functioning, and a "task list" reminds the user of future plans for changes or additions to the site.

FrontPage Editor is the module in which each page is actually designed. The user may choose from about fifty different "schemes" found in the "format" menu, which combine color combinations with font and bullet styles; unfortunately, these may not be customized in any way, but different schemes may be used for different pages. Templates and wizards are also available, as well as a file of clip art. Animation of highlighted text is another option in the "format" menu. Words may be selected to spin, spiral, drop in from the top of the page, or zoom in and out on the page, among other options, simply by clicking the desired animation effect. A continuous text "marquee" can also be set up; the user chooses the direction and speed of the motion. Page transition effects may also be chosen from this menu, allowing one page to dissolve into another, or to disappear in a "wipe," stripe, or checkerboard pattern, to name a few of the choices. Linking buttons may be transformed into "hover" buttons, which change color when touched by the cursor.

Simple interactive forms are easy to create in FrontPage with some minimal typing of values and specification of how to tabulate and store the data collected. To divide and organize pages, a variety of frame formats is offered. Another feature is the imagemap, a free-form "hot spot" which turns any image on the page into a hyperlink.

A hit counter, which records the number of site visitors, and a search form, which searches the entire site for desired words or phrases, can be set up. In order to function, these features require additional FrontPage server extensions to be loaded onto the server that hosts the Website; this software is available from Microsoft free of charge.

During the editing process, many of the special effects created by FrontPage are not visible, but a tab at the bottom of the screen enables the user to switch from the editing mode to a "preview" mode, which is supposed to show how the page might look in a Web browser.[1] Another tab opens the HTML mode, where the code for the page can be seen and edited; a third tab returns the user to the normal "what-you-see-is-what-you-get" editing mode.

A great drawback of FrontPage 98 is that several of the animation features are created with code that is not standard HTML and that cannot be interpreted by Web browsers other than Microsoft's Internet Explorer 4. When using a browser that is not compatible with "dynamic" HTML, many of the effects will not appear–page transitions will appear as a simple segue, and animated text will sit motionless on the page. This is a serious limitation for Web authors who want to communicate with the world at large, and not only with those people who upgraded to Windows98 (which includes Internet Explorer 4). However, FrontPage pages do look almost the same even without the special effects; the color schemes, graphic animation, and hover buttons do function in other browsers.

Netscape Composer is available free when downloaded as a part of the Netscape Communicator package; when sold on CDs (with accompanying documentation), the same package sells for $25. It can be downloaded or ordered from Netscape's product information page at http://home.netscape.com/comprod/sales/index.html. Microsoft's FrontPage 98 sells for $100; their product site includes a tutorial that can be found at http://www.microsoft.com/frontpage/tutorial/tutorial.htm.

NOTES

1. Recorder's Note: This feature was rather disappointing in the demonstration, as several of the special effects could not be seen.

PLENARY SESSIONS

Internet Publishing Update: Assessing the Impact of Changes in Publishing Technology on Libraries

Mark Walter

SUMMARY. Changes in publishing technology are redefining the economics and even the structure of serials. In a speech to the NASIG audience, the author describes three technology trends that will impact the relationship among authors, publishers and libraries: the shift to digital masters; the rising importance of the Web and its impact on the economics, manufacturing and distribution of publishing; and the growth of the World Wide Web as the gateway to what people get from libraries. For each, a set of pressing, as yet unresolved issues is presented. The author suggests that during this transition period, when serials are published in both printed and electronic form, publishers and libraries work together to establish standard practices for the coming age of all-electronic journals. *[Article copies available for a fee from The Haworth Document Delivery Service: 1-800-342-9678. E-mail address: getinfo@haworthpressinc.com]*

The NASIG community stands at a very interesting juncture in the history of journals. On the one hand, we have more journals being published in print today than ever before. But on the other hand, electronic journals, in combination with the Web, are redefining our very definition of the term "serials." For the first time in the history of journal publishing, technology is going to force us to change our notion of the public record.

Mark Walter is Editor, Seybold Publications.

[Haworth co-indexing entry note]: "Internet Publishing Update: Assessing the Impact of Changes in Publishing Technology on Libraries." Walter, Mark. Co-published simultaneously in *The Serials Librarian* (The Haworth Press, Inc.) Vol. 36, No. 1/2, 1999, pp. 69-77; and: *Head in the Clouds, Feet on the Ground: Serials Vision and Common Sense* (ed: Jeffrey S. Bullington, Beatrice L. Caraway, and Beverley Geer) The Haworth Press, Inc., 1999, pp. 69-77. Single or multiple copies of this article are available for a fee from The Haworth Document Delivery Service [1-800-342-9678, 9:00 a.m. - 5:00 p.m. (EST). E-mail address: getinfo@haworthpressinc.com].

After nearly two decades of experiments with electronic delivery of conventional print journals, we are now witnessing the transformation of journals as we know them. That transformation will not take place overnight. It is clear, however, that it will have a profound impact on both publishers and libraries, and, of course, on the way researchers report their findings and read about the findings of their colleagues.

BACKDROP: THE MOTIVATION FOR JOURNALS

Before delving into technology, I'd like to take a moment to place technology in context. From a researcher's perspective, journals are the way to publish one's research, to establish credentials. There is much that could be said about whether universities ought to change their emphasis on publishing research as a criteria for promotion and tenure, but for our purposes here, I'll take the point of view of the consumer.

Where is the reader headed? In a nutshell, readers are headed online. They expect to see research sooner; they expect to see better filters; they expect to see research linked to related materials; and they expect that electronic media will be the transport for getting their hands on the actual data. That's the customer you all serve.

It's also useful to keep in mind the business forces that are at work here, and the objectives of the players, because technology will impact the symbiotic relationship between libraries and publishers.

Historically, libraries have been the keepers of the archive and in many cases the center for accessing the journals. Librarians know how to categorize and catalog research materials, and they are adept at helping researchers find information.

Publishers have been the traditional conduit for researchers to get their findings published. Over the years, publishers have developed expertise in the peer-review process, in manuscript preparation and markup, and in the production of collections of papers in what we know as a journal. Whereas the library is a nonprofit service center, the publisher is usually running a for-profit operation. Some serial publishers are nonprofits, of course, but even at nonprofits there is pressure to run the business as efficiently as possible.

So this is where we have been. But in the past couple of years, technology has thrust itself to the forefront of many of the issues the NASIG group faces. Technology is expanding the boundaries of the term "serials," forcing us to examine and adapt our practices to an age of digital documents.

DIGITAL MASTERS

For many journals, especially those in the technical sciences, the printed page will soon no longer be the master record of the published results. Yes, it contains the authored paper, and maybe illustrative pictures or text; but for the first time in the history of serials, we are now publishing journal articles in which some of what is contained in the article does not appear in print.

Take a very popular example, namely, publishing articles in Adobe's Portable Document Format (PDF) for display or printing from an Acrobat viewer. Acrobat pages are a faithful master of the printed page, but they also can contain other information. For example, they might contain original color illustrations or photographs that were reproduced in black and white in the printed journal. The reason for including the color originals in the Acrobat version and not in print is purely economical–it costs much more to print all pages of a journal in four colors than it does to include color in an Acrobat file being delivered on CD-ROM or online. In electronic form, there is no penalty, other than larger files, for including color photos.

Another typical Acrobat addition is the use of links. What used to be just links to other pages of the Acrobat document are now routinely links to places on the Web. As with Hypertext Markup Language (HTML) versions of journal articles, often these links have no counterpart in print. For example, it's now routine in many journals to link citations to their abstracts or even to the full text of the article being cited.

It is now also possible to attach and embed sound, animation and video files to the original document. These are not widely used in journals today, in part because of technical challenges, but as those go away, what is to keep researchers from demanding this freedom? From the researchers' point of view, an animation may do a better job of illustrating a point than sixteen pictures reproduced in sequence. A 3-D model, which cannot be rendered except in two dimensions on paper, may be the best way to present a new physical structure.

In short, the electronic journal will have capabilities that are not economically feasible, and sometimes not technically possible, to produce in print.

ADDED COSTS

Making straight PDFs from articles that will be published in print is a trivial exercise for the publisher. But adding other information, especially links, introduces new complexity into the production process.

Bookmarks may be generated automatically, but inline links to external Websites may not be: It depends on the composition system being used, and how well it accepts and recognizes URLs (Universal Resource Locators) in the document. In many applications, the URLs provided by the author must be converted by hand or by a software conversion program into links that are recognized in the page makeup program, before the PDF is generated. There also can be additional steps in preparing graphics and full-text indexing. Though a trivial cost once they are set up, they still must be done.

The point is that even for a page-based metaphor, there are costs associated with creating digital masters. The more value I add to the electronic product, the higher my costs.

IMPLICATIONS AND QUESTIONS

The implication is obvious: the digital rendition of articles may contain information (such as an attached animation) that is not displayed in print. In addition, the digital version may have features, such as active links, that are not features of print.

The issue I'll raise is one many libraries already face: If the PDF file contains things that the printed version does not, which one is the master that gets archived? At what point do we say that the printed version is a derivative of the electronic and that the electronic one is the master?

BEYOND PAGES

It gets worse. Many STM (Scientific, Technical, Medical) publishers are converting their articles to SGML (Standard Generalized Markup Language). This conversion separates the form from the content and enables the publisher to encode the structure of the content–the hierarchy of the headings, for example–in a way that is independent of the page.

It also means that their master file is not a digital page at all; in fact, presentation is applied when the publisher prepares a document for a particular medium. So it gets formatted in pages for print and formatted as HTML for the Web.

The implication is that we will begin to move away from the page metaphor. In the near future, the display of HTML will improve beyond what it is today. In the years ahead, Web browsers will be able to display XML (Extensible Markup Language)–a simplified version of SGML–and they will read style sheets that come much closer to what we have for print composition than what is possible in Web browsers today. As that happens we will move farther away from printed pages as a reasonable archive of the journal.

So we are left with some basic questions: What is the archive? Is it what was published in print? Is the HTML created for the Web? Is The SGML source or an aggregate of source and published materials?

Publishers consider the SGML source their master, because that is what they will use to create HTML and to create future renditions of their electronic journals. But what about the libraries? There has been considerable debate in NASIG circles about libraries having the right to receive the digital archive of e-journals they purchased. Yet do libraries really want unformatted SGML files?

The reality is that as journals become electronic and grow to become part of a networked hyperlink corpus, only the publisher will be in a position to maintain that corpus, to keep its links up-to-date and to refresh the display of original material in a format that is compatible with everchanging technology.

Maybe libraries are being gouged on prices. But libraries should also understand that publishers are making an investment they've never had to make before. A database that handles logical pointers (instead of links to physical files) isn't cheap. And neither is modifying all of the citations to turn them into SGML so that authors' names are coded as authors and are therefore easily linked to databases or abstracts or even to the cited works.

The trend in publishing today, one that we at Seybold believe will continue for the foreseeable future, is for publishers to add value to the electronic versions of the things they publish. That means adding value to the content itself. It also means giving content additional context, for example, real links from cited works to an online database of other works by that author.

It is likely that publishers will continue to add this value to satisfy the demands of their readers and to differentiate their products. It's also likely that a majority of libraries will not have the resources or expertise to take on this task. That means that the industry will have to grapple with a new paradigm for archiving. If publishers cannot be trusted to keep their material indefinitely, then libraries and publishers together will have to figure out a new way to ensure preservation of historical documents that exist only in digital form.

WEB DELIVERY AND CUSTOM PUBLISHING

The Web is changing the economics as well as the content of serial publishing. Karen Hunter of Elsevier put it very well last February when she spoke at the annual meeting of the Professional Division of AAP. "The Web was a godsend to us. We no longer had to design the user interface, buy and deliver the software for searching and displaying the documents, and supply the hardware to run it on." It is a big help to libraries, too, to finally move away from each CD-ROM having its own software and user interface.

In industrialized nations, we now have a nearly ubiquitous delivery target, and the economics of this new medium are radically different than with print or CD. Though the cost of adding each user is not zero, the raw cost of manufacturing and delivery is significantly less than in print. In particular, on the Web we can do something that simply was not economically feasible in print, namely, custom journals.

Among the leading STM journal publishers, the trend is to enable subscribers to select their favorite articles, save their frequent queries, or bookmark their favorite topics. The direction is to utilize the economics of the Web to tailor the product to the reader's preferences. This trend moves the serial business away from one of mass production of a single product to one in which a large database or web is the basis for many customized products.

IMPLICATIONS

It's not a quantum leap, then, to see that once publishers have articles categorized, they can allow subscribers to pick their own topics of interest. Publishers can let readers decide what part of the issue is published to them. They can let readers decide if they want the articles e-mailed to them or accessed from a Website. The notion of seeing a journal as one static entity begins to break down in favor of a new model: a corpus of research.

Eventually (and this will happen first in specialty journals with small subscriber bases), publishers will ask: Why bother printing at all? Why not let printing be done on demand by the customer? The technology is in place to do this today, and soon it will become more affordable to do so.

QUESTIONS

The questions, then, are not technological ones, but business ones: Is the library willing to maintain profiles for all the subscribers from its patrons? If the library pays for the subscription, how do I charge? Will the researcher kick in some extra money for these features? If print dies out, what becomes of the century-old tradition of volumes and issues? This is already happening in encyclopedias. Some editors envision a day when there will be no more editions. There will be only one, ever changing edition: the Web one.

So far, e-journals have maintained the notion of editions. But that is an artifact of a publishing process grounded in print. We publish editions because we're on a cycle of publication–quarterly, monthly, weekly. Only now is the publishing community beginning to slowly adapt to publishing on a continuous cycle. Look around at sites that do not have print counterparts. Do they hold a story for the next edition? Or do they put it up when it's ready?

Serials evolved because mass printing and ubiquitous postal service created an economical way to distribute research. Over time, the volumes and issues of journals also became a convenient and unambiguous way for researchers to cite previously published works. But if technology alters the dynamics and economics of publishing–as I believe it is doing today–then before long we may need a different convention for citing works, one that takes into account this notion of continuous publishing. The NASIG group, for which serials hold special interest, is a good one, I believe, to explore this future and establish standard practices for the industry to follow.

THE WEB AS THE FOCAL POINT OF COMPUTING

The third trend is that the Web is becoming the focal point for computing. In that context, the library's homepage becomes the front door to the virtual electronic library, one that is always open and one that I can visit from the comfort of my dorm room, apartment or house.

As this trend continues, libraries will face increasing pressure to devote precious resources to maintaining that digital library. There is considerable value in cataloging not only internal but also external information, in making the catalog accessible to patrons and in maintaining access privileges to online serials hosted at publishers' sites. But it will also take resources, enough that one can ask if libraries will also bear the burden of maintaining unique customer profiles for thousands of patrons and hundreds of journals.

WHAT ABOUT LIBRARIES CUTTING OUT THE MIDDLEMAN?

In that context, it's worth examining the idea that libraries could adopt a new model for serials, one that bypasses the publisher altogether. After all, the libraries already have the site; they catalog the articles; they could also publish and host the source for their faculty or for journals in specific disciplines.

I believe that some journals will indeed be published this way. The questions are: How good will they be? Will they be prestigious enough to count for tenure? Is the library–and more to the point, is the school–willing to make the investment necessary to become a publisher, even an electronic one?

Even though the distribution costs will go down considerably, editorial costs for high-quality, peer-reviewed journals, will remain. Consider the payment to editors to make sure peer review happens; the maintenance of the database of peer reviewers; the copyediting, proofreading, and production costs. (A cynic might say that there is always the indentured servant, otherwise known as the grad student.) There will also be the costs of converting the data to SGML, of storing the accumulated material, of making print-ready versions for those who request it, and, most of all, of hyperlinking the cited sources and keeping the links up-to-date.

Readers notice quality, and quality does not happen by accident. So while this model may work in some cases, it is likely, at least in the short term, that they will be the exception, not the rule. Consumers like the speed of self-publishing, but they not be willing to give up the quality they've come to expect from professional journals. Publishers will be forced to shorten their publication cycles without sacrificing quality and features. In most cases, the school and its library will be hard pressed to keep pace.

CONCLUSION

Technology has a way of creeping from novelty to indispensable aid. For many people, e-journals are still a novelty–a nice comple-ment, but not necessarily a replacement for receiving the printed prod-uct. But a new generation of researchers view the world differently: they go first to the electronic archive and print out from that if they want to read from a paper page. As our culture moves increasingly in that direction, not just for journals but also for news, directories, reference, catalogs and all manner of published material, libraries and publishers will have to ask themselves how they want to handle print.

These changes in technology will not arrive wholesale overnight, but they are already occurring, and the pace of technological change is steadily increasing. For a group such as this one, there are serious issues to be addressed, and now is not too soon to begin sitting down together to decide how you want to shape serials in a way that will serve your interests.

Technology will beckon consumers; it will entice the researcher to ask for more in the way of electronic journals. It will be up to the library community, in cooperation with publishers, to manage expec-tations, to decide what technologies to accept and which ones to reject; to decide what conventions of print to keep and what can be left behind.

I don't have the answers to these difficult questions, but if I stimu-late you to start and continue those discussions, I will have succeeded. We are at a very interesting juncture in the history of journals. And you, the members of NASIG, are the ones who will help shape its future course.

Publishing in the New World

Patricia S. Schroeder

The following is an audiotape transcription by Marguerite Horn, with revisions by Patricia Schroeder. Bracketed information has been added to clarify a citation, sentence, or abbreviation. Italics were added for citations.

SUMMARY. Intellectual property rights are threatened by current trends in publishing and by the changing market. In this presentation, Patricia S. Schroeder, an advocate for intellectual property rights, describes the need for understanding and cooperation and for support for legislation to protect authors' rights. *[Article copies available for a fee from The Haworth Document Delivery Service: 1-800-342-9678. E-mail address: getinfo@haworthpressinc. com]*

Thank you all so much, and thank you, Judy. That's very nice. Thank you for inviting me back to my favorite state, Colorado. For those of you from Texas we always said, "Be glad that I haven't had time to iron our state because it would be bigger than Texas." We'll just keep the wrinkles in Colorado because we like those mountains, but just think of how big Colorado could be if we flattened it out! It is a delight to be here. And I'm glad to see that some of you are going to try the casinos tomorrow. Let me tell you, they're no different than

Patricia S. Schroeder is President and Chief Executive Officer of the Association of American Publishers, Inc.

Marguerite Horn is Head of the Cataloging Department, State University of New York at Albany.

[Haworth co-indexing entry note]: "Publishing in the New World." Schroeder, Patricia S. Co-published simultaneously in *The Serials Librarian* (The Haworth Press, Inc.) Vol. 36, No. 1/2, 1999, pp. 79-91; and: *Head in the Clouds, Feet on the Ground: Serials Vision and Common Sense* (ed: Jeffrey S. Bullington, Beatrice L. Caraway, and Beverley Geer) The Haworth Press, Inc., 1999, pp. 79-91. Single or multiple copies of this article are available for a fee from The Haworth Document Delivery Service [1-800-342-9678, 9:00 a.m. - 5:00 p.m. (EST). E-mail address: getinfo@haworthpressinc.com].

casinos anywhere else–leave your wallets here and you'll have a better time. I'm thrilled to see so many wonderful people from America's most prestigious university research libraries–that is wonderful and I know how difficult your task is. So I am thrilled that you've all selected this wonderful place to come.

If I am speaking slowly, it's because I feel like I'm 125 years old this morning. I always enjoy being on a campus. It seems like all of us just got out of school, and we can carry that little fantasy around until we come back to a campus. I woke up earlier this Saturday morning, being on eastern time, and so I was walking up on University Hill where students live in these little apartments–none of them have had their lawns mowed and they all look exactly like they looked when I was in school–that isn't any different. But to be walking up there early in the morning, and seeing all the beer cans and the cups sitting all over the yard, and the doors still propped open with a phone book or something. I thought, "My word, here I am up, dressed and walking around, and their party just ended a few moments ago!" It was like you just walked into this scene. That ended my fantasy that I just got out of school! More time has passed than I care to admit.

But it's always great to come to Boulder and see that great blue sky in the morning and breathe the air. It is just fantastic. We always say Colorado is the nation's lungs where Americans come to breathe. Citizens worked very hard getting oxygenated fuels and all sorts of things to lessen the smog that we had here for a while, and we are very proud of that. So we certainly hope you get outdoors and enjoy it!

And we constantly have a fight (as you drive around and look) between bulldozers and the Front Range. And lately the bulldozers seem to win. Boulder is an interesting town, for those of you who are interested in town planning, in that it has had the most restrictive growth measures of any Colorado town; the rest have all just kind of yielded. So Boulder still looks absolutely marvelous; the only problem is–the price of the housing has gone straight up. It's a very interesting place to get involved in the growth debate. We have had that growth debate going on in Colorado since World War II where we were a little backwater and suddenly a lot of people came out here during the war, really liked it, decided to stay and then the natives got really owly about "Who are these people moving in here?" Colorado has gone through the whole series of bumper stickers: "If God meant Texans to ski, he'd have made bullshit white." Really wonderful things like that.

And those very threatening ones where they'd have a Colorado license plate that said "Native." Of course, most of these people with those bumper stickers meant they had lived here ten years, rather than two!

It has been a marvelous state to represent for twenty-four years. I had a great time writing the book [*24 Years of Housework and the Place Is Still a Mess: My Life in Politics*], which is now in its third printing, so we're having a lot of fun with it. If you get a chance, take a look at it, because I think it gives you a little flavor of Colorado politics. It also tells you we're not known for dress out here. One of the things that I pointed out as coming from here, which has always been very casual when it comes to dress, there's always somebody from New York who comes to Denver, turns up their nose and says, "It wouldn't be hard to be the best dressed woman in Denver." And we're like, "So be it, we don't care." I got elected and went to Washington in 1972 with a two-year-old and a six-year-old, and the town was absolutely on its ear. They could not believe somebody would elect a woman with a young family to come to Congress. So this is the whole story about that, but when you look at the pictures in the book, you also understand, I was dressing like a Coloradan in Washington, which was quite shocking to many. But you all remember in 1976, the Carters came, and they were really rather casual. But one of my favorite stories was 1981 when I knew the place had changed and I was in deep do-do. I was at an inaugural party at the Reagan inauguration. First of all, so many minks gave their life for that event it was unbelievable. I kept thinking, "Well, at least the mink farms in Colorado must be doing well up in the mountains." I'm at this party, and in my typical Colorado background not being too clued in on the rich and beautiful, and some woman comes over and says to me "Who's dress is that?" and I said "It's mine!" I suddenly realized there was no way to pull those words back in and swallow them and that I was the one that looked like the fool, not her, and it was indeed in a different day! But it was great fun to be able to just tell those things because you really get the texture and flavor of what's going on.

There are so many issues that we could talk about this morning, but you're going to be talking about them in great detail all weekend, and you're going to be talking with other people who are nationally recognized as experts. I'm nationally recognized as a generalist! I'm proud to be a generalist because I think the challenge for every American as we end this decade, end this century, and end this millennium is to try and think a little bigger. I think about this a lot in another capacity I have as head of an institute in Boston called the Institute for Civil Society. We are trying to stir thought on how does America get back to the de Tocqueville civil society that Europeans and other people saluted in this country and many of us fear has eroded quite a bit! Certainly in Congress it has eroded quite a bit. And what is "it?" There is a large group of people wanting to define the civil society as political correctness, Miss Manners, "I'm civil and you're not unless you agree with me." Those are not traditional American definitions of civil society. We've always had very vigorous debates, but the kind of debates we had when I got to Congress were debates on facts. There was no more polarized debate in this country than there was on the Vietnam War, and in 1972 I walked into the middle of that debate at thirty-two years of age. Suddenly I was also in the middle of the impeachment decision on Nixon, and, of course that was a rather polarized debate, you can imagine! But we dealt with what we thought were the facts, and the other side dealt with what they thought were the facts. Citizens tried to find out what they really believed. And I think one of the things that has happened lately is that instead of debating and dealing in the facts, we immediately go for the personal. If you don't agree with me, I start attacking you personally. Or your mother's lineage or whatever. What does that have to do with the issue? And if you're just a citizen trying to watch this, you don't come away with really any more information. It looks like a food fight. So, how do we get people back into the facts and out of personal attacks? Research librarians must be very frustrated also. You have probably never seen so many fact-free debates as we have had in this nation on issues, and the less you know the louder you yell, and the more you try to go for emotional hot buttons. It's getting more and more difficult to sort out where it is we are and what it is we should believe. Talk radio rules the 90s.

The other thing that I must say has happened in this country is that the National Rifle Association has defined how all politics work and it makes me very sad. What do I mean by that? The National Rifle Association put together this incredible organization. And you've got to respect it. You've got to respect it because it got its way–everyday, any day it wanted it. The NRA got all sorts of people to join. They had a way to crank out mail and postcards and alerts overnight in seconds that could come back into Washington and scare the bejeezus out of any elected official that ever thought about doing anything they didn't want done. Most of the time, and I hope this doesn't shock you, what they told their members was a bit of a stretch (that's the nicest way I can say it). Because cynicism runs so deep about politicians, people totally believed the NRA's "facts!" I remember I had a bill (as an example) making it a federal crime to pack in your checked luggage a loaded gun (that sounds pretty reasonable and easy, doesn't it?). And the reason I had it was we had had many baggage handlers at the Denver airport killed handling baggage. You know how people all get into hobbies and go out and buy all new stuff? People decided they were going to go hunting for the first time, and they were going to go hunting in Colorado. They'd go buy a fancy rifle, and they'd have the guy load it at the store so they wouldn't have to remember all the process, and then they pack it up and take it out there. If you're the baggage handler you don't appreciate this! I want to tell you they had posters of me printed all over with bull's eyes on 'em. I was "gonna take away your gun." This bill was "the camel's nose in the tent." This was going to be the "end of the second amendment." I would send my bill back to people and say, "This is really all it is." Citizen cynicism is so deep they'd say, "No, send the real bill. This isn't the right one."

People don't understand that while we have standards about what you can say and can't say when you advertise toothpaste or when you advertise anything else (if it is incorrect, you can sue), we don't have those standards for political speech. If one makes a statement about a car that's not right, you can sue. In politics there are no rules. The first amendment allows you to say anything you want to say. And, so, as a consequence, we have learned that people operate much more from fear than feeling good about their causes. Even the right wing found that when they took over the Congress, their membership dropped way off. It was much easier to organize if you could say, "Democrats are in control and they're gonna do this and they're gonna do that. Send in your money and save the world." Well, if your guys are in control, you're not as interested in sending your money in. So, we learned it is more rewarding to keep people all riled up. Probably everyone of us today has gotten riled up about some stuff that very often is distorted. And, I think, all of us need to take pause, take a look, figure out where we're going, figure out where we've been. How do we play in this new environment that hardly any of us can totally understand? But that is going to be the real challenge. So I hope you have lots of time to do that up here this weekend, where we think because Colorado's a little bit higher, we see things a little clearer! And maybe the vision all comes back for where we're going. Dream on!

Most people are very surprised to find out that I really spent all my life in Congress investing a tremendous amount of time in learning about intellectual property. People look at you, like, "Why would you do that?" You certainly don't get any press for that. Most people pay absolutely no attention to it. Most people are aware that I did a lot of things on women's issues and on the Armed Services Committee and all of that, but never on intellectual property. So, why did I spend all of this time in that area? Well, I think of late, I feel much better that I did, because it meant that what I thought when I first got to Congress has really turned out to be true. And that is–as you look at this nation in the post-NAFTA era and the post-GATT era and you look at this global village that we're in–the most important thing we're going to be able to do for American jobs in the next century is intellectual property. I don't think Americans are going to be able to compete very often making things with their hands. We're just seeing this huge auto strike. As of today, GM is totally shut down. That strike is basically about moving stuff offshore–let's be perfectly honest. In this post-NAFTA environment, they don't like it. I understand that. If I were an auto worker, I wouldn't like it. But it's going to be very hard to stop corporate boards from doing whatever they can do to cut costs. In this global economy, they can pretty much do what they want to do. This is a very difficult game that we are in right now.

Nevertheless, let me tell you, if you missed it, what the May 7 statistics said about intellectual property. On May 7 Senator Hatch and Senator Leahy released the intellectual property part of our country's economy. It showed that the fastest growing part of our economy–it's growing three times faster than the rest of our economy–is around the copyright industries. Is that stunning? It is larger than automobiles; it is larger than agriculture. The number one export from this country now is intellectual property. It used to be the number one export was airplanes–Boeing. It's a really interesting shift from products hands made to products heads make. I think this is going to happen more and more, and I'll tell you why. If you look at the Internet, 82 percent of the people using the Internet on the globe speak English. Now we can debate about whether this is a good thing or a bad thing, but let me tell you that English is now the lingua franca–let's be perfectly honest. And almost everybody is using English as their resource material. Think of the great American textbooks that have been done for the professions. If you are studying engineering anywhere on the globe or medicine anywhere on the globe or anything you want to think of anywhere on the globe, you are probably going to be reading texts in English. The other side of the coin is they were probably pirated! It's very frustrating to be in my new role. There's good news/bad news. Every Chinese university is using our textbooks; bad news, not one of our companies has gotten a dime in copyright. So if you figure our legitimate exports are now number one, think of where we would be if we didn't have this piracy going on.

And the piracy is so much easier than it's ever been. People who publish books have been very late coming to this. The people who produce music figured it out much faster because the technology got them earlier. The same thing happened with movies and the same with videos. But with books all you could do was go xerox the whole book somewhere–that's a little cumbersome, takes a lot of time, and most people didn't want to do that. But now you can scan it and each copy is just as clear as or better than the first one. That's a whole new challenge.

The other thing is the technology now is so doggone good–I mean it really is so good and so easy–that we forget that because it is so easy to copy anything you create; we forget it isn't any easier for you to create it than it was a millennium ago. Creation has not been made easier by technology. So, creativity is no easier than it ever was. In fact, I would profess it's more difficult because more and more things are being produced all the time. So to be creative and crisp and fresh and something that people really want to see, it's a lot harder. But if it's so easy to copy what you do, it's very easy then to just diminish what you did as a creator. We should never diminish creators because this great American creativity has really taken over the world culture almost, is something we should be terribly proud of and protect. Bottom line, it's twenty-first-century jobs for the young people we are educating.

If you look at the Constitution, the only place where the word "rights" is used in the body of the Constitution is vis-à-vis patents and copyright, which is very interesting. All the rest of the places the words "rights" are used are in the Bill of Rights, amendments to the Constitution. Probably the last president who really understood this was Lincoln. Lincoln was a patent and copyright lawyer, and he used to always say the reason intellectual property rights were in the body of the Constitution is our forefathers understood totally how important it was to fan the fires of this creative American genius that we've created. So for years and years and years copyright has been some arcane thing that we keep lawyers behind a door down at the end of the hall to deal with. And now suddenly the whole universe is changing, and how do you apply that law to what's happening today? How do we look at the overall job context? Where are we going?

On campuses, when I was teaching at Princeton, I got into constant fights with young people, because they kept saying to me, "You're going to work for the big publishers." And I would say, "Well just a second." They had all bought into the digital futures coalition which says everything should be free–and you know these kids, they're great: they scan all their textbooks up there, they do everything, they trade software, sound recordings. They have these co-ops going where copyright is the last thing they're thinking about. But I would say to them, "What is it you plan to do when you graduate from here? If you're going to be a steelworker, you're doing the right thing, I guess, economically, but if you're planning to do what I think you're probably going to be doing and what most Princeton grads are going to be doing, your behavior right now is pretty stupid, because you're strangling your future before you even got it!" And nobody has really challenged them to think that way, and I think we'd better get them thinking that way. Maybe there's another vision of where this country is moving post-GATT, post-NAFTA, but I don't think there is. I think we all ought to be preparing them properly for what it is they're probably going to be doing and how important it's going to be to compete there globally in the e-commerce environment.

Look, what is it that this country has done so well? You people have been at the forefront of it. We have figured out how to organize volumes and volumes of technical, professional, and difficult information and make it accessible. There's going to be a greater need for that than ever before because every minute there's more and more of this stuff being generated out there. You can go out on the Internet, and you can find information all over the place, but it may be wrong. (I hope that doesn't come as a shock!) It hasn't been vetted. You'd be really running a very high risk if all you did was go out from site to site, pull it down and rely on it. Navigating this information flood is going to get more and more difficult for the average person. And it's going to be very important to figure out what we all do in that environment. You will be key.

I think the people who deal in copyright want to be able to use the Internet for e-commerce so we can deliver our stuff as rapidly as everyone else. Right now it makes no sense. You can do e-commerce with Amazon.com to order a book (which goes really fast), but then the book comes by snail mail. Well, why does it come by snail mail? Because if you did it by e-commerce (there are ways that you can have machines that can make a book–that's not a big deal), but you can't protect that copyright–somebody can break that software, get in there, and your book is gone. Basically, many Americans are more and more investment bankers in copyright, because, if others can copy your work without paying you, I don't know how you eat. Now in these debates, I hear all sorts of things, like, "Well, didn't those songwriters write those songs so people will sing them and listen to them? Aren't they happy that people are listening to them? What else do they want?" I'll tell you, they want food, money, mortgage payments, etc. "Didn't authors write these books so people would read 'em?" However, no one ever says that to the technology people. Think about this–the technology people have been brilliant in getting into our minds. No one ever says, "Didn't they make those computers so we could use them? What do you mean they want us to pay for them?" Or "Didn't they make this table or didn't they make this mike for us to use? What do you mean we have to pay for them? Come on! They should be so happy that we're using their products." Think about how our culture uses that argument against intellectual property, but we would never use that argument for real property. Basically for our own national interests we should be aggressively protecting intellectual property, but we're shooting ourselves in the foot.

And look at this debate that's been going on in Texas that has been absolutely making me wacko. Some argued the state should buy every seven-year-old a laptop, and they'd never have to buy anything again for them. And they are winning! They were on the Today Show again last week. Matt Lauer says to a Texas advocate, "Isn't that pretty expensive, at least for the first initial [outlay]?" "Oh it won't be much at all–just an electronic thing they put at their desk." Well, first of all, that's a total duck, and the guy should have been hit real hard on that. But secondly, it's not like "If you build it they will come." Buy this computer, just plug it in and write in "second grade" and the programs all come up; "third grade," the program comes up. "K-12" it's all there. It's magic. It's cheap. No problem. Maybe they know there's no content contained in the laptop and are going to let all these kids go out on the Internet and find what they want! Well, what some are gonna find will bring down every public school system in America! You don't just do that. Literacy is terribly important, but it is the on ramp to the information highway. People have got to learn to read first, and they have got to learn to process stuff. And we all know that a young child looking at a screen, the brain goes into that passive alpha state. When they are young, they need books and interaction with adults and talking and being read to. And that's how you build the neurons in the brain and the synapses. And yet somehow we're convincing everybody that all we have to do is buy a little palm screen for kids, and it will sit there and stimulate them even more!

I came in a whole different generation where our whole neighborhood gathered around the two TVs to watch Kukla, Fran, and Ollie. So, I realize that I am a troglodyte and will just stipulate that. But I feel like I'm suffering from attention deficit disorder 90 percent of the time in this society, as you're getting bombarded by all this stuff. And we're all going to feel more and more like it. And it's a real challenge to figure out how we process this. And people are going to be coming to you. You're going to be the people that they look to. And they're going to be looking to this country because the great thing this country has done is show how to organize museums, with phenomenal information that people can process as they walk through, and libraries and textbooks and all sorts of things. We just should be very proud of that. Yes, we know we gave the world Elvis–that's great. But we also did this, too. We often forget the intellectual part of what we did. This country has more brain factories (i.e., research universities and top global universities) than any place else on the planet. And that came with everybody working together to present material in a way that people can process, learn, grow, and then move on. So we ought to be very proud of it. And we ought to be talking to each other, figuring out how we hold that intellectual lead.

Language is so important, and people keep saying, "You belong to the big book publishers!" And I say, "Barnes and Noble is bigger than any publisher in America, but they're not big. The telephone companies, each one of them is bigger than all publishing together–but they're 'Baby Bells.' " Language is interesting, but it tells you how publishers were asleep when they got a label slapped on them. And it has kind of poisoned that water as everybody snarls and hisses at each other, trying to figure out a twenty-first-century agenda.

The other thing I've been amazed about in the whole publishing, library, copyright area has been how polarized the community is. I look at the movie industry, the recording industry, and the software industry and, knowing human beings, I really don't believe that the screen writers, the film directors, the actors, and everybody else love the film companies more than the authors and the agents and everybody love the publishers. I just don't think that they do. But they have learned that when they come to Washington it's "rumps together, horns out." When our groups come to Washington they're all beating each other up–they just bring their fights right to the capital with them.

I remember saying to some of the writers one day, "I honestly don't understand you. You are working on the side of no copyright." "Well, that's right," they said, "because we don't think we're getting enough from the publishers." And I said, "Well, great! That's how we'll end the argument. If copyright goes away, then you won't have any argument with the publishers!" And they said, "Well, that's not really fair. It won't go away." Well, I don't know how you can think it won't go away if you've got the authors out there saying "We don't want copyright–get rid of copyright." What are you talking about? This is a great populist notion–you can have everything for free. Show me the American that says, "No, I really want to pay. No, please make me pay, I'm dying to pay!" It's not going to happen. So, somehow we come in and continue all of these fights rather than talking to each other trying to figure out where it is we can all work together.

Copyright provides the cake for this nation to eat. Who gets what size piece of the cake is a process that goes on in negotiations after you've preserved the cake. If you haven't preserved the cake, obviously you don't have to worry about piece sizes. Authors hire agents, agents go to publishers. Authors say, "Why didn't you get me more money?" and the agents say, "Well, the publishers are greedy." Who wants to help the greedy! Basically all of us need to know much more about copyright law. If I were head of an authors' group, I would be sure they knew the in's and out's of copyright law. I always found in politics, anytime you had to kiss through a picket fence–i.e., the author's here, the publisher's here, and the agent is the picket fence–there's always potential for problems, not to mention splinters in your lips!

As you know, in Congress we have been working very hard on trying to get the WIPO [World Intellectual Property Organization] implementation through–this is a treaty that was signed a year and a half ago in Geneva by one hundred and twenty or thirty countries. We think it's very important that the United States ratify it, because if the United States does not ratify it, then no other country really cares. They'd just as soon take our stuff for free. If we don't do it, the Europeans are going to do it first through their Eurosystem, and then they will be the new lead dogs in intellectual property. I'm not very anxious about conceding to them. And if you think you don't like what's here, remember in the European system they don't share our concept of fair use. Our system is very different from their system. And the countries who implement the bill in this new global environment may be able to impose laws on everyone else. Basically, at the moment, WIPO embraces standard U.S. copyright law, which allows more user rights than Europe does. If we drop the WIPO implementation ball in this Congress, I think you're apt to see the Euros do it or the whole thing implodes and nothing happens. For our country, it's a huge problem if WIPO does not pass because the Internet will look like yellow pages in the sky. I prefer seeing the Internet being used to transmit your content information more quickly, but it won't happen unless rights holders are protected.

What does the treaty basically say? It basically is a prohibition against creating a commercial technology that is exclusively built to destroy a software program that's protecting copyright. Now this isn't really hard. Many say the treaty will be impeding technological progress. If I have a burglar alarm in my house and somebody invents a way to defeat that burglar alarm, that happens to be a crime in every state in the union. Nobody's saying "Hey, the law is impeding technological progress!" The law is very specific about how this technology must be something that was invented to sell to others to defeat your security architecture protecting your copyright. That sounds like breaking and entering to me. Why are we so uptight about this? Other than this anticircumvention provision, the treaty is basically U.S. copyright law. Who knows what it's going to be when it gets done? The Senate renamed it, in its wisdom, to the Digital Millennium Copyright Act. You gotta love the Senate. They always have to make things almost too grandiose. It was, like, please! The Digital Millennium Copyright Act? We haven't even had the printing press for a millennium! So who knows what a millennium's going to bring? But we know we need global protection for rights holders to do e-commerce on the net and the WIPO treaty is the road map.

Everything is changing. Who ever thought Europeans would surrender their passports? Who ever thought that they would be surrendering their currency? Europricing is here. I was with the British book publishers, and they're frantic. Since they're not in the Euro, do they put on books the Euro price? Clearly they're going to want to sell them in Europe! We fight change because we understand what we have now and fear the law of the unintended consequences if laws change. But, we must have change to compete globally, just like the Euros are having to do changes to compete.

I think Colorado is the proper place to try and do some out-of-the-box thinking about the course corrections needed. I honestly believe research libraries are going to be more important than ever before. Because while you have all of this publishing going on–self-publishing–it's going to be more and more critical to sort, sort, sort, and find what's real. And people are going to be desperate for that kind of service, after they get over discovering the novelty of, "Oh, look at this!" We're like babies discovering their hands. But once you get through that stage, then one wants focus. You're going to be very key in that. There will be a bigger and bigger demand for good content of high quality. But we won't keep the high-quality content unless people pay for it. I'm sorry–money is a motivator. People can't afford to volunteer. You need the high-quality content going with the high-level technology. The laws should find a way so that it doesn't become "either/or." Too many people think, "Well, we've got to spend the money on the technology or we won't look modern, but we don't have enough money to spend it both on technology and content, so then the content should be free." Well, again, that's very shortsighted for this country's future workers.

Thank you for letting me come here. I'd be happy to answer questions about anything that you would like to ask. And I again welcome you to Colorado. Thank you very, very much.

It's Personal, It's Digital and It's Serial: Trends That May Affect Higher Education, Publishing and Libraries

Ellen J. Waite-Franzen

SUMMARY. What are some of the important trends to watch that may affect the way information is delivered and used? This paper looks at emerging technologies and social trends to provide some thought-provoking questions for higher education, publishing, and libraries. Scenario planning is presented as a way to look at and plan for a world that is quickly changing and impacted by technology. *[Article copies available for a fee from The Haworth Document Delivery Service: 1-800-342-9678. E-mail address: getinfo@haworthpressinc.com]*

I want to commend the folks who chose the conference title, "Head in the Clouds, Feet on the Ground." This is a wonderful maxim for these times. My intent for this paper is to take this maxim and relate it directly to our world in higher education and libraries. All of us, whether we are in education, libraries, publishing, technology or industry, need to stop and take a 30,000-foot view of the many destinations that are possible. We need to see the many different paths that we

---

Ellen J. Waite-Franzen is Associate Provost for Information Services, University of Richmond.

All URLs cited in this paper were current as of the date the paper was presented (June 21, 1998).

[Haworth co-indexing entry note]: "It's Personal, It's Digital and It's Serial: Trends That May Affect Higher Education, Publishing and Libraries." Waite-Franzen, Ellen J. Co-published simultaneously in *The Serials Librarian* (The Haworth Press, Inc.) Vol. 36, No. 1/2, 1999, pp. 93-112; and: *Head in the Clouds, Feet on the Ground: Serials Vision and Common Sense* (ed: Jeffrey S. Bullington, Beatrice L. Caraway, and Beverley Geer) The Haworth Press, Inc., 1999, pp. 93-112. Single or multiple copies of this article are available for a fee from The Haworth Document Delivery Service [1-800-342-9678, 9:00 a.m. - 5:00 p.m. (EST). E-mail address: getinfo@haworthpressinc.com].

can take to get to those destinations. And while the rocks in our paths need our attention, we won't get to our destination if we only focus on what is three feet in front of us. I have three goals for this paper.

My first goal is to introduce a particular planning methodology, scenario planning, that is useful when the future is not clear, when our destinations are not known.

My second goal is to present trends and technologies that I believe are predictors of a very different future. These could be thought of as the possible paths to our future state.

And my final goal is to tie the first two goals together. I will pose some questions, based on the trends, that we must ask about our future. These questions should help us to begin to think about possible scenarios for our institutions, our libraries and ourselves.

SCENARIO PLANNING

I came across scenario planning in two books recommended to me by amazon.com, my favorite bookstore. The first is *Scenarios, the Art of Strategic Conversation,* by Kees Van Der Heijden.[1] And the second is *The Living Company, Habits for Survival in a Turbulent Business Environment,* by Arie De Geus.[2] De Geus worked for Royal Dutch Shell for thirty-eight years and also is widely credited with organizing the concept of the learning organization.

De Geus explains in this book how, over the years, Royal Dutch Shell embraced all the current planning methodologies and trends as they arose. These included bottom-up planning, management by objectives, and a process they called the unified planning machinery. Traditional methodologies, such as strategic planning, rely on a list of typical industry predictions, and the creators of the plan build a case around those predictions. De Geus contends that our typical strategic planning methodologies focus on one future, and that future normally looks very much like today.

Shell found that the problem with these methodologies was the failure or the inability of the methodology to respond to turbulent times and the unpredictable changes in the world. For the oil industry these turbulent, unpredictable times were the rise in power of OPEC in the 1970s and the collapse of oil prices in the 1980s. The industry had not predicted those major events. Fortunately for Shell, back in the 1970s, they had started another planning process that was running alongside their traditional strategic planning methods. And the process they were using is called scenario planning.

De Geus and his colleagues at Shell used the work of David Ingvar, the head of neurobiology at the University of Lund, in their development of this methodology. Ingvar's research shows that the human brain is constantly attempting to make sense of the future. Every moment of our lives we instinctively create action plans and programs for the future. These plans are then sequentially organized as a series of potential actions and the brain stores them in our prefrontal lobes.

Ingvar believes that we visit these possible futures and remember our visits, and he calls this "a memory of the future." It is an internal process within the brain, related to man's language ability and to perception. It helps us sort through a plethora of images and sensations coming into the brain by assigning relevance to them. We perceive something as meaningful if it fits *meaningfully* with a memory that we have made of an anticipated future.

Why have we evolved with this enhancement? Ingvar notes that an obvious reason would be to prepare us for action once one of these futures materializes. We will not perceive a signal from the outside world unless it is relevant to an option for the future we have already worked out in our imaginations. The more memories of the future we develop, the more open and receptive we will be to signals from the outside world.[3]

Scenario planning builds on the organization's memory of the future. As I view scenario planning, it is a very complex and difficult planning methodology. When an organization uses this technique, the organization examines a variety of possible events and impacts, often looking at the worst case as well as the best case. It must then develop a portfolio of responses to the possible futures. Scenario planning requires us to take a long view to help us plan different paths of action if different things happen. Not one plan . . . many plans. And it requires that we look beyond our normal indicators for our possible futures.

The following questions illustrate the difference between typical planning methodologies and scenario planning. For Shell, the typical planning methodology would start with questions such as:

- Based on what we know today, will the price of oil fall?
- Will competitors expand into our business?
- Will the OPEC disband?

And then the debate begins among the managers, and no conclusions, or right answers, arise. Or the managers reach consensus and agree that, yes, the price of oil will fall, and then construct a plan based on that now accepted fact.

Using scenario planning, De Geus points out, the questions would be slightly different, but the answers would be radically different.

- What would we do if the price of oil falls or rises?
- What would we do if Microsoft expands into our business?
- What would we do if OPEC disbands?

When managers are asked these types of questions, they need to respond with different action plans and scenarios, based on a number of different futures.

In our institutions today, we all know that something radical is going to happen to us in the next three, five, ten years. What this will be we have a hard time articulating and, in fact, spend much time debating. While we often debate the vision, we do not develop the actions we should take if a particular future does indeed come to pass. We are caught in a "Catch-22" situation. We cannot plan for our future because we cannot agree on our future. My experience at the ACRL conference in April 1997, as a member of a panel responding to Eli Noam's vision of the future for higher education, is an example of this impotent kind of discussion. None of the panelists or Noam discussed the possible actions higher education should take if the economic world of education really does change. Instead we debated the vision.

In the final section of this paper, based upon the trends that I am about to present, I am going to pose some scenario questions that should provoke our thinking and that should lead to more productive discussions on our personal and institutional futures.

THE TRENDS

Our desktop computers are getting faster, and disk storage continues to drop in cost. The June 18, 1998, *New York Times* lead article in the *Circuits* section stated what we all know: "No matter how carefully you shop, one thing is almost certain, in ninety days or less, a better, faster, cheaper computer will be available. The frantic pace of change in the computer industry guarantees that today's cutting edge technology will be dull within two years."[4] Technological change is happening faster than even our technological forecasters predicted a year ago, and penetration into the home is also on high speed. In June, *PC Magazine* reported that computers have reached a 45-percent penetration in U.S. homes. In homes with higher income, the penetration is 65 percent. Over $100,000 income, the penetration is 70 percent.[5] And while most of us are still focused on the speed of our desktop computers (when will it go to 500MHz? January 1999), there are other developments beyond desktop speed and storage capacity that are worth our attention and may in the long run affect our educational and information environments more than a 1000MHz computer.

What are some of those trends? For over a year, I have been collecting Websites, articles, and ads for new products as well as keeping track of developments in the technology and information areas. When I was reviewing my folder to prepare for this paper, three groups emerged:

- Group I is *Ubiquitous Computing*. This group includes developments in computers, hardware, devices, and networking technologies.
- Group II is *Ubiquitous Information*. This group includes developments in electronic information, its creation and its distribution.
- Group III is *Social Trends and Reactions to Ubiquitous Computing and Ubiquitous Information.*

UBIQUITOUS COMPUTING

Ubiquitous is word that is now popping up whenever the words "computing" and "technology" are around. It is a word that is conveying the change in how the technology industry is approaching future products and services. *Ubiquitous* means existing or being everywhere at the same time; constantly encountered; widespread. It is a word that conveys volume or magnitude. It is not a word that would have been coupled with computing ten years ago, although I found the first signs of it being used in earnest in the research labs about five years ago. Given the meaning of ubiquitous, then *ubiquitous computing* means computing everywhere, all of the time. Computing is widespread; it is integrated into our environments.

Mark Weiser, of Xerox's Palo Alto Research Center, on his Website (http://www.ubiq.com/hypertext.weiser/UbiHome.html) takes responsibility for the concept of ubiquitous computing. Ubiquitous computing is the third era in computing. The first era was the mainframe era, big computers shared by a select group of people. Now, we are possibly at the end of the personal computing era, person and machine sharing the desktop. Next comes ubiquitous computing, or the age of calm technology, when technology recedes into the background of our lives but is ever present. Before we can have truly ubiquitous computing, we need to have the communication infrastructure and network in place for the ubiquitous network.

UBIQUITOUS NETWORKS

PC Magazine says "historians will label the years 1995 to 2005 the Decade of Wireless."[6] I want to give you a little personal history here on wireless. Wireless was a hot ticket back in the mid-90s. Wake Forest University used wireless to solve some of the campus infrastructure and access problems when it went to its laptop requirement for students. But almost as soon as it became hot, it died. Two things happened: The wireless technology development came to a standstill and applications started eating up bandwidth. In May 1997, at a conference that I attended on technology in business schools, a leading expert in network technology pronounced wireless "dead, dead, dead."

One year later, wireless, big and fat, has re-emerged as a major player in our world. The leap in development happened. Wireless has a life for a number of reasons. Perhaps the most important is that the corporate world needs wireless; the consumer needs wireless. There is nothing so compelling to industry as real unmet need. Why do we need it? One reason is that the most difficult part of any network is what is called "the last mile." This is that wire into the house or the office that is often provided by the local telephone provider and is often not up to the same standards as the rest of the network. But what if "the last mile" weren't a problem? Our problems with communicating with our personal portable devices as well as many of our physical connection problems would be solved.

Another related development in this area of ubiquitous networking includes satellite networks rather than fiber networks. Even though "the last mile" is the biggest problem in the physical network, laying the fiber to our homes, offices and institutions is not easy, and the expense of providing it and servicing it is significant. Satellite networks that will serve our digital world are serious business and will be part of our day-to-day network soon. I admit that six months ago when *Newsweek* ran an illustration of the Microsoft/Bill Gates satellite concept, I made fun of it. No more. Motorola now has fifty-one satellites in orbit that are supplying information; two other competitors are putting up test satellites. Bill Gates backs one of the competitors, Teledisc.

A project in the MIT Media Lab is called BodyNet (http://clark. lcs.mit.edu/bodynet.html), a kind of "personal local wireless network" that integrates various digital information appliances. Interoperability among most such devices–watches, cameras, cellular phones, laptop computers–is now all but nonexistent, thus restricting their flexibility and accessibility to the worldwide digital network. But imagine if this were not the case. Initial BodyNet work includes the development of languages and software to coordinate these personal appliances so that they work together and share information.

PERSONAL DIGITAL ASSISTANTS (PDAS)

Other evidence of ubiquitous computing is the evolution of the personal digital assistant, PDA, or handheld device. The "personal digital assistant" is one of those other phrases that has emerged into our everyday technology language this past year. The personal digital assistant or PDA comes in all sizes and flavors. We have many PDAs that have traveled with us from the music world; they include the Walkman and Discman. No jogger can do without one of these.

But PDAs are becoming more important to everyone, and the development in the PDA market is astounding. The world is swiftly moving from the desktop computer doing everything to having a gadget that does one or two tasks well, at a price that is affordable for the typical consumer.

Cell phones are personal digital assistants. And some of them are getting smarter; they can be cordless phones and cell phones; they know when they are in or out of range without any intervention from us. (This gets back to the developments in the ubiquitous network.)

The PalmPilot (http:palmpilot.3com.com/home.html) may well be the best-known emerging multi-tasking device in this category. While I heard a faculty member describe a PalmPilot as a sledge hammer looking for a nail, I also have many colleagues and friends who are tied to their PalmPilots, who find them more useful than a cell phone. The fact that PalmPilots are available at Bloomingdales, as well as at any computer store, leads me to think that this is one device that is being widely adopted.

Another device that has caught my attention is CrossPad, or a portable digital portfolio (http://www.cross-pcg.com). A CrossPad looks just like a typical leather portfolio. It has a pad of paper on it, and a special pen. The pad digitizes the notes, which are then transferred to the word processor in the PC.

Handheld computers that run either Windows CE or the full Windows suite such as Toshiba's Libretto, or the Compaq handheld, are a few steps up in functionality from the palmhelds although they are slightly larger. You can actually write or edit a document or do a PowerPoint presentation with these computers. Windows CE is also showing up inside appliances other than computers, including car radios that respond to voice commands, as well as a forthcoming video game from Sega called Dreamquest.[7]

Here's more evidence of ubiquitous computing: digital cameras. Gameboy has the coolest digital camera (http://www.nintendo.com/gbcinfoseek.html). What makes it cool? Its price of $45. We can all own this device that records thirty images at a time. You can customize the images, paint them, import them to Gameboy games, export them to a computer. And while these are PDAs that store information, they also allow us to create new content that could not be created without them.

When we talk about ubiquitous computing these are the types of computers that first jump to mind, but there are other PDAs that provide information, they don't just act as storage devices for our information.

MORE PERSONAL DIGITAL ASSISTANTS

Global positioning devices tell you where you are and how to get where you want to go. Though still a little flawed, they are getting better. The *New York Times* recently reviewed them, and while global positioning devices are not foolproof, they are certainly on their way to full functionality.[8]

For a person like me who is addicted to the Weather Channel, my very own Accu weather pager (http://www.weatherpager.com) for $9.95 a month, might be a great personal assistant. This little device provides regional weather forecasts and advisories. While cars might be the largest personal assistants that we own, finding a radio station that one wants to listen to is often a challenge. Is it worth $9.95 a month to get the type of music or news you want, without commercials? A new satellite network is being developed that consumers can subscribe to that guarantees fifty different channels of commercial-free radio wherever the car is located (http://www.cdradio.com).

Pagers have undergone much development and are no longer just pagers; they can send detailed messages as well. Even watches are getting into the communications field; Seiko has one that reminds me of a Dick Tracy watch/phone. The Seiko Website (http://www.messagewatch.com) for this device says:

> A full Feature SEIKO® digital watch pager that is also your personal pager, extended answering machine, and news channel, weather forecaster, lottery numbers, sports scores, financial information, ski and surf reports, custom alpha messages, reminder notification, email custom notification and more! Batteries even last an average of 18 months in normal use.[9]

And they adjust automatically as you cross time zones. And does it have a price that allows many people to purchase it? Yes. The price of the watch pager starts at $49.95.

SPEECH RECOGNITION SOFTWARE

One of the developments that will make computers useable by more people is the integration of speech recognition software. The computers' abilities to communicate with humans still lags behind its other capabilities. Speech recognition is changing this. Continuous dictation software is available now and is under fast-track development. Two packages, Dragon (http://www.naturalspeech.com) and Via Voice from IBM (http://www.ibm.com/viavoice), are less than $200. Speech is predicted to be the interface of the future and will make computers useable for many people who lack keyboarding skills. Speech recognition is still a first-generation product, but widespread adoption is predicted, and the Gartner Group predicts that by 2001 this will be a standard interface with our computers.

FUTURE DEVICES

While you might not think of smart cards and electronic cash as personal digital assistants or part of the ubiquitous computing environment, they are, and they will make our lives easier.

Electronic books are emerging once again. Three new devices are scheduled to be released in fall 1998. The Softbook, the Rocket ebook and the EB Dedicated Reader are the newest attempts at replacing the printed book with an electronic equivalent. The text of the book is downloaded into the devices, and each device can hold more than one book. A possible use for the electronic book is to replace highly used reference books or textbooks. Or, if the cost drops from the $300-$1600 range, to store all our vacation reading on one small device.

There are also some interesting developments in research labs. At the MIT Media Lab (http://www.media.mit.edu), research includes eyepiece computers that recall peoples' faces and names based on security software that is currently available.

MIT's Media Laboratory professor, Michael Resnick, has developed digital Legos that are Lego blocks with miniature computers (http://el.www.media.mit.edu/groups/el/projects/programmable-brick). Using their desktop machines, children can write instructions for the computer and using infrared signals send the instructions to the block. While computers and toys have been linked for years, this development goes further, since the child, not the manufacturer, programs the toy.

Going to the extremes, there are wearable computers or ubiquitously ubiquitous computers. In MIT's Media Lab, researchers and students are hard at work integrating computers into or onto our bodies and into our everyday settings (http://lcs.www.media.mit.edu/projects/wearables/). One of the doctoral candidates, Thad Starner, does all of his computing using a wearable computer. The display is in his eyeglasses. The processor is carried on his belt. He controls it with a stylus that resembles a remote control (http://testarne.www.media.mit.edu/people/testarne/).

Bradley Rhodes, a doctoral candidate at MIT, has a project that is referred to as the "remembrance agent" (http://rhodes.www.media. mit.edu/people/rhodes/RA). This application examines the files, the e-mail, the articles, the Webpages you are looking at and recommends other files, e-mails, articles, Webpages that might be important to your situation. While this agent is a PDA, it also extends into my second watch area of ubiquitous information.

UBIQUITOUS INFORMATION

If ubiquitous computing means that computers are so embedded in our daily life that we don't notice them, then my concept of ubiquitous information carries that same idea of providing us with the information we want and need, when (or as) we need it. The remembrance agent goes beyond computers making our communications and tasks easier; it goes to the heart of many of our worlds, significantly affecting what information we will see and review.

In this watch area, there are a number of projects and developments in new information-focused collaborations, knowledge management, knowledge-based systems, and in information production and distribution. These projects will be catalysts for change and are foretelling of a very different future of information retrieval and delivery.

KNOWLEDGE MANAGEMENT SYSTEMS

The Gartner Group at their Gartner Group Predicts conference reported that knowledge-based systems are seeing a

> resurgence of interest due to the new distribution medium of the WWW, which changes the economics of knowledge based system development. Gartner predicts that intelligent agents will emerge from their highly specific functions to become a widespread metaphor underlying much of the future of software development.[10]

While knowledge management has been on the agenda in the IT industry for a number of years, has anything tangible happened in this arena? The answer is yes. DuPont has a knowledge management process up and working in Richmond, Virginia. Polymer engineers share information in a knowledge management system that uses software from the software developer Warren-Forethought Inc. (http://www.mockingbird.com/info/highlights.htm). This system contains information or knowledge culled from DuPont's staff in manufacturing plants and corporate offices. It provides training as well as information on daily development and manufacturing issues. The plant employs a fraction of the staff of a traditional facility because of this system.

Another re-emerging technology is content filtering. Perfect content filters will provide us with only the information we need; no more, no less. This is also an area where there is a resurgence in development geared toward the corporate environment because of the amount of information corporations need to review and use.

An example of a content filter producer is grapeVINE (http://www.gvt.com/index2.htm). GrapeVINE filters information off the Web, and its primary customer base is corporate. Their Website states:

> grapeVINE solves the problem of keeping the enterprise informed by enabling and stimulating the sharing of key experiences and knowledge. It enhances Netscape Compass Server by allowing people to be informed of content on the Internet and their Intranet without being overloaded with irrelevant information.[11]

Closely related to content filters are push technologies. Push technologies aggregate content and push it to us. Push technologies are also being used in corporations to distribute company data. Some of the well-known push program companies are BackWeb, PointCast, and Marimba. Push is an important concept in the knowledge management portfolio. One site (http://www.strom.com/imc/t4a.html) that is current as of May 13,1998, lists forty-two different current push technology companies and their products.

Push is one technology to watch closely in the next few years. Gartner reports on the "hype cycles" for different technologies. When a new technology becomes available, there is high expectation for the technology to change the world. Then we go through a period of disenchantment with the technology when it cannot perform to that level of expectation. Some technologies die at this point; others go back to the labs and undergo more development. Or the world changes enough that the technology becomes useful. The last wave in the cycle is the wave of realism as the technology re-emerges and finally meets expectations. Push technology has gone through the first two waves, and Gartner predicts that it is a technology that is finding its place in our information world.

The Gartner Group also predicts that knowledge management systems are going to trigger a revolutionary leap, rather than an evolutionary leap, in the power of information technology and information delivery. If we can filter information and put together the right data to create knowledge, this will provide a great leap in our educational and corporate information systems.

DIGITAL CONTENT

Beyond the traditional conversions of print to digital, other developments are taking place in content creation and content ownership. We must acknowledge that the proliferation of business and commercial content on the Web is a new development. Corporations and businesses are creating content and distributing it on their Websites. Information that was previously not available at all, either internally or externally, is now available online. And this is useful information both for the consumer and the industry. Practically every national corporation has a Website. Every major national newspaper has a Website. This is free, useful, valuable information that was not available to the consumer three years ago.

And there is information on the Web that the consumer does pay for, but that now she/he can get easier and faster and often times with added enhancements. Just one genre example here. Music librarians should know about sheet music online sites. Sunhawk (http://www. sunhawk.com), in the state of Washington, allows you to download the first pages of sheet music to try out; or if you have the right plug-in, they will play it for you. If you want it, you buy it, download the full score, and print it out. There are other similar sites which even include a religious music site:

- http://www.halleonard.com
- http://olga.com
- http://www.downeast.net/ppm
- http://www.sheetmusicdirect.com
- http:// www.worshiptogether.com

Other projects that could directly affect libraries include new collaborations between institutions. At Johns Hopkins, the Community of Science (http://www.cos.com) is a possible forerunner of universities and research centers collaborating together to register researchers and then to share research information amongst the membership. Research is shared electronically, at the will of the producer. Other organizations, such as the mathematicians, and groups of universities, such as ARL and CIC, that already collaborate in other areas are considering similar initiatives aimed at sharing the research output of the faculty. Obviously, if this scenario becomes widely successful, it could do away with scholarly publishing and distribution as we know it.

Digital personal archives are beginning to get some attention. The *New York Times* recently had a think piece on the subject.[12] What happens when a person dies and the majority of their output has been digital? How will this affect our archives in the future? Will we print out the files on paper and catalog them, or will they only exist in their digital environment? Will we be able to share the archives widely and make files ubiquitously available, therefore solving a problem of providing access to primary source documents?

THE LIBRARY OF THE FUTURE

Among other projects in the MIT labs are some that are targeted at changing our concept of the library. MIT's Library 2000 (http://www.lcs.mit.edu/web-project/Brochure/ltt/ltt.html) project describes their project in the following terms:

> The project's approach is pragmatic: to develop, build, and prime with data a prototype test-bed of an on-line electronic library using the technology and system configurations expected to be economically feasible in the year 2000. Our basic hypothesis is that the technology of on-line storage, display, and communications will soon make it economically possible to place the entire contents of any library on-line and make them accessible from computer workstations located anywhere. Our vision is that one will be able to browse any book, journal, paper, thesis, or report using an ordinary personal computer, and follow citations by pointing–the report or paper selected should pop up immediately in an adjacent window. The following is an important part of the

project: Our goal is not to invent or develop any of these evolving technologies, but rather to work out how to harness them.[13]

Another MIT group, The Personal Interface Architecture group (http://www.lcs.mit.edu/web_project/Brochure/pia/pia.html), addresses one of the central questions of this new technology: How should one interact with the flood of digital information soon to become available to the individual? In short, they ask, "How do you touch a planetful of bits?"

Another MIT project, called the Livingroom of Tomorrow (http://clark.lcs.mit.edu/LOT.html), seeks to reinvent our living spaces so that we can naturally and comfortably receive this deluge of information.

And MIT's Library Channel (http://clark.lcs.mit.edu/LC.html) project, meanwhile, is developing new technologies that will essentially bring the resources of the public library into the home–or perhaps into one's back pocket–through the earlier mentioned BodyNet and the Livingroom of Tomorrow.

These are the developments that have caught my attention in the summer of 1998. (If you are reading this paper in the summer of 1999 or 2000, you are probably chuckling over all the obvious developments that I missed that are now impacting you as you read this paper.) These aggressive developments and trends do lead to the next watch area, the impact on our societies and cultures.

SOCIAL TRENDS AND REACTIONS TO UBIQUITOUS COMPUTING AND UBIQUITOUS INFORMATION

What are some of the trends that result from the development in ubiquitous computing and ubiquitous information? First and perhaps foremost is the development that I call "The Unquestioning Faith in the WWW and its Future."

The WWW has quickly transitioned from a research network to an unstable academic work area, a playground, and a major business medium. Web commerce is growing at a steady and significant rate. Dell does $3 million a day on the Web, the travel industry generates $2 million a week. In 1997, we did $2.8 billion worth of business via the Web; by 2000, the U.S. Department of Commerce predicts we will do $12 billion.[14]

Providing Web access and services is a major business initiative for our telephone, cable, television and software industries. WebTV, while not an instant success, is getting a share of the market and may well be a precursor of other information technologies and services that extend into our homes.

Practically every major corporation has a Website, and the number of sites is growing rapidly. More importantly, more useful information is being provided at each site. Let me give you an example from my personal experience. I am a great fan of IKEA stores, but there are not many of them in the U.S. In late 1997, I went on the Web and searched for IKEA.com (http://www.ikea.com). Sure enough, I got a page. But it was basically an empty site that said, "Thanks for visiting." Nothing else, not even a very interesting graphic. I went to the page in June 1998, and it is now a fully developed Website that showcased many of their product offerings. I could not order products yet, but I expect the next time I go to it, I will be able to do so.

I regularly shop on the Web. *Amazon.com* (http://www.amazon. com) is my favorite bookstore. *Www.Harry and David.com* (http:// www. harryanddavid.com) is my favorite site for presents for the in-laws. *B&B on the Beach* has my favorite site for renting a home on the outer banks in North Carolina (http://www.bandbonthebeach. com). The United Airlines site (http://www.ual.com) is my favorite site for plane reservations and car rentals, even though I usually fly USAir. I could go on and on, but there are many consumers like me, and our numbers will grow. I save time; I find what I want easily and quickly; and I can do it in the middle of the night, or Sunday mornings, or whenever I have time.

COMPUTERS AS COMPUTATION, COMMUNICATION, COLLABORATION TOOLS

The evolution of computers from tools for computation to tools for communication to tools for collaboration is the second trend. Our first use of computers was to compute, usually in isolation. Then computers evolved into communication devices. Now the computer is seen as a collaboration device. Gartner is using this terminology, as is Microsoft. At Wake Forest University, their earlier experiment with ubiquitous computing promoted computers as communication devices. In 1998, at a spring meeting on their experience, the phrase was "computers to enhance collaboration." We are deliberately moving into the era of shared ideas, shared creation and shared space; and computers are making this easier. As computers play larger roles in assisting with communication and collaboration, their importance in our homes, our offices and our schools will increase.

CONNECTING AS A NATIONAL AND INTERNATIONAL INITIATIVE

Clinton, Gore and Gingrich are not the only national leaders who are pushing connectivity to our schools and homes. France has a highly developed network. Japan is investing in running fiber to every residence in the country. Over fifty-five million non-English-speaking people use the Internet, according to Euro-Marketing Associates. Emarketer, an Internet research group, predicts that the number of Internet users from outside the U.S. will begin to outnumber U.S. users by 1999.

The goals of this initiative are often related to the communication trend mentioned above, but the potential exists for computers to serve in collaborative initiatives as well. This initiative will have a tremendous impact on our higher educational institutions as more children are connected earlier in their lives.

ACCEPTANCE OF TECHNOLOGY AND EXCITEMENT ABOUT IT

Computers prices are dropping and will continue to drop. In fact, they are dropping faster than predicted. In January 1998, the prediction was that in five years or less, if you can afford a TV, you will be able to afford a PC. In July 1998, the $500 233MHz computer is available, a price that was predicted to appear in late 1999. Today school systems are being wired and standards are being developed to include technology as part of the curriculum of K-12. But there is a trend that goes beyond availability; there is excitement about technology. "The net generation," as Don Tapscott has labeled our youngsters, are the instigators of the excitement.[15] While adults may perceive that children have learning and attention weaknesses, embracing technology is not one of their weaknesses. Children are comfortable with computers and technology. Like it or not, they will push our world forward into integrating technology even more into our lives.

PLANNING OUR FUTURES

The real voyage of discovery consists not in seeking new lands but in seeing with new eyes.

–Marcel Proust

This paper has covered two major topics: scenario-planning essentials and trends in technology and society. This leads to the final section, the final challenge, tying this all together. What are our possible futures in higher education when we think of the trends of ubiquitous computing, ubiquitous information, and the resulting social changes? We cannot doubt that our institutions, our libraries, and our jobs will change as a result of technology's impact. The crystal balls, however, are not very clear on how all of the technological, social, cultural and political changes will come together and affect our institutions and our lives. We do not have an accurate view of our future world. While we cannot precisely forecast our future, we can pose questions in ways that will first make us acknowledge that we must begin to plan for a different environment and secondly, prompt us to develop scenarios or future memories. The goal is not to have *the* plan, but to have many plans that can be called upon given the actual environment.

The scenarios and questions that follow are to serve as catalysts for you and your environment and I hope that they stimulate you to develop other scenarios that are relevant to your institution and your professional life.

SOME SCENARIOS TO CONSIDER

It is 2001. The initial consortial efforts of higher education institutions have evolved into many new collaborations, including a major scholarly electronic publishing and distribution initiative. Scholarly publishing, as we know it in 1998, no longer exists. The creation, aggregation, distribution and access are all done by a centralized association. What are the possible roles for faculty and libraries in this environment? Describe the possible ways that this will affect your library's physical environment. Describe the technological infrastructure that your campus would need to implement this future.

Distance learning is indeed a reality that even top-tier institutions are heavily engaged in providing. What are the possible actions that your college or university should take to position itself for this reality?

MIT's Library 2000 project is out of the lab and into the home. Microsoft has acquired the rights to the software and bundles it with Office 2000. Every user of Office 2000 has the benefit of a robust knowledge management system. What roles do librarians play in an environment where our major services are now delivered electronically to our patrons?

It is 2005. Information arrives in the library digitally and it is organized by the MIT/MS 2000-KM system. Although the library still purchases books on demand, they arrive ready to shelve. What roles do librarians play in this scenario?

It is 1998. Review the PDAs available today. Brainstorm on all the possible uses of the PDAs in the academic environment. Describe ways for your institution to integrate them into the university environment.

It is 2001. Students arrive on campus equipped with many personal digital assistants. Describe the PDAs of the year 2001 that you think students will use in their leisure and academic life. How will these PDAs integrate with the library and with the services that the library provides?

It is 2005. You are twenty-seven years old and a new graduate of the University of Illinois' School of Library and Information Science. What has your education prepared you to do in the world?

It is 1998. You are forty-five years old. You expect to work for another eighteen years. You are a serialist. You have worked in technical services for your entire career, but you are now the last librarian in this ARL library's technical services division. You know that within the next two years the university library's plan is to have no librarians in the division. The creation and dissemination of scholarly information continues to evolve. What are the possible roles that you can play in the library's new organization? How will you make our educational and information worlds a better place?

It is 1998. Your challenge is to develop scenarios that fit your institution, your library and your life.

I end this paper with a quote from Yogi Berra that I believe characterizes our future and also the art of scenario planning: "When you come to a fork in the road, take it."

NOTES

1. Kees van der Heijden, *Scenarios, The Art of Strategic Conversation.* (Chichester: John Wiley and Sons, 1996).

2. Arie de Geus, *The Living Company, Habits for Survival in a Turbulent Business Environment.* (Boston: Harvard Business School Press, 1997).

3. Ibid., 34-37.

4. Peter H. Lewis, "Bigger, Faster, More 3-D," *New York Times* (18 June 1998): D1.

5. Jake Kirchner, "PC Prices: How Low Can They Go?" *PC Magazine* 17, no. 5 (10 March 1998): 30.

6. Frank J. Derfler Jr., "Wireless Communications," *PC Magazine* 17, no. 11 (9 June 1998): 198.

7. Joe Hutsko, "Windows 95 and Its Smaller Sibling," *New York Times* (4 June 1998): E8.

8. Katie Hafner, "Scooby Doo, Where Are You?" *New York Times* (14 May 1998): E1.

9. *Seiko Messagewatch*. Available: http://www.messagewatch.com.

10. David House, Eric Schmidt, and John Roth, "What's Coming Down the Pipe (or Fiber?" (panel discussion at 'Gartner Group Predicts the IT Marketplace,' San Diego, Calif., April 7-9, 1998). Audiovisual copy available at http://events.audionet.com/events/gartner/predicts98/whatscoming/.

11. "Products," *GrapeVINE Technologies*, par. 1. Available: http://www.gvt.com/index2.htm. 21 September 1998.

12. Lou Grinzo, "In a Life's Digital Flotsum, A Bittersweet Balm For Death's Sting," *New York Times* (7 May 1998): E7.

13. *Library 2000*. Available: http://www.lcs.mit.edu/web-project/Brochure/ltt/ltt.html.

14. "Internet Growth So Swift It's a Blur," *Richmond Times-Dispatch* (16 April 1998): A1.

15. Don Tapscott, *Growing Up Digital: The Rise of the Net Generation.* (New York: McGraw-Hill, 1997).

CONCURRENT SESSIONS

How I Learned to Love Neodata

Marcia Tuttle
Chuck J. Vanstrom
Mark Earley

SUMMARY. Neodata is the world's largest magazine fulfillment center, with offices located in Boulder. Long a source of problems for serials and public service personnel, the fulfillment center has changed recently, thanks to both electronic technology and the work of subscription agents. The scope of the fulfillment center's business has expanded from providing mailing labels and performing other circulation services for magazine publishers to telemarketing, claimed issue supply and 800-number customer service for a wider range of publishers. *[Article copies available for a fee from The Haworth Document Delivery Service: 1-800-342-9678. E-mail address: getinfo@haworthpressinc.com]*

Marcia Tuttle is a library serials consultant in Chapel Hill, North Carolina.
Chuck J. Vanstrom is Vice President for Industry Relations, Centrobe.
Mark Earley is Vice President of Information Services and Products, Centrobe.

[Haworth co-indexing entry note]: "How I Learned to Love Neodata." Tuttle, Marcia, Chuck J. Vanstrom, and Mark Earley. Co-published simultaneously in *The Serials Librarian* (The Haworth Press, Inc.) Vol. 36, No. 1/2, 1999, pp. 115-132; and: *Head in the Clouds, Feet on the Ground: Serials Vision and Common Sense* (ed: Jeffrey S. Bullington, Beatrice L. Caraway, and Beverley Geer) The Haworth Press, Inc., 1999, pp. 115-132. Single or multiple copies of this article are available for a fee from The Haworth Document Delivery Service [1-800-342-9678, 9:00 a.m. - 5:00 p.m. (EST). E-mail address: getinfo@haworthpressinc.com].

INTRODUCTION

In this session a librarian and two magazine fulfillment center officers presented their perspectives on a service that the fulfillment center provides primarily for publishers of mass-circulation magazines.
Tuttle introduced fulfillment centers in general. Next, Vanstrom and
Earley presented their company, Centrobe, as a case study of a specific
fulfillment center. (Until May 1998, Centrobe was called Neodata
Services, Inc. Neodata is the term used by Tuttle in the early parts of
the session.) Tuttle spent a day at Neodata (located in Boulder County,
Colorado) in 1993 and came away very impressed by the work its
employees do. One might say that she began to love Neodata right
then. However, preparing for this session, she realized that there have
been many changes in five years, some even within the preceding few
weeks. Following Vanstrom and Earley's case study of Centrobe,
Tuttle covered library problems and solutions.

WHAT ARE MAGAZINE FULFILLMENT CENTERS?

When someone mentions Neodata, each librarian probably has his
or her own definition of the company. One may say, "It's serial acquisitions' (or the subscription agent's) biggest problem." Or, "It's a
post office box in Boulder, Colorado." I have heard, "Neodata is
really a bunch of computers with no people anywhere around." And
maybe some would say, "It is a helpful person who answers an 800
number and gets me the missing issue." One's own definition of
Neodata and other fulfillment centers depends on one's experience
with them.

In 1985 I published an article on fulfillment centers that was full of
little digs such as these: "Almost certainly a transfer order from direct
to an agent or from one agent to another will go wrong." "It appears
to us all that we are struggling to communicate with self-sufficient
computers, and we always lose the battle." And then there is this one:
"Almost certainly junk mail asking us to subscribe to the same magazines over and over comes from fulfillment centers; it is one of the
things they do best."[1]

To the serial acquisitions librarian, magazine fulfillment centers are,
to use current jargon, outsourcers that publishers of popular magazines

use for periodical circulation, that is, ordering and distributing. The fulfillment center is an intermediary between the publisher and the subscriber, in some ways similar to the relationship between the library serials department and the subscription agent. Its service consolidates orders and renewals for many publishers just as the subscription agent does for a large number of libraries. However, the publisher's outsourcer's efficiency does not necessarily work to the advantage of librarians; this process can add a second intermediary for libraries (although not for individual subscribers), and thus put another step in the ordering procedure for subscription agents.

The fulfillment center is able to provide economies of scale in magazine circulation and distribution through a combination of automation and tremendous volume. Because of its investment in technology and the volume created by serving many publishers, the fulfillment center is able to perform these functions far more efficiently than a single publisher could, thereby saving the publisher a significant amount of money. The service is most economical for mass-circulation magazines, although the use of state-of-the-art technology makes it possible for even some publishers of scholarly journals to take advantage of the fulfillment center's services.

Processing orders and renewals for more than 400 large-circulation magazines creates a gigantic volume of mail each day. Some days Neodata receives more than one million pieces of mail! On her visit Tuttle saw rows and rows of computers and computer operators entering data and handling the checks that come with some of the mail. Malina Silva, her host that day, described this as "heads-down work." Regulations required that employees stop their processing hourly, raise their heads, stand up, and perform certain exercises to ward off repetitive motion injuries. If they did not exercise, they were not eligible for workmen's compensation. There definitely are people at Neodata!

The fulfillment center has traditionally dealt with the subscriber's address label, with its lines of letters and numbers, which then goes either in print or electronically to the periodical binder. There were no magazine issues visible anywhere during Tuttle's visit. Everyone has seen these labels, perhaps on personal subscriptions, with what look like scraps of a name, a street number, a ZIP code. Once a gentleman from Communications Data Services (CDS), another large fulfillment center, explained the "key line" or "match code" (each company has its own name for it), and Tuttle could do a pretty good job of interpreting the information, but things have changed! Figure 1 and Figure 2 show examples of today's mailing labels, one from Neodata and the other from Time, Inc.'s own fulfillment company in Tampa, Florida.

Some mailing labels are still printed on paper and pasted onto the issue. (In Figure 1, the clue is the small half circle at the top and bottom center of the label.) Others are produced by ink-jet printers and go directly onto the magazine (Figure 2). It is easy to pick out the pieces of a name or an address and the expiration date. Other letters and numbers are not so obvious. Computer operators are able to code

FIGURE 1. *Better Homes and Gardens* Mailing Label

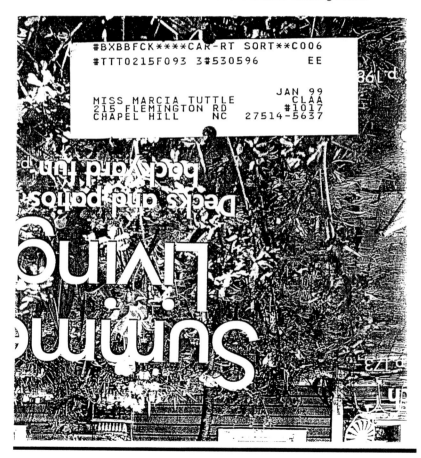

FIGURE 2. *Time* Mailing Label

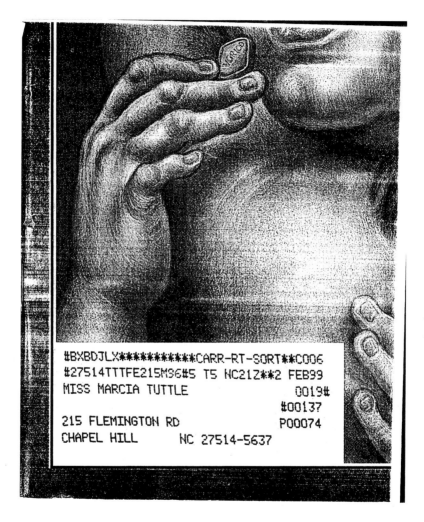

```
#BXBDJLX***************CARR-RT-SORT**C006
#27514TTTFE215M36#5 T5 NC21Z**2 FEB99
MISS MARCIA TUTTLE                0013#
                                 #00137
215 FLEMINGTON RD                P00074
CHAPEL HILL        NC 27514-5637
```

just about any information the publisher wants on the mailing label or in their customer database; for example, demographic data that can be used for special promotions. The fulfillment center can then generate sophisticated management reports for its clients for various purposes.

While placing orders and printing mailing labels is a major part of the fulfillment center's business, it is in processing renewals, especially multi-year renewals, that the real profits lie–individual subscriber renewals, that is! The efficient magazine renewal depends on matching the letters and numbers on the renewal order form with those on the existing mailing label. Employees scan the orders into the computer, and if the key line matches, no problem: the invoice is sent, the check is deposited or the credit card charged, and the renewal is completed. One can see that library orders do not fit this procedure easily. Today librarians prefer one-year subscriptions because of uncertain funding. They also have customized order forms spelling out the library's or the parent institution's requirements, such as four copies of the invoice or the mailing address in a very specific format. Furthermore, librarians do not like to make exceptions to their processes that work well for them.

A related service the fulfillment center offers is placing inserts in magazines, millions of magazines! They call these "blow-ins"–the ones that fall out when you pick up the magazine (Figure 3)–and "tip-ins"–the ones that have a corner bound in the issue. As irritating as they may be to a subscriber (library or individual), they are profit-

FIGURE 3. *Publishers Weekly* Blow-in

SAVE OVER $46

SEND NO MONEY NOW

YES! I want to SAVE OVER $46 off the cover price. Enter my one year subscription to Publishers Weekly today for just $169!

H709U

☐ Payment enclosed.
☐ Bill me.

Charge to: ☐ VISA
☐ Mastercard   ☐ AMEX

Name   (Please print)

Title

Account No.   Company

Exp. Date   Address

Signature   City   State   Zip

For faster service call: 1-800-278-2991. Outside U.S. call: 310-978-6916.

Florida residents please add applicable sales tax. 1 year Canada $219 (includes GST); all other countries, air delivery $299. Remit in U.S. funds.

able marketing devices for the journal itself, related publications, or a product advertised in the magazine.

As lucrative as mailing labels and renewal inserts are, the fulfillment center's work does not stop there. The aforementioned 1985 article concluded: "Given the impact computerization is making on our professional and personal lives, it is certain that fulfillment center managers will not be satisfied with their present limited function."[2] In fact, these companies have expanded their operations to include a whole range of marketing services such as direct mail advertising (including sweepstakes), 800 phone numbers for customer service (Figure 4), holiday gift subscriptions (Figure 5), telemarketing, fund raising, association membership services, mailing list rental, and television offers ("Operators are standing by . . ."). Even "Ask Abby" (Figure 6) seems to use a fulfillment center!

Librarians have long been concerned about the consolidation of subscription agencies, with the larger ones buying out the smaller and less highly automated ones. The situation is the same with magazine fulfillment centers. Within the last decade the giant Neodata of Boulder bought Meredith in Des Moines, Iowa; Kable News Company of Mt. Morris, Illinois, bought Fulfillment Corporation of America (FCA) of Marion, Ohio. With the possible exception of the Tampa, Florida, facility owned by Time, Inc., Neodata and CDS are the only very large fulfillment centers left. Is there an impact on journal prices from this consolidation? It is difficult to tell.

WHO DO FULFILLMENT CENTERS SERVE?

Let there be no misunderstanding: *publishers* are fulfillment centers' clients. The "customer" in "customer service" is the publisher, not the subscriber. If, as recent articles indicate, many publishers are placing more emphasis on service to subscribers, the fulfillment center will contract to do so; if not, it doesn't happen. While it may seem that the 800 telephone number service may be for the subscriber's benefit (and it certainly is helpful–please note the telephone number in Figure 3), the fulfillment center provides that service primarily for the publisher and does so because the publisher is willing to pay for it. Thus, the subscriber is the secondary client of the fulfillment center. *Library* subscribers, however, constitute only a small percentage of those who receive mass-circulation magazines. Economies of scale demand that fulfillment centers cater to the majority.

FIGURE 4. *MacWorld* 800 Number

IDG
INTERNATIONAL DATA GROUP

April 1997, Volume 14, Number 4   Macworld (ISSN 0741-8647) is published monthly by Macworld Communications, Inc. Editorial and business offices: 501 Second St., San Francisco, CA 94107, 415/243-0505. Subscription orders and inquiries should be directed to 800/288-6848 or 303/604-1465. Subscription rates are $30 for 12 issues, $60 for 24 issues, and $90 for 36 issues. Foreign orders must be prepaid in U.S. funds with additional postage. Add $18 per year for postage for Canada and Mexico subscribers. Add $69 per year for postage to all other countries. Periodicals postage paid at San Francisco, California, and at additional mailing offices. **Postmaster:** Send address changes to Macworld, P.O. Box 54529, Boulder, CO 80322-4529. Printed in the U.S.A.

SUBSCRIPTION SERVICES

PC World Subscriber Services, P.O. Box 55029, Boulder, CO 80322-5029
INTERNET: http://www.pcworld.com/resources/subscribe/customer_service/
E-MAIL: pcwhelp@neodata.com
PHONE: In U.S. other than CO   800/234-3498
              In CO and outside U.S.   303/604-1465
              New orders   800/825-7595

CENTROBE, AN EDS COMPANY: A CASE STUDY OF A MAGAZINE FULFILLMENT CENTER

Neodata, the largest and best-known fulfillment center, no longer exists. It has been merged with three other related companies to form Centrobe, an organization that performs far more fulfillment functions

FIGURE 5. *National Geographic Traveler* Gift Letter

Give NATIONAL GEOGRAPHIC TRAVELER.
Save when you order more than one subscription!

Just $17⁹⁵*

for the first subscription
(or your renewal).

Only $10⁹⁵

for each additional subscription.

TRZAXH3 527514TTTFE215M95

***************** 3-DIGIT 275
MARCIA TUTTLE
215 FLEMINGTON RD
CHAPEL HILL NC 27514-5637

☐ Please extend my subscription to NATIONAL GEOGRAPHIC TRAVELER for one year (six issues).
Return entire form with payment instructions. Correct address if necessary. Thank you!

~ited-Time
~fer!
PLEASE RUSH!
Holiday Gift Order Enclosed.
⁹97.

Please send NATIONAL GEOGRAPHIC
TRAVELER *as a gift* to...

Gift For:
Please print (Mr., Mrs., Miss, Ms.)

Street

City

~. Zip Code

Please place first-
class postage here.

Traveler
PO BOX 63016
TAMPA FL 33663-3016

1. Fu~
   or your ~.
2. Additional gifts. ~
   Quan~ .
3. Add sales tax for orders sent ~.
   MD (5%) and DC (5.75%)...........
4. Total cost of order (1) + (2) + (3) = $ ____

Payment Instructions:
☐ My check is enclosed for.................$ ____
   Make payable to NATIONAL GEOGRAPHIC TRAVELER.
☐ Please bill me after January 1, 1998.

Annual rate in the U.S. for first subscription or renewal. All prices in U.S. funds.

~e gift cards will
~ur recipients.

Thank you!

Trav~ ~r

FIGURE 6. "Ask Abby"

ʻ.. we can
ːr.

He's in Texas and I'm in Penn-
ʻlvania, but I will write.

With all my love and thanks
— CARMEN

DEAR CARMEN: My pleasure. Write again and keep me posted.

Send questions to Dear Abby, P.O. Box 447, Mount Morris, IL 61054.

tion
he ha
them.
In h
believe
to pos
proved
underp
His i

than simply supplying mailing labels for magazine issues and processing subscription renewals.

EDS, the parent company of Centrobe, provides information technology and services worldwide. It has more than 100,000 employees at sixty-seven locations in nineteen countries and revenue of about $14 billion. Centrobe itself has more than ten thousand employees in fourteen countries, leading to 350 million customer relationships. Centrobe offers the world's largest direct marketing services and consists of its Manufacturing and Retail Division; Communication, Utilities and Financial Division; Marketing Services; Media and Entertainment (Publishing Fulfillment Services); and International Services.

Neodata began as a division of Esquire, Inc. in 1949 and was acquired in 1968 by A. C. Nielsen. In 1984 Dun & Bradstreet merged with Nielsen, and in 1990 Hicks, Muse, Tate & Furst, Inc. acquired Neodata and merged it with TMI Corporation, a telemarketing, fulfillment, and distribution services company. The following year Neodata acquired Meredith Corporation's product fulfillment operation, and in 1992 it bought Wiland Services Inc.'s database marketing services. Another acquisition was the Lacek Group, a customer loyalty programs company, in 1995-96. Neodata itself was acquired by EDS in August 1997, and in May 1998 it merged with two other EDS divisions (dbINTELLECT and EDS' CustomerSolutions) to form Centrobe, which combines the customer service specialties of its four precursors. Each group had its own emphasis. The Lacek Group created customer loyalty programs (e.g., frequent flyer programs), and dbINTELLECT concentrated on sophisticated databases using "advanced graphics to display complicated customer relationships." Neodata, of course, concentrated on direct marketing and fulfillment; EDS CustomerSolutions ran "call centers that handle both complicated and simple requests."[3]

The Media and Entertainment Group within Centrobe is the division that performs the services affecting librarians' work, but subscription fulfillment is only a small part of that group's efforts. In addition to magazine publishers, clients include software publishers, video/music publishers, entertainment organizations, associations, and even the U.S. Postal Service. Services beyond subscription fulfillment include product fulfillment and distribution (e.g., books, prizes, merchandise, premiums, etc.), list order fulfillment, marketing database services, membership services, and loyalty services. Some of the largest publisher clients are Meredith, Conde Nast, Petersen, Ziff Davis, Newsweek, Times Mirror, U.S. News, and Hachette-Filipacchi.

Marketing services performed by Centrobe include much work with databases of subscriber lists and other accumulations of names and addresses. Today's technology–and the company lives or dies by its technological sophistication–enables Centrobe to offer list "merge/purge" (i.e., deleting duplicate names from a combination of several lists), a marketing database for special promotions, list rental, Internet service offerings, and list enhancement, among other services.

The term "agent" is interpreted slightly differently by Centrobe than by serials specialists. To the company, an agent is any intermediary between the subscriber and Centrobe, and this definition includes such activities as sweepstakes and school or club fund-raisers. However, the other agents do not have the problems that library subscription agents and their customers have with the fulfillment center, because they have individuals, not libraries, as subscribers. At the same time, though, attempted renewal by these subscribers without using a renewal card from Centrobe can create match-up problems.

Some years ago Neodata personnel, working with library subscription agency representatives, grouped all agency subscriptions into a separate, centralized operation within the company and staffed it with a supervisor having long-term management experience. This section could accept orders on magnetic tape, and its personnel continued to work with the subscription agencies and other agencies to bring their systems into compatibility. The agents could then receive management reports, accounting reports and other data that they might need, all of which benefit the library subscriber, as well as the agency and Centrobe. Discussions continue between Centrobe and the library subscription agencies in strong efforts to resolve problems that remain. For example, fulfillment centers are working now with vendors to develop a standard information format that can be used with any fulfillment center. One must remember, though, that sometimes there is little that can be done about a difficult situation, because the publisher, not Centrobe, makes decisions such as how many back issues can be stored for claims and replacements.

After its acquisitions in the early 1990s, perhaps inspired by the success of the "agency room," Neodata introduced the Customer Service Center (CSC) concept. Whereas before, each individual task had been performed in one or more of twenty-four separate facilities in the Boulder area (e.g., order entry, lettershop, warehouses, and telephone service), now CSC brought all services for a customer together in one building with an overall general manager and allocated staffing resources to specific customers. There are six CSCs for magazine fulfillment. This change enabled Neodata to customize services for their publisher clients and to involve them in the process. In addition, employees "develop a better understanding of each publication's mailing cycle (and unique requirements). Then, when subscriber questions arise, each representative can get right to the problem at hand."[4] Merging the four EDS companies in 1998 only enhanced the ability to give publishers the service they need. Centrobe lists the CSC benefits as improved cycle times, focus on quality programs, enhanced communications, and client partnerships.

More recently, Neodata put into place "a mammoth software system" named NCORE (Neodata Customer Oriented Relational Environment).[5] One of the products of NCORE is named NCOREAccess, a desktop query and reporting tool. By using NCOREAccess, Centrobe clients are able to answer their own questions and design their own reports without waiting for Centrobe personnel to do it for them. In addition, publisher Websites often have links to Centrobe so that subscribers can communicate directly with Centrobe customer service representatives via the Internet.

Looking toward the future, Centrobe is beginning to increase use of fax, voice mail, the Internet and electronic mail as means of communication.

Also, a popular new service for subscribers is credit card orders with rapid dispatch of the first issue. An example is the experiment conducted by Neodata for *Wired*: "Last year, in conjunction with Neodata, the monthly offered subscribers 12 issues, with the first issue sent overnight, for $39.95, tacking on a delivery cost of $10 per subscription. In another test, *Wired* paid for delivery."[6]

HOW DOES THE FULFILLMENT CENTER CAUSE PROBLEMS FOR LIBRARIES?

Remember that the *publisher*, not the library, is the fulfillment center's customer. This reality means that efficient library processes, so important to serials staff members, do not always work with periodicals distributed by Centrobe and the other companies. The problems appear in all of the serial acquisitions functions: ordering, receiving, claiming, and dealing with letter mail. Let's take them one by one.

First, ordering. All libraries, but especially public library systems, are likely to have multiple subscriptions to the magazines that fulfillment centers handle, for example, *Better Homes and Gardens*, *Newsweek*, and *Travel and Leisure*. Many serials staff members have had the surprising experience of discovering that they have paid for one five-year subscription instead of the intended five one-year subscriptions. The error can occur whether the orders are direct or through an agent, although direct orders using renewal notices with their replicas of the library's computerized mailing label can sharply reduce the chances of its happening. Some vendors are able to match their renewal orders electronically with the separate orders in Boulder, Mount Morris, or Tampa. Another remedy is to go ahead and order multi-year subscriptions if you possibly can. These magazines are not expensive, the departure from policy will not have much impact on the budget, and there is usually a saving in a long-term order.

Another problem with magazine orders can be a library address that is too long to fit onto a computerized mailing label. Most individual subscribers do not have this problem, but often the institution whose library orders serials has requirements for information on the address label and sometimes for the arrangement of these elements. If the address consists of too many lines or too many words, the fulfillment center employee who records the subscription must abbreviate the address to make it fit. For a long time there was no standard for address labels, but now there is one, and serials librarians would do well to learn its space limitations.

A final related problem, and probably the most serious difficulty in ordering and renewing these subscriptions, is the occasional change of the start date to another month or week. The difference can be slight, for example, one month, or it can be more significant, perhaps four or five months. The result for the library is duplicate issues at one end of the subscription and gaps at the other. The practice of sending renewal notices far in advance of expiration date is profitable for the publisher, who can earn interest on the early payments and save postage and labor on future renewal notices not sent, but it can cause trouble for the library. Sometimes the renewal order will not reach the fulfillment center in time to be renewed without a lapse in service, but there is another reason for the change of start date. This reason is the fulfillment center's obligation to the publisher client to supply the total number of copies of a magazine that its advertisers have paid for.

Advertising rates are based on a range of subscriptions; the more copies, the higher the cost of the advertisement. There is an agency, called the Audit Bureau of Circulations (ABC), that monitors the number of subscriptions distributed. In fact, ABC has a permanent branch office at Centrobe. If the number of subscriptions that advertisers have paid for drops below the floor of that range, the fulfillment center must start new subscriptions immediately to make up the difference. If there are more copies distributed than advertisers have paid for, new subscriptions or some renewals may be held until the next issue or until they are needed. So far as I know, there is nothing the library subscriber or the subscription agent can do about this beyond using renewal notices with address label data.

Libraries have fewer receipt problems than they have order problems, but again, subscribing to multiple copies of a title can cause confusion. Many academic libraries pay each copy on a separate fund and need to distinguish among copies. A more difficult situation arises when one copy stops coming and the check-in staff member cannot tell which one it is. Sometimes the library can place a bulk order for the number of subscriptions it wishes to receive. They will come together in a single package with a single mailing label. In this case, if one copy stops coming, they all stop coming!

It is in claiming that fulfillment centers have made the most progress in accommodating subscriber needs, especially library needs. Whereas claims, which nearly always come only from librarians (or perhaps from serials librarians with personal subscriptions?), used to be ignored or the subscription automatically extended, now all (or almost all) fulfillment center periodicals have an 800 number listed for customer service. In this case, the subscriber *is* the customer, the publisher's customer. There is no 800 service unless the publisher pays for it! In addition, some publishers pay their fulfillment center to warehouse a certain number of back issues to fill library claims. Apparently, some publishers will accept a request for a missing issue made over the 800 line and fill it from their own stock. I suspect this was the case when I claimed my personal subscription to *Time* magazine. I was warned that it would take three weeks or a month for the missing issue to arrive. Today, publishers and fulfillment centers are experimenting with electronic mail customer service. For domestic subscribers it is hard to see how that could improve on 24-hour interactive telephone service, but for foreign subscribers, particularly librarians, it is sure to be welcomed.

A library serials department can run afoul of periodical delivery dates if its staff members do not record the receipt date and the claimer does not remain aware of the receipt date of each issue. This date can be more significant than the cover date. For example, fulfillment centers print labels for some monthly magazines two months before the cover date and send them to the binder, who ships the issues a full month before the date printed on the cover. Thus, the library should receive the July issue in early June. If the claimer waits until August, or even mid-July, to mail or telephone a claim, it may not be possible to obtain the issue. It is likely that whoever holds the extra issues–publisher, binder, or fulfillment center–has disposed of them to the second-hand market.

A serials department's letter mail is always a challenge, and the activities of the magazine fulfillment center do not make processing the mail any easier. Librarians, how many copies of a sweepstakes mailing does your library get? Subscription agents, how many copies of unnecessary renewal notices do your customers send you?

Centrobe and the other companies manage a thriving and profitable exchange or sale of periodical subscriber lists. Publishers Clearing-House and American Family Publishers want their "official finalist notification" to go to persons likely to subscribe to magazines, and our libraries' names are on all the mailing lists. The sweepstakes sponsors are selling magazines. In fact, they are considered "agencies" by fulfillment centers. If one should respond personally to one of these sweepstakes, his or her name goes on a mailing list of respondents, which is then rented to publishers or other sweepstakes sponsors. There is a service called "merge/purge," which should eliminate duplicate mailings, but again, the client would have to pay for it. I doubt if these particular clients want the mailing lists shortened.

As for the flood of multiple renewal notices, the coded label should identify to the fulfillment center which subscriptions are through vendors and block these mailings, but apparently it does not work that way. The serials staff member's options are (1) to ignore the notices and risk lapsed subscriptions, (2) to check each notice to verify that either it is through a subscription agent or it does not need to be renewed yet, or (3) to pack up all the notices and ship them off to the vendor, making your customer service representative there do all the work. (Watch your service charge!) In addition, should the library's or the subscription agent's renewal order not match up with the expiring order, the renewal notices will continue to come and finally turn into "We-Miss-You-And-Want-You-Back" notices. Even if one has ignored all the communications until this one, now is the time to verify that the library has paid someone for the renewal and to verify that the journal is coming.

WHAT CAN LIBRARIANS DO?

There must be something librarians and subscription agents can do about their difficulties with mass-circulation magazines. I do not want to say, "Know your enemy," because Centrobe is not our enemy. But I cannot say, "Know your partner," because they are not our partner, either. Centrobe is the *publisher's* partner, and the circulation functions they perform are one of the ways publishers keep subscription prices as low as they can. The economies of scale are enormous! If each publisher had to acquire the electronic equipment and hire its own staff, to say nothing of losing the fulfillment center's volume postage discounts, magazine prices would rise noticeably.

Let me phrase the solution this way: Understand Centrobe and play their game. Centrobe is far more important to librarians and subscription agents than we are to Centrobe. Chuck and Mark generously agreed to come and talk to us and listen to us. They have helped us to understand their company's requirements and the ways they have adapted their workflow to accommodate libraries' and vendors' needs. Librarians can do no less than hear what they say and adapt procedures where they can.

Without question, most of the progress in resolving library problems with fulfillment centers has resulted from the work of subscription agencies, particularly EBSCO, whose own profitability depends on efficiency. Representatives of the large domestic agencies regularly visit Centrobe, CDS, and the other companies and work with them to smooth the processing of library orders, renewals, and claims. One must mention the incredible work done by Bill Randolph of EBSCO before he retired. In addition, over the years Bill made available to me notes of his meetings with fulfillment center personnel so that I could learn "their game." EBSCO has also hosted meetings in Birmingham for officers of the fulfillment centers to discuss mutual problems and solutions. Vendors' publisher relations personnel meet with publishers using fulfillment centers to inform them of their library customers' needs. It is the client publisher who can change circulation procedures, not the fulfillment center. Further, the subscription agents educate their library customers and implement processes that can resolve problems; for example, several years ago a newly devised two-part claim postcard, sent by the library claimer directly to the magazine's subscription address, allowed the library to bypass the agent and save perhaps a week or more in getting the request to the source of the issue. EBSCO has also written a short brochure, available from the company, about working with magazine fulfillment centers.

As I have said, my own visit to Neodata was a real eye-opener. I came away with great respect for the work this company does and I have even more respect now, realizing how it both changes with the needs of its publisher clients and anticipates future needs. Lest I seem too starry-eyed, I must say that the visit did not resolve my library's fulfillment center problems–but it did help! I began to understand why we sometimes had duplicates and gaps. It was useful to be told that Neodata and the publishers preferred telephone claims to written ones, because our serial acquisitions assistants also preferred to telephone. I saw that the 800 number service had strict quality control measures in place, which was comforting.

There have been almost no articles in the library press about fulfillment centers, but marketing periodicals, often available full-text through InfoTrac, ABI/Inform, and Dialog, are full of them. The magazine business journal *Folio* is a good place to find these articles, as is *InformationWEEK*. The *Denver Post* also publishes Centrobe press releases and occasional feature articles. Not only will one learn of current changes and trends, but it is also possible to track histories of the companies and mergers. Fulfillment centers have Webpages, as well, for information about the companies and their services.

NOTES

1. Marcia Tuttle, "Magazine Fulfillment Centers: What They Are, How They Operate, and What We Can Do about Them," *Library Acquisitions: Practice and Theory* 9 (1985): 46-47.

2. Ibid., 49.

3. Leyla Kokmen, "Customer Service is the Goal," *Denver Post*, May 19, 1998. Much of the information in this paragraph came from Kokmen's article.

4. Jenna Schnuer, "Treat Subscribers as Customers," *Folio: The Magazine for Magazine Management* 25 (1997): 169.

5. Menda Zetlin, "From Fulfillment House to Strategic Partner," *Management Review* 85 (1996): 33-37.

6. Ibid., 170.

CONSORTIAL ACQUISITIONS
OF SHARED ELECTRONIC JOURNALS

Consortial Acquisitions
of Shared Electronic Journals

Adolfo Rodriguez

Presenter

Nancy Newsome

Recorder

SUMMARY. Universidad Nacional Autónoma de México is a multicampus university, one of the largest in the world, with installations in most of the states. It faces some of the challenges and opportunities for resource

Adolfo Rodriguez is Director General, Universidad Nacional Autónoma de México.
Nancy Newsome is Serials Librarian at Hunter Library, Western Carolina University.

The following report was prepared by Nancy Newsome and also appeared in the *NASIG Newsletter*, September 1998.

[Haworth co-indexing entry note]: "Consortial Acquisitions of Shared Electronic Journals." Newsome, Nancy. Co-published simultaneously in *The Serials Librarian* (The Haworth Press, Inc.) Vol. 36, No. 1/2, 1999, pp. 133-135; and: *Head in the Clouds, Feet on the Ground: Serials Vision and Common Sense* (ed: Jeffrey S. Bullington, Beatrice L. Caraway, and Beverley Geer) The Haworth Press, Inc., 1999, pp. 133-135. Single or multiple copies of this article are available for a fee from The Haworth Document Delivery Service [1-800-342-9678, 9:00 a.m. - 5:00 p.m. (EST). E-mail address: getinfo@haworthpressinc. com].

sharing that apply to consortia in the United States. The university is acquiring electronic journals and intends to serve as the base for a consortium involving most of the public universities in Mexico. *[Article copies available for a fee from The Haworth Document Delivery Service: 1-800-342-9678. E-mail address: getinfo@haworthpressinc.com]*

This session described the experience of the Universidad Nacional Autónoma de México (UNAM) in acquiring electronic journals for its multiple campuses. Adolfo Rodriguez began by giving a description of the university itself as background for his talk. It is a state (federal) university and is free to all citizens. The major research of Mexico takes place at UNAM. Some faculty (about 8 percent or 2,000) are devoted entirely to research, while the rest are regular faculty. Librarians and computer specialists are considered academic staff. In all, about 34,800 in these categories are employed at UNAM to provide service to 268,612 students enrolled in the various undergraduate, professional, and graduate programs.

The libraries of UNAM produce Liburnam, which is the national union catalog of academic libraries for monographs and is used as a cataloging instrument for a lot of university libraries in the country. Other catalogs produced there include serials (Seriunam), maps, Latin American articles on social sciences, and Latin American articles on science and technology. The library system includes 140 departmental libraries, one central library, and one coordinating office. Technical processes and information technology efforts are centralized. The total holdings include 3,830 serial titles, 15,025 paid subscriptions, and 13,581 subscriptions received through exchange or donation, for a total of 28,606 subscriptions. The libraries currently receive 443 electronic periodicals, 214 of which are free. The free electronic journals must be peer reviewed to be added to the collection. Currently they are working on installing the Elsevier package of 1,100 electronic journals. They are also currently in negotiations with Academic Press, Blackwell, OCLC, EBSCO, and Ovid. When making selection decisions, they are not concerned with duplication of titles among the different databases.

UNAM can be looked at as an institution with different locations or as a consortium of academic libraries. They have approached and have been approached by other universities to form consortia. There are both problems and benefits of a consortial arrangement. One of the problems concerns the legal agreements. There are translation problems and jurisdiction problems on an international basis. There is also the question of how to divide the cost among the participants.

Some of the benefits can be seen in the ability to access more titles more quickly. Some say working through a consortium can also save money, but this is not necessarily the case. Not all titles in a collection will be used, additional staff are often needed for administration, and there is the possible loss of archiving ability.

Another possible problem lies in the fact that there are so many types of consortia along with many different ways of licensing and pricing of products. There are also many ways to buy a product–through aggregators, vendors, and the producer. Dealing with how the product is accessed is yet another problem, with choices ranging from IP address to access via password (which is a huge problem, considering the number of students and faculty at UNAM). Funding is another problem for UNAM: the Minister of Education must be convinced that purchase of this type of information is needed.

A consortium provides users with two important services–content and connectivity. It used to be that a consortium shared one core collection and those shared materials were unique to each location. In the electronic environment, the same materials are shared in electronic format via a local server, which in UNAM's case is a machine with large storage capacity. This changes the way collection development is approached, in that journal titles chosen should be useful to a large number of the libraries. It also raises questions such as, What will happen to the union catalogs? Will we have one shared catalog instead as collections become more homogeneous?

In conclusion, Rodriguez stated that the problems are not easy to solve, but in Mexico they are trying, since despite the difficulties, the results are beneficial.

COPING WITH THE DIGITAL SHIFT: ARCHIVING AND OTHER ISSUES TO CONSIDER

Coping with the Digital Shift: Archival Purpose and Responsibility

Lizabeth A. Wilson

SUMMARY. Now that electronic journals are becoming a reality and publishers are offering electronic versions of a large number of print journals, librarians must make decisions about subscribing to the electronic version, continuing the print subscription, or subscribing to both. New questions arise, such as the following: Who will store the electronic version? What happens if the library discontinues its subscription? Will the electronic version become the primary mode of access/distribution, with print as a backup? What will happen if publishers forbid ILL of electronic versions? The presentation will address these and other issues, with particular emphasis on the latest developments in archiving. *[Article copies available for a fee from The Haworth Document Delivery Service: 1-800-342-9678. E-mail address: getinfo@haworthpressinc.com]*

Lizabeth A. Wilson is Associate Director of Libraries for Public Services, University of Washington Libraries.

[Haworth co-indexing entry note]: "Coping with the Digital Shift: Archival Purpose and Responsibility." Wilson, Lizabeth A. Co-published simultaneously in *The Serials Librarian* (The Haworth Press, Inc.) Vol. 36, No. 1/2, 1999, pp. 137-147; and: *Head in the Clouds, Feet on the Ground: Serials Vision and Common Sense* (ed: Jeffrey S. Bullington, Beatrice L. Caraway, and Beverley Geer) The Haworth Press, Inc., 1999, pp. 137-147. Single or multiple copies of this article are available for a fee from The Haworth Document Delivery Service [1-800-342-9678, 9:00 a.m. - 5:00 p.m. (EST). E-mail address: getinfo@ haworthpressinc.com].

Remember a long, long time ago (well, not that long ago), when the decision to subscribe to a journal was simple and straightforward? Remember when the number of people involved in the life of a subscription was relatively limited–the selector, serials and collection maintenance staff, and the reader?

Libraries assumed that there would be space on the shelf, lights to read by, and convenient photocopiers that worked. The patron only needed to be able to read and maybe use an index to benefit from journal collections in libraries.

Libraries had ordering, cataloging, binding, and shelving down to a fine art. We had national standards and local traditions for cataloging. We had routines in place. We knew what a title cost, or at least thought we did. Our most contentious discussions were over whether we shelved by call number or title.

When it came to canceling journals, it was equally simple–often hard, painful, contentious–but simple. We could identify our duplicates. We could measure usage. We could sort by price. We could count on interlibrary loan to get needed articles that were not in our collection.

Then, along came electronic journals, and the story changed. It was fun at first, as we experimented and played with this new format. I remember hearing about this *Bryn Mawr Classical Review* and wondering if this was the harbinger of the future. There were so few e-journals that one could keep track of them by counting on one's fingers. Some heroic soul could even keep a master list of them all, at least for a while.

We talked about whether or not e-journals should be included in the catalog. Should we link the e-journals directly from the bibliographic record? We began piloting ways to catalog e-journals. My cataloging colleagues at the University of Washington asked us public service types for some titles to catalog. Could we identify a couple of ongoing value? We had to hunt pretty hard.

We got excited about the additional value that e-journals provided. Distributed, "24-by-7" access. Time and place independence. We could better serve our distance learners, our faculty at the teaching hospital a bridge and congested traffic away, the student who pulls the all-nighter and works at hours many of us no longer see except on New Year's Eve. We embraced the enhanced searching possibilities and welcomed embedded linkages. We heard testimonials from users on how distributed access to journals transformed how and where they could work. We looked forward to the integration of e-journals with discovery and retrieval tools. One-stop research might just become a functioning reality.

At the same time, the decision process for acquiring and licensing e-journals began slowing down. Some would say it was more like paralysis. Some libraries created new positions or reallocated staff to manage this process. The overhead was enormous. The once simple selection process became complex and sometimes cumbersome as the number of individuals grew who needed to be involved to make it all work. For the first time, the ring of decision makers extended well beyond the library.

The selector and acquisitions, serials, and cataloging staff were still involved. But now consultation was needed with a wide range of players: library systems, public service staff, campus networking, academic department computing, printing services, consortial partners, facilities and equipment managers, purchasing agents, and university legal counsel.

Each new e-journal, or package of e-journals, presented unique questions. Pricing seemed idiosyncratic. Packaging took on unpredictable forms. Bundled paper and electronic titles. Bundled electronic journals and indices. "Thou-shalt-not" caveats began appearing on licensing agreements. Patterns were hard to see.

We began to long for the romanticized days of the print journal past. It was all so simple then. We tried applying the existing procedures that worked so well with print journals to this new world. You couldn't blame us for building on our existing schema. We used the same approach in the development of the early online catalogs. We automated the card format, even though studies showed that only trained library staff could decipher a catalog card. And we did the same when teaching databases. We used print indexes as our conceptual framework even when the parallels did not exist.

The protocols and traditions for subscribing and canceling didn't work anymore. When we had two print subscriptions and the budget cuts came, we would cancel the second copy. Or if we had a print and microform copy, we kept the print. Print was our backup. It was our archive. We knew how to manage it.

I would like to share my view, as a public service administrator, of the e-journal digital shift we are experiencing. My perspective has been broadened recently, due in large part to the shift I have been describing. At my institution, we are experimenting with a new collection development approach, which seeks to align information resources development and user services. It is driven by, among other factors, the issues inherent in electronic journal selection, maintenance and support.

Those of us in academic libraries share a common goal of providing seamless access to electronic journals in support of faculty, student and staff information needs. We seek to integrate these resources fully into our local information systems and service programs. We recognize that we need to work with vendors, publishers, consortia, associations, faculty and students to find ways to reach this goal. At the University of Washington, we strive to create and promote an atmosphere where information and ideas are readily accessible and freely exchanged. To fulfill this mission, we are committed to providing essential resources, regardless of format or location.

How can we meet our goals and fulfill our missions, when there are so many unanswered questions, when the decision process has become so complex, and when the costs keep shifting under our feet? How do we speed the decision-making process? How do we decide what to order? What to cancel? When to take a pass?

I suggest that we need principles and guidelines to help us shape these decisions. Agreement on what those principles should be appears to be emerging in the library community. I recommend that you become familiar with three documents which address such principles and guidelines:

- Principles for Acquiring and Licensing Information in Digital Formats[1]
- Principles for Licensing Electronic Resources[2]
- Statement of Current Perspective and Preferred Practices for the Selection and Purchase of Electronic Information[3]

If your institution is like mine, you are using these documents as you develop local principles and practices.

What will allow libraries to move forward in the acquisition, maintenance and archiving of e-journals? I offer my own personal list of "deal breakers." If these items are not satisfactorily addressed, the deal is off and the e-journal is not acquired or licensed:

- *Governing Law.* Agreements need to recognize governing law to be that of the jurisdiction of the subscribing institution. If this is not reflected in agreements at the University of Washington Libraries, it will not get past our attorney general's office.
- *Year 2000.* Products and resources need to be Year 2000 compliant, or the order won't get out of university purchasing.
- *Definition of Authorized Users.* This entails settling on an acceptable definition of "authorized users." I will explore authorized users in more depth later in this paper.
- *Integration.* The ability to integrate electronic journals with local environment, platforms and systems is a key requirement.
- *Standards.* Electronic resources need to be based on current standards in use by the library community. Data formats should follow industry standards and be fully documented. Data should be platform-independent and available in a multiplicity of formats.
- *Authentication.* Authentication systems cannot be a barrier to access by authorized users.
- *Fair Use.* Licenses and purchasing agreements must permit and support the "fair use" of all electronic journals.
- *Pricing and Costs.* "No cancellation" clauses that require the library to continue paying for print subscriptions to be able to obtain the e-version are unacceptable. The electronic resource should cost less than print unless there is substantial added value. Libraries and their users need to define what added value is and what it is worth. Reasonable costs must take into account the library's internal processing costs.
- *Archiving.* Agreements must address archival access and state archival responsibility. Perpetual licenses should be awarded when content is purchased.

I would like to address three issues in more depth: users, integration, and fair use. In the following paper, Andrea Keyhani addresses pricing and packaging; integration; authorization systems; and digital archives. She also provides an update on development in these areas.

USERS

As a public institution with a broad mandate to serve the state of Washington, our "authorized users" include faculty, staff, students and on-site, walk-up users of the campus. As we move toward more distance education and seek to build an information infrastructure which supports "24-by-7" learning and research, what constitutes the university is defined by relationship. To describe the university in terms of its acreage is no longer a workable notion. The university in its physical and virtual manifestations is wherever research and learning takes place. This might be at the kitchen table, in the residence hall, at the marine labs on an island in Puget Sound, in the traditional campus classroom or lab, or in the field. Our users also include others directly served by the university through its managed laboratories and other research and instructional facilities and programs, K-12 educators, and outreach programs. We are committed to working with information providers to create mutually acceptable mechanisms for authentication of authorized users. We ask vendors to link their access control mechanisms to our authentication infrastructure. We avoid systems built on individual passwords and user identification.

INTEGRATION

Integration is key to delivering seamless access to electronic journals. In line with its mission to best serve faculty, students, staff and extended partners of the university, my library is moving to an information environment in which the Web will serve as its primary gateway. The Web gateway provides a uniform platform to integrate a wide variety of local and remote resources and discovery, delivery, and service tools.

The amount and range of material delivered through the Web already exceeds that available through any other protocol. An increasingly complex range of electronic resources is being produced including traditional literature databases, full-text systems with sound and images, numeric databases, image collections, and multimedia materials. Our current mixed environment of electronic resources cannot take advantage of filtering devices and metasearch functionality that a common integrated system can include. It does not aid users in filtering the mass of information now available and can create significant barriers to access. One of the key challenges in transitioning to a single gateway will be to provide tools that cross over the range of available resources and that can grow in complexity over time with Web developments. Print journals continue to be critical resources, and referring to them within this integrated electronic environment is another key challenge.

It is now technically possible to integrate a full complement of self-service features and tools including linking to document delivery, borrowing services, profiling, and automatic updating in the libraries' information system. A Web gateway to information resources integrated with services and tools will empower our faculty, students, and staff to meld information content pervasively and conveniently into their coursework, research, and practice.

In order to take advantage of, and incorporate, emerging and emergent technologies and resources, we need modularity and interoperability. We need extensibility and reusability. We need to integrate electronic resources and systems we don't control which reside on remote servers. To facilitate integration, we support both formal and de facto industry and community standards.

With this intent in mind, electronic journals and any associated features and capabilities should be accessible from institutionally-supported computing environments. Data should be platform-independent and available in a multiplicity of formats. We need to be able to integrate e-journals easily into our local systems and services. We need electronic journals which adhere to universal access design principles and are compatible with existing adaptive technologies for users with disabilities. We need to allow for personalized or customized views of e-journals as our users create "MyLibrary" or "MyJournal" sites using templates supported by the library.

FAIR USE

The concept of fair use is an important one for institutions of learning and research. It is highly relevant and must be retained in the electronic journal environment. We seek licenses that permit and support the fair use of all information for noncommercial, educational, instructional, and scientific purposes by authorized users, including unlimited viewing, downloading, and printing, in agreement with the provisions in current copyright practices. Libraries have a valuable tradition of sharing journal articles among themselves through interlibrary loan through fair use rules. It is important to review licenses and understand how the contract will affect participation in interlibrary loan before signing.

A couple years ago I was part of a focus group on electronic journals and archiving. The focus group was made up of directors and associate directors of academic libraries. We were asked, "What must happen before libraries will accept e-journals, before they will cancel their print copies of journals and depend on electronic access?" It was unanimous. We needed access to a perpetual, reliable, and "for-always-ever-after" archive. We needed that archive to be supported by an entity we trusted. The sponsor of the focus group heeded our advice and proceeded to work on the development of a perpetual electronic journal archive.

If that focus group were brought back together today, I think the advice might be somewhat different. We still would recommend a reliable archive, but we would suggest that we have learned that more than an archive is required. We have learned that it is not just about technology. The technology questions can be and are being solved. The real issues are the economic and user questions.

Let me explain. First, the economic issues. Economics will force us to shift more quickly than we might prefer. We can't keep up with the price increases for print journals. How will we be able to add on the electronic subscriptions? The costs implicit in maintenance of print journals–the shelving, the binding, the building–disappear in the electronic world, but they are costs that we do not recoup. They are not part of our material budgets. Someone else pays these costs. They are amortized. They are hidden.

Similarly, the cost of identifying duplicate titles in print and through large package purchases of databases is high. It requires systematic review of holdings, allowance for unpredictable changes in the titles in the packages, and cumbersome record changes. We back-burner it, because it is not yet part of our routine.

Second, the most critical issue is how well e-journals serve our users. Initially, I viewed this question as one of user acceptance and adoption of electronic journals. I have changed my mind. I now recognize that electronic journals and their print counterparts are not duplicates or substitutions for one another. Because of their different functionality and use, they are apples and oranges.

Beth Rossner, American Association for the Advancement of Science (AAAS), reports that *Science* magazine's 26,000 paid, online subscribers want both print and online versions.[4] We are certainly hearing the same thing in our focus groups and surveys at the University of Washington. The print is used one way and the online another by the same researcher. Is the digital shift segmented? Is the digital shift generational? I think so.

Change (the journal of the American Association of Higher Education) gives special praise for Peter Grenquist's article, "Why I Don't Read Electronic Journals." Professor Grenquist offers his reasons for not reading e-journals:

- The difficulty of reading a screen and establishing the source and authority of the text
- The absence of convention–titles, headings, careful punctuation, indentation, paragraphing, and page breaks–that facilitate use
- The jumbled incoherence of computer display
- The inability to markup an article or to find and use it again conveniently
- The inability or uncertain legality of transmitting an article to a friend[5]

"Just mail me the journal," concludes Grenquist.

A recent report from the University of Illinois at Urbana-Champaign recommends that the library not make a large investment in electronic, full-text materials at this time. The report concludes:

> At this point in time, electronic products are often inferior and more expensive than print options. Most people prefer the readability, portability, and ease of annotation that print provides. Display technology is getting better, but we are at least a decade away from electronic copy that equals the quality of print. Traditional peer-reviewed, archival-oriented publications are such a critical part of our promotion and tenure decisions. We, as well as experts in the field, do not fully understand the impact of electronic content on professional societies and the academy. Authors have not learned how to fully exploit electronic media. Electronic content is still largely in print format. For example, in contrast to print journals, including images is not expensive in electronic text. Images are on an equal footing with words.[6]

However, we have others eager for more e-journals. On library surveys just concluded at the University of Washington, a top priority for the libraries for the next five years, according to undergraduate students, should be the provision of more electronic full text. Many undergraduates are members of a digital generation and have been raised in a world of robust and ubiquitous electronic media. Learning and research is a "plug-and-play" experience for many. They are unaccustomed to, and impatient with, learning sequentially and expect access anytime, anyplace. Consider the University of Washington senior student in business who responded to the survey, saying: "What I love about the computer is that while I'm downloading something from a home page I can be doing three other things at the same time rather than wasting my time running around trying to find where the journal is. I can just sit at my desk and it will take me an hour rather than three." Consider the University of Washington medical student doing clinical rounds in rural Montana. Access to the electronic journals is a lifesaver, and that is not an exaggeration.

The decision to cancel a print title, when the electronic archive is guaranteed, is not as simple as I had anticipated a couple years ago. At the same time, we may be beginning to see a shift in the notion of archival purpose and responsibility. Ross Atkinson suggests that if a digital mentality emerges, we and our users may "become increasingly accustomed to some forms of information loss in some circumstances (not only of physical but also intellectual content) . . . we must expect the iron grip of the warranty syndrome to loosen: librarians will no longer be inclined to see as an essential function the provision of total access forever to every object for which they assume responsibility."[7]

CONCLUSION

The digital shift truly is uneven. The choices are not easy. The routines are not in place. The costs are not known. Until they are, we need to continue developing standards and guidelines, listen continually to our users, enter into campus conversations about the unsustainable status quo environment of journal publishing and the possibilities in electronic scholarly communication, engage in meaningful dialog with producers, aggregators, and publishers, imagine new models such as those supported by the SPARC,[8] and actively support our users. If we take these actions, we will manage a digital shift that ultimately provides seamless access to electronic journals in support of faculty, student, and staff information needs.

NOTES

1. University of California Libraries. Collection Development Committee, *Principles for Acquiring and Licensing Information in Digital Formats*. Available: http://sunsite.berkeley.edu/Info/principles.html. September 26, 1998.

2. Association of Research Libraries et al., *Principles for Licensing Electronic Resources*. Available: http://www.arl.org/scomm/licensing/principles.html. September 26, 1998.

3. International Coalition of Library Consortia (ICOLC), *Statement of Current Perspective and Preferred Practices for the Selection and Purchase of Electronic Information*. Available: http://www.library.yale.edu/consortia/statement.html. September 26, 1998.

4. Association of American Publishers, "Annual Conference Report," *Professional/Scholarly Publishing Bulletin of the Association of American Publishers* (February/March 1998): 1.

5. Peter Grenquist, "Why I Don't Read Electronic Journals," *Change* 30, no. 2 (March/April 1998): 9-10.

6. *Final Report of the Task Force on the Future of the University Library.* University of Illinois at Urbana-Champaign, par. 3, "*Technology, Recommendation 13.*" Available: http://www.uiuc.edu/providers/provost/taskforce.html#fr3. September 26, 1998.

7. Ross Atkinson, "Managing Traditional Materials in an Online Environment: Some Definitions and Distinctions for a Future Collection Management," *Library Resources and Technical Services* 42 (January 1998): 18.

8. Scholarly Publishing & Academic Resources Coalition (SPARC) is a partnership project of the Association of Research Libraries and other educational and research organizations. Its mission is to be a catalyst for change through the creation of a more competitive marketplace for research information. For further information, consult the SPARC website at http://www.arl.org/sparc/index.html.

Coping with the Digital Shift:
Four of the Thorniest Issues

Andrea Keyhani

INTRODUCTION

As electronic journals become a real option for serious consideration by libraries, various library organizations, such as The International Coalition of Library Consortia, the University of Washington, and the University of California Libraries, have drawn up guidelines for acquiring and licensing digital information. The guidelines are based on careful evaluation of libraries' shrinking budgets in the face of rising serials costs, lack of storage space, library workflows, and user needs. Libraries note the potential benefits of electronic serials, but also quake at the thought of inaccessible electronic files caused by lack of preservation, changing technology, or publisher requirements.

This paper addresses four of the thorniest issues raised by library consortia: pricing, authorization systems, integration, and permanent digital archives. These issues are problematic not only for libraries, but also for publishers, because they are issues of the digital world.

PRICING AND PACKAGING

One focal point of the guidelines is pricing. The organizations mentioned above suggest the following pricing guidelines:

Andrea Keyhani is Manager of Publisher Relations with OCLC Online Computer Library Center, Inc.

[Haworth co-indexing entry note]: "Coping with the Digital Shift: Four of the Thorniest Issues." Keyhani, Andrea. Co-published simultaneously in *The Serials Librarian* (The Haworth Press, Inc.) Vol. 36, No. 1/2, 1999, pp. 149-162; and: *Head in the Clouds, Feet on the Ground: Serials Vision and Common Sense* (ed: Jeffrey S. Bullington, Beatrice L. Caraway, and Beverley Geer) The Haworth Press, Inc., 1999, pp. 149-162. Single or multiple copies of this article are available for a fee from The Haworth Document Delivery Service [1-800-342-9678, 9:00 a.m. - 5:00 p.m. (EST). E-mail address: getinfo@haworthpressinc.com].

- The cost for electronic content should be less than its print equivalent, unless there is considerable added value.
- Content and access costs should be separated.
- Libraries should have the option to purchase the electronic version without having to pay for the print subscription.
- Site license pricing should be based on the anticipated number of actual users, as opposed to the total campus population.
- Publishers should not expect libraries to shoulder the entire cost of development and marketing of electronic products. Costs for electronic products should be low enough to encourage experimentation and widespread use.[1]

CURRENT PRICING MODELS

Current pricing models offered by publishers for electronic journals are varied, with the most popular being a bundled print and electronic package, aimed at preventing cancellation of print subscriptions. Among the ECO (Electronic Collections Online) publishers offering a bundled package, the majority offer the electronic content for 1998 at no additional cost. Thus, for the price of the print, subscribers can now obtain the electronic content as well. While some publishers view this as a special introductory offer, others have decided to stay with it, at least for awhile. The advantage of this package is that it provides a good opportunity for libraries to try out the electronic version, at little additional cost, of journals already subscribed to in print. Publishers can market the extra benefits of their journals and maintain or even expand their subscription base.

Publishers who are offering a bundled package with a surcharge for the electronic version generally charge anywhere from 10 to 50 percent more for the package over the print-only cost, with the majority being in the range of 15 to 20 percent. Site licenses are considerably more and are premised on campus-wide usage. Pricing for site licenses is still very much in the conceptual stage for most small publishers, while a few organizations, such as Academic Press (http://www.apnet. com/www/ap/aboutie.htm), have clearly defined pricing. Consortia are forcing publishers to formulate site license pricing (a non-issue prior to electronic journals), with the expectation of significant discounts for consortia members. A consortial model that has attracted considerable attention and has been successful is the Academic Press model, which deals exclusively with consortia, is based on prior-year expenditures and a minimum fee, and provides all participants of a consortium with access to the collective holdings of the group.

Publishers offering electronic-only subscriptions are still in the minority. Pricing for e-only subscriptions generally range from 75 to 100 percent of the print price, with the majority in the 90 to 95 percent range. Two good examples of discounted electronic journals are Johns Hopkins University Press and Blackwell Science.

Are libraries ready for electronic-only subscriptions? Given discounted pricing, as well as the guarantee of perpetual access and a permanent archive, libraries will certainly consider e-only subscriptions very seriously. While it is true that few libraries have given up print so far, it is also true that few publishers have offered electronic-only subscriptions that meet those criteria.

FUTURE PRICING MODELS

Per-article sales. Although the subscription model is the most comfortable one for publishers, per-article sales hold some attraction as an additional revenue source. Initially, per-article sales were viewed with great trepidation by publishers, who feared the demise of their entire subscription base if libraries could purchase individual articles. More recently, however, a number of publishers are looking at this model as providing not only additional revenue but also greater exposure for their journals, primarily from users who find the article as part of an aggregated collection of journals from many publishers. As libraries are provided with statistics on per-article sales by aggregators such as OCLC, the libraries may find it more economical to subscribe to a journal for which there are a significant number of per-article sales. Purchasing an individual article online has clear advantages over traditional ILL or document delivery, in that the articles are available immediately and in a highly readable format equivalent to the print.

Per-article subscriptions. A model that encompasses both the individual article and the subscription model is a subscription that spans a collection of journals and provides a set number of individual articles from that collection. The collection could be limited to a publisher or could represent an aggregated collection from multiple publishers. A variation on this theme would be a subscription to a *virtual* journal: a collection of articles on a particular subject area, pulled from a number of different journals. Publishers could collate articles from their own journals. With publishers' permission, aggregators could offer a far more comprehensive virtual journal, collating articles from many publishers' journals.

AUTHORIZATION SYSTEMS

Authorization systems should not be a barrier to access by authorized users, defined as faculty, students, and walk-up users not formally affiliated with the library. The *site* (covered by the site license) should include every campus location, on-site and remote, and any location where authorized users might be, at home and abroad. The issue of distance learning further complicates the definition of authorized users.

Ensuring that only authorized users have access to electronic data is clearly an issue of importance to publishers, who have always been concerned about the ease with which electronic information can be illegally disseminated to unauthorized users. There are a number of methods currently used by aggregators and publishers, some of which can at least partially accommodate the requirements specified by the libraries. The most popular are:

- IP address recognition,
- authorization/password, and
- proxy servers.

IP address recognition. This is the most popular method today. The institution provides the publisher/aggregator with a range of IP addresses, and all users must enter the system under one of those addresses. In the case of aggregators connecting users to the publisher's server, both the aggregator and the publisher must be able to recognize the user's IP address. The upside for IP address recognition is that the library does not need to distribute authorizations, which could be illegally disseminated. Users simply log on through the campus network, which automatically carries the appropriate IP address to the publisher's server. The downside involves users who cannot connect to the campus/institution network and must use a SLIP or other type of connection to log on to the publisher's server. Unless the institution offers its own SLIP connections, SLIP connections coming through Internet service providers carry a different IP address each time a user logs on, and therefore cannot be identified beforehand.

Authorization/password. A unique authorization and password is generated by the publisher/aggregator for an institution or an individual. The upside is that users, regardless of location, can access the system if they know the authorization and password. The downside involves the security of the authorization, which can be disseminated easily to unauthorized users. Libraries are most hesitant to distribute such information, especially if their access fee is based on a certain number of simultaneous users. Clearly, it is to the library's advantage to keep the usage under tight control. Additionally, many data licenses place responsibility for ensuring copyright compliance on the library. Again, tight control can minimize the risks of copyright violation.

Proxy servers. OCLC provides Common Gateway Interface (CGI) scripts to libraries who wish to use authorization/password but do not want to disseminate the number to their users. The library authenticates its users through its own server and then automatically tacks on the authorization/password as it passes them through to the publisher/aggregator's server. Under this scenario, users access the library or campus server, where they are authenticated by entering their campus ID. Once they pass this point, users are then referred to the publisher/aggregator's server. The benefits of this method are that users do not need to know the authorization number, and they can access the publisher/aggregator's server from any remote location. However, this method requires creation of an authentication system. Additionally, any problem with the proxy means that large groups of users do not get access until the proxy is fixed, and the proxy is also a single point of potential security problems. Finally, the double handling required by going through a proxy server can mean response-time delays for the users.[2]

AUTHENTICATION SYSTEMS

It is necessary to differentiate between authorization systems, such as the ones mentioned above, and authentication systems, which validate an individual user logging on to a network operating system. Authentication systems establish who a user is by comparing a user's ID against an authorized list, and are frequently the basis for the proxy server and IP address recognition scenarios described above.

Authentication systems can be quite sophisticated, such as Kerberos and digital certificates, or they can be based on a simple identification number issued to a user, such as a PIN or student ID number. A white paper on "Authentication and Access Management Issues in Cross-Organizational Use of Networked Information Resources" has been drafted by Clifford Lynch of the Coalition for Networked Information. The goal is to identify relevant issues and lay the foundation for standards development in access management. Lynch finds cryptographic certificates to be the most viable option in a large-scale networked environment for a number of reasons: they can accommodate multiple affiliations and access rights; they offer strong security and interoperability across institutions; and also, support for certificates (unlike Kerberos) is starting to appear in Web browsers and other commercial software. There are cost and logistical problems associated with certificates (they are difficult to distribute and complicated for users to install), but the biggest potential problem concerns user privacy, since the certificates contain specific information about the user. However, there may be ways of authenticating the user, then masking the user's identity as he/she is passed through to the remote server, thus combining external anonymity with internal accountability.[3]

INTEGRATION

Integration is key to creating the one-stop shopping service that libraries seek for their patrons. Clearly, it is not enough to offer bibliographic databases that simply contain references to full-text material, nor is it enough to produce electronic full-text files from a single publisher with no links to anything else. The optimal service should connect

- bibliographic databases with full-text,
- local system files to full-text,
- full-text references to the primary articles, and
- Full-text references to bibliographic databases for further research.

In addition, the ideal service should

- aggregate journals from many publishers,
- create cataloging records for electronic journals for a library's local system,
- update holdings records in OCLC's WorldCat to reflect the library's acquisition of electronic journals, and
- notify users that a library holds the print copy.

Aggregation provides an easy way for libraries to integrate full text into their systems. Eliminating the need to create links to a potentially large number of publisher sites, aggregators collect the data from many publishers and offer it in a single location.

ARCHIVING

An archive is an organization that preserves information for access by public or private communities. The explosive growth of digital information brings new challenges to archiving, as it becomes painfully clear that digital information is easily lost, corrupted, or changed. The technology evolution is causing some hardware and software systems to become obsolete in just a few years, potentially rendering those data inaccessible that are dependent on these systems. It is important that those producing, maintaining, and accessing the data be active participants in long-term preservation planning to minimize life-cycle costs and enable long-term preservation.

ARCHIVING INITIATIVES

A number of digital preservation initiatives are aimed at investigating ways to preserve data in a standardized fashion that can be used by any archive. The Task Force on Digital Archiving, which was sponsored by the Commission on Preservation and Access, was the first initiative to identify critical archival issues and has spawned a number of other projects and initiatives.[4]

OAIS. The National Archives and Records Administration is organizing a Digital Archive Standards workshop to be held in late June 1998, with the purpose of identifying potential digital archiving standardization topics and assessing interest in developing the standards. The basis for discussion is the draft Open Archival Information System (OAIS) Reference Model, which has been developed by the Consultative Committee for Space Data Systems, which is part of NASA.

The OAIS Reference Model addresses in detail the areas of data submission, archival storage, data management, access, and dissemination.[5] It also addresses migration of data to new media, the role of software in preservation, and the exchange of data among archives. The model should be applicable to any archive.

The OAIS model advocates creation of an Information Package, which contains Content Information and Preservation Description Information (PDI). The PDI is the key to long-term preservation, and is divided into four types of information:

- *Provenance:* The source and ownership of the content and its history. An example is a copyright statement.
- *Context:* Describes how the content relates to any other information. Examples are DDC numbers and related data sets.
- *Reference:* One or more unique identifiers for the content, such as ISBN or DOI (Document Object Identifier).
- *Fixity:* A protective measure to preserve the integrity of the content, such as encryption, a digital certificate, or a checksum.

Packaging Information ties the content and the PDI into a single entity. If the content is on a CD-ROM, for example, the Packaging Information would include the ISO-9660 volume/file structure on the CD-ROM as well as the actual CD-ROM.

The OAIS model also describes responsibilities that an archiving organization must assume:

- *It must establish criteria for information.* The organization must determine the kind of information it is willing to accept. The criteria may include subject matter, source, uniqueness, data format, standards compliance, and physical media.
- *It must assume control of data to ensure long-term preservation.* Whether the organization is the owner or the custodian, it must be able to make and implement decisions about data migration and access.
- *It must determine designated consumer communities.* The organization must be able to determine which communities are likely to access the information and ensure that the information is understandable to those communities.
- *It must ensure that information is understandable and fully documented.* Certain scientific content, such as data sets, may be understandable only to its producers unless there is sufficient information describing the meaning of various fields. Similarly, the content should be fully documented down to the bit level, to ensure that new software can replace the software originally used to create the content.

- *It must follow established preservation policies and procedures.* The organization needs to establish policies for backups and data migration.
- *It must make the information accessible.* The organization is responsible for making the information available to its designated user communities by creating easy-to-use interfaces, and offering secure access to the data, which protects the data from unauthorized use as well as tampering.

CEDARS. A new three-year project on digital archives is CEDARS, which is funded by the Joint Information Systems Committee (JISC) in the UK. CURL (The Consortium of University Research Libraries) will lead this project. CEDARS will address strategic, methodological and practical issues and will offer guidance to libraries regarding digital preservation. The main objectives are to (1) promote awareness of the importance of digital preservation among all of the stakeholders, and (2) to provide guidelines to libraries to help ensure the long-term preservation of digital resources in their collections.[6]

Digital Collections: A Strategic Policy Framework for Creating and Preserving Digital Resources is a study conducted by the Arts and Humanities Data Service and funded by JISC.[7] A publication draft, now available, includes a good introduction to the issues involved in creating and preserving digital information, implementation guidelines, and case studies. The organizations interviewed represented legal deposit or copyright libraries, institutional archives, funding agencies, research-oriented agencies, and cultural heritage organizations, among others.

The study emphasizes the need for careful management and planning of digital information from the point of creation, and suggests that the costs for preserving digital resources are heavily dependent on decisions made at various stages of their life cycle. The life cycle of digital resources can be broken down into three phases: (1) data creation, (2) data and collection management and preservation, and (3) data use. The way in which data is created (formatted, compressed, and encoded) will affect how it is managed, used, and preserved in the future. Data and collection management and preservation involve many policy decisions about selection of materials to be preserved and for how long. It also involves decisions about how and where to store the data, how often to refresh the data, what kind of disaster recovery procedures are required, and when to migrate the data onto new media or into new formats. Finally, data use is dependent upon legal requirements, why it was created, where and how it is stored, and under what conditions it should be accessed. The study makes the point that few organizations involved with digital resources have control over their entire life cycle. For example, data creators control how the data is produced, but few of those creators have traditionally been interested in the long-term preservation of the data. Similarly, the organizations most involved with preservation, such as libraries, have little influence over how resources are created.

The use of standards was acknowledged as key to reducing costs for long-term preservation by all respondents. However, there is currently little consensus as to the best standards to use, and there is clearly a need to do research and cost analyses on "best practices." Data creators who are not interested in long-term preservation are unlikely to adopt standards, especially when those standards are more costly or more difficult to implement than other methods that produce desired short-term results. The study recommends demonstrating the long-term cost effectiveness of the higher investment in standards, metadata, and data documentation. The study suggests that funding agencies can play a key role in determining how resources are handled throughout their life cycle. It also suggests that no single organization can preserve all digital materials, and that cooperative agreements can help divide responsibility for different subject areas or materials.

WHO IS TAKING RESPONSIBILITY FOR ARCHIVING?

As discussed in the AHDS study mentioned above, a number of disparate organizations are involved in various archiving projects, most of which can be considered "demonstrator" projects: experiments to judge the efficacy of a particular archiving scheme, establish standards, and continue to identify issues. Organizations surveyed in the study include the Center for Electronic Records of the National Archives and Records Administration (NARA), the Public Record Office in the UK, the Inter-University Consortium for Political and Social Research (ICPSR), the Natural Environment Research Council in the UK, the National Library of Australia, and the British Library, among others. Organizations such as the Commission on Preservation and Access in the United States have spearheaded initiatives to lay the groundwork for international archiving through its Task Force on Archiving of Digital Information, which I described in considerable detail last year at this meeting. JISC, as described above, is also taking a strong role in funding studies to identify the issues required to establish a national archiving policy. Thus far, no broad-based government initiatives that encompass nationwide data have been announced.

A handful of scholarly publishers are in the process of formulating their own archiving policies, though some, like Elsevier, have publicly stated that it is too early to formulate a long-term policy. Most journal aggregators have made similar statements, or have stated that they are not in a position to assume archival responsibilities. In contrast, OCLC has taken a strong position on archiving and has made it a cornerstone of its Electronic Collections Online (ECO) service. All publishers participating in ECO must agree to allow OCLC to establish an electronic archive and to provide perpetual access to subscribers. To ensure perpetual access online to volumes subscribed to, OCLC has created a subscription profiling system that captures volumes and dates (including gaps) for each journal subscribed to, and incorporates that information into the library's unique authorization. To create a permanent archive, OCLC has committed to either migrating ECO content to new data formats as current formats become outmoded or to continue to support the software required to view outmoded formats.

Within the academic library community, the twelve member libraries of the Committee on Institutional Cooperation (CIC) are building the CIC Electronic Journals Collection (CIC-EJC). The CIC libraries hold 57 million volumes, more than 17 percent of the collections holdings of the Association of Research Libraries. In 1991, the CIC began creating an archive of freely available electronic serials. However, it soon found that "an uncataloged, unsearchable collection whose contents were not examined regularly by collection staff could not be of widespread, long-term, or consistent value to scholars because it offered no assurance that the collection was complete, current, and worthy of preservation."[8] Based on this project, the CIC began developing the CIC-EJC prototype encompassing collection policy, organization, bibliographic control, and access policies for electronic journals. Although the CIC is currently pointing to publishers' sites for access to the journals, it is also building a permanent archive of all titles in its collection by storing the data on disk and backing it up to tape.

The National Digital Library Federation is a consortium of twelve research university libraries, the Library of Congress, the National Archives, and the New York Public Library, committed to archiving digital information.[9] Each member of the group has pledged to undertake a project having to do with one of these three areas: (1) discovery and retrieval, (2) intellectual property rights and economic models, and (3) digital archiving. Garrett makes a point of differentiating digital libraries from digital archives, where digital libraries are repositories for collecting and providing access to digital information, but may or may not create long-term digital archives.[10]

PERPETUAL ACCESS VERSUS PERMANENT ARCHIVES

A distinction must be drawn between the concept of a permanent archive versus the concept of perpetual access. For example, Johns Hopkins University Press's Project MUSE offers perpetual access to its subscribers by issuing an annual nonsearchable CD-ROM archival disc as well as allowing libraries to load the archive locally, thus ensuring that libraries retain ownership of the materials. However, Johns Hopkins is making no claims of establishing a permanent archive.[11] Although Hopkins has gone a long way towards accommodating the libraries' demand for perpetual access, there are clear limitations for long-term archival use of CD-ROMS. Moreover, most libraries are not in a position to create their own digital archive.

Organizations creating permanent archives may not necessarily offer perpetual access. For instance, the Association for Computing Machinery has mapped out a plan to maintain an archive of its publications. However, users that drop their subscriptions lose access to all back issues.[12] A number of other publishers also require ongoing subscriptions, viewing the electronic content as an expanding database to which subscribers have complete access, but only so long as their subscriptions are current. The matter is complicated by "forward" hypertext linking used by some publishers to establish links from backfiles to current files. Given the existence of such links, it is difficult to prevent backfile-only subscribers from using links to new articles in current files.

Thus, the issue of perpetual access and permanent archives has become more complicated and will continue to be thorny as publishers and aggregators take advantage of electronic publishing capabilities, which allow linking backward and forward as well as to external databases and referenced journals that may or may not be subscribed to by the user. The DOI (Document Object Identifier) system, which offers publishers a means to separate and identify parts of a document and links to related information, has good potential for handling this complexity, though it produces a new level of financial complexity should publishers decide to charge for every element identified.

As described above in the archiving initiatives, there is much work to be done in developing standards for archiving, as well as in determining what should be archived, and perhaps most importantly, who should take responsibility for archiving. In the meantime, the initiatives are raising the level of importance of the archiving issues and of trying to get the buy-in of all parties involved, especially the creators of the digital files. It is increasingly clear that there are no simple solutions to archiving, though it is equally apparent that resolutions and standards need to be put in place quickly, lest we lose an important part of our cultural heritage.

CONCLUSION

Affordable pricing, comprehensive integration, secure yet remotely accessible authorization systems, and a guarantee of a permanent electronic archive are just a few of the criteria formulated by libraries as they contemplate purchasing electronic journals. In the face of budget cuts, rising serials prices, a plethora of publisher websites, and limited storage space for print journals, the criteria are reasonable and basic to the success of electronic publishing programs. Publishers/aggregators and libraries must be prepared to work together to deal with these issues.

NOTES

1. International Coalition of Library Consortia (ICOLC), *Statement of Current Perspective and Preferred Practices for the Selection and Purchase of Electronic Information.* Available: http://www.library.yale.edu/consortia/statement.html. 19 June 1998; University of California Libraries Collection Development Committee, *Principles for Acquiring and Licensing Information in Digital Formats.* Available: http://sunsite.berkeley.edu/Info/principles.htm. 22 May 1996.

2. Clifford A. Lynch, "The Changing Role in a Networked Information Environment," *Library Hi Tech* 15, no.1-2 (1997): 30-38.

3. Ibid.

4. Commission on Preservation and Access and the Research Libraries Group, *Preserving Digital Information: Report of the Task Force on Archiving of Digital Information*. (Washington, D.C.: Commission on Preservation and Access, 1996).

5. Consultative Committee for Space Data Systems, *Reference Model for an Open Archival Information System (OAIS)* (Silver Spring, MD: White Book, 1998).

6. *Cedars Project*. Available: http://www.leeds.ac.uk/cedars/. 19 June 1998.

7. Arts and Humanities Data Service, *Digital Collections: A Strategic Policy Framework for Creating and Preserving Digital Resources*. Available: htp://www.ahds.ac.uk/manage/framework.htm. 24 April 1998.

8. Bonnie MacEwan and Mira Geffner, "The Committee on Institutional Cooperation Electronic Journals Collection (CIC-EJC): A New Model for Library Management of Scholarly Journals Published on the Internet," *The Public-Access Computer Systems Review* 7, no. 4 (1996), 7. Available: http://info.lib.uh.edu/pr/v7/n4/macewan.7n4.html. 26 September 1998.

9. Susan E. Feldman, "It was Here a Minute Ago!" *Searcher* 7, no. 9 (October 1997): 52.

10. John R. Garrett, "Task Force on Archiving of Digital Information," *D-Lib Magazine* (September 1995). Available: http://www.dlib.org/dlib/september95/09garrett. html. 26 September 1998.

11. Ellen Finnie Duranceau, "Archiving and Perpetual Access for Web-Based Journals: A Look at the Issues and How Five Ejournal Providers are Addressing Them," *Serials Review: EJForum* (in press).

12. Garrett.

EMERGING TRENDS
IN JOURNAL PUBLISHING

Emerging Trends in Journal Publishing

Liz Pope

SUMMARY. Electronic journals, especially Web journals, offer new challenges as well as new opportunities for publishers. Electronic journals require an entirely new workflow and demand an entirely new set of publishing skills. This leads publishers to look for new ways of doing things that are being found more and more by strategic partnerships, collaborative outsourcing, and even insourcing. In this session, the presenters will review the major issues and challenges faced by publishers and report on emerging trends in journal publishing today. Focusing on the traditional print product as well as on the development of the "new" journal, the presenters will relate the cultural, technical, and structural changes that have arisen from the shift from paper-centric publishing to a combination of paper and electronic. At the heart of this change is the need to adopt a publishing system that processes journal content as electronic data, rather than as static typographic images, and manages the electronic journal archives to ensure continued access to the links and electronic features that matter to readers. *[Article copies available for a fee from The Haworth Document Delivery Service: 1-800-342-9678. E-mail address: getinfo@haworthpressinc.com]*

Liz Pope is Vice President, Business Development, Community of Science.

[Haworth co-indexing entry note]: "Emerging Trends in Journal Publishing." Pope, Liz. Co-published simultaneously in *The Serials Librarian* (The Haworth Press, Inc.) Vol. 36, No. 1/2, 1999, pp. 163-174; and: *Head in the Clouds, Feet on the Ground: Serials Vision and Common Sense* (ed: Jeffrey S. Bullington, Beatrice L. Caraway, and Beverley Geer) The Haworth Press, Inc., 1999, pp. 163-174. Single or multiple copies of this article are available for a fee from The Haworth Document Delivery Service [1-800-342-9678, 9:00 a.m. - 5:00 p.m. (EST). E-mail address: getinfo@haworthpressinc.com].

BACKGROUND

Scientific, technical, and medical (STM) publishing is a well-established sector of the publishing industry. The size of the market has been estimated conservatively at $2.5 billion annually, according to a Salomon Brothers report.[1] More than 90 percent of this business is derived from some 2,000 research libraries worldwide, where currently less than 5 percent of the revenue is from electronic products. In the next five to ten years, the electronic contribution is expected to increase to 70 percent. Scholarly journals are the most profitable and the most time-sensitive sector of the industry. Journal publishing is also unique in that scientists are both the creators and the consumers of the information that is produced. As currently constructed, scientists, operating under "publish or perish," contribute articles for inclusion in publishers' journals to secure tenure. Peer review is essential and a recognized component of the journal publishing system.

While the growth of scholarly information can be seen in all fields of learning, increases have been most dramatic in the sciences (13 percent per year for scientific and technical journals), where output doubles every 5.5 years.[2] The increased output has severe implications for research libraries, especially in scientific fields. Due to budgetary constraints, research libraries are being forced to reduce acquisitions and cancel journal subscriptions in core subject areas. Library funding is moving away from the focus on self-sufficient collections toward cooperative collection development and resource sharing. Tensions have thus emerged within the scientific community. Scientists continue to expect that their libraries will be well stocked. On the other hand, librarians find it increasingly difficult to maintain adequate levels of resources and to provide increasing access to electronic resources in a context of restricted budgets and the growing body of knowledge.

CHALLENGES AND OPPORTUNITIES

We are in a period of history where the advancement of technology is moving at an astounding rate. It seems that no sooner does a technology appear than its market is threatened by another more advanced application. In conjunction, recent innovations in the Internet client-server systems have enabled widespread access to new database and electronic publishing applications. The most important is the development of the World Wide Web, a collection of servers operating on a set of common Internet protocols. A number of freely available clients or browsers such as Netscape Navigator and Microsoft Explorer allow computer users to connect to Web servers. These clients have made advanced electronic publishing applications accessible to any individual with a computer and an Internet connection.

In particular, electronic journals or electronic versions of journals that are also available in print can be delivered over the Web to the end user's desktop. Once the information is in electronic form, it can be made available in a variety of formats. Powerful software tools can also be provided. The challenges and opportunities of the new digital world include:

- *Customization:* Personalizing tools such as hyperlinks, reader profile filters, information agents, and database marketing help to fine tune a journal to the audience of one.
- *Timeliness:* Web publishing is faster and more convenient than paper-based media, collapsing the closing schedules for both the editorial and the advertising function.
- *Comprehensiveness:* No physical library can possibly compare to the mountains of information available at a keystroke on the Internet.
- *Searchability:* Interface design and search engine; searching through a comprehensive database is a major editorial advantage over print, useful for retrieving a nugget of data, but more importantly, helping the reader sift and filter raw data into useful knowledge.
- *Economy:* For the publisher, library, and reader; Web media are cheaper to produce than print-based media and audiences expect the Internet to be more economical, one way or the other.
- *Transaction:* Participation, forums, games; lets the reader interact with the author, order directly from an online catalog, and participate in the creation of the text.

Publishing on the World Wide Web has been anticipated as an exciting possibility, offering unlimited, global distribution combined with the chance to integrate networked hypertext and multimedia. But the reality of Web publishing today is one of mixed results. Although Hypertext Markup Language (HTML) is a good electronic delivery medium for many texts, it is often a poor choice for representing source documents.

The Web isn't just technology, although its operation depends on it. The Web does have a technical basis as a client/server system for hypermedia communication. But all the fancy interactive software in the world will not convince you or anyone to use the Web. Now that the desktop publishing revolution has freed communicators from the oppression of three-dimensional film, paper and plates, smart publishers are offering their customers a new generation of interactive products and services that go far beyond traditional ink-on-paper technology.

The immediate problem of the Web is that one finds that there is no shortage of information, but instead extreme difficulty in accessing it. In the print world, the experience of primary publishers in the area of indexing is limited. As such, primary publishers of traditional print journals will have to concentrate their energies on developing their expertise in indexing, searching, and marketing as they move their journals onto the Web. Initially, most publishers have been most interested in defining interactivity as the consumer being able to describe and receive information they need. Such a system will enable readers to request and receive journal articles directly at their desktop.

APPROACHES TO ELECTRONIC PUBLISHING

Publishers interested in offering their journals in electronic form on the Web face a confusing assortment of options. Some, for example, putting tables of contents and article abstracts on the Web, are easy and fairly inexpensive to implement if the original composition files are well prepared. Publishing the full text of a journal electronically introduces other issues, such as the display of tables, equations, special characters, and illustrations. In addition, Web publishing needs to adapt to rapidly evolving browser technology. Finally, there are several standards competing to provide the best way of creating, managing, and delivering text-based information via the Web.[3] The following discussion addresses these different standards and how each can be used to create an effective information management environment.

PDF (PORTABLE DOCUMENT FORMAT)

PDF, the portable document format, was designed by Adobe Systems, Inc. in order to provide a system-independent method of delivering page-based information. PDF files are an easy by-product of Post-Script composition files used for print journals. They are created by printing to a PDF driver or by "distilling" a PostScript file. The resulting PDF file can be read using a tool from Adobe called Acrobat Reader. This tool is available free from Adobe and can be downloaded from their Website or any one of their affiliates.

Advantages: PDF provides electronic pages with impressive page fidelity. Type, graphics, and color are all reproduced as they appear on the hard copy original. In addition, hot links and other electronic object types, such as sounds and movies, can be added to the PDF file. PDF files are inexpensive to create and are used by several companies, including most journal publishers, to deliver page-formatted information on the Web. Because the end user receives a document that looks like paper, training costs are also low.

Disadvantages: PDF creates large files with little structural information. PDF files are not nearly as flexible as other electronic formats because they were designed for viewing on paper, not to provide a way of delivering intelligent document structure to a user. Although Adobe has products available that can index many different PDF files for cross-document searching and navigating, there is little support for searching. That is, navigation is limited to "turning" pages from section to section and "scanning" the page for text of interest.

Another problem is page fidelity. PDF files are not necessarily pixel-by-pixel replicas of a page that might be printed by the document owner. This is partly due to the fact that fonts used to create the original document might not be on the machine that eventually views the document.

HTML (HYPERTEXT MARKUP LANGUAGE)

Supported by over 100 million Web browsers, HTML is becoming the de facto standard for transmitting information between people on-line. Because of the simplicity and low cost of HTML, a large information base has been created, making HTML even more valuable.

Advantages: HTML browsers are very powerful and cheap or free; a vast range of information can be delivered to the browser using a combination of third-party add-ins and server-side content support. HTML document browser interfaces are easy to build into existing products because of the simplicity of HTML code. HTML is easy to learn because it is simple; there are only a few dozen tags and not all are used in most situations. HTML works across systems that are otherwise unrelated; any Webpage can link to another publicly accessible page simply by just entering the address.

Disadvantages: HTML's simplicity, while making it valuable as a basic method of delivering simply structured information, causes it to fall short of being a long-term method of delivering complex information types. HTML is a weak presentation tool, lacking even the most fundamental page-oriented formatting capabilities, such as hanging indents, white-space control, justification, kerning, and hyphenation. However, because of the nearly universal compatibility, Website designers are working around these problems by using tables to simulate multiple columns and indents and GIF graphics to create certain designs with type and white space. In such cases, HTML itself has become a shell that contains the real markup.

Because it does not allow for creating custom tags or presenting tags with different styles, HTML is also a weak markup tool. There is no real modularity of hierarchical relationships between elements. This limits HTML to delivering page-oriented information instead of being a method to deliver intelligent information. HTML provides linking, but it is only a one-to-one link, and requires an anchor on the target end in order to access anything within the document. HTML's instability is another problem. First there was HTML, then HTML+, followed by HTML 2, then a series of specifications in level 3, and now a level-4 HTML. Plus, browser manufacturers have created extensions to the "standard" HTML (like "blink" and "center" tags), causing other manufacturers to play catch-up.

The combination of this instability and HTML's simplicity has caused a situation where there are numerous codes that break when presented to a browser. This problem had made both Webmasters and users frustrated, causing them to seek out a better solution. One way HTML advocates are trying to extend HTML is by promoting the ability to create more customized styles in HTML using cascading style sheets (CSS), a technical recommendation of the W3C (World Wide Web Consortium). CSS separates structure (HTML markup) from format (how it looks).

SGML (STANDARD GENERALIZED MARKUP LANGUAGE)

SGML is an international standard that is more than ten years old. It was originally designed to provide a way of describing text-based information so organizations could exchange information easily. Since then, SGML has become valuable in describing information sets that allow document owners to overcome the restrictions of paper-only publishing. SGML provides a way of creating markup languages customized for each document type and of separating the content from eventual formatting.

Advantages: SGML is not tied to a particular operating system or application, and so it is portable from one platform to another. It is a standard maintained by the International Standards Organization (ISO). Because of its standing as a stable standard, there are many products available in several categories, from editors to document management solutions to typesetters and web delivery applications. Several vendors are providing tools and support for each category. SGML does not provide a fixed set of tags but rather a syntax for creating your own tags. Several industries have formed consortia for the purposes of creating common tag sets to exchange information using their terms and expressions.

Disadvantages: SGML is complicated to understand and difficult to integrate into an application. SGML requires a "parser" that is difficult to write and maintain. Since SGML was created in the early days of desktop computing, it is overly concerned with maximizing limited memory and disk space by providing a complex set of "minimization" rules and exceptions. This complexity results in SGML being more expensive than a simple tag set like HTML. Each document must have a "document type definition" created, which requires the owner of the document to perform a "document analysis" to discover its structure. Still, there is a relatively small market for SGML, so the pool of individuals who have experience in document analysis and document type definition design are hard to find and expensive to keep on staff. Finally, because of the complexity of the standard, and the smaller market for vendors, tools that support SGML are more expensive than those that support HTML.

XML (EXTENSIBLE MARKUP LANGUAGE)

XML is a new technical standard of the W3C. Because XML uses SGML as its core technology, it is portable between systems. XML is easy to learn. It is also easy to learn to write programs that can process XML documents. When the designers of XML started to work on the standard, they had ten design goals:

- XML shall be straightforwardly usable over the Internet.
- XML shall support a wide variety of applications.
- XML shall be compatible with SGML.
- It shall be easy to write programs which process XML documents.
- The number of optional features in XML is to be kept to the absolute minimum, ideally zero.
- XML documents should be human-legible and reasonable clear.
- The XML design should be prepared easily.
- The design of XML shall be straightforward and concise.
- XML documents shall be easy to create.
- Terseness in XML markup is of minimal importance.

These goals led the development of XML and helped the design committee stay focused on what was important. An XML "well-informed document" processor can be written in a few days, and a parser that reads "valid" XML documents takes less than a week to write. This means that users can include XML processing capabilities in their products, as Microsoft did with Internet Explorer 4.0.

XML, because of its simplicity and the advent of the "well-informed document" concept, is a natural candidate for use on the Internet, providing complex formatting possibilities plus the ability to perform advanced searching and navigation functions. Time will tell if the goals of XML have been reached. XML has already made quite an impact, more than SGML has received in over ten years. XML has inspired the imagination of content providers by giving them a simple, extensible, vendor-independent way of describing and exchanging information that HTML has failed to do. Finally, XML has the potential of delivering good-looking presentation with high-quality structure that PDF cannot match.

WEBSITE DESIGN OBJECTIVES

The discussion in this section addresses several website objectives. The relative importance of each objective depends on a site's application-specific characteristics: the kinds of documents being accessed, the volume of information being managed, and who is providing the content. Objectives include:

- *Creation:* Ease of data creation
- *Accessibility:* Accessibility to Web search engines

- *Sensitivity:* Context-sensitive searching
- *Maintainability:* Ease of maintenance
- *Luminosity:* Illumination of off-site resources

It should be easy for content providers to create and modify documents. HTML does a fairly good job meeting this goal. HTML has a simple tag set, and with the help of a high-quality HTML editing software package, it is not hard to learn enough HTML to create goodlooking, easy-to-read documents. Editing SGML documents, on the other hand, can be cumbersome when the DTD is complex.

Several search engines with publicly accessible HTML user interfaces are available for use in locating resources on the Web. These search engines rely on "Web spider" programs that traverse the Web to build their search indexes. Therefore, in order for a Website's documents to be searchable using these Web search engines, the documents need to be in the form of static HTML (or plain text) files. Document creators have the option of providing their own keywords to a search engine through HTML's "META" tag, which can be used to specify/name pairs describing arbitrary characteristics of the document. However, different search engines may use different "META" syntax, because HTML does not dictate any particular set of properties.

If context-sensitive searching is required, then the data should be structured in an application-specific manner, i.e., according to an SGML DTD. Therefore, this objective conflicts with the accessibility objective. The proposed MCF (Meta Content Framework) uses XML syntax to specify information about the content of a Web document. If MCF is implemented in Web browsers, then Website designers will no longer be forced to choose between the accessibility and sensitivity objectives.

Once the total size of all static HTML documents in a Website grows beyond a few hundred kilobytes, it becomes necessary to spend a lot of effort maintaining the site. This requires checking for dead hyperlinks, making sure information is up-to-date, and maintaining consistency between the documents. HTML provides no support for any of these tasks. The degree to which a Website provides hyperlinks to documents on other Websites is called the site's luminosity. Although luminosity is generally seen as a good thing, off-site hyperlinks should be used with discretion.

WEBSITE DESIGN OPTIONS

Whatever the electronic publishing plan, good digital files are necessary. Well-prepared, consistently tagged files will be the most useful; and if those files are in SGML, they will be even more adaptable. A customized, database approach offers an almost unlimited range of electronic publishing options, from simple and inexpensive ASCII-based interfaces with simple structured queries to highly graphic, menu-driven products. A Website designer using SGML has several decisions to make. In particular, the designer must address the two issues that follow.

SOURCE DOCUMENTS

The designer must decide whether to represent the source documents as HTML conforming to an HTML DTD or to use a DTD specifically tailored to the Internet's requirements. Each approach has its advantages and disadvantages. It is usually easier for content providers to author documents in HTML than to use an application-specific DTD. On the other hand, documents conforming to an application-specific DTD can be searched using an SGML search engine according to the structures in that DTD. Therefore, using SGML-conforming HTML to represent source documents favors the creation objective, and using an application-specific DTD favors the sensitivity objective.

DYNAMIC versus STATIC HTML

Until more Web browsers support the display of SGML documents, the majority of SGML-based Websites will need to display their SGML source documents as browser-ready HTML. Even if the source document is SGML-conforming HTML, all entity references and marked sections must be normalized. Therefore, an SGML-based site design needs to include an SGML-to-HTML translator to render the SGML source as browser-ready HTML. While the implementation of a translator is straightforward, the designer needs to decide whether the translation should be done a single time after a document is created or modified. There are advantages and disadvantages to both approaches. Generating the browser-ready HTML dynamically simplifies the Website's design because it eliminates the need to keep statically generated HTML documents synchronized with the SGML source. However, dynamically generated documents are not accessible to external search engines. In addition, dynamic generation of HTML requires the use of CGI (Common Gateway Interface), a standard for applications with Web servers. CGI adds overhead to the server, in addition to the processing required to generate an HTML document. Frequent requests to generate HTML from SGML on demand can degrade Web server performance. However, keeping the SGML source and the HTML consistent requires an infrastructure for configuration management. The larger the number of documents in a Website, the more sophisticated the data management needs to be. A large site requires a high powered relational or object database management system to keep track of the associations between the SGML source and the browser-ready HTML.

CONCLUSIONS

In today's world of rapid technological change, no one can predict precisely what tomorrow's electronic publishing solutions will look like. However, most scholarly publishers agree that their future business will depend on the strength of their computer connectivity to the Internet and other networks, especially the linkages to key customers and suppliers. To survive, publishers must choose a technology strategy that will allow them to adapt and deploy new publishing systems quickly, without disturbing their current infrastructure or impacting their ability to do business. One of the biggest mistakes is to choose a strategy that limits flexibility in the future.

As emerging Internet and Web technologies push the envelope of what can be done online, content creators, managers, and users struggle just to keep their knowledge and skills current. However, the opportunities of the networked world demand far more of us; just keeping up with technology is not enough. As new technologies continue to change the way we gather information and communicate, the real leaders will be the ones who can renegotiate these relationships.

NOTES

1. "The Electronic Revolution: In the Beginning Was the Word," *Salomon Brothers UK Equity Research Report*, February 1997, 40.

2. Joseph J. Branin and Mary Case, "Reforming Scholarly Publishing in the Sciences: A Librarian Perspective," *Notices of the AMS* 45, no. 4 (1998): 476-77.

3. Brian E. Travis and Dale C. Waldt, *The SGML Implementation Guide: A Blueprint for SGML Migration* (New York: Springer-Verlag, 1995).

STM X-REF:
A Link Service for Publishers and Readers

Gerry Grenier

SUMMARY. Linking out from reference citations within online STM (science, technology, medicine) serial articles is an issue of growing importance for readers and content providers alike. This paper touches on the current state of linking activities and discusses on a high level the creation of a linking service that will facilitate resource discovery by the end user and automatic link creation by the publisher of online serials. *[Article copies available for a fee from The Haworth Document Delivery Service: 1-800-342-9678. E-mail address: getinfo@haworthpressinc.com]*

INTRODUCTION

The number of online scholarly peer-reviewed journals is growing rapidly. According to the Association for Research Libraries,[1] the number currently stands at 1002 as compared to forty-seven in 1996. This emergence is due to at least three factors that are driving the expansion of the World Wide Web at large: (1) evaporation of geographic and time barriers to information; (2) improved resource discovery in the form of more intelligent, easy-to-use search tools; and (3) hypertext linking. Having overcome most of the back-office operations and infrastructure issues necessary to put their journals online,

Gerry Grenier is Wiley InterScience Development Director, John Wiley & Sons, New York, NY.

[Haworth co-indexing entry note]: "STM X-REF: A Link Service for Publishers and Readers." Grenier, Gerry. Co-published simultaneously in *The Serials Librarian* (The Haworth Press, Inc.) Vol. 36, No. 1/2, 1999, pp. 175-185; and: *Head in the Clouds, Feet on the Ground: Serials Vision and Common Sense* (ed: Jeffrey S. Bullington, Beatrice L. Caraway, and Beverley Geer) The Haworth Press, Inc., 1999, pp. 175-185. Single or multiple copies of this article are available for a fee from The Haworth Document Delivery Service [1-800-342-9678, 9:00 a.m. - 5:00 p.m. (EST). E-mail address: getinfo@haworthpressinc.com].

publishers are now focusing their efforts toward enriching their offerings with features that are unattainable in the print medium. Hyperlinking is one area in particular that is attracting high user demand and increasingly high publisher investment. Original scholarly work is (generally) published as a print article in a peer-reviewed scholarly journal. Original publication spawns the subsequent creation of related electronic objects that include a full-text HTML (Hypertext Markup Language) version, a full-text PDF (Portable Document Format) version, abstracts created by various secondary services, and author-created supporting material (Figure 1).

The original work and its family of related objects currently are published in isolation of each other, each object ignorant of its siblings. The STM publishing community is working to develop hypertext linking systems in order to create a more useful web of resources. Many

FIGURE 1. An STM serials article and some of the objects that are spawned upon publication.

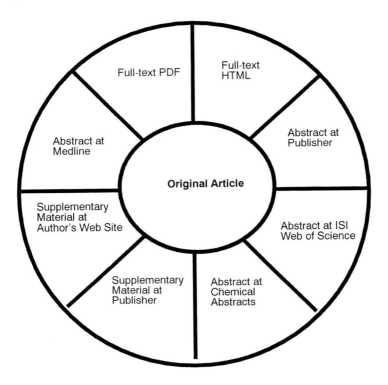

linking arrangements have been created between content providers and the National Library of Medicine, the ISI Web of Science, and Chemical Abstract Services, to name a few. These arrangements are dependent upon business agreements (I use the term "business" regardless of whether money is exchanged) between the two agencies. This practice results in a different link mechanism for each different business relationship, as well as an uneven level of service to the user, who, we must remember, moves from journal to journal ignorant of the publisher and the publisher's services. The current practice also results in a very cumbersome link-building process that is certainly manageable on a small scale, but one that presents problems on a larger scale.

Barriers to link building and the problem of uneven citation linking can be overcome if the STM publishing community can agree on standards that can be used to create a link lookup service that holds meta-information obtained from all providers of scholarly content. The collective result would be a comprehensive metadata database that can be used to resolve lookup queries originating from any citation of the original work. Hypothetically I will term this service "STM X-REF." Hyperlinks that take advantage of such a service would be easier to create and would offer the kind of comprehensive linking that readers require.

Creation of such a service has three components: standards agreement, technical implementation, and business considerations. Standards agreement is underway. Technical implementation of a project this size has precedence (for example, the larger search engines such as Yahoo, or the bookstore, Amazon.com). The larger question that lurks is, who could own and administer this service, and what impact will the service have on the existing STM industry?

A REVIEW OF CURRENT LINKING

I will describe linking from a primary publisher's perspective. Links are described as coming inward from an external source or going outward to a resource from citations in published serial articles.

Examples of inward links include those originating from secondary services: within an abstract at Medline or, say, the ISI Web of Science, to the full-text HTML or PDF at the content provider's Website. Outward links are those originating from other primary publishers: external citations to Wiley articles made in non-Wiley journals to the full-text HTML or PDF at our Website, for example.

Currently these links are created as the result of a business agreement and exchange of technical details between two organizations. A publisher, Wiley, for example, might inform Medline that in order to link into the full-text PDF file for any article within Wiley Inter-Science, Medline should build a link consisting partly of static information combined with dynamic article-related qualifiers, such as:

www2.interscience.wiley.com/zcgi/wiley-bridge?ID=issn,volume,opening page

    Static   Dynamic

The static information identifies the server. The dynamic information is built at the point of link creation. A link, then, from Medline to an article in the *American Journal of Medical Genetics* (ISSN 0148-7299) volume 81, page 275 would read:

www2.interscience.wiley.com/zcgi/wiley-bridge?ID=0148-7299,81,275

Some publishers (American Physical Society, for example, at http://publish.aps.org/linkfaq.html) publish their link syntax for anyone wishing to build a link into journal article abstracts. Their link syntax, while similar to Wiley's, uses a different method to identify the journal. For example, "http://publish.aps.org/abstract/PRD/v55/p1/" links the user to the abstract appearing on page 1 of volume 55 of the journal *Physical Review D*. These are but two examples of similar yet different pathways into STM journal content.

To turn to an examination of outward linking, let's take a hypothetical example from a large STM publisher who produces as many as 36,000 STM articles per year. Included in these articles are citations to roughly 750,000 articles in the STM serials literature. Creating links for these 750,000 citations can be costly and time consuming. The link creator must determine:

- if there are any potential electronic objects that relate to this citation
- the location of the related objects (who is the publisher and what inward links do they offer?)
- the link pointer
- the degree of link persistence

In order to link to resources at, say, Medline and ISI Web of Science, the publisher must create two links using two separate processes. The process to create Medline links takes advantage of the Medline batch citation matcher: the publisher submits a single file for each article's citations, noting for each citation the ISSN (or journal title or abbreviated journal title), the year of publication, volume, opening page and author. Not all of these fields are required, but completing the set furthers the probability of an exact match. The Medline batch citation matcher returns a unique ID for each article, and the publisher appends that Medline ID to a base URL provided by Medline.

Linking to an abstract of the same work at the ISI Web of Science would require Wiley to first obtain a base URL format from ISI and then append the ISI unique identifier for each article citation. The ISI identifier could be the DOI (Digital Object Identifier) or it could be an identifier unique to ISI. It is certain that it will not be the same identifier as the one used at Medline. Once the publisher completes the processing of these links, the appropriate links are inserted into the HTML (Figure 2).

FIGURE 2. Example reference citation page using currently available linking mechanisms.

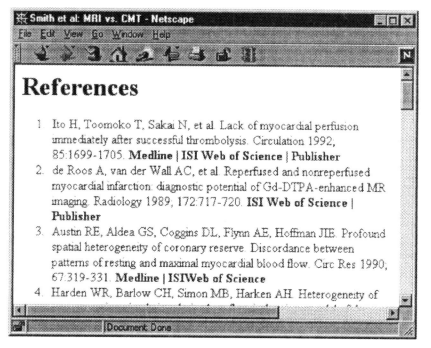

AN ALTERNATIVE UNIVERSE:
CREATING SMARTER HYPERLINKS
(ONE-TO-MANY LINKING)

Current linking in the STM journals community can be described as a one-to-one relationship, that is, one link leads immediately to one resource. One-to-one links are certainly an improvement over "pre-Web hyperlinking" (or lack thereof). However, we need to take a step forward and create *one* link that leads to many related Web resources (Figure 3).

FIGURE 3. (a) Current links are generally a one-to-one relationship. (b) A link service would facilitate one-to-many relationships.

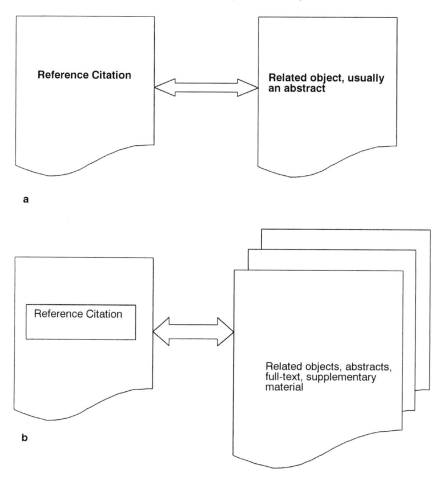

A one-to-many linking service can be realized through the creation of a metadata database that holds information about all objects that relate to original works in the STM literature.

Links utilizing the lookup service would be in the form of a query that demanded a list of all the available Web resources that relate to this work. The link service would return a single link-resource page, giving the user a single rich source of links to follow. I like to think of this as a "smart Yahoo" for the STM publishing community.

CREATING LINKS TO THE LINK SERVICE–OVERVIEW

With the existence of STM X-REF, creation of links would be greatly simplified. A content creator would simply create a link that passed a standard unique identifier to the STM X-REF. This unique identifier would be appended to a base URL pointing to a local lookup server. For example, a typical link would read "www.linkservice.com/ unique_identifier" where the unique identifier could be the ISSN, volume and opening page number, or indeed a "dumb number" (such as the DOI) that uniquely identified the work. This process would eliminate the need to discover the availability and source of links, leaving that task to STM X-REF.

With Standard Generalized Markup Language (SGML) coding becoming the norm, it would leave publishers (primary and secondary) with the task of creating a holder for a unique identifier within their SGML-coded data.

UNIQUE IDENTIFIERS

Standards creation can be a difficult hurdle to overcome. The creation of the ISSN led to a much more efficient trade in serials publications. As individual articles now are becoming important as a unit of trade, the creation of a unique article identifier will be the glue that holds article-related services together. Current work in this area is encouraging, the most promising being the work of the International DOI Foundation (IDF), at http://www.doi.org.[2,3,4,5] The creation of the International DOI Foundation was an important step forward in institutionalizing a framework from which a standard article identifier could be created.

The existence of a unique article identifier for a *work* would allow the owner of an object related to that work to use the work ID and embellish that ID with attributes such as type and location of content. In plain terms, the encoding in the identifier would declare to incoming queries at STM X-REF, "I am a full-text PDF file related to the work titled 'Preparation and properties of SBS-g-DMAEMA copolymer membrane by ultraviolet radiation,' by Yang, Jong and Hsu, published in the *Journal of Biomedical Materials Research*, and you can reach me at the following URL."

METADATA STRUCTURE

Agreement on the minimum metadata structure needed to describe the content maintained by STM X-REF is as important as the unique identifier itself. The International DOI Foundation, among others, has identified metadata as an urgent priority.[5,6,7,8,9]

OBJECT REGISTRATION

Content creators would register metadata descriptions of their STM-related objects with the STM X-REF. The metadata description will include

- the original work's unique identifier
- an object type attribute identifier (i.e., full-text, abstract)
- a link pointer attribute to the object
- access rights attributes

Success of the STM X-REF lookup service would be dependent upon a steady and timely feed of metadata from STM content providers.

END USER BENEFITS

With the metadata database in place and the links to it included in online STM reference sections, the user would be provided with one-click access to a collection of all the registered objects for any work

(Figure 4). STM X-REF would return a page of resources that relate to the cited article (Figure 5). Each resource would have an access indicator, informing the user of any potential barriers to the object. Clicking on a resource link would bring the user directly to that resource, with, of course, any access restrictions that are in place at the site holding the resource.

BUSINESS CONCERNS

Can a service such as the hypothetical STM X-REF be a viable business concern? Certainly, if there is a need and demand, then success should follow. When considering STM X-REF as a business concern I should emphasize that this service is not a search service, but rather a lookup service. Metadata will not contain abstracts, and therefore will be of limited search value except, of course, for known-item searching.

Revenue could be generated by service agreements with publishers as well as advertising that could be placed on the referral pages.

Potential owners of such a lookup service could be drawn from primary and secondary STM publishers or current Internet portals wishing to expand their services into niche markets. Indeed, the size

FIGURE 4. Reference citation page showing one link that leads to STM X-REF–a hyperlinking lookup service.

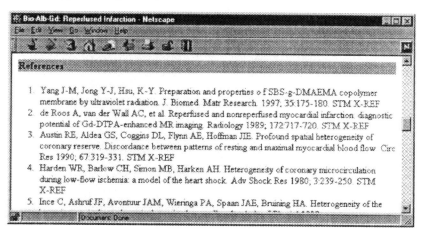

FIGURE 5. Look-up results page from the hypothetical hyperlinking look-up service STM-XREF.

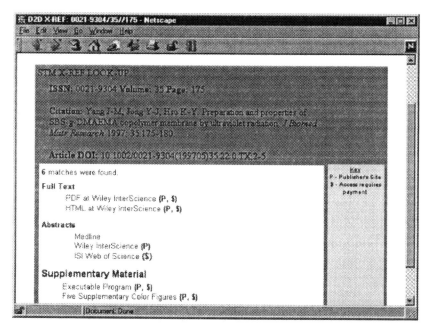

and potential of a service could well spawn a new independent player in the STM community.

CONCLUSION

The state of hyperlinking between STM serials, while an improvement over "sneaker-net" hyperlinking of just five years ago, is one area of added value that needs improvement. When I think of today's linking and compare it to a world with a link lookup service I am reminded of a quotation made by the late R. Buckminster Fuller, who said:

> If you are in a shipwreck and all the boats are gone, a piano top buoyant enough to keep you afloat that comes along makes a fortuitous life preserver. But that is not to say that the best way to design a life preserver is in the form of a piano top. I think that

we are clinging to a great many piano tops. . . . (*Operating Manual for Spaceship Earth*)

I hope that at the least this idea of STM X-REF will stir librarians, publishers, authors, end users, and entrepreneurs to build that better life raft.

NOTES

1. *Directory of Electronic Journals, Newsletters, and Academic Discussion Lists.* 7th ed. (Washington, DC: Association of Research Libraries, 1997).

2. Mark Bide, *In Search of the Unicorn: The Digital Object Identifier from a User Perspective.* Available: http://www.bic.org.uk/bic/unicorn2.pdf.

3. International DOI Foundation. Available: http://www.doi.org.

4. International Standard Work Code (ISWC). Available: http://www.nlc-bnc.ca/iso/tc46sc9/iswc.htm.

5. Norman Paskin, "Information Identifiers," *Learned Publishing* 10 (1997): 135. Available: http://www.elsevier.nl/homepage/about/infoident.

6. Dublin Core Initiative. Available: http://purl.oclc.org/metadata/dublin_core/.

7. EDITEUR. Available: http://www.editeur.org/.

8. Godrey Rust, "The Right Approach," *D-Lib Magazine*, July/August 1998. Available: http://www.dlib.org/dlib/july98/rust/07rust.html.

9. UK Metadata Working Group. Available: http://www.bic.org.uk/rights.html.

Scholarly Journals in the Electronic World

Peter B. Boyce

SUMMARY. Above all, the electronic information environment is interlinked. Links can knit together the scholarly references, citations and data sources for the user as never before, bringing the whole web of distributed information resources right to the reader's desktop. A certain amount of infrastructure and degree of cooperation is needed to make this happen effectively. The field of astronomy now benefits from such an infrastructure, which has been named Urania. Links and other electronic resources comprise much of the value of an electronic journal, but make the job of maintaining an electronic archive more difficult. Users of the electronic scholarly journals in astronomy have developed new expectations for speed of production, ease of use, and ability to update links and features, and a demonstrated degree of permanence in electronic journals. These expectations are fundamentally changing the way publishers must look at the journals they produce. *[Article copies available for a fee from The Haworth Document Delivery Service: 1-800-342-9678. E-mail address: getinfo@haworthpressinc.com]*

INTRODUCTION

The electronic, interlinked world of scientific publishing is very different from the world we have known of individual journals containing individual articles. The differences have major implications for

Peter B. Boyce is Senior Associate for Electronic Publishing for the American Astronomical Society.

[Haworth co-indexing entry note]: "Scholarly Journals in the Electronic World." Boyce, Peter B. Co-published simultaneously in *The Serials Librarian* (The Haworth Press, Inc.) Vol. 36, No. 1/2, 1999, pp. 187-198; and: *Head in the Clouds, Feet on the Ground: Serials Vision and Common Sense* (ed: Jeffrey S. Bullington, Beatrice L. Caraway, and Beverley Geer) The Haworth Press, Inc., 1999, pp. 187-198. Single or multiple copies of this article are available for a fee from The Haworth Document Delivery Service [1-800-342-9678, 9:00 a.m. - 5:00 p.m. (EST). E-mail address: getinfo@haworthpressinc.com].

the traditional journals, for the traditional database providers and for the libraries. Preparation, distribution and maintenance of electronic documents require a degree of interdependence among all the steps in the information chain, from author to reader, which is unheard-of for paper journals.

Small changes in the electronic manuscript may have enormous consequences later in the production process, introducing complexities which can, and should, be avoided by establishing effective feedback and communication among all parties.

The need for effective communication up and down the information chain suggests that we can function best if we adopt a new mode of working. Instead of dealing with vendors and customers in a confrontational mode, we at the American Astronomical Society (AAS) have found that the best results are obtained by viewing electronic publishing as a collaborative and cooperative venture. First and foremost, we must remember that we are in the business of facilitating the delivery of information, and that new tools and new techniques made possible by the Internet and computer technology will enhance the production, storage, location and retrieval of information. The AAS embarked upon the development of electronic journals in 1991 with a diverse team made up of users of scholarly journals. As described by the author,[1] the AAS Electronic Publishing Development Team sought advice and feedback from the library community, other users, authors and the current journal production staff. We avoided being unduly influenced by the journal production procedures in use at the time. In fact, we eventually redesigned the whole journal production process, which resulted in adding a full set of electronic features, generating an archival quality electronic database using the Standard Generalized Markup Language (SGML), and producing the journals more rapidly and at less overall expense than paper alone was costing in 1992.

WHAT IS AN ELECTRONIC JOURNAL?

There are a number of differing definitions of an electronic journal, ranging from a journal with only the abstracts online to the full-featured, highly linked information resource (a.k.a. journal) as exemplified by the AAS's *Astronomical Journal*.[2] Not everything that goes by the name of "electronic journal" deserves that name. We steadfastly maintain that collections of abstracts do not a journal make. We equally steadfastly maintain that a collection of page images delivered electronically also do not qualify as a true electronic journal, since they only amount to electronic document delivery of paper journals. An electronic journal is not a collection of unlinked, separate articles. It is not a set of static pages in a particular format which is fixed for all time. And, by our measure, a journal available only in Portable Document Format (PDF) is not a true electronic journal either, a view shared by all the participants in a plenary session on the future of the scholarly journal presented at the 1998 meeting of the Society for Scholarly Publishing.[3]

We define an electronic journal as a *linked, permanent* information resource for *transferring* reliable and accurate information from the producer to the reader. These three important characteristics are the hallmark of a good electronic journal, and each defines an important manner in which the new electronic communication regime differs from that of the paper journal. Let's inspect them in more detail. We will explain how links are critical. But, the underlying *raison d'etre* of a journal is to transfer information. A good electronic journal makes that easy. Finally, we have come to expect the information in a scholarly journal to be permanently available. Electronic journals must have demonstrable longevity.

LINKS

An electronic journal must have copious links, for two purposes: for navigation within the article and the issue and for connectivity to other relevant resources. Applied intelligently, navigational links can ease the burden of reading articles on the computer screen and even provide new capabilities which enhance the transfer of information to the reader, which we will speak about later. A table of contents (TOC), either as an explicit list or as a "contents" frame, for each article with links to the various sections and back to the TOC is a great help to the reader. Links from the text to the reference page are an obvious necessity, but reverse links from each reference to the spot in the text where it is discussed are equally important. Reverse links from the references to the text offer a new way for readers to browse an article. Readers who work on the same specialty can go directly to the reference list (which must appear in alphabetical order and preferably is downloadable as a separate page), find their own papers referred to, and by means of the reverse link, jump directly into the text to see what the author said about their work. Links to and from tables, plates, figures, video clips, etc., are additional important aids to browsing and navigation within the article.

But readers of the electronic *Astrophysical Journal*,[4] which has been available for three years, are quick to tell us that the links to the referenced articles, both to the abstracts and to the full text of the articles, add the greatest value to the electronic edition. Our journals also link to subsequent electronic articles which refer back to the article being read, a capability impossible to duplicate in the paper version. We call these "forward links" or "citations." Links to outside databases and other information sources outside the article and outside of the specific journal are also important. In the system we have put together for astronomy, the electronic journal article is but one part of a distributed resource, linked forward and backward in time to other articles, abstracts, and additional databases. The electronic information resources in astronomy are widely distributed, yet are heavily interlinked, and will become even more so.

The wealth of electronic information that can be accessed via the gateway of the well-linked electronic journal article is growing. For active academic scholars, time is a precious resource, and the flood of available information is growing daily. The challenge is to locate and recover relevant material. Quick connections from a journal article to information judged to be relevant by the author and editor are a boon to busy researchers.

With the electronic journal now serving as a gateway to additional information, the boundary where the journal ends is growing indistinct. In the electronic environment, this is as it should be, but it leads to issues of reliability and permanence of such supplemental material, namely, material which is not under the control of the journal. In the highly interlinked environment of the World Wide Web (WWW), producers and readers alike are becoming ever more dependent upon working cooperatively with a high degree of trust and responsibility. The academic community, with its overarching credo of scholarship and intellectual integrity, is in a prime position to create a cooperative, integrated electronic information resource. An example from astronomy shows how well this can work.

URANIA

In order to make an effective, linked electronic information resource, a protocol and set of standard names for articles must be in place. No general standards existed when we started, so we had to devise our own. Working with the NASA-supported Astrophysics Data System (ADS)[5] and the global set of astronomical data centers,[6] we developed a working system of common standards, naming conventions, and cooperative protocols which have made it possible to link the astronomical literature together into a system of interlinked resources that bring information to the researcher's desktop anywhere in the world where there is an effective connection to the Internet.

A second necessity for an electronic information system is a way to find and retrieve relevant articles. For this, astronomy turns both to the ADS and to the astronomical databases. The ADS has a system of searchable abstracts for astronomy's core literature that has proven to be a popular resource. In addition, the astronomical databases provide an object-oriented system by which comprehensive information about a specific star, galaxy or other object can be retrieved, along with links to the articles where the specific data were published.

Another requirement is a name resolution system by which a link can be directed to the symbolic name of an article without having to hard code the actual physical location of the article (or piece of data). Symbolic names are permanent, while the normal Uniform Resource Locator (URL) is dependent upon where the item is physically stored and is not permanent unless special precautions are taken. Moreover, the symbolic names also make it possible to maintain mirror sites for the major online information resources in astronomy.

The historical literature, a major component of any information system, also needs to be available electronically. Again, astronomy turns to the ADS, which is engaged in a project to scan the full-text pages of the major historical literature in astronomy and make them available online. Each article is accompanied by its reference and citation lists, which are linked to the full articles as well as to the current electronic journals. To complete the full electronic resource, the current electronic journals are linked to each other as well as to the ADS system of abstracts, which, in turn, provides the links to the full-text page images of the older literature and to the holdings of the data centers.

To emphasize the importance of this cooperative effort, we have called this enabling infrastructure "Urania," named for the muse of astronomy.[7] Urania is not a collection of objects. It is not a product to which libraries can subscribe. It is not a consortium. It is the underlying infrastructure that makes possible the interconnectivity that characterizes the dissemination of electronic information in astronomy. The smoothly functioning links that connect the references, citations, data, and historical literature are the result of a standardized naming system,[8] excellent cooperation among the various organizations that are providing the information, and our simple, but functional, name resolution system. As described by Boyce et al.,[9] the science of astronomy is now reaping the benefits of a distributed, interoperable system for the exchange of information.

TRANSFER OF INFORMATION

A good electronic journal is designed so as to transfer information effectively. We have already spoken of the convenience afforded by the intelligent use of links for navigating within an article. But an intelligent design calls for more than just the use of links. Format, speed, ease of use, and permanence are important expectations of our readership.

Readers use the electronic journal in two ways: browsing to locate articles they want to read, and saving the articles for a thorough reading off screen. These two uses require different formats. In browsing, speed of transmission, easy navigation and a format adapted to easy reading on the screen are important. On the other hand, readers want to print out the selected articles of interest. In this case, high-quality printing in a page-oriented format is important. Good electronic journals are available in multiple formats adapted to these two different uses.

Adobe's PDF system produces page images in which it is possible to insert links and that have some form of navigation between different pages. However, PDF images are not matched well to the screen format, do not usually have links inserted in them, and are several times larger than the same material sent encoded in Hypertext Markup Language (HTML). We make our journals available in three formats, PDF for printing, HTML in one file per article, and HTML broken up into one file per section. The latter format makes it possible for readers who may be using a slow connection to load only the abstract before they spend the time necessary to load the whole article. As early as 1996, readers of the *Astrophysical Journal Letters* showed their preference, choosing one of the HTML formats over the PDF by a factor of six to one. Informal surveys confirm that readers use the HTML version to browse for important articles and then print the article locally using the PDF format. This pattern simply mimics the usage of paper journals, where readers find important articles and then photocopy them for inclusion in a working notebook for later use.

But there is more to scholarly electronic journal design than the PDF versus HTML question. Many journals include too many graphics which take time to transmit but carry no significant information. Some of the worst examples are complicated graphical images that are used in many journals as linking "buttons." Using underlined text as the link anchor can significantly reduce the time it takes for a page to load over a modem connection. Transmission speed is highly desired by our readers, especially those around the world who may be trying to access the journal from countries with less than adequate connectivity. Even in the U.S. and Europe, transmission can be agonizingly slow during busy periods. In a scholarly journal, the rapid transfer of information should take precedence over cute graphics.

In the future, electronic journals will have to go beyond a reproduction of the capabilities already available in the paper versions. The transfer of information can be greatly enhanced through the use of color images, video clips, three-dimensional representations, machine-readable data tables, and even embedded math fragments and working algorithms. There will be a wide and growing variety of electronic features in the journal of the future. Doctors will see video demonstrations of heart operations. Ornithologists will hear bird songs. Readers of clinical medical journals will be able to calculate risk factors for individual patients by going to online journal articles and plugging information into "live" equations. Finally, astronomers will be able to manipulate 3-D images of star clusters and replay simulations of galaxy collisions contained in refereed journal articles. All these things have been demonstrated today in single articles. The future will see such things become commonplace in the journals, profoundly increasing the ability to transfer information and concepts from the author to the reader.

On the WWW, color is as inexpensive as black and white but carries significantly more information. We have many authors who submit color images for the electronic edition and black and white images for the printed version, thus avoiding the costly color printing process. The authors are assuming implicitly that the electronic, not the paper, version of the article is the authoritative copy. There is no significant concern, as measured by the informal feedback we receive, that the paper version does not contain the complete information. We can see emerging in the astronomical community a growing expectation that the electronic version has primacy over the paper version. Implicitly, our community is assuming that the electronic version, with all the electronic enhancements, will be available into the foreseeable future.

PERMANENCE

Scholars advance knowledge by building upon the work of those who have preceded them. To be of value, the record of that work must be available. It must endure through time. In the electronic world, the text and illustrations must remain available–with links that continue to function, with video clips, live math fragments, and other electronic features that continue to work and be accessible by the then-current technology through the years. The preservation and archival maintenance of electronic material will become more and more of a problem. Preserving effective access to the individual articles as the technology changes will be difficult. In the electronic era, it will be sufficient no longer to find a storage location for a file or two where the material is stored and left like a book on a shelf. No storage medium lasts forever. Electronic material will have to be actively managed to prevent deterioration of the material to the point where it becomes unreadable.[10] The problem of deterioration is not unfamiliar to librarians who have witnessed the physical deterioration of 1920s journals that were printed on acidic paper and are now crumbling to dust under the reader's fingers. The same process happens in the electronic era; the time scale is simply faster. The electronic journal has the added complexity of maintaining working links and remaining accessible in a world of rapidly advancing technology. As electronic journals incorporate more and more links, preserving the links as well as the textual material will be even more difficult. Yet this will have to be done. This is a serious problem to which, in general, not enough consideration has been given.

The AAS has stepped up to this challenge. First, working with our publishing partner, the University of Chicago Press, we have reworked our publishing process to translate incoming manuscripts into an archival quality electronic form that uses SGML to encode all the features of the article. Working in SGML, and in a cooperative fashion with the ADS, we can insert reference and citation links efficiently and almost automatically at an early stage in the process. From the final SGML database we can derive the HTML, the PDF and the paper versions of the article that the public sees. As new versions of the standard browsers appear with added capabilities, we have modified the automatic translation software to incorporate those new capabilities into the HTML version of the articles. In fact, we have remade the entire set of electronic issues to incorporate new features. Since such rederivations can be done automatically, this has not proven to be a burden on the operating budget of the journal. This experience gives us the confidence to promise that we will actively maintain the electronic versions of our journals for the indefinite future.

In addition, just to ensure that we will be able to maintain the electronic journals in a widely accessible form, we are assigning a small percentage of current subscription income to an archival maintenance fund. Every five years the fund will have accumulated to the point where we can afford to completely redevelop the automatic translation program and to retranslate all our electronic material into a new format, even if we have to augment the process with a significant amount of manual work. We feel confident that we have proven our ability to maintain the electronic archive in a widely accessible form for as long as we remain the publishers.

USER EXPECTATIONS

Our readers expect several things from their electronic journals. Maintenance of scholarly integrity is one such expectation. With the growing amount of information of questionable accuracy appearing on the WWW, and access to information becoming available to readers who may not have the capability to judge for themselves the reliability of such information, the scholarly electronic journals will become welcome islands of quality in the growing sea of information available to readers.

The readers are interested in seeing the material as rapidly as possible. To this end, the AAS and the University of Chicago Press have worked to revise the whole production process to focus on producing first the electronic version, from which can be derived the paper version, which requires a longer time scale for publication. The electronic version of each paper is posted, article by article as soon as they are ready, within three weeks of acceptance by the scientific editor. This is a major breakthrough in the dissemination of information, and other scientific societies are following suit.

Readers will also come to expect that the information on the WWW represents the latest, updated material. Yet, the scholarly journal implies an integrity of the material, i.e., that it has remained unaltered since it was accepted for publication. These two conflicting requirements do not seem to be compatible. We can expect to see a new type of information resource arise in astronomy, similar to the genome and protein molecule databases in biology, which are a compilation of up-to-date, and presumably best, estimates of the values of measured information. Such new online sources of the "latest and best measurements" will exist side by side with the "traditional" scholarly electronic journals, which remain unchanged after publication. But even the traditional scholarly journals will have to point to the latest citations and updated material in their electronic versions.

CONCLUSION

We are working in a new environment, and the implications about how we must change to make effective use of the new capabilities are enormous. Electronic documents will be assembled from pieces located in several places. Even today, one year of the *Astrophysical Journal* is made up of about 250,000 interlinked files. We will soon see electronic documents assembled on the fly, to match the reader's capability to access and process electronic information. Different readers could see technically different presentations that depend upon their computer hardware, their native language and their expressed preferences.

It is very difficult for us to envision the enormity of the long-term changes that are happening today. Historically, we have always overstated what will happen in the short term as a result of the introduction of new technology. But we have consistently failed to envision the effects of the fundamental revolution brought on by the growth of the WWW.

As an example, consider the planning and conduct of conferences. No sweeping predictions were made about how the Internet would change how this is done, but look at the reality. Just five years after the introduction of Mosaic made the WWW generally accessible, it has become a major tool for conference organizers. Conferences are now put together by individuals located in far-flung locations without using paper mails. Hotel reservations, conference registration, and distribution of the program are all accomplished over the WWW. The proceedings are often made available over the WWW. This is a remarkable change over a short time. The same pace of change is taking place in the scholarly information enterprise, and we in the scholarly publishing business will have to abandon many of our past habits and older modes of thinking if we are to remain relevant and successful.

NOTES

Dr. Peter B. Boyce was the executive officer of the American Astronomical Society during the start-up phases of the AAS's electronic publishing development, and was the senior associate for electronic publishing for the last three years. He is now the principal of his own consulting firm, P. Boyce Associates. Without the cooperation and contributions of the Urania coalition, astronomy would not have the effective system it now has. Without the cooperation and encouragement of the editors of the AAS journals, we would not have the high-quality electronic journals that are a critical element of the Urania collaboration. Sarah Stevens-Rayburn of STScI and the astronomical library community have provided helpful insight into the needs of the users. Most of all, I am indebted to Evan Owens of the University of Chicago Press and Chris Biemesderfer of Ferberts Associates, who have been valuable members of the AAS Electronic Publication Development Team and have provided the clarity of vision and the technical know-how to actually make this all happen.

1. Peter B. Boyce and Heather Dalterio, "Electronic Publishing of Scientific Journals," *Physics Today* 49 (January 1996): 42-47. Available: http://www.aas.org/~pboyce/epubs/pt-art.htm. 14 September 1998.

2. Available: http://www.journals.uchicago.edu/AJ. 14 September 1998.

3. David Pullinger, editor of *Nature*; Peter Boyce, AAS; Richard Lucier, The Digital Library, University of California; Robert Bovenschulte, American Chemical Society.

4. Available: http://www.journals.uchicago.edu/ApJ. 14 September 1998.

5. G. Eichhorn, A. Accomazzi, C. S. Grant, M. J. Kurtz, and S. S. Murray, "New Capabilities of the ADS Abstract and Article Service," in *Astronomical Data Analysis Software and Systems VII*, Astronomical Society of the Pacific Conference Series, vol. 145 (San Francisco: Astronomical Society of the Pacific, 1998), 378. The abstract can be found on the ADS itself at http://adswww.harvard.edu/.

6. Two major data centers are the Centre de Données astronomiques de Strasbourg (http://cdsweb.u-strasbg.fr/CDS.html) and the NASA Extragalactic Database (http://nedwww.ipac.caltech.edu/).

7. Available: http://www.aas.org/Urania. 14 September 1998.

8. Urania is now based on a "Bibcode" identifier, which is derived from a volume, page, year naming scheme and is ideally suited to identifying articles published in a scholarly journal. The bibcode, also known as "refcode," was developed during the 1980s as a cooperative effort among the astronomical data centers, notably NED. The bibcode system has served astronomy well. It provided a simple, workable method to get started in developing methods for inserting effective links into electronic documents. We look forward to integrating the bibcode system into a more generalized standard whenever one becomes universally adopted.

9. Peter B. Boyce, Evan Owens and Chris Biemesderfer, "Electronic Publishing: Experience Is Telling Us Something," *Serials Review* 23, no. 1 (fall 1997): 1-9.

10. John Garrett and Donald Waters. *Preserving Digital Information: Final Report and Recommendations* (Washington, D.C.: Commission on Preservation and Access, 1996). Available: http://www.rlg.org/ArchTF. 14 September 1998.

EVALUATING ONLINE RESOURCES: NOW THAT YOU'VE GOT THEM, WHAT DO YOU DO WITH THEM?

Measures of Cost Effectiveness in Electronic Resources

Chuck Hamaker

SUMMARY. The high cost of online and Internet-based resources makes evaluating their utility and cost effectiveness an ongoing concern. While it is not difficult to measure aspects of the cost, use, and effectiveness of online resources, many related issues are unresolved, including defining terms, analyzing statistics, and protecting user confidentiality. *[Article copies available for a fee from The Haworth Document Delivery Service: 1-800-342-9678. E-mail address: getinfo@haworthpressinc.com]*

Chuck Hamaker is Assistant Director, Technical Services, University of North Carolina, Charlotte.

[Haworth co-indexing entry note]: "Measures of Cost Effectiveness in Electronic Resources." Hamaker, Chuck. Co-published simultaneously in *The Serials Librarian* (The Haworth Press, Inc.) Vol. 36, No. 1/2, 1999, pp. 199-205; and: *Head in the Clouds, Feet on the Ground: Serials Vision and Common Sense* (ed: Jeffrey S. Bullington, Beatrice L. Caraway, and Beverley Geer) The Haworth Press, Inc., 1999, pp. 199-205. Single or multiple copies of this article are available for a fee from The Haworth Document Delivery Service [1-800-342-9678, 9:00 a.m. - 5:00 p.m. (EST). E-mail address: getinfo@haworthpressinc.com].

MEASURES OF COST EFFECTIVENESS
IN ELECTRONIC RESOURCES

Probably the most under-discussed topic in the literature on evaluating electronic resources is evaluation after the contract is signed. We have a large and growing literature on evaluating content, connectivity, usability, user level, authority, source, types of pricing from multi-user to per-search, FTE and every possible concatenation.

Contract negotiations between consortia and publishers and vendors have created numerous pricing options, patterns, even breakthrough approaches. Sources who had previously only charged "per hit" have written "unlimited use" contracts based on their experiences in what is a new and rapidly growing market. Evaluation after the ink is dried on the contract has tended to be couched in very formal terms. Time-outs, simultaneous use, downtime, how quickly items load, currency of the data, connectivity issues and the like dominate contracts. Cost effectiveness measures, though often assumed in negotiations, are seldom measured against a scale the parties to the agreements would jointly recognize. Part of this is just the idiosyncratic nature of institutions and individuals, but part of it is because we have not developed even a general taxonomy to "think" about evaluating electronic resources other than through service, content or usability issues. If those goals are met (i.e., if the "purchasers" or licensees are happy about those issues), future decision making, how the product will really be judged outside the "specs" is not an issue that is "quantified."

Part of this goes back to the old failed philosophy of print acquisitions: if it's good, they'll pay our price. Or as Keith Courtney said to me when I was much younger and more naive, at Bryn Mawr at the first NASIG conference, "At the end of the day, you have to have what we publish and you will pay our price." For publishers, this has meant in their heart of hearts they believed the innate quality of their product justified whatever price they could get, and many librarians with bottom-line responsibility for purchasing believed it too.

In the online and electronic resource environment, the question, because the costs are inescapable and quite high, of why we continue purchasing a product or service is one that is reviewed more thoroughly and more often than in the print environment and by a wider range of hands. Gone are the days when a single individual could successfully commit an institution to an annual outlay of tens of thousands of dollars based solely on her expertise.

The arguments, the "justifications" that I often hear from librarians and administrators sound suspiciously, to me, little different from the justifications I heard for expensive, seldom-used titles in the print environment. And the rush, almost "gold rush fever," that has ensued to provide "content" for institutions has often meant few questions are asked in the initial purchase or contract. Quality, content, usability–end of discussion!

In fact even in the print environment we believed somehow that what we purchased was in part justified by usage either current or future. When use studies show even the most hard-headed idealist ("it's-good-so-you-have-to-buy-it" specialists) that per-use costs for some print products are in the thousands of dollars (and I refer you to Tina Chrzastowski's statistics as reviewed by Steve Bensman and Stanley Wilder in a 1998 *LRTS* article),[1] then even the mandarins of selection have had to take stock.

In the electronic environment we cannot escape evaluating numbers. Hypothetical usage, theoretical usage, the "I-put-it-back-on-the-shelf-after-I-looked-at-it" usage literally do not count. "I have six hundred students in my class who must use this" isn't a justification for anything the second time we hear it if there is no usage data to back it up. Of course, that doesn't stop some people (including librarians) from making that argument in the absence of data or even in the face of detailed usage data disproving the assertion.

What usage is in any particular resource is, of course, variable, depending on the resource itself. No matter what "usage" is, a cost per use can and should be ascertained, whether through negotiation for data from the producer or vendor, or through interpreting "use" data derived from transaction logs. Anyone who has looked at detailed transaction logs knows that the data reported must be screened, massaged, interpreted to be useful. In some systems, even a "fake" use looks "real" unless you know what data fields in the log to examine. Often, "interpreting" a log or log summary requires a lot of feedback from those who created the log.

Those who use UnCover's Gateway systems know only too well that the detailed raw log of articles ordered is a messy bit of data. You have to know that a repeat of the order number, for instance, doesn't mean a repeat of an order, but that one order number (if other fields are complete) is valid and the other a "dup" in the system's inner work-ings, and that an order that repeats the same title isn't a "dup" if the pagination is different. Interpreting all these details, knowing what the log actually means, is critical for interpreting "use." Every resource with "report" data that I've seen is the same. You can't just add the numbers up.

Let's assume in this most perfect of perfect worlds that in fact you get "good enough" numbers you can use for evaluating "usage" of a resource. What do you do with the "numbers?" What's the compara-ble? How can you compare one "unique" resource and its utilization and cost per use (whatever or however that is interpreted) with any-thing?

Let me begin with a caveat. No individual in an institution will normally have all the pieces to see the cost of an electronic transaction. As in the heyday of hyperinflated journal costs, the people making the "retain" decisions may only be marginally sensitized to cost issues, and the people paying the bills probably do not have enough of a context to "value" a use, just as the individuals lobbying for a particu-lar continuing service may not have a comprehensive perspective on the cost.

A case in point is IAC's extremely useful products, like their full-text periodical indexes. Cost per use is generally irrelevant, contracts are often for unlimited use, but cost per use for a similar product, EBSCO's full-text product in OCLC's suite of services, is a common pricing option. From a generalist's perspective the type of material covered is similar. A question not generally asked is: Is cost per article in OCLC's version of EBSCO's product similar to the cost per use of IAC's "unlimited" use? In one institution both products were avail-able to end users without cost to them. Surprisingly (and hardly an endorsement one way or the other of the products themselves), the "unlimited" use products when compared to the "pay-per-use" prod-ucts were almost identical in per-use costs. There's something strange in this picture, and it's not the products themselves. It is, quite frankly, marketing of the products to the institution and its users, integration (or lack thereof) and access options. Now my guess is that neither OCLC nor IAC know that their products are priced comparably (in terms of this institution's use), and logic (without data) would never suggest they are comparably priced. As for per-use versus "unlimit-ed" use, in terms of future potential for cost containment, it is more cost effective for the institution to market one product more than the other. The folks at IAC might be surprised to learn that their product for this particular institution and its users is no more cost effective than per-article pricing! And the librarians who initially made the decisions in the context of their institution's needs wanted both.

Every product, no matter what its cost is consciously or unconsciously, should be defined before purchase, then evaluated after use in one of three general "cost" categories, and defended (if rationally approached) depending on those categories. There are "low-cost-per-use" products, designed normally for a general audience. Full text aggregators often fall in this category, where there is a large degree of substitutability based on content. What "low cost per use" means has a wide range, from a few cents to a few dollars. FTE pricing, unlimited-use pricing, per-hit pricing, even number of simultaneous users–whatever the contractual price basis for the material–is almost immaterial because use will be converted to implied per-text, per-hit/per-use pricing, regardless of who is accessing the material. Because of its nature and the fact there are numerous competing and similar products, the bottom-line comparison is ultimately going to be price per use. If the material is of a general nature, that bottom-line per-use cost had better be low and its use high. If I were selling this kind of product, I'd be giving away "how to" material. If not, it will be replaced even if all contractual obligations are met. The aggregators of this type of material have as much stake in their compilations' (1) being marketed to the library's local constituency, (2) being easy to access, and (3) being well and widely known and used among the target user population as do the institutions paying the bills. If content is roughly equivalent, then cost per use is going to be a major factor. The only factors that might override that are accessibility and ease of use, including utility of search engine(s) and speed of delivery.

The next category I call, for lack of a better term, mid-range resources. They are more specialized (normally) than the low-cost-per-use products and often get bundled with the low-cost non-differentiated products. If bundled, there may be a slight premium for using them, and often they are available as stand-alones targeted for higher-priced offerings to specialized clientele. Generalist aggregators often include them because the aggregator's target audience would never be reached by the more specialized marketing that exposes the product to its original audience, and the specialized audience seldom has access to the "low-cost" variant. They are often excluded by the licensing agreements. Lexis/Nexis was a typical example of this medium-range product, at least in the "educational discount" model, for many years. It was and continues to be priced one way to the premium market (a reporter for *Forbes* once told me the librarians wouldn't let him use it because it cost too much) and another to the nonspecialist market or novice market-educational discount pricing schemes or FTE pricing. These are lagniappe sales for the specialist producer. The bottom line for evaluation could still, due to the nature of the content, be per-use pricing if evaluators can obtain data on either transaction logs or summary use statistics. I hope they do. Because of the nature of the products it contains, I suspect librarians will cut some slack on per-use evaluations because of the perception of the value (non-monetary) of the content.

The third almost unconscious gradation is of course the "high-price-per-use" product. My instinct is that this will vary significantly by institution and by subject. "High" for me might not be "high" for you. In this arena, libraries or consortia almost demand user information. It becomes critical to know exactly who is using or accessing or retrieving the information. The "privileged" user or department may even be sharing the costs. I put in this category such pricey items as *Web of Science* or even *Current Contents* and per-article use or premium pricing for full-text for sci-tech and other expensive journals. "Who uses it and how much?" is a necessary question, even though it might go against our instincts, and the privileged users who have access to these products normally recognize that their personal use will be monitored, much as individuals with long distance phone privileges assume their use will be monitored. Some of these services are primary research full-text journals, highly specialized research databases, specialized nontextual data sources, premium-priced electronic adjuncts and add-ons to print sources. I put even well-known products like UnCover in this category, many of the specialized indexes and abstracts and most of the premium-priced document delivery and/or full-text products targeted to scholarship. My advice to publishers and other purveyors of specialist information: make your premium-priced products indispensable electronically before they are priced as rare jewels, or suffer the consequences. Relatively low levels of use even at relatively high per-use pricing are probably acceptable, but high price and no use won't be. The lesson of utility is being learned too well at other price points to assume it won't apply in the premium market. The only thing that increases utility is ease of access, ease of use. Too many premium-priced products are designed to be user-unfriendly and create unnecessary bars. It is future cash flow and use levels, not the current picture, that will determine the long-term viability of these products. One thing the large aggregators have learned is that the "introduction" curve, the utilization curve, is something that takes time. Unlimited-use contracts normally accelerate in the third year. It is experience that has taught the aggregators that lesson. To pass these unspoken tests, the high-priced specialty products will have to meet the same test: utilization, even though the numbers will be smaller. Or, to restate Ward Shaw's aphorism from Becky Lenzini, "Communication is King, Content only a Prince."

I hope I've made my point. Utilization data for electronic resources is not optional. It is the key to continued contracts. Interpretation is critical. The vendor or library that ignores it does so at its own peril. The library will overpay, and someday wake up, or the vendor will be caught unaware, surprised, even offended, when the product is dropped.

NOTE

1. Stephen J. Bensman and Stanley J. Wilder, "Scientific and Technical Serials Holdings Optimization in an Inefficient Market: An LSU Serials Redesign Project Exercise," *Library Resources & Technical Services* 42 (1998): 147-242.

Statistical Measures of Usage of Web-Based Resources

Jim Mullins

At ALA's 1997 Midwinter Meeting in Washington, D.C., the JSTOR Users Group met. At this meeting, the need to provide use statistics for journals available through JSTOR was raised. Kevin Guthrie, JSTOR president, agreed to form a task force to advise JSTOR on how statistics could be gathered and disseminated to the members. The Web Statistics Task Force was formed at the meeting. Members appointed to the committee were David Farrell, University of California-Berkeley, Chair; James Mullins, Villanova University; Kimberly Parker, Yale University; David Perkins, California State University-Northridge; Sue Phillips, University of Texas; Camille Wanat, University of California-Berkeley; and Kristen Garlock, JSTOR, ex officio.

During the spring of 1997, the task force worked on the project. At ALA's summer 1997 meeting in San Francisco, David Farrell provided JSTOR members with an update of the task force's work. He reported that while the project was progressing, it was becoming evident that the issues associated with electronic Web usage statistics were greater than initially anticipated. As the task force communicated with librarians and vendors, it became increasingly more apparent that a national guideline was needed to enable librarians and electronic vendors to collect and disseminate the statistics necessary to evaluate usage of an electronic resource.

Jim Mullins is Director, Falvey Memorial Library, Villanova University.

[Haworth co-indexing entry note]: "Statistical Measures of Usage of Web-Based Resources." Mullins, Jim. Co-published simultaneously in *The Serials Librarian* (The Haworth Press, Inc.) Vol. 36, No. 1/2, 1999, pp. 207-210; and: *Head in the Clouds, Feet on the Ground: Serials Vision and Common Sense* (ed: Jeffrey S. Bullington, Beatrice L. Caraway, and Beverley Geer) The Haworth Press, Inc., 1999, pp. 207-210. Single or multiple copies of this article are available for a fee from The Haworth Document Delivery Service [1-800-342-9678, 9:00 a.m. - 5:00 p.m. (EST). E-mail address: getinfo@haworthpressinc.com].

The charge to the task force was expanded to

- Identify units of measurement
- Explore the capability of vendors and systems for Web-based products to record and measure use
- Devise analytical models and report formats for evaluating and applying use measurements

Representatives of various electronic resources available through the Web were contacted. They represented various types of resources including index, abstract, full-text book (e.g., encyclopedic) and full-text periodicals. Each presented a different twist to the challenge. The task force continued to work through the spring of 1998.

Since a member of the task force was from JSTOR, it was possible to experiment with various statistics-gathering and distribution options through the auspices of JSTOR. JSTOR created a program that enabled the collection of data for each institution's use of JSTOR titles. This information was then made available to member libraries. Because confidentiality was considered critical, statistical access was not available to any institution other than that generating the data. In order for a multiple-institution comparison to be compiled, all data from member institutions were combined in a category format—large, medium or small. A single institution's statistics could then be compared to the average for the category into which that institution fell (e.g., Villanova University's statistics were compared to the average for medium-sized libraries).

In the spring of 1998, the task force solicited input about the guidelines that had been completed at that time. The newly formed International Consortium of Library Consortia (ICOLC) reviewed the guidelines and gave its approval. As librarians, vendors and publishers review the guidelines, the task force anticipates that new areas will be identified. It is also likely that new developments in the field of electronic publishing will require updating and revision of the guidelines.

Below is the current version of the guidelines. The task force does not consider the guidelines to be complete, and as it continues development it invites comments and suggestions. Please direct comments to web.statistics@umich.edu.

GUIDELINES FOR STATISTICAL MEASURES OF USAGE OF WEB-BASED RESOURCES (APRIL 1998)

I. Measurement Elements for Abstracting & Indexing Services (e.g., EconLit and the A&I portion of a mixed database such as ABI/Inform) & Full Text Databases (e.g., reference works like *Britannica Online* and journal providers like AP/IDEAL and JSTOR): Priority measurement elements are *italicized*. Statistics should reflect usage from a resource provider's main and mirror sites.
   A. *Number of queries* (Searches) categorized as appropriate (Note: number of sessions (Logins) may be substituted in the event number of queries is not available
      1. By database
      2. By IP address/locator to subnet level
      3. By special data element passed by subscriber to vendor (e.g., account number)
   B. Number of turnaways due to contract limits (e.g., requests exceed simultaneous user limit)
   C. Number of items examined (i.e., marked or selected, downloaded, e-mailed, printed):
      1. *Citations* (for A&I databases)
      2. *Journals* (for full-text databases) broken down by title, ISSN, or other title identifier as appropriate
         a. Tables of Contents
         b. Abstracts
         c. *Articles* (or essays, poems, chapters, etc., as appropriate)
         d. Other (e.g., image/AV files, ads, reviews, etc., as appropriate)
   D. Usage levels
      1. Per time period
         a. *Queries or Sessions, Turnaways*
            1. By day, month, year
            2. By time of day
         b. *Peak simultaneous use* as appropriate
      2. Per interface used
         a. By Web, Telnet, or Z39.50 as appropriate
   E. Total hours of server downtime by month as appropriate
II. Privacy and User Confidentiality: Statistical reports or data that reveal confidential information about users must not be released

by resource providers without permission. Providers do not have the right to release statistical usage information about institutions without permission.

III. Comparative Statistics: Resource providers should provide comparative statistics that give participants a context in which to analyze statistics for their institutions. A grouping for purposes of comparison might be compiled by the resource provider (e.g., statistics from an anonymous selection of similar institutions), or it might be a grouping composed on demand (e.g., statistics from all campuses in a consortium, presented either anonymously or not, as desired by the participating institutions).

IV. Access/Delivery Mechanisms/Report Formats: Access to statistical reports should be restricted by IP address or another form of security such as passwords. Institutions should be able to allow access to their usage data by other institutions if they desire. Resource providers should maintain access to tabular statistical data through their Website (updated monthly), which a participant can access, aggregate and manipulate on demand. When appropriate, these data also should be available in flat files containing specified data elements that can be downloaded and manipulated locally. Resource providers are also encouraged to present data as graphs and charts.

TELECOMMUNICATIONS AND IT INFRASTRUCTURE IN THE DELIVERY OF ELECTRONIC INFORMATION

Telecommunications and IT Infrastructure in the Delivery of Electronic Information

Christopher J. Duckenfield

SUMMARY. As libraries increasingly rely upon electronic means to retrieve and distribute information, library staff must develop relationships with telecommunications and information technology organizations. This presentation examines the possible forms of those relationships and the changing roles of library staff. *[Article copies available for a fee from The Haworth Document Delivery Service: 1-800-342-9678. E-mail address: getinfo@haworthpressinc.com]*

The subject of this presentation is relationships; in particular, relationships between library personnel and telecommunications and in-

Christopher J. Duckenfield is Vice Provost, Computing and Information Technology at Clemson University.

[Haworth co-indexing entry note]: "Telecommunications and IT Infrastructure in the Delivery of Electronic Information." Duckenfield, Christopher J. Co-published simultaneously in *The Serials Librarian* (The Haworth Press, Inc.) Vol. 36, No. 1/2, 1999, pp. 211-224; and: *Head in the Clouds, Feet on the Ground: Serials Vision and Common Sense* (ed: Jeffrey S. Bullington, Beatrice L. Caraway, and Beverley Geer) The Haworth Press, Inc., 1999, pp. 211-224. Single or multiple copies of this article are available for a fee from The Haworth Document Delivery Service [1-800-342-9678, 9:00 a.m. - 5:00 p.m. (EST). E-mail address: getinfo@haworthpressinc.com].

formation technology personnel. In order to have relationships there must be some commonality of interest, so I'll begin by discussing those interests as they are today and as they may be in the future.

If you have any doubts about the future impact of technology on library science, then you should read the conference schedule. Just about every single presentation relates to technology and the library. The subtitle of the conference is "Serials Vision and Common Sense," and obviously the vision of the organizers, presumably reflecting the views of the membership as a whole, is that the future of library serials management lies with technology. You would think that you were at a computer center user-services conference, given the number of talks about Hypertext Markup Language (HTML), Webpage design, browser selection, and the like.

So, the fact that I am an information technology manager does not make me as out of place as might first appear. Both library and information technology professionals see technology as the key to our future, and we see a convergence of interests that we need to decide how we are going address.

HOW DO EACH VIEW OURSELVES AND EACH OTHER?

Librarians view themselves as professionals, but they also view themselves as faculty and are accorded that status by their institutions. They embrace the traditional concept of a university as a collection of scholars focused around a library. Since the university is focused around the library, they believe that the library should be untouchable, in particular exempt from budget cuts. In this they can count on widespread public support, since the public also associates libraries with universities. Actually, the public associates books with universities and so can accept the central role of the library.

This support by the outside world is a two-edged sword because librarians feel that the outside world does not understand the modern library; in particular, the outside world does not understand the place of serials in the modern library and the economic issues surrounding serials acquisition and management. However, the public will provide support precisely because they don't understand the role of the modern library. They will support buying books but aren't so ready to support buying new library technology.

Computer people view librarians as a group that has managed to take an out-of-date concept of what a library is and persuade university administrators and faculty that librarians should be viewed as faculty members. They have raised the academic freedom flag, invoked the images of book-burning, and gained a status they don't deserve. They dabble in technology that they only partially understand and place unreasonable demands on computing staff, either at the front end in what they ask for, or at the back end when they fail at something they have tried to do themselves and need bailing out. They get special budgetary treatment when it is obvious that the future lies with technology.

Computer people view themselves as being at the center of the modern university. Without them the university could not hope to function. Everyone else in the institution is a 9-to-5 drone. Computer people work all the time. They are in the office in the wee hours of the morning when the rest of the university is asleep. They could all go down the street and earn twice as much money (an article of faith among computer people, whether or not they have ever tested its validity). Instead, they work long and hard for meager wages making things easy for faculty who work just a few hours a week.

Librarians view computer people as spoiled brats with minimal social skills who just want to play with the latest technology. Customer service is a foreign notion to these people. You can't get them to deliver the technology that libraries want; there is always some problem if you suggest some software or hardware. What they give you doesn't work the way you want it. And for this these kids get paid handsomely and always seem to be getting job upgrades. They can't be counted on to be around when they are needed. They claim to work all sorts of hours, but where are they when everyone else in the world is working? It is no comfort to know that the computer people were working all night if, when you come to work in the morning, your computer doesn't work and there are no computer people around to fix it.

Obviously the picture I have just painted is somewhat overdrawn, but there are enough elements of truth in it to make it evident that librarians and computer people have a different tradition. They have approached and viewed their roles very differently. With their worlds moving closer together their views of those worlds and their respective places in them must change if they are to successfully serve their institutions in the future.

WHERE DO WE SEE OURSELVES
AND EACH OTHER MOVING?

As is apparent from this conference, and just about any other library conference, librarians have embraced technology. The advent of the personal computer and the ensuing development of publishing software, the ability to deliver multimedia documents over the Web, and the development of sophisticated search engines have opened up a whole new world of possibilities for libraries. Librarians can see what the technology will make possible and the more aggressive among them are actively trying to make their visions of the future into reality.

The difference between technology today and technology of fifteen to twenty years ago is that today users aren't at the mercy of the technologists. Much of the technology is available to and affordable by the general public. Librarians don't have to wait for the computer center to buy sophisticated hardware and software before they can implement a new technology-based service. Very often they can do it themselves at modest cost. As a result, libraries, even libraries that do not have formal computing staffs, have employees who feel comfortable with computing technology and have developed enough expertise to implement new services using their new-found knowledge.

As they become increasingly comfortable with technology, librarians are, to some degree, taking on some of the characteristics of the despised technologists. They fall in love with the technology for technology's sake, buying hardware and software constantly; they work odd hours stuck in front of their PCs; and they start to show up at computing conferences and meetings at least as often as at those for libraries.

As librarians become more like the technologists, so the technologists are starting, rather late in the day, to take on some of the characteristics of the librarians. They are showing an interest in customer service. Libraries have always stressed customer service, which is, by their definition, finding out what the customer wants and then providing it. This is a foreign concept to technologists. Their view of the world was always that they knew best about technology. What the customer said he wanted was not necessarily what he needed. The technologist knew best what the customer needed, and it was the technologist's job to provide what he knew was needed rather than what he had been asked for.

This change in attitude did not come about because the technologists suddenly saw the error of their ways. It was forced on them because their customers, with easily-used technology available to them independently of the computer center, were increasingly bypassing the experts. The technologists were put in the position of having to explain what they were doing in providing service and solving problems, and they had to show a new tolerance for different technical opinions.

Librarians have moved into new technological territory that was previously the preserve of the computer center. The computer center has been forced to work with the library for defensive purposes, if for nothing else. Where will this lead?

ARE LIBRARIES AND COMPUTER CENTERS CONVERGING OR DIVERGING?

New frontiers have been opened up for the more adventurous to cross. The interests of libraries and computer centers are converging if that is how the two groups want to play the game; that is, there are now areas of common interest, but will they want to develop those interests in common?

What was once the exclusive preserve of the computer center is now open for libraries to lay claim to. The library can, if it so chooses, go its own technological way. It can set up its own system and run it the way it likes. It is not beholden to the computer center for all its support.

Library and computer center could well be headed for competition over the newly exploding area of technology in the classroom. Who will win out in the bid to be the provider of support services to faculty who want to integrate technology into the curriculum?

As the computer center adjusts from a strong, central organization to a more distributed support organization, and the library expands its role as a study center, there is also potential for competition in providing traditional computer center services such as computer labs and consulting services. Of course, what are potential areas of competition could also be areas of cooperation.

WHAT HAS TO BE DONE TO PROMOTE THE BEST INTERESTS OF THE INSTITUTION?

People cannot be expected to ignore their own self-interest and just focus on the interests of the institution. You can be sure that when, during some particularly contentious discussion, you hear the statement, "After all, we all work for the same university," that what you are actually hearing is code for "Just quit arguing and do things my way." No one is going to sacrifice self-interest just because they work for the same university.

Some might say that it is the cynical way, others might call it the American way, but "enlightened self-interest" is what we count on to make our world work. We add the adjective "enlightened" to justify the apparent selfishness of this approach, but what we seek is an acceptable compromise that gives something to everyone. The success of this strategy depends upon the participants' willingness to compromise or seek consensus. Some people are either just too selfish or too principled for this to work, and in that case all you can do is hope that the surviving vision or visions does in fact support the institution as a whole.

Margaret Thatcher is quoted as saying that "consensus is the triumph of expediency over principle." If you have a Margaret Thatcher around, you had better either just give in or batten down the hatches and do the best you can with what you've got. Compromise is not in the cards.

Since this presentation is about relationships, let's assume that compromise is not entirely out of the question, and that librarians and computer people are willing to work together to define and redefine their respective roles. It is this willingness to work together and to not take rigid stands either on turf or on technical solutions to problems that is the key to developing a library and information technology support structure that meets the needs of the institution and the people involved.

IS IT POSSIBLE TO ORGANIZE FOR SUCCESS?

Many people don't like to deal with people. When they get into positions of management, they try to create an organizational structure that determines employee behavior and makes unnecessary any significant manager/employee interaction. They try to organize for success. The United States is perhaps the shining example of organizing for success. Its institutions have proven to be remarkably stable no matter what individual personalities and egos came along. Even on as grand a scale as the United States, however, individuals have been able to threaten those institutions.

On a small stage a big personality can be dominant. The structure of the organization can be overwhelmed by an individual, maybe several individuals, so the institution is not necessarily protected by its structure. Strong personalities at the head of the library and the computer center can not only assure that one will not be consumed by the other, but can also lead to missed opportunities for joint development projects in areas of mutual interest. Conversely, combining library and computer center under a single head could ensure a focusing of resources on broader-based projects, but could also result in a skewed vision of the project as it appears to the director.

Certainly, an institution can organize for failure. That is, it can organize itself and set up budgetary mechanisms that would make it very difficult for it to function effectively. One has to assume that no institution would deliberately do this, but if it is likely to occur then it will be in the area of information technology.

Since the area of computing is still relatively new, and since many administrators did not grow up with computing, there is sometimes a tendency to try to fit computing into some already established structure. Merging the library with the computer center is a typical example. In other cases more experimental structures are attempted. None of these structures will guarantee that computing and information technology will be well managed and controlled, or that the computer center and the library will work well together, or that new technologies will be explored to the benefit of the institution.

No matter what the structure, the key to success lies in the relationships among the participants. This occurs at two levels: first, the willingness of individuals to work together for the common good; second, the ability of those individuals to create the working relationships and operational structures to take advantage of technology for the benefit of the institution as a whole.

RELATIONSHIPS AND STRUCTURES

The traditional administrative structure for library and computer center within a university is for them to be distinct entities, each with its own director. In the early days of automation many libraries were able to function independently of the computer center. Library automation consisted largely of automating the card catalog, and turnkey systems could be purchased that ran independently of the institutions' computing operations. Relatively few institutions used their entire existing computing network to access library systems.

The advent of the personal computer and the continued development of computer networks both pushed libraries and computer centers together and at the same time helped push them apart. The library wanted to provide access to library databases from the personal computers that were appearing in faculty offices and student labs. This required cooperation with the computer center, which had responsibility for the faculty and student data networks.

On the other hand, as the power of desktop computing was made available to the general user, library staff developed a certain expertise and confidence that led them more and more to seek their own counsel in regard to planning for technology and to develop in-house support structures.

In this new world where a computer user can purchase a high-powered computer over the phone for just a few hundred dollars, and where sophisticated software and peripherals are cheaply available, who needs a computer center? This thought went through the minds of both library and computer center personnel. Computer centers were put on the defensive as they saw their traditional position eroding. Many of them, unable to adjust and define a new role for themselves, effectively withered away, replaced by a collection of distributed networks and support structures. What remained of the old computer center was a mere shell of its former self.

Most computer centers have reinvented themselves to some degree. They have gathered networking into themselves and have become kinder and gentler. The smarter ones have reached out to help users rather than waiting for the users to come to them, and they have recognized that in a distributed world of computing, the users have alternatives to the computer center.

Now we all live in a computing world that is no longer focused around a computer center. The computer center may well exist and offer excellent services, but it is not the only source of such services. There are a variety of places to go to get help, and the more self-confident ones can even go it alone if need be. There are incentives to work together and incentives to work apart. Everything is in a constant state of flux and competition.

When we look across the country at various universities, we no longer see the same structure replicated everywhere. We see a wide variety of structures and relationships that have developed to provide services of one kind or another. It is the willingness to form such relationships and work together for the common good that will enable us to take full advantage of information technology. Nowhere are the possibilities greater than in the area of library services.

It is essential that librarians, while gaining a knowledge of what technology can do for them, not be so seduced by the technology that they forget their roles as librarians. It is equally essential that computer center people recognize that many users, including librarians, can now be expected to have knowledge and opinions regarding technology that are deserving of consideration. The technological field is no longer a private domain, and it will take a shared effort to properly exploit it.

The overall structure of information resources that you have to deal with could be anything from the traditional separated library and computer center, to the library and computer center under a single head, or any one of a number of hybrids. Suffice it to say that you will have to learn to deal with coworkers who may or may not have the same service goals as you, or who may or may not speak the same language. Your supervisor may come from a completely different professional background than you, and you may be asked to provide services for which you were never trained.

None of us is going to be able to remain in our closed little world, dispensing services for which we were trained, to people with whom we can readily communicate, using technologies with which we have been familiar for a long time. We can expect to have to discard a lot of knowledge that we spent years accumulating, learning something new, and discarding that in its turn. My background was originally in mathematics, whose truths are universal and unchanging. It was extremely difficult, once I got into computing, to come to terms with the fact that the brightest of computer programmers became experts in a field in a matter of months rather than years, and were time and again able to throw that knowledge away and become experts in something else without apparent concern.

Now we'll take a look at some of the groupings and relationships with which you may be confronted. I hope that as part of this discussion today you will share with the people here any experiences that you may have had in working with unusual organizational structures. The more experiences you hear about, the better prepared you will be if called upon to work in a different structural environment.

RELATIONSHIPS WITH TELECOMMUNICATIONS PERSONNEL

The relationship between any group and the telecommunications group is often very tense. While everyone occasionally feels pressure in their jobs, network services people are expected to function under constant pressure. Whether it is in the computer center, in the library, or a separate group, the network services support group tends to have a different view of the world than those with whom they work.

Network services functions in an atmosphere of constant crisis. Everything it does is in crisis mode. Because the demand nationwide for qualified network support personnel is so great, Network services tends to be understaffed. Its people run from crisis to crisis (and every network problem is a crisis for the person who can't work as a result), constantly bombarded with questions about when this problem or that is going to be fixed, and never getting the time to properly plan for network growth and improvement.

Network services people believe in order but live with disorder. One of their primary aims is to bring order to their working lives. They therefore are very interested in a network structure that is stable, manageable, and predictable. Unfortunately for them, the tools that they need to provide that stability, manageability, and predictability tend to fall into that invisible infrastructure area that is too often starved for funds.

Network services is a victim of the word "infrastructure." When we think of an infrastructure we think of something that we invest a lot of money in once every twenty years and pretty much ignore in the meantime. Network services might get funds for cabling, servers, and routers–the components of the physical network–but funding for the invisible support tools, such as network management software and problem diagnosis software and hardware, is much harder to obtain.

A logically designed network, with an adequate number of support staff provided with up-to-date hardware and software for network management and problem diagnosis, is the dream of the network services professional. They often find themselves in conflict with the people they serve, who want the maximum amount of end user service. Network support staff want to use some of their resources to provide the network management support as opposed to putting it all into direct services.

This is exemplified by the different approaches to network design often seen in the network service groups attached to the traditional computer support groups compared to the approach sometimes taken in network support groups attached to end user offices. A long-time network support person will want to use the most intelligent switches and routers, use the most sophisticated network diagnosis tools, and not add anything to the network that cannot be supported 100 percent. The newer, departmental support groups, on the other hand, are much more prepared to go with cheaper switches that might switch just as fast as their intelligent counterparts, but lack diagnostic, encryption, or other functions. They are more prepared to trade more switches for less intelligence.

The trick for library personnel, as it is for many other groups that are to some degree involved in telecommunications, is to find the right balance between the two extremes. That balance may come at a different point on the support continuum for different organizations, but a recognition that the telecommunications support group has its own, and possibly different, philosophy of network management is half the battle to finding that balance.

NEW LEARNING ENVIRONMENTS

There is a great deal of interest these days in utilizing technology in the educational process. It is not acceptable to say "in the teaching process" because that is no longer politically correct in educational circles. Now we are interested in collaborative learning or asynchronous learning, or some equivalent terminology. Here I'll use the term "collaborative learning."

Educational theory now holds that there are "multiple intelligences." The number quoted is eight. The theory is that there are different forms of intelligence, and people with different forms of intelligence learn in different ways. Some people learn by hearing, others learn by doing, others learn best through pictorial representations, and so on. Unfortunately, the traditional way of teaching is to teach to the 10 percent or so who are receptive to the teacher standing in front of the class and lecturing.

Collaborative learning aims to change the entire learning environment so that communication between faculty and student is more than one way, so that students can work singly or in groups, utilizing resources outside the confines of the classrooms, and to broaden the range of intelligences served. The primary tool for facilitating this new learning environment is technology.

Creation of a collaborative learning environment involves several groups. Librarians may have a hard time staying out of this. The collaborative learning bandwagon is picking up speed and you will be expected to get on board. The federal government is starting to put a lot of money into research into the effectiveness of different learning models using technology, and where the federal government leads, the charitable foundations will surely follow. Right on their tails will be the universities as they chase the research dollars.

Some very crude initiatives are being implemented. Perhaps the most obvious are the requirements by some universities that all students have a laptop computer. Supposedly, they are going to study the impact of that requirement on the learning process. The more cynical among us might speculate that the reason for requiring all students to have a laptop is not because the university curriculum requires that all students have a laptop, but so that it can say that all students are required to have a laptop. It is actually a legitimate research project to inquire into the effects of a ubiquitous laptop program, but the real research is likely to be a good deal more granular. Future research will take specific approaches to teaching and learning to see how best to apply technology to reach the various intelligences and the most number of intelligences at the same time.

Institutional, as opposed to individual faculty, approaches to collaborative learning usually involve several different groups. An example would be a collaboration between the training arm of the computer center, a center for research in the use of technology in the curriculum, a faculty development center, and the library.

STRUCTURES TO EXPLOIT NEW TECHNOLOGIES

Clemson University is developing the Collaborative Learning Environment (CLE), a set of tools and services that will allow all faculty easily to integrate the use of technology into the curriculum, both as an administrative tool and as a teaching and learning tool. The lead role is being taken by the Division of Computing and Information Technology, but with important contributions from the library, and anticipated support from newly created centers for faculty development and instructional technology research. One of the features of the CLE that helps meet the library's goals is the management of electronic reserve materials. Materials in electronic format that are on reserve for specific classes will be automatically restricted to the students in those classes. Access will be through a single identification of the student to the network and will not require any special passwords or setup by library or computer center staff.

In this model the library is not assuming any new responsibilities, but is collaborating with the computer center to develop a system that meets the library's service requirements in an electronic age.

Another collaborative effort occurred at the University of Delaware, a leader in the use of technology in teaching, where the aforementioned four groups collaborated to create a Faculty Institute on Teaching, Learning, and Technology.

The University of Delaware offers a series of workshops in January and June of each year that it calls Teaching, Learning and Technology Faculty Institutes. These workshops cover a wide range of topics, but all are designed to provide faculty with the tools and the skills they need to use technology to improve the way they teach and the learning experience for their students. One whole track is devoted to using the technological services of the library, and using the Web and the Internet to supplement library services.

A key aspect of the Delaware program is a concerted effort to focus faculty attention on technology by covering a broad range of applications of information technology to teaching and learning, and doing that over a concentrated period of time. Delaware attempts to coordinate its information technology support services, including those of the library. The library is considered a key information technology service provider.

At the University of Iowa the library is the key player through its TWIST initiative. TWIST is a three-year, foundation-funded program to encourage faculty to use technology in innovative ways in the classroom. The project is driven by the library. In TWIST, library staff, particularly library discipline specialists, work with individual faculty to develop multimedia materials for use in their classes. TWIST also produces and maintains a wide range of resources for those wishing to learn how to apply technology in their classes. These include online tutorials, learning guides, and links to other sites.

At the University of Oregon the library plays the lead role in integrating the use of technology into the curriculum. The library itself houses the Instructional Media Center, which delivers educational services to remote sites using such technologies as two-way satellite transmission. The library also operates several Information Technology Centers, which provide faculty, students, and researchers with access to a wide range of technologically-based resources. In addition, the library has the responsibility for coordinating the university's efforts to improve the educational environment through technology. The New Media Center, which assists faculty in developing multimedia class materials, and the Teaching Effectiveness Program, which helps faculty and graduate assistants improve their teaching, are linked to the library through the library's Academic Educational Coordination unit.

WHAT ROLE SHOULD THE LIBRARY PLAY?

In general, the library as an organization should feel less threatened than the computer center. The faculty is the ultimate seat of power at the university, and the library is much more entrenched in the mind of the faculty than is the computer center. The library has an academic legitimacy that the computer center typically does not. The computer center is therefore much more likely to be inward looking and the library may well have to play the role of initiator in any collaborative venture.

It is clear, from looking at the numerous examples around the country, that partnerships can be developed to the benefit of the library, the computer center, and the institution. It is also clear that the actual role played by the library in such partnerships can vary enormously. In some the library is the junior partner, in others an equal, and in others it is clearly the leader. What is certain is that if the library wants a role, there is a role for the library to play.

The new world of information technology is filled with opportunities for libraries, but librarians cannot be sure just what their roles will be in that new world. Library staff should be prepared for any role and any partnership. Some roles will be there for the taking; others will be thrust upon you. If libraries and computer centers are to serve their institutions to the best of their abilities, they must be prepared to work together to define relationships that take maximum advantage of their respective talents and that best fit the goals and ambitions of the institutions they serve.

YOU MAY ALREADY KNOW THE ANSWER

You May Already Know the Answer

Janet Swan Hill

SUMMARY. It is tempting, when faced with an unfamiliar publication medium or access device, to assume that existing rules, practices, and mechanisms are unable to cope with the wonders and complexities of these materials and tools. It gives us a superior feeling to announce that we must rid ourselves of stuffy thinking and cut our ties to an illogical past. It may be harder, and it is certainly less flashy, to approach novel situations with the assumption that the principles that have guided us in the past are still relevant, and that the practices and rules that apply to other materials and situations may also be applicable to this one. Concentrating on similarities, common interest, and shared principles may be less exciting than considering ourselves or our situation to be unique or unprecedented, but it is likely to yield more useful and lasting results. *[Article copies available for a fee from The Haworth Document Delivery Service: 1-800-342-9678. E-mail address: getinfo@haworthpressinc.com]*

Janet Swan Hill is Associate Director for Technical Services, University of Colorado, Boulder.

[Haworth co-indexing entry note]: "You May Already Know the Answer." Hill, Janet Swan. Co-published simultaneously in *The Serials Librarian* (The Haworth Press, Inc.) Vol. 36, No. 1/2, 1999, pp. 225-245; and: *Head in the Clouds, Feet on the Ground: Serials Vision and Common Sense* (ed: Jeffrey S. Bullington, Beatrice L. Caraway, and Beverley Geer) The Haworth Press, Inc., 1999, pp. 225-245. Single or multiple copies of this article are available for a fee from The Haworth Document Delivery Service [1-800-342-9678, 9:00 a.m. - 5:00 p.m. (EST). E-mail address: getinfo@haworthpressinc.com].

The topic proposed to me when the invitation to speak was tendered was "Cataloging Issues in the Online Age," which is wonderfully broad. As often happens, the invitation came when I was in the midst of writing another paper, and I had just reached the point of discovering that one whole area that I wanted to cover wouldn't fit into the time allotted, and it occurred to me that the subject I was going to have to leave unexplored for the one paper might actually suit NASIG's purposes better than it fit into the other paper. So if you want to think of it that way, this is actually a second-hand sermon. Before I go any further with it, though, I need to proffer two warnings, and to admit one thing.

The first warning: This is not going to be erudite. This is the last day of your conference. You're all tired. It's summertime in Colorado, and somehow "erudite" doesn't seem to be called for.

The second warning: I'm very opinionated. I was brought up in a household where holding, discussing, and expressing opinions was valued, and I went to a small college where forming, discussing, and expressing opinions was expected. To me, life is a seminar, and active participation in the discussion is required.

Finally, the admission: I'm not a serials cataloger. I have cataloged serials, but it was a long time ago. What this means is that I'm not going to insult you by trying to give concrete serials-specific cataloging instruction. I'd just look silly, and you'd all be justifiably annoyed at my presumption.

EXPERIENCE AS A TEACHER

Because this paper is based on my personal point of view, and because my point of view is derived from my experiences, I'm going to start out in a somewhat unorthodox manner by telling you what those experiences have been. In effect, I'm going to deliver a highly specialized biographical sketch, concentrating on those experiences that are of significance to the points I'm going to make.

Part of what influences my opinions is that I've been in librarianship a long time. I attended library school the year the *Anglo-American Cataloging Rules* were introduced. OCLC didn't yet exist. What was known as the "MARC Project" was in its infancy, and not even the people at the Library of Congress had too clear an idea what machine-readable cataloging records might eventually be good for.

After graduation, I went to the Library of Congress as a Special Recruit (now called Intern), and spent several months moving from department to department with the rest of my class, meeting people, learning what could be learned in such brief encounters and getting a little practice at various jobs, and then I took my first permanent professional position as a funny format cataloger–specifically, as a map cataloger.

One of the experiences that stands out most vividly from my time as an intern consisted of a pair of encounters: in serial cataloging, and serial records/bindery. In serial cataloging we learned that they were so far behind in cataloging serial titles that they'd made a policy not to catalog a serial until its first volume was bound. A week or so later we went to serial records/bindery where the people doing the presentation proudly told us that they had just decided not to bind any serials until they were cataloged. One of us somewhat hesitantly raised his hand and asked if they'd consulted with serials cataloging first, whereupon a most interesting discussion ensued. My understanding is that soon thereafter, the departments got together and resolved the problem. It was an interesting early lesson.

As a map cataloger, I cataloged monographic maps, as well as sets, series, subseries, serials, atlases, facsimiles, photoreproductions, microforms, aerial photographs, stereographic pairs, remote sensing imagery, globes, relief models, looseleaf services, stick charts, coloring books, kits, napkins, pencils, playing cards, placemats, and a shower curtain. But mainly, I cataloged maps . . . lots of maps. I created and/or reviewed several hundred authority records every two weeks, and I compiled and edited LC's Map Cataloging Manual. For all the years I was in the Geography and Map Division, I experienced trying to provide access to materials that were not represented in the main catalog of the library, and with lobbying for their inclusion.

In working on the cataloging manual, my fellow catalogers and I discovered time and again the ways in which map catalogers had gone astray, either inadvertently, through lack of routine contact with catalogers of more "mainstream" materials, or through the belief that "those people" just didn't understand the cataloging needs or the special complexities and properties of cartographic materials. Time and again my fellow catalogers and I examined the variations from mainstream practices that we found and explored the reasons for them, and time and again we concluded that the materials and the users were better served by having maps handled as much like books as could reasonably be managed. Over and over again we would find that practices that seemed harmless or even useful when viewed only in the context of a separate file were "distinctions without a difference," in that they provided no substantial benefit to anyone but posed some problems simply by being different–or they were confusing when viewed in the context of a mix of materials–or they contributed to an actual or perceived barrier to incorporation of cartographic materials into the general catalog, and thus, they contributed greatly to decreased accessibility to the very materials that we cared so much about.

After seven years I left LC and went to Northwestern University Library as head of its catalog department. While there I participated in the development of the NOTIS integrated library automated system, perhaps the first complete system to treat serials as "just one more format." To this end, I had to provide strong encouragement to serials catalogers to abandon some treasured idiosyncratic practices and to begin regarding themselves and the cataloging they produced as another part of the overall enterprise, instead of as something free-standing and independent.

At Northwestern I had occasion to gain agreement from catalogers of various kinds of materials that they would adhere to standard practices, only to have them try later to renege, saying they hadn't realized how much work it would be. I had several opportunities to engineer incorporation of other groups of materials into the central catalog, and in the process to consider and then reject special treatment of them, and to see afterwards the vindication of decisions to treat them as much like everything else as was reasonable. On the other hand, I was a willing party to Northwestern's development of a policy to selectively run counter to standard cataloging practice for serials, and to utilize latest entry cataloging in those instances when catalog access seemed better served by it (this practice has since been abandoned). I was also instrumental in the negotiations whereby Northwestern became one of the pilot participants in the program that later became NACO (Name Authority Cooperative), from which BIBCO (Bibliographic Cooperative) and eventually PCC (Program for Cooperative Cataloging) developed.

It wasn't until I left LC and went to Northwestern that I began to get involved in the work of the profession at large in any serious way. But

I started big. My first committee assignment was on the Committee on Cataloging: Description and Access (CC:DA), which is the committee within ALA that is given the authority to develop recommendations and policies for the revision of the *Anglo-American Cataloging Rules.* I served on that committee in one capacity or another for a total of eleven years, six of them as the ALA representative to the Joint Steering Committee for the Revision of the Anglo-American Cataloguing Rules, which is the six-member international committee that actually writes the rules. This service on CC:DA spanned the period in which the cataloging community came to grips with the implementation of AACR2 and de-superimposition. CC:DA dealt with these issues and also handled the political tinderbox that was microform cataloging. While I was on the committee, we worked on the rules and principles governing every sort of material. We worked to apply the rules to machine-readable data files, later renamed "computer files." We made major revisions to rules governing the cataloging of audio-visual materials, sound recordings, kits, and interactive multimedia, as well as working out troublesome problems for legal materials, scores, and serials. In each of these discussions, it was necessary for every member of the committee, no matter what her/his own background, to examine all proposals and problems in light of the rules as a whole, to compare the way in which this sort of material was handled as compared to all other sorts, and to discern and then apply the underlying principles of cataloging to them all. I also did astonishingly nit picky things, such as chairing two subcommittees charged with assuring consistency of indention practice and consistency of ellipses throughout the rules. You haven't lived until you have tried to determine whether an ellipsis is in italics or not.

Other professional service that is relevant to my talk today includes serving on a "think tank" to discuss the cataloging of interactive multimedia, serving on the task force that began the consideration of issues associated with cataloging multiple versions of the same intellectual entity, and being part of a working group whose task it was to compare all extant ISBDs and to harmonize their language and provisions from one format to another. While on the Joint Steering Committee, I was part of the effort to get AACR2 into machine-readable form, and part of the effort that led to the "future of the rules" conference recently held in Toronto.

After twelve years at Northwestern, I left to come to the University of Colorado as head of technical services. Many of the experiences here have been analogous to experiences at LC and Northwestern, including the realization that the fight against wandering out of the mainstream is never ending. Among the most telling experiences have been those that illustrated richly the pitfalls of doing things on the cheap, and those that have illustrated the pitfalls of indulging in non-standard practice.

LIFE'S LITTLE LESSONS

I hadn't intended this paper to be an autobiography. In fact, it started out quite differently, but at one point, as went I back over what I'd written to try to get it into some more coherent order, it fell into place in this form. I'm glad it happened, though, because it's interesting to look back this way. None of us is completely in control of our own careers: We take advantage of opportunities that come our way, or those that we can engineer, and we pursue our interests, but our interests may change, or circumstances may change them for us. So it's a bit of a surprise to see so many unifying themes coming to the surface.

What I'm going to do next is, referring to the circumstances described above, I'll "tease out" some of those unifying themes and lessons learned, and expand on them. You'll note that although many refer to a less automated environment, all are nevertheless relevant to the online age, and although many came as a result of experiences with various formats, they are nevertheless relevant to serials.

The first of these lessons is that everybody thinks their own stuff is the most special. In the course of nearly thirty years in librarianship, I have worked closely with a wide variety of materials and an even wider variety of catalogers. I can say with utmost conviction that with only one or two exceptions, there is no group of catalogers that does not believe that the materials they work with are more complex and difficult to handle than any other materials, or that their materials are not misunderstood, or that in order to do a competent job of handling them, you need specialized education or experience, or a special "bent." They may not say so straight out, but their behavior and their conversation reveal it.

- Serials catalogers truly believe that their materials are the most difficult to catalog.

- Music catalogers are utterly convinced that music materials pose the greatest difficulties to catalogers.
- Audiovisual catalogers know in their heart of hearts that nobody but they can possibly understand or appreciate the extent and seriousness of the problems their materials present.
- Catalogers of electronic and digital resources are sure that the problems they face are more difficult to handle than anybody else's.
- Microform catalogers believe that the problems they deal with are harder to handle than the problems inherent in other materials.
- Special collections and archival catalogers bask in the certainty that the cataloging they do is more difficult and complex and detailed than any other kind.
- The same kinds of things can be said of catalogers of maps, graphic materials, legal materials, government documents, religious materials, materials in non-Roman alphabet vernaculars, or any other kinds of material you care to name.

The only exceptions I can think of are catalogers of children's materials (though they might actually argue with this) and generalist catalogers of books. The only reason that book catalogers don't think they are special is that they aren't allowed to. There are so many other groups of catalogers out there saying, "You can't possibly understand because what you do is so straightforward," that the book catalogers have come to believe it. I don't.

In fact, every group of catalogers except the children's materials catalogers and the book catalogers is right. Every group of catalogers is special, and every group of materials poses particular problems that are in some way more difficult, complex, or problematic than others. Every group of materials benefits from but does not require having those who catalog them have some specialized background in the materials or the subject matter. I say "benefits from, but does not require" because in the course of twenty years of hiring catalogers, I've discovered that it is a lot easier to teach a good cataloger about the material, than it is to teach a noncataloging subject, language, or format specialist to be a good cataloger.

All of these groups of catalogers need to continue to believe that they are special, but it would do everyone–including, in the end, our users–a lot of good if these catalogers would recognize that they are not unique in their "specialness." We really ought not be able to hear a choir humming "Nobody Knows the Trouble I've Seen" in the background when we talk to catalogers with a special constituency.

There are very real problems that arise from an exaggerated view of your own specialness and others' "ordinariness":

- It creates resentment on the part of others, which makes cooperation difficult and unlikely.
- It creates barriers to communication, in that it contributes to a belief that others have nothing to offer, so not only do you not go seeking information or advice from others, but you may reject any that comes along as coming from someone who couldn't possibly understand.
- It creates barriers to information, as information is sought only from those who occupy your own niche, and information not phrased in the jargon of your own group is rejected as being irrelevant or as missing the point.
- It creates barriers to imagination, as each special group speaks mainly among themselves, thus denying themselves the stimulation of ideas that come from a broader perspective and from discussing other people's problems and solutions, and they also deny themselves access to solutions that may already exist.
- Because of these things, isolation contributes to ineffectiveness and increases the likelihood that bad decisions will be made, both through not availing yourselves of the assistance of others, and through making decisions that may be good for you, but bad for someone else.

An exaggerated sense of your own specialness and of others' inability to comprehend your problems leads to each special group of catalogers looking at their world from inside a cage, looking out from between bars, though the bars are essentially of their own making and are largely imaginary.

The second and third of the lessons I draw from the experiences detailed above are that (2) every novel situation tends to be treated at first as if it requires novel handling, but (3) very few situations turn out to be as novel as they were at first thought to be. To illustrate this point, let me return to a description of that think tank I mentioned. Back in the early days of interactive multimedia, when catalogers were just beginning to recognize that they were going to see more and more examples of computerized information resources that allowed user interaction with text, graphics, and sound, catalogers that had to handle such materials got quite agitated. They sought guidance among themselves, and many seemed convinced that these items represented a whole new species of material that was going to require an entirely different approach to cataloging than anything that had come before. Rumblings were heard about the inadequacy of AACR2 to handle them. Into this fray stepped Sheila Intner, who organized a meeting to discuss the matter and to develop a position or proposals that could be presented to CC:DA and that would thereby influence the direction of rules revision. The meeting took place over two very long days during an ALA annual conference in Atlanta. About twenty cataloging experts were invited to attend, many of whom had experience in rules construction and revision and many of whom were specialists in computer file cataloging. Most of us went into the meetings assuming that we were going to find it necessary to propose major modifications to the cataloging rules. We were prepared to consider the possibility of having to write a new chapter.

We saw demonstrations and examples and heard discussions of how the materials were intended to be utilized, and then we began trying to sort out the problems. Early discussion seemed to focus on the differences between these materials and others, but before too long a surprising pattern began to emerge. Time and again, we found ourselves saying things like, "Yes, but this is completely analogous to X," or, "Y already takes care of that," or, "The same reasoning in the case of these other materials led us to decide Z." By the time we were halfway through our schedule, we were looking at each other in astonishment, realizing that in fact these materials, which had at first seemed radically different from others, and which had at first seemed to present so many unique problems, and which had at first seemed to cry out for major rules modifications and special treatment, in fact had many more similarities to other types of materials than differences, and none of the problems presented could not be reasoned through by applying the principles that underlay the extant rules. In the end, much to our collective amazement, we concluded that interactive multimedia were well accommodated by the present rules, needing essentially nothing more than the creation of their own smd (special material designator) and some relatively minor modifications to various rules, such as additional examples to make it explicit or implicit that this rule or that applied also to interactive multimedia.

This is just the clearest example I could cite of something I have seen happen again and again. Some imaginative publisher starts producing a new format of material or presenting an old format in a different way, and at first it is assumed that the rules don't handle it. More often than not, the catalogers who are closest to the materials will set forth the problem with an air tinged with "So there" or "Figure this out, I dare you" or "See, we really do have weirder problems than the rest of you." More often than not, however, applying the underlying principles and seeking guidance from the existing rules for all types of materials will reveal that the rules do successfully accommodate the evolutionary variants and unusual instances, and often it will be discovered that some other format of material has some of the same characteristics and problems, and that a successful way of handling them has already been found.

This should be comforting to us. It should enable us to get that "deer-in-the-headlights" look of stark terror out of our eyes as we think about electronic journals, or cataloging the Web, or about the evolution of materials away from either serial or monographic to something closer to "continuous publication." It would also be good if it reminded us of the larger whole of which we are a part, and alerted us to the necessity of understanding and acknowledging that there is much of value that can be found in the experiences and expertise and viewpoints of those who catalog other things, and that either they, or we, or both of us, may indeed already know the answer.

Remember that I talked about an exaggerated sense of your own specialness and a belief in others' inability to comprehend your problems leading to catalogers looking at the world from inside a cage? It's not a closed cage; the door is open. The walls aren't even continuous, but we have to know enough to walk out. Have you ever called a dog that was on the other side of a fence? The dog tries to come to you. It may try to get under the fence, and it may run back and forth a bit along the fence, but it's not smart enough to go looking for an open gate or for the end of the fence. You can point toward the open gate, but the dog looks at your hand, not at where it's pointing. Sometimes, just by accident, the dog will happen upon the open gate and come through. We're supposed to be smarter than that. We're supposed to be able to find solutions to our problems. We ought to be clever enough to go looking for openings and to take advantage of them. In fact, since we built the fence we ought to be able to recognize that there's no need for it, and to take it down entirely.

The fourth and fifth lessons are also paired. They are that (4) virtually every example of nonstandard or substandard treatment turns out to be a mistake in the long run, no matter how clever or necessary it seemed at the time, and (5) virtually every decision to handle something according to the full standard repays the effort that you put into it.

Here I would like to cite the patron saint of catalogers, Arnold Wajenberg. Arnold was the principal cataloger at the University of Illinois at Urbana Champaign, and in a speech he once uttered a truism so telling that I have remembered it ever since and have paraphrased it complete with a corollary. Arnold said that "if you follow a nonstandard practice, some day, someone, somewhere will curse your name." My corollary is that "if you follow a substandard practice, some day, someone, somewhere will curse your name . . . and if you stay long enough at your present job, chances are, it's going to be you."

This was true in 1985 when Arnold said it, and it becomes truer with every passing day. The reasons that it is becoming truer specifically have to do with the increasingly online environment in which we are working and where we do all of our work watched over by a group of monsters who cannot bear not being paid attention to, who are always hungry, and who can become destructive if they are not fed and cared for. Those monsters are system migration and revision, record sharing, union databases, and rules revision.

Thinking back over three decades of experience, I have difficulty coming up with an example where following a nonstandard practice, or pursuing a substandard practice turned out to be an indisputably good idea. The closest I can come for nonstandard cataloging is the decision at Northwestern to do latest entry cataloging on those serials that met a carefully drawn list of criteria, but even when we were using the automated system it was designed to work well with, it still caused some problems vis-à-vis our bibliographic utility, and Northwestern no longer follows this practice. A case of substandard cataloging that did not backfire was a decision not to do full subject analysis for locally produced dissertations. The best that can be said for this was that it caused no serious problems. We knew from the beginning that it would not provide the kind of subject analysis we wanted and that public services people would rather we didn't cut back, but in that instance, it was a choice between utilizing the subject access afforded by *Dissertation Abstracts*, or running more than a year behind with getting the records on the database at all.

It took me a while to think of even these two little examples. On the other hand, I can readily come up with instance after instance when following a nonstandard or substandard practice has caused long-term difficulties. A particularly delicious example is that of "saved fields." Here at CU, we used to use the CARL automated system. The system was originally written on behalf of, and used by the Colorado Alliance of Research Libraries, which is a group of libraries, none of which has ever been all that richly endowed, and to which, therefore, ways to save money have always been seductive. In the relatively early days of system use, in the interests of not having to buy more computer storage space, the eyes of those in charge lit on the fixed fields. The CARL system made no use of fixed fields at that time, so it was decided to do without them. All of the fixed fields in existing records were removed and "saved" on tapes. As new records were received from OCLC, fixed field data was stripped and "saved" offline. There was no way to access it. Time passed.

When I arrived at CU, it took me a long time to realize that my problem in looking for fixed field data wasn't that I hadn't figured out how to find it, it was that the fields simply weren't there. Horrified, I began lobbying for restoration of the data. By this time many of those who had made the original decision were gone. Databases had gotten large enough so that being able to manipulate records using fixed field data began to look like a good thing to want to do, and not being able to do so was now seen as a weakness in the system, which was by this time being marketed. So after a few years, the data were restored. Or, to be more accurate, there was an attempt to restore it. Some data was just plain lost forever, and I am not talking about a few records. I am talking about upwards of 90,000 records in our database that still have empty fixed fields. Loss of this data interferes with catalog retrieval, made system migration incredibly difficult and added substantially to its cost, is creating problems for moving materials to remote storage locations, and will pose a heavy workload as we join other libraries to create an online Colorado union catalog.

This was a particularly dreadful idea with particularly far-reaching results. Most of the other illustrations that come to mind are also egregious, because it's usually the horrible examples that you remember. The fact that smaller-scale decisions with less far-reaching impact don't make the same splash doesn't mean they should be any less well considered, because they also can cause harm. Some examples of these would include:

A. Generically bad ideas that simply lead to poor retrieval or complicated workflow, such as

- A decision by a branch library to use general and specific subject headings. This always sounds like an added service when anyone suggests it, but it adds extraneous headings to a database that may already be bordering on too large to search easily. It produces search results that are imprecise. It leads users to make false assumptions about how to retrieve materials, which can in turn lead to failed searches. It also raises the question of whether you have sufficient resources to add general headings to items with copy, or whether you just add them to the minority of materials you do originally.

- A decision made by our own serials department at a time, I hasten to add, that predates anyone who is in the department now, to catalog analytics, but not to make shelflist cards. Inability to find out, short of canvassing the entire card catalog, what analytics have been cataloged has created a variety of problems, especially in relation to attempts to do retrospective conversion and inventory control.

B. Shortsighted bad ideas that are based on the needs or capabilities of the current situation without adequate thought to the future.

- A decision by a university library to cease tracing series. The decision was made primarily because of the difficulties associated with card filing. When the library moved to an online catalog, in which "card filing" is not an issue, much valuable access had been permanently lost.

- Any decision to delete information from a bibliographic record just because your catalog doesn't use or display it. The saved fields fiasco is a grand example of such a problem. A lesser example might be stripping other classification numbers only to discover as you join a union catalog that the centrally-assigned number you have stripped away is going to be a shared subject retrieval mechanism.

- Any decision to use a MARC field in a way other than intended. An example of this would be a decision to use the 508 field for performers as your means of offering retrieval by these persons' names, instead of by providing added entries. Names in the notes field are not under authority control. They may be accessed through different indexes and may not even be indexed in the next system you implement. Another example would be recording local information in nonlocal note fields, and then migrating to a system in which 590s and such are stripped out.

C. And let's not forget the bad ideas that arise from too narrow a focus.

- We have a great example of a good idea gone wrong here at CU. Many years ago, in an effort to get a popular sheet music collection under some control, instead of creating even semi-standard records, an entirely separate database was begun, using DBase, and defining records that consisted of a very few "MARC-like" fields of limited size. These records have caused us trouble ever since. In order to get them into the central database, special programming had to be performed at a special cost. But the fields are still short, the headings not under authority control, the titles are not in OCLC, and the records required special and expensive programming to migrate them from CARL to our present automation system.
- Less spectacular but equally unfortunate decisions can be reached through too great a familiarity with your own materials and users and too little familiarity with other materials and users, or through a conviction that your own problems are so special that consideration of "the norm" is a waste of time. Examples would be map, catalogers or audiovisual catalogers, or serial catalogers, or music catalogers listening to their users and introducing some aberrant practice without considering how it affects the catalog as a whole, or being unable to imagine what use someone could make of some piece of data and ceasing to supply it, only to discover later that there was another constituency that relied on it.

So far I've talked about "The Dark Side." Now for the good side of "The Force": virtually every decision to handle something according to the full standard repays the effort that you put into it.

A good example of this would be what happened with the curriculum materials at Northwestern. This was a fairly large collection of primary and secondary school textbooks and teachers' materials that were used by the education department. Even well after Northwestern had begun doing its cataloging in machine-readable form, these materials were given only brief manual records. Unfortunately this meant that they also had to circulate manually, and eventually this was a problem. So the catalog department was asked to convert the records and was told that all we needed to do was take the brief records and transcribe them "as is" because, so it was said, almost no one used the materials and it wasn't worth the effort. But we couldn't bring ourselves to do a substandard job, so we converted the records, we enhanced them in their description and access points, and we put them under authority control. And lo! circulation of them went up by more than 100 percent. It appears that it wasn't that no one had wanted to use the materials before, it was that when they were not accessible in the same way as other materials, no one knew they were there.

As with the bad examples, it's the spectacular ones that stand out, but that doesn't mean that you are not daily reaping the benefits of doing things up to standard. The absence of problems may not be something you can quantify, but it's a positive thing nevertheless.

This paper so far has worked like a funnel. First there were those formative experiences, that led to six lessons, which have in turn led me to the following two generalized issues:

- The first is that all of us, and especially catalogers of special materials, must make a constant and conscious effort to remember the big picture and to remember that everything affects everything else. There is essentially nothing you can do in your own department or unit that does not have some impact on what happens elsewhere. We are all like flies on a spider web. If I wiggle, every other fly feels it. If you flap your wings, I can tell. If any of us makes too great a fuss, the spider finds us all.

The more isolated you are in your own unit, the less likely you are to see the vital interconnections, and therefore the more likely you are to make a decision that you or others will later regret. It may be anything but a mild regret, because repairing an error, or changing your mind and trying to bring records up to standard later takes more time and trouble than it would have cost to do it right in the first place, if indeed repair is even possible.

- The second issue is that we must cling to our principles and re- member our purposes. We are all in for a bit of a bumpy ride from now on. The materials we handle, and the systems we han- dle them with are undergoing rapid evolution. It's not going to be possible to stick doggedly to the same old practices, but you do need to stick to your principles in pursuit of your purposes. The changes we are undergoing will buffet us with the need to deal with unprecedented circumstances and to solve unexpected prob- lems. As we feel pressured to deal with these problems rapidly, if we don't keep our overriding purposes and underlying principles in mind we are vulnerable to making mistakes on our own, and if we don't know and can't articulate these principles and purposes we are ill-equipped to counter bad ideas pushed by those on high.

First you have to know what your principles and purposes are, and not everyone does. Even if you yourself have them clear in your mind, you cannot rely on others having a good grasp. Even if you have a good understanding of them, it's still amazingly easy to lose sight of them and to begin making and justifying decisions as if the tasks were more important than the product, or to think that your own circum- scribed purpose is or ought to be the purpose or goal of the entire enterprise.

An example of losing sight would be this: We buy information resources to satisfy the needs of our clientele. We catalog these materi- als to make them accessible to users. We use copy to make the catalog- ing easier, quicker, and cheaper. But people can begin to view using copy as an end rather than as a means, and build up a complex body of procedures that can become so involved and time consuming that it takes more time and may cost about the same as original cataloging. If that happens, it's time to rethink our policies.

Having an appreciation for the principles that underlie the catalog- ing rules will be one of your greatest helps in figuring out how to face unusual challenges. Some of the principles of the *Anglo-American Cataloging Rules* that may be especially important these days include these:

- The rules are actually a code, that is, they are not just an aggregate of specific instances but are instead written with reference to common principles. Therefore, even though the specific instance you have in hand may not be explicitly addressed in the rules, your problem may nevertheless be covered.
- AACR abandoned the pretense of omniscience in catalogers that was characteristic of earlier rules. They are instead written to enable a cataloger to put together a description largely based on the information s/he has in front of her.
- AACR is built on the principle that analogous situations should be dealt with analogously across formats.
- It is taken as an article of faith that there are more similarities than differences among the various types of materials, and that it is in the interests of all to try to emphasize the similarities while accommodating the differences, rather than to emphasize the differences.

This leads me finally to the last segment of my paper: A look to the future. First, something in the very near future. So near, in fact, that many of you may already have experienced it–system migration. It's fairly well accepted by now that most libraries will not be using the same automated system forever. Anyone with an ounce of sense and awareness who has undergone a system migration knows that it's not something you want to do often, but it's something that most of us are probably going to have to go through, perhaps several times. Even if you don't migrate from one system to another, it's highly likely that the system you keep will undergo significant revision to all or some of its parts.

Given the reality of system migration or significant system upgrade, the best, most heartfelt advice I can give to anyone is to resist all temptations to establish nonstandard practices, and begin now to discontinue any that you have created in the past and to make plans for how you might find and fix the nonstandard records you already have. Nonstandard records and nonstandard practices are inevitably trouble. They don't load right, if they load at all, they interfere with record overlay, they display wrong, they put information in the wrong indexes, and they create a host of other problems. It is impossible to predict how a particular piece of data will be used in the future or how it will be manipulated, but it is possible to know that your records will be at variance from the norm if you devise and follow a nonstandard practice, and it is reasonable to expect that systems will be designed to accommodate standard records.

I know how tempting it is to do "something special" for your users, or your materials, or your circumstances, and I know how easy it is to look at something and say, "It's such a little thing, and it makes such a difference to our users." Unfortunately, odds are that despite your good intentions, it's not going to turn out to be a little thing in the end, and the difference it will make to your users and to the body of users in general may turn out to be largely negative.

At this point I'd like to quote more fully from Arnold Wajenberg's conference summary delivered following the ALCTS Classification Institute in 1985:

> Deviating from standards always gets you into trouble. It is very seldom that you can say "always" about anything in cataloging and classification, but I have come to the conclusion that no matter how good the justification for saying, "In this case I don't like what the cataloging rules require, or what the classification schedule requires, or what the standard subject heading is. It is obviously wrong, so I'm going to do the obviously right thing and make my own rule . . . and I'll commit my library to it." If you follow through with that intent, someday someone will curse your name for leaving him or her a mess to cope with. Following standards is more important than ever as libraries become more automated and as they simultaneously decentralize and integrate their operations. More and more often smaller units within our larger umbrella organizations are performing cataloging, and attempting to cooperate not only with each other, but also with other libraries across the state and the nation, and even the world. Whenever any of these units deviates from standards in cataloging or classification, in MARC coding, or in any other aspect of bibliographic control, it makes it harder for those units to use other people's work efficiently, and it also makes it harder for other people to use the deviant institutions' work.[1]

Something else that we almost certainly have to look forward to is major revisions in the rules for descriptive cataloging, and a large part of that impetus will come from basic changes in the nature of seriality, or more precisely, changes in the bibliographic universe that have made it essential to come to grips with the increasing variety and volume of materials that are neither monographic nor serial, but which are simply "nonstatic" or "ongoing."

Back when I went to library school, it wasn't hard to tell the difference between the monographs and the serials. There weren't (relatively speaking) all that many different kinds of serials, and there were only a few kinds of materials that didn't fit well into either category–annuals, for instance, which could be handled without undue strife as either monographs or serials, and looseleaf services, of which there were mercifully few. But that was in the days of print and analog. Time passes and things change. Ever since the introduction of digital materials, both serials and monographs have seemed to "melt" (I'm picturing movie special effects, in which something that was distinct and hard edged begins to soften, and then to droop, and then to flow, so that in the end you can hardly recognize what it started out as), until now we have a lot of materials that are not, as the rules so quaintly put it, either "complete in one part or complete, or intended to be completed in a finite number of separate parts,"[2] and neither are they "issued in successive parts bearing numeric or chronological designations and intended to be continued indefinitely."[3]

Interactive multimedia was not the "new species" we feared it was, but it looks as if serials and monographs have interbred, and they have produced a new species. After years of study and work, the Multiple Versions Task Force in ALA finally had to admit that the rules as they stood could not do what would be best for intellectual entities issued in multiple versions. But even so, the camel was still walking. The explosion of nonserial, nonmonographic "ongoing" publications, however, may be all that the camel can take.

There is no question that serials experts can have a great deal to contribute to the conversation about how to incorporate reflection of that "third dimension" of a publication–its susceptibility to alteration of content over time–in the cataloging rules for all materials.[4] After all, you have been routinely dealing with the bibliographic undead for a very long time, and now we are going to have to figure out how to handle bibliographic immortals.

I urge you to get involved. And by involved, I mean within the system. This means getting involved with those bodies that contribute to the *Anglo-American Cataloging Rules*. In the U.S., unless you work for the Library of Congress, this means ALA. Further, it means working through the ALA committee that contributes to the rules, the Committee on Cataloging: Description and Access, or, on any of the thirty-two organizational units from which CC:DA accepts nonvoting liaisons, including one from the Serials Section of ALCTS, who is advised by the Committee to Study Serials Cataloging. CC:DA operates both as a whole and through task forces that often include volunteers who are not members of the committee itself, so there are a number of avenues by which you can contribute.

The proliferation of information resources that are not monographic, that share a critical feature with serials–that of being ongoing–will almost certainly affect more than the cataloging rules. It's not too great a leap to assume that it will also have at least some impact on the organization of cataloging operations; it may be that the impact will be profound.

At first glance it might be thought that all of those "not-monographic" materials will necessarily flow into serial cataloging units, but my guess is that while this might be true for a time, eventually these materials will go where most of the staff is. After all, while they are not monographic, they are also not serials. It may even be that once the dust settles, and we have figured out how to handle these "neither-here-nor-there" creatures, that we will find fewer and fewer reasons to keep serials and monographic catalogers apart.

So what are we left with?

- A future in which we must make all of our decisions in the knowledge that system migration and system upgrade will be a frequent occurrence, and thus we must plan for making these occurrences as nontraumatic as possible, which argues strongly for following standards.
- A future in which the spectrum of variation among the materials we handle will both broaden and also even out, so that while the number of differences may increase, the differences may themselves become relatively small, and instead of materials becoming more different from each other, they may eventually begin to look more like each other than ever before.
- A future in which the standards in use will be modified to reflect the profound changes in the materials.
- A future in which the organizations we build may need to be modified to reflect the changes both in the materials and our means of handling them

That looks like a future in which there will be lots of questions to be dealt with. But I submit that if we will accept that we are more alike than different, and that all materials are more alike than different, and that the same principles form the basis for all of our rules and practices, and that if we will bother to learn, remember, honor, and apply those principles, we will find that in fact, and in essence, we already know the answer to many of the questions, we just have to find them.

NOTES

1. Arnold Wajenberg, "Summarizing the Preconference," in *Classification of Library Materials*, ed. by Betty Bengtson and Janet Swan Hill. (Neal-Schuman: New York, 1990), 186.

2. *Anglo-American Cataloguing Rules*, 2d ed. (Chicago: American Library Association, 1988), 620. The Glossary definition of "monograph."

3. Ibid., 622. The Glossary definition of "serial."

4. Jean Hirons and Crystal Graham, "Issues Related to Seriality." Available: http//www.nlc-bnc.ca/jsc/confpap.htm. Paper prepared for the International Conference on the Principles and Future Development of AACR, Toronto, 1998. The concept of the three dimensions of publications is first broached in the introduction (p. 4).

MEETING END USER NEEDS IN THE ELECTRONIC UNIVERSE: A DIALOGUE

Meeting End User Needs in the Electronic Universe: A Dialogue

Trisha L. Davis
Richard G. Ham
Taissa Kusma

Presenters

Susan Andrews

Recorder

Trisha L. Davis is Head, Continuation Acquisition Division, Ohio State University.
Richard G. Ham is Professor in the Department of Molecular, Cellular, and Developmental Microbiology, University of Colorado at Boulder.
Taissa Kusma is Director of Online Product Development for Academic Press.
Susan Andrews is Serials Librarian at Texas A&M University–Commerce.

The following report was prepared by Susan Andrews and also appeared in the *NASIG Newsletter*, September 1998.

[Haworth co-indexing entry note]: "Meeting End User Needs in the Electronic Universe: A Dialogue." Andrews, Susan. Co-published simultaneously in *The Serials Librarian* (The Haworth Press, Inc.) Vol. 36, No. 1/2, 1999, pp. 247-251; and: *Head in the Clouds, Feet on the Ground: Serials Vision and Common Sense* (ed: Jeffrey S. Bullington, Beatrice L. Caraway, and Beverley Geer) The Haworth Press, Inc., 1999, pp. 247-251. Single or multiple copies of this article are available for a fee from The Haworth Document Delivery Service [1-800-342-9678, 9:00 a.m. - 5:00 p.m. (EST). E-mail address: getinfo@haworthpressinc.com].

SUMMARY. The advent of electronic products has had enormous impact on all players in the information chain. Users struggle to find secure, current, comprehensive, well-structured and easily searched electronic sources. Librarians struggle to fund and acquire rights to access these electronic sources needed by their users. Serials vendors and aggregators struggle to acquire the rights to deliver content from publishers. Publishers struggle to meet the demands of end users, librarians, serial aggregators and their own production costs. This session addresses these issues and asks, "Where do we go from here?" *[Article copies available for a fee from The Haworth Document Delivery Service: 1-800-342-9678. E-mail address: getinfo@haworthpressinc.com]*

Connie Foster, serials coordinator at Western Kentucky University, introduced the three speakers, who represented three perspectives on end user needs in the electronic universe.

Trisha L. Davis, head of the Continuation Acquisition Division at Ohio State University, proceeded to give a basic introduction of the session. She explained that it was intended to be a dialog between a librarian (Davis), a publisher (Kusma), and a normal end user (Dr. Richard G. Ham). The dialog was intended to be focused on the normal end user in 1998 (Dr. Ham). At that point, Davis introduced Dr. Richard G. Ham, professor of Molecular, Cellular, and Developmental Biology at the University of Colorado, Boulder.

Ham gave us an outline of what the ideal system for the normal end user would be. The first need on his list was quality and convenience. Readability of text and clarity of illustrations should be at least similar to the printed journal. Currently, there are two formats being used: Hypertext Markup Language (HTML) format (had a good printed page, but did not like the figures) and Portable Document Format (PDF) format (looks like a real journal page, prints out nicely and has good figures, but is hard to read on screen). Neither format was as nice as the printed journal, but the advantage was accessibility anytime, anyplace. Readability and clarity both require high-definition monitors, according to Ham, and any online format is limited by the amount of material that will fit on the screen. A related important feature was the ability to move freely and quickly between text and figures. Screen size limits usually do not allow text and figures on the same page, as well. Ham thought that online should come as close to flipping pages of a paper copy as possible. Finally, fast response time with servers that respond rapidly and do not become overloaded during peak times was a must. Ham believed that distribution and display systems must be fast and not be subject to overload.

The second major necessity of the ideal system addressed the ability to locate articles. This included the ability to browse contents and identify articles of interest, as well as search for topics (e.g., links), and the need for long-term archival maintenance (paper often outlasts online information).

Thirdly, the normal end user, according to Ham, must be permitted "fair use" copying. Detailed analysis involves highlighting, rereading, and writing in the margins, and reviewing a topic required being able to lay out paper copies side by side on a table. He also said that researchers need to be able to accumulate papers closely related to current work and students must be able to copy papers used in teaching. Ham also wondered what the policy would be with regard to downloading items to a user's computer?

Accessibility was the fourth ideal. There should be enough machines for convenient access and access should be at least as easy as for individual print issues. Multiple concurrent users for the same article should also be possible. Remote access was considered a major reason for buying online journals, so online users should be able to access from their offices, after hours, and from home.

The next consideration was definition of authorized users. Can anyone on campus use the journal, will researchers with academic appointments have remote access, will any online access to the campus library allow online journal use, and finally, how would access be controlled and who would be responsible for the control?

Subscription costs were also a major consideration. Ham noted that library materials costs are rising faster than library budgets and that currently libraries are trying to cancel journals and have little hope of the financial situation improving in the near future. He also pointed out that online journals are generally more expensive than print, although they are frequently packaged with the print version (at a higher price tag), and the online journal subscriptions alone are not usually available. Ham felt that online publishing should cost less than paper (no mailing or paper costs), and he believed that libraries are seeking cost-saving alternatives.

Ham's last consideration was infrastructure costs. He pointed out that most campuses are facing budget shortfalls, while high-resolution monitors, printers, etc. are costly. On the other hand, he still believed that libraries needed high-quality monitors, good-quality printers, good maintenance and service (another expense). Faculty offices would need the same equipment. Distribution and security systems would also be needed (another expense), as well as a reliable permanent online archive, which might reduce the need for library shelf space and related costs.

Trisha Davis briefly responded to Ham at this point. She said that she had found two articles addressing this subject, one from 1988 and one from 1994. She pointed out that in 1988 most people weren't on the Internet and used paper copies and that the 1988 article mentioned many of the same things that Ham had discussed. Davis also pointed out that although we had identified our problems ten years ago and are still having them, we are currently using online journals anyway. The 1994 article said that we would adopt new roles and drop old ones. Davis thought that we have added roles but not dropped the old ones.

Davis went on to say that quality and ease of use are additional library concerns and burdens now. Serials librarians now have to communicate with high-tech people and deal with a large range of equipment, which is an additional burden and also creates a need for educating ourselves. She felt that we are all struggling with archiving, "fair use" and licensing. She did say that publishers have come a long way with the licensing concerns, excluding ILL and archiving. On the subject of costs, Davis felt that funding has shifted to high-visibility projects and not mundane daily needs. She suggested that we need to carefully consider our problems so that we can communicate them to those who need to know.

Davis made two final and important points on keeping end users happy. First, work hard with consortia. She also stated that each of us has to speak loudly and clearly to licensing negotiators about our needs. Her second point was that it is important to consider our role with serials agents. We need to tell them our needs, and they may be able to help us with licensing, interfacing and so on. Davis felt that we have gone from a relationship of buying anything that the end user needed to having to meet the end user's needs as best we can without letting him know all of the problems involved.

Taissa Kusma, director of online product development, Academic Press, was the last-minute substitute for John Cox, who was to have been the publisher representative for the dialog. She started with a brief introduction, indicating that she believed that there had been a lot of changes in the last decade, including the relationships between publishers, customers and vendors, and a move from CD-ROM to full-text online, which led to the first exposure of end user needs. She felt that what end users wanted (ease of use, browsability, indexing, etc.) was different from what librarians wanted (complex and fast searching capabilities). Kusma believed that the publisher is now closer to the end users, but now many are dealing with consortia as the middleman. She said that some publishers, like Academic Press, try to get needs from both the consortia and the libraries, but that there are still communication problems. She also pointed out that usage is not automatic. She suggested keeping usage statistics and using surveys in addition to advertising what you have.

Regarding clarity and quality (in response to the two previous speakers), she pointed out that they depend on implementation and that cost is involved, since higher quality creates larger files. Kusma also mentioned that navigation depends on implementation as well and that PDF does not extend to more complex searches. She also said that publishers are putting resources into establishing links these days and a great deal of progress has been made in linking indexes and abstracts to articles. Publishers are also aware of the desire and importance of archiving and the current lack of guarantees. OCLC is being looked at as a possible long-term archiving entity. However, the specifics of future access are still being worked out. User authentication was considered to be an issue that is progressing, with remote access having clearly defined limits, while in-library use is free to all who walk in. As far as costs go, Kusma said that most leasing agreements have a price increase cap which can help keep the price down. She also pointed out that the same costs are still there for online journals as for print, except for the mail costs (for online-only journals). Costs still include development, maintenance, customer support (a new cost and higher than anticipated) and a different production stream (more tagging of articles, etc.).

A brief question and answer session followed, and then Davis concluded the dialog with a few remarks regarding the ILL debate. She felt that the main problem was that a few librarians have abused their usage of ILL, which has caused publishers to be cautious about their policies in this area.

PRICING OF SCIENTIFIC, TECHNICAL AND MEDICAL (STM) PUBLICATIONS

Serials Pricing–An Agent's View: Trends and Characteristics of Higher Education Funding and STM Journal Pricing

Allen Powell

SUMMARY. This session explored the current and future pricing of STM information distribution with three speakers representing the subscription agent, the nonprofit publisher, and the library perspectives. Allen Powell presented current pricing characteristics and trends of STM journals published in print and electronic formats. Malcolm Getz focused on journal publishers who contemplate distributing their titles in electronic format and are concerned that revenues will remain sufficient to sustain operations should print sales decline. David Stern discussed mod-

Allen Powell is Vice President and Chief Financial Officer, EBSCO Subscription Services.

[Haworth co-indexing entry note]: "Serials Pricing–An Agent's View: Trends and Characteristics of Higher Education Funding and STM Journal Pricing." Powell, Allen. Co-published simultaneously in *The Serials Librarian* (The Haworth Press, Inc.) Vol. 36, No. 1/2, 1999, pp. 253-262; and: *Head in the Clouds, Feet on the Ground: Serials Vision and Common Sense* (ed: Jeffrey S. Bullington, Beatrice L. Caraway, and Beverley Geer) The Haworth Press, Inc., 1999, pp. 253-262. Single or multiple copies of this article are available for a fee from The Haworth Document Delivery Service [1-800-342-9678, 9:00 a.m. - 5:00 p.m. (EST). E-mail address: getinfo@haworthpressinc.com].

els of alternative information delivery and pricing packages that attempt to maintain a relatively stable revenue base while allowing for the customization of purchase profiles for organziations and research communities. *[Article copies available for a fee from The Haworth Document Delivery Service: 1-800-342-9678. E-mail address: getinfo@haworthpressinc.com]*

It has been said the only two certainties in life are death and taxes. Perhaps it is time to add a third item to this exclusive list–that prices of scientific, technical, and medical (STM) publications will increase over time at an average annual rate in the range of 10 to 12 percent. This appears to be a grim reality, just like death and taxes, to library professionals whose task it is to acquire, manage, maintain, and facilitate access to STM information. This reality is especially disturbing as higher education funding and, more specifically, library funding have not been increasing at a rate proportional to that of price increases of STM material.

LIBRARY FUNDING

According to the U.S. Department of Education, the average annual rate of revenue increase per higher education institution (HEI) from 1990 to 1994 was 5.7 percent. During this same period, the average annual increase in higher education outpaced the United States' Consumer Price Index (CPI), which increased at an average annual rate of 3.2 percent. The average annual increase in higher education revenue was calculated based on the total current funds revenue of all public and private two- and four-year institutions as reported by the Department of Education.

The Department of Education also reported details of the allocation of total current funds revenue by source. These figures indicate an increasing proportion of HEI revenue is being provided by tuition and fees, while funding from state and local government has decreased. From 1990 to 1994, the average annual percentage revenue increases by source were as follows: tuition and fees, 8.7 percent; auxiliary enterprises, educational activities, hospital and other, 6.9 percent; federal government, 5.6 percent; gifts, grants, contracts, and endowments, 5.4 percent; and state and local governments, 2.1 percent.

Department of Education records indicate over this same time period the average total HEI library expenditure rose an average of 4 percent annually. Since librarians generally operate on a fund basics accounting policy and normally utilize all allocated funds, it is reasonable to assume overall library funding is not increasing as fast as college and university revenues. Over this same period, the annual funding gap was roughly 1.7 percent. Said another way, libraries appear to be receiving an even smaller portion of the college and university revenue pie.

There is a caveat to this conclusion. If libraries do not report figures in a consistent manner from year to year, this could potentially increase or decrease the actual funding gap, if one exists. Further, if libraries receive benefit from expenditures allocated to other HEI cost centers there may be a smaller funding gap or no gap at all; for instance, costs associated with computer and communication hardware and software, license fees, etc., which enable students and library patrons to access information, may be charged in total or through some sort of allocation to other non-library centers.

This caveat must also be kept in mind when considering statistics from the Association of Research Libraries (ARL) for a more recent time period. Figures obtained from the ARL Website indicate that from 1993 to 1997, ARL expenditures rose at an average annual rate of 4.3 percent. This growth rate is similar to the 4 percent annual growth rate for HEI libraries during the earlier time frame presented above. In explaining the methodology used to arrive at the ARL expenditure growth rate, we extracted total materials expenditures for the 108 university research libraries in the U.S. and Canada for 1993 from the ARL Website. This group of 108 universities was treated as the "base" group for purposes of computing changes in expenditures from year to year. Universities added to ARL after 1993 were excluded from the study. The sum of total library expenditures for these 108 institutions for each year was divided by the previous year total to arrive at an annual percentage increase for each period. These increases were then averaged to produce the final average annual increase percentage presented above.

The same methodology was used to determine the average annual increase in ARL serial expenditures. Again, the caveats mentioned earlier apply, and the figures reveal that the average increase in serials expenditures was 5.5 percent. From these numbers we concluded that serials expenditures are consuming a larger portion of total library expenditures. During this time frame, the CPI increased at an average annual rate of less than 3 percent. Based on this, it is not unreasonable to assume that while library budgets are not keeping pace with total HEI revenue, they are growing at a rate which is marginally ahead of general inflation.

JOURNAL PRICES

At first glance, this funding trend does not appear to be overly negative. However, it must be put into the context of the pricing trend of STM information. As was mentioned in the beginning, prices of STM serial publications have been rising by 10 to 12 percent annually. When the funding trend is coupled with the price increase trend, the inevitable long-term result will be fewer journal purchases. Indeed this has been the reality in the library industry for some time.

What disciplines of STM material are driving these "high" price increases? The *1998 Periodical Price Survey* published in the April 15, 1998 issue of *Library Journal* gives us some insight. The survey includes an in-depth study of the almost 3,000 titles included in the ISI *Science Citation Index*. The study indicates that from 1994 to 1998, the average annual price increase of all journals in the index was 12 percent. The average cost of all journals in the index was $771. Table 1 details the seven disciplines in the index with prices higher than the index average.

Physics and chemistry lead the way with the most expensive journals. Table 2 shows that over the last four years the average price of a journal in the index rose by 57 percent.

TABLE 1. Average Journal Price by Scientific Discipline for 1998

Discipline	Price
ISI Science Citation Index	$771
Technology	$775
Math & C.S.	$860
Engineering	$867
Biology	$891
Astronomy	$1,088
Chemistry	$1,577
Physics	$1,601

TABLE 2. Price Increase by Discipline (1994 to 1998)

Discipline	1994	1998	% Incr.
Astronomy	$746	$1,088	46%
Math & C.S.	$567	$860	52%
Physics	$1,036	$1,601	55%
ISI Sci. Cit. Index	$491	$771	57%
Chemistry	$1,007	$1,577	57%
Biology	$557	$891	60%
Engineering	$523	$867	66%
Technology	$458	$775	69%

The seven most expensive disciplines are displayed in ascending order based on total percentage price increase from 1994 to 1998. Technology had the highest increase at 69 percent. Table 3 presents the same seven disciplines in terms of average annual percentage increase.

Evaluating STM journal prices by discipline of study can be helpful when trying to estimate future expenditures. Analyzing pricing based on country of origin can also be useful. The *Library Journal* price study shows the average price of the 1,372 U.S. journals in the *Science Citation Index* was $480. The average price of the 1,594 non-U.S. titles in the index was $1,020, more than two times the average cost of a U.S. journal. From 1994 to 1998, U.S. titles increased at an average annual rate of 11.7 percent versus 12.1 percent for non-U.S. titles.

Studies like the *Library Journal* survey, which track price increases of such indexes as the ISI indexes, are useful. They are even more so when prices by discipline and country of origin are considered in relation to a library's holdings. However, these studies should not be the only tools used to forecast journal price increases, as a library's collection may not mirror an index. As an example, consider Table 4, which compares both the number of journals and the total cost of the ISI index to the actual profile of the average academic library that places substantially all of its U.S. and non-U.S. journals with EBSCO.

U.S. titles comprise forty-six percent of the titles in the index versus 70 percent of the titles for the average library. Likewise, there is also a difference in total cost. U.S. titles comprise only twenty-nine percent of the expenditure of the index versus 46 percent for the average library. One conclusion is that U.S. titles account for a disproportional amount of the number of titles in comparison to total overall serials expenditure.

TABLE 3. Average Annual Price Increase % by Discipline (1994 to 1998)

Discipline	% Increase
Astronomy	10.0%
Math & C.S.	11.1%
Physics	11.6%
ISI Science Citation Index	12.0%
Chemistry	12.0%
Biology	12.5%
Engineering	13.5%
Technology	14.1%

TABLE 4. Percentage of Titles and Expenditure by Publisher Origin

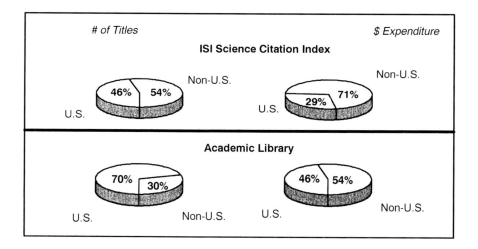

From this comparison, it is evident that an individual library's current collection should also be considered when estimating future price increases. This type of customized approach to collection analysis and forecasting has become a staple in the library industry. One of EBSCO's functions as an agent is to help with this type of approach by offering customized reports such as the historical price analysis and customized budget analysis, as well other essential collection development reports.

History often gives us a glimpse into the future. This is why we have focused primarily on what has occurred historically with regard to library funding and journal pricing. However, we should not necessarily depend solely on the past when forecasting the future. Indeed, the best place to go for information on what journal prices will be in the future is to those who determine the future, namely, the publishers. To help our customers budget, we annually contact major STM publishers and ask them for their estimated price increases for the upcoming year.

We also have discussions with publishers to determine the factors influencing the price increases. Over the years, publishers' responses and insights into pricing factors have been similar, with three primary factors driving journal price increases: normal inflationary business increases (wage, benefits, supplies, postage, machinery, etc.), information expansion (resulting in additional pages, volumes, and issues), and cancellations. The last of these three, cancellations, is noteworthy because publishers' indications that cancellations (decreased units sold) increase prices supports the notion that the demand for STM material is not price elastic. Put simply, lowering the price of an STM journal will not result in a greater-than-proportional increase in demand for the journal. Conversely, an increase in price will not necessarily result in greater-than-proportional decrease in demand. Year-in and year-out, on average, the sum impact of the three components above has consistently resulted in average price increase estimates from publishers for STM journals in the 10 to 12 percent range.

Of course, when a publisher's native currency is different from a library's native currency, a fourth element, currency conversion, comes into play. This is why librarians should evaluate their collection in terms of country of origin when budgeting, as was mentioned earlier. Table 5 shows how the strengthening and weakening of the dollar have impacted prices of the titles included in the *Science Citation Index* from 1994 to 1998.

As you can see, U.S. journal price increases remain in a relatively tight range (10.7 percent to 12.6 percent) over the period. Non-U.S. publication price increases, however, ranged more broadly from a low of 6.7 percent in 1998, when the dollar strengthened, to a high of 20.2 percent in 1996, when the dollar weakened considerably. In order to keep libraries abreast of foreign currency developments as well as budget for the upcoming year, EBSCO produces an annual price projections study that covers a five-year period showing currency fluctuations and the impact on serials costs.

TABLE 5. Price Increase History, Science Citation Index

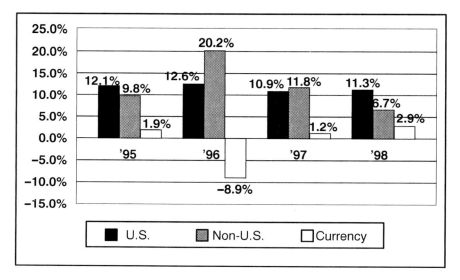

ONLINE JOURNALS

There is now a fifth element which may likely impact STM journal prices. This is, of course, the online journal. Pricing models for online journals are still in a relatively embryonic stage, as are functionality and usability issues surrounding this new medium. Attitudes and views of publishers appear to change frequently, and publishers are testing various pricing models in an effort to find that which offers an acceptable revenue stream.

EBSCO reviewed the pricing methodologies of fifty of the largest STM publishers currently offering online journals through agents. Of the fifty pricing models, 78 percent tied the delivery of the online format to the purchase of the print journal itself. This is somewhat understandable as one of the major uncertainties connected to online journals is archiving and access to back issues. Coupling online with print addresses this issue. The remaining 22 percent offered online whether the print was purchased or not. A detailed look showed pricing methods of the 50 publishers broken down as follows: 54 percent, online comes free with purchase of print; 24 percent, online offered only in a print/online combination price more than print; 8 percent, online available in a stand-alone subscription priced more than print; and 14 percent, online available as a stand-alone subscription price less than or equal to print.

The number of publishers offering online journals continues to expand rapidly as does the number of online journals. In February of 1997, EBSCO's database of title listings contained 850 priced online journals. The number of online journals available through EBSCO has grown exponentially, and as of June 1998, the database contained more than twenty-seven hundred online journals. This figure, of course, does not include online journals from publishers who do not allow ordering of their online journal through subscription agents.

EBSCO is optimistic that these publishers will in time make their online journals available through agents, as the market has voiced this desire. We are also convinced that there will be a vital role for agents and others who seek to fill the role of aggregator in the world of online journals. The aggregator's role will be to help libraries manage online subscriptions efficiently and in a cost-effective way. This will be done when libraries and publishers turn to the aggregator for authentication and access management of online journals. Aggregators will offer a variety of Web-based services that authenticate, or provide a "gateway," to full text through several methods: Internet protocol (IP) address, user name, user password or a combination of these. These services will provide a single familiar interface with a single search engine that enables users to seamlessly search for and access online journals from multiple publishers. Administrative features will also provide librarians with a single source for ordering, processing and invoicing of both print and online journals–traditional functions subscription agencies have always provided. One source for both print and online journals provides all the traditional services of an agency, plus combined reporting and analyses for both print and online journals.

In addition to the administration and management of online information, successful aggregators will also offer integrated research solutions. Library patrons in the near future will be able to conduct a keyword search in an online database that will allow them to know immediately if the full text is available in a package database to which they subscribe, an online journal to which they subscribe, or to a print journal in their holdings. When full text is not available, users can be automatically prompted to electronically order an article through a document delivery service.

Will the advent of electronic journals and the vision of integrated information services favorably impact the disparity between higher education funding for the acquisition of STM information and the actual cost of acquiring this information? If history is any indicator of the future, it is likely this disparity may continue even in light of new offerings presented by the world of electronic information. It is not unrealistic to expect that this tension will continue for the foreseeable future unless there is real change in the marketplace regarding issues such as the ownership of intellectual property, control of the publishing process, the price elasticity of demand of STM material, and the criteria for faculty promotion and tenure.

Electronic Publishing in Academia:
An Economic Perspective

Malcolm Getz

The Library at Washington University reports 150,000 hits per year on its electronic, networked *Encyclopedia Britannica* at a cost to the Library of four cents per hit.[Baker, 1996] This rate of use seems to be an order of magnitude larger than the rate of use of the print version of the document in the library. At the same time, the volunteer Project Gutenberg whose goal was to build an electronic file of 10,000 classic, public domain texts on the Internet has failed to sustain itself.[1] The University of Illinois decided it could no longer afford to provide the electronic storage space and no other entity stepped forward to sustain the venture.

A first lesson here is that production values, the quality of indexing and presentation, the packaging and marketing of the work, matter. Those ventures that take the approach of unrestricted free access don't necessarily dominate ventures that collect revenues. When a shopper asks "What does it cost?" we can naturally respond, "What is it worth to you?" Electronic communication among academics is growing

Malcolm Getz is Associate Professor of Economics, Vanderbilt University.

The author appreciates the help of Elton Hinshaw and the American Economic Association in understanding its operations and the comments of Paul Gherman, David Lucking-Reiley, and Flo Wilson on an earlier draft of this essay.

This paper is published in the form in which it appears in the *Journal of Electronic Publishing* (Ann Arbor, MI: University of Michigan Press, September 1997). [Web terms have been capitalized for consistency with the rest of the volume.–Ed.]

[Haworth co-indexing entry note]: "Electronic Publishing in Academia: An Economic Perspective." Getz, Malcolm. Co-published simultaneously in *The Serials Librarian* (The Haworth Press, Inc.) Vol. 36, No. 1/2, 1999, pp. 263-300; and: *Head in the Clouds, Feet on the Ground: Serials Vision and Common Sense* (ed: Jeffrey S. Bullington, Beatrice L. Caraway, and Beverley Geer) The Haworth Press, Inc., 1999, pp. 263-300. Single or multiple copies of this article are available for a fee from The Haworth Document Delivery Service [1-800-342-9678, 9:00 a.m. - 5:00 p.m. (EST). E-mail address: getinfo@haworthpressinc.com].

when it is valuable. In contemplating investments in electronic publishing, the publisher's, and indeed academia's, goal is to create the most value for the funds invested. Generally, the freebie culture that launched the Internet represents only a subset of a much wider range of possible uses. Many quality information products that flow through the Net will be generating revenue flows sufficient to sustain them.

The *Encyclopedia* gives a second lesson, namely, that the costs of electronic distribution may be significantly less than print. Serviceable home encyclopedias on CD now cost about $50 and *Britannica CD '98 Multimedia Edition* is $125, a small fraction of the $1,500 price for the 32 volume print edition of the same *Encyclopedia*. *Britannica* also offers a World Wide Web subscription at $85 per year or $8.50 per month with a discount to purchasers of the print or CD product. The World Wide Web service is updated thrice annually and offers more articles than the print edition. Of course, the price charged for a given format may reflect differences in the price elasticities of demand. Nevertheless, the lower price for the electronic product is consistent with a considerable cost advantage.

Indeed, the latest word processing software includes tools that will allow anyone who uses word processing to create documents tagged for posting on the World Wide Web. Essentially, anyone who owns a current vintage computer with sufficient network connection can make formatted text with tables and graphics available instantly to everyone on the Net. The cost of such communication is a small fraction of the cost of photocopying and mailing documents.

An important consequence of the dramatic decline in the cost of sharing documents is the likelihood of a dramatic increase in the quantity of material available. Everyone who writes may post the whole history of their work on the web at little incremental cost. Availability is then hardly an issue.

The challenge to academia is to invest in services that will turn the ocean of data into sound, useful, compelling information products. The process of filtering, labeling, refining, and packaging, that is, the process of editing and publishing, takes resources and will be shaped by the electronic world in significant ways. This essay is concerned with this process.

SCHOLAR

Begin with first principles. Academia may become more useful to our society at large by communicating electronically. When electronic scholarship is more valuable, our institutions will invest more.

Scholarship plays three roles in our society. First, academia educates the next generation of professionals, managers, and leaders. Second, it makes formal knowledge available to society at large, stimulating the development of new products, informing debates on public policy, and improving understanding of our culture. Third, it develops new knowledge. Digital communication ought ultimately to be judged by how well it serves these three activities, teaching, service, and research. Consider each in turn.

Access to networked, digital information is already enhancing education. More students at more institutions have access to more information because of the World Wide Web. About 60 percent of high school graduates now pursue some college, and President Clinton has called for universal access to two years of college.[Burd, 1997] The importance of the educational mission is growing. Of course, today networked information is sporadic and poorly organized relative to what it might someday become. Still, the available search services, rapid access, and the wide availability of the network are sufficient to demonstrate the power of the tool. Contrast the service with a conventional two-year college library whose size depends on the budget of the institution, when access often depends on personal interaction with a librarian, and where a student must plan a visit and sometimes even queue for service. Access to well-designed and supported Web-based information gives promise of promoting a more active style of education. Students may have more success with more open-ended assignments, participate in on-line discussion with others pursuing similar topics, and get faster feedback from more colorful, more interactive materials. Integrating academic information into the wider universe of Web information seems likely to have important benefits for students when it is done well.

Similarly, many audiences for academic information outside the walls of the academy already use the World Wide Web. Engineering Information, Inc. (EI) for example, maintains a subscription Website for both academic and non-academic engineers.[Engineering Information] A core feature of the service is access to the premier index to the academic engineering literature with a fulfillment service. But EI's

Village offers on-line access to professional advisers, conversations with authors, and services for practicing engineers. Higher quality, more immediate access to academic information seems likely to play an increasing role in the information sectors of our society, including nearly every career where some college is a common prerequisite. Higher education seems likely to find wider audiences by moving its best materials to the networked, digital arena.

In the business of generating new knowledge, the use of networked information is already accelerating the pace. Working papers in physics, for example, are more rapidly and widely accessible from the automated posting service at Los Alamos than could possibly be achieved by print.[Los Alamos National Labs] In text oriented fields, scholars are able to build concordances and find patterns in ways impossible with print. Duke University's digital papyrus, for example, offers images of papyri with rich, searchable descriptive information in text.[2] In economics, the web gives the possibility of mounting data sets and algorithmic information and so allows scholars to interact with the work of others at a deeper level than is possible in print. For example, Ray Fair maintains his 130 equation model of the US economy on the Web with data sets and a solution method.[Fair] Any scholar who wants to experiment with alternative estimations and forecasting assumptions in a fully developed simulation model may do so with modest effort. In biology, the Human Genome Project is only feasible because of the ease of electronic communication, the sharing of databases, and other on-line tools.[Genome Database] In visually oriented fields, digital communication offers substantial benefits, as video and sound may be embedded in digital documents. Animated graphics with sound may have significant value in simulation models in science. In art and drama, digital files may allow comparative studies previously unimaginable. Digital communication, then, may have its most significant consequence in accelerating the development of new knowledge.

The pace of investment in digital communication within academia may well be led by its value in education, service broadly defined, and research. In each case, institutional revenues and success may depend on effective deployment of appropriate digital communication. Of course, individual scholars face a significant challenge in mastering the new tools and employing them in appropriate ways. It is also worth emphasizing that not all things digital are valuable. However, when digital tools are well used, they are often significantly more valuable than print.

PUBLISHER

The evolution of the digital arena will be strongly influenced by cost and by pricing policies. Cost is a always a two-way street, a reflection, on the one hand, of the choices of authors and publishers who commit resources to publication and, on the other, of the choices of readers and libraries who perceive value. Publishers are challenged to harvest raw materials from the digital ocean and fashion valuable information products. Universities and their libraries must evaluate the possible ways of using digital materials and restructure budgets to deploy their limited resources to best advantage. Between publisher and library stands the electronic agent who may broker the exchange in new ways. Consider first the publisher.

The opportunity to distribute journals electronically has implications for the publishers' costs and revenues. On the cost side, the digital documents can be distributed at lower cost than paper. The network may also reduce some editorial costs. However, sustaining high production values will continue to involve considerable cost because quality editing and presentation are costly. On the revenue side, sale of individual subscriptions may, to some degree, yield to licenses for access via campus intranets and to pay-per-look services.

PUBLISHER COSTS

The central fact of the publishing business is the presence of substantial fixed cost with modest variable cost. The cost of gathering, filtering, refining, and packaging shapes the quality of the publication but does not relate to distribution. The cost of copying and distributing the publication is a modest share of the total expense. A publication with high production values will have high fixed costs. Of course, with larger sale, the fixed costs are spread more widely. Thus, popular publications have lower cost per copy because each copy need carry only a bit of the fixed cost. In thinking about a digital product, the publisher is concerned to invest sufficiently in fixed costs to generate a readership that will pay prices that cover the total cost.

There is a continuum of publications, from widely distributed products with high fixed costs but lower prices to narrowly distributed products with low fixed costs but higher prices. We might expect an even wider range of products in the digital arena.

To understand one end of the publishing spectrum, consider a publisher who reports full financial accounts and is willing to share internal financial records, namely, the American Economic Association (AEA). The AEA is headquartered in Nashville but maintains editorial offices for each of its three major journals in other locations. The AEA has 21,000 members plus 5,500 additional journal subscribers. Membership costs between $52 and $73 per year (students $26) and members get all three journals. The library rate is $140 per year for the bundle of three journals. The Association had revenues and expenditures of $3.7 million in 1995.

The AEA prints and distributes nearly 29,000 copies of the *American Economic Review* (AER), the premier journal in economics. The AER receives nearly 900 manuscripts per year and publishes about 90 of them in quarterly issues. A *Papers and Proceeding* issue adds another 80 or so papers from the Association's annual meeting. The second journal, the *Journal of Economic Perspectives* (JEP), invites authors to contribute essays and publishes more topical, less technical essays, with 56 essays in four issues in 1995. The third journal, the *Journal of Economic Literature* (JEL), contains an index to the literature in economics, indexing and abstracting several hundred journals, listing all new English-language books in economics, and reviewing nearly 200 books per year. The JEL publishes more than 20 review essays each year in four quarterly issues. The three journals together yield about 5,000 pages, about 10 inches of linear shelf space, per year. The index to the economic literature published in JEL is cumulated and published as an *Index of Economic Articles in Journals* in 34 volumes back to 1886, and distributed electronically as *EconLit* with coverage from 1969. The *Index* and *EconLit* are sold separately from the journals.

This publisher's costs are summarized in Figure 1. Some costs seem unlikely to be affected by the digital medium, while others may change significantly. The headquarters function accounts for 27 percent of the AEA's budget. The headquarters maintains the mailing lists, handles the receipts, and does the accounting and legal work. It conducts an annual mail ballot to elect new officers, and organizes an

FIGURE 1. American Economic Association Expenses 1995

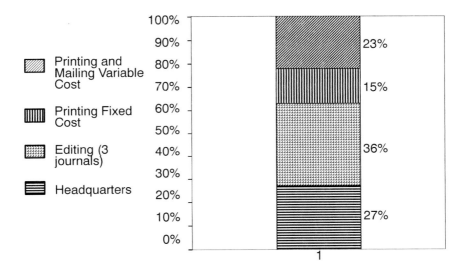

Source: Elton Hinshaw, "Treasurer's Report," *American Economic Review*, May, 1996 and unpublished reports.

annual meeting that typically draws 8,000 persons.[3,4] The headquarters function seems likely to continue in about its current size as long as the AEA continues as a membership organization, a successful publisher, and a coordinator of an annual meeting.[5] Declining membership or new modes of serving members might lead to reduction in headquarters costs. In the short run, headquarters costs are not closely tied to the number of members or sale of journals.

The AEA's second function is editing, the second block in Figure 1. Thirty-six percent of the AEA's annual expenditures goes to the editorial function of its three journals. Eighty-eight percent of the editorial cost is for salaries. The editorial function is essential to maintaining the high production values that are necessary for successful information products.

Operating digitally may provide some cost saving in the editorial function for the *American Economic Review*. The editors could allow manuscripts to be posted on the Internet, referees could access network copies, and dispatch their comments via the network. The flow of some 1,600 referee reports that the AER manages each year might occur faster and at lower cost to both the journals and the referees if the network were used in an effective way.[6] However, the editorial cost will continue to be a significant and essential cost of bringing successful intellectual products to market. Top quality products are likely to have higher editorial costs than lower quality products.

The top two blocks shown in figure 1 describe the 48 percent of the AEA's total budget that goes to printing and mailing. These functions are contracted out, and have recently gone through a competitive bid process. The costs are likely to be near industry lows. The total printing and mailing costs split into two parts. One part doesn't vary with the size of the print run and is labeled as fixed cost. It includes design and typesetting and thus will remain, to a significant degree, as a necessary function in bringing high quality products to market.[7] The variable-cost part of printing and mailing reflects the extra cost of paper, printing, and mailing individual paper issues. These 23 percent of total Association expenditures, $800,000 out of $3.7 million total, might be reduced considerably by using distribution by network. However, as long as some part of the journal is distributed in print, the Association will continue to incur significant fixed costs in printing.

In short, distribution of the journals electronically by network might lower the AEA's expenditures by as much as 23 percent.[8]

PUBLISHER REVENUE

Figure 2 summarizes the American Economic Association's revenues in six categories. Thirty-eight percent of revenue comes from individual memberships. Another five percent comes from the sale of advertising that appears in the journals. Nineteen percent comes from the sale of subscriptions, primarily to libraries. Another 19 percent comes from royalties on licenses of the *EconLit* database, most of these royalties come from SilverPlatter, a distributor of electronic databases. Less than half of one percent of revenues come from selling rights to reprint journal articles. Finally, 17 percent of revenues come from other sources, primarily income from the cumulated reserves as well as net earnings from the annual meeting.[9]

Distributing the journals electronically by network seems likely to change the revenue streams. What product pricing and packaging strategies might allow the AEA to sustain the journals? If the journals

FIGURE 2. American Economic Association Revenues 1995

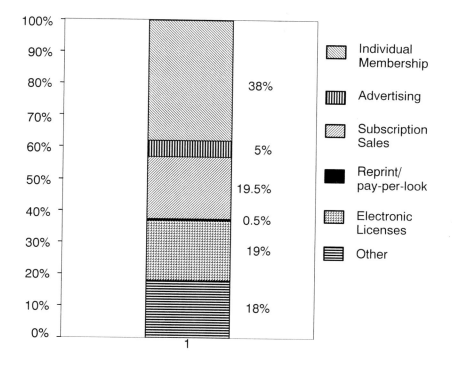

Source: Elton Hinshaw, "Treasurer's Report," *American Economic Review*, May, 1996 and unpublished reports.

are to continue to play an important role in the advance of the discipline, then the Association must be assured that revenue streams are sufficient to carry the necessary costs.

If the library subscription includes a license for making the journals available by network to all persons within a campus, then a primary reason for membership in the Association may be lost. With print, the main distinction between the library subscription and the membership subscription is that the member's copy can be kept at hand while the library copy is at a distance and may be in use or lost. With electronic delivery, access may be the same everywhere on the campus network. The license for electronic network distribution may then undercut revenues from memberships, a core 38 percent of AEA revenues.

The demand for advertising in the journals is probably motivated by distribution of journals to individual members. If individual subscriptions lag, then advertising revenue may fall as well. Indeed, one may ask the deeper question of whether ads associated with electronic journals will be salient when the journals are distributed electronically? The potential for advertising may be particularly limited if the electronic journals are distributed through intermediaries. If a database intermediary provides an index to hundreds of journals and provides links to individual articles on demand, advertising revenue may accrue to the database vendor rather than the publisher of the individual journal.

The AEA might see 43 percent of its revenues (the 38 percent from member fees plus the 5 percent from advertising) as vulnerable to being cannibalized by network licensure of its journals. With only a potential 23 percent saving in cost, the Association will be concerned to increase revenues from other sources so as to sustain its journals. The 20 percent shortfall is about $750,000 for the AEA. Here are three strategies: (a) charge libraries more for campus-use licenses, (b) increase revenues from pay-per-look services, (c) enhance services for members so as to sustain member revenues. Each of these strategies may provide new ways of generating revenue from existing readers, but importantly, may attract new readers.

THE CAMPUS LICENSE

The Association could charge a higher price to libraries for the right to distribute the electronic journals on campus networks. There are about four memberships for each library or other subscription. If membership went to zero because the subscriptions all became campus intranet licenses, then the AEA would need to recoup the revenues from four memberships from each campus license to sustain current revenues. If network distribution lowered AEA costs by 20 percent, then the campus intranet license need only recoup the equivalent of two memberships. Libraries currently pay double the rate of memberships, so the campus intranet license need be only double the current library subscription rate. That is, the current library rate of $140 would need to go to about $280 for a campus-wide intranet license for the three journals.[10] Of course, many campuses have more than one library subscription, say one each in the social science, management, law, and agriculture libraries. The Association might then set a sliding scale of rates from $280 for a small (one library print subscription) campus to $1,400 for a large (five library print subscription) campus.[11] These rates would be the total revenue required by the Association for campus-subscription assuming that the library's print subscriptions are abandoned. A database distributor would add some mark-up.

The campus intranet rate for electronic access is easily differentiated from the print library subscription because it provides a license for anyone on the campus intranet to use the journals in full electronic format. This rate could be established as a price for a new product, allowing the print subscriptions to continue at library rates. Transition from print to electronic distribution could occur gradually with the pace of change set by libraries. Libraries would be free to make separate decisions about adding the campus intranet service and, later, dropping the print subscription.

Individual Association members could continue their print subscriptions as long as they wish, reflecting their own tastes for the print product and the quality of service of the electronic one as delivered. Indeed, individual members might get passwords for direct access to the on-line journals. Some members may not be affiliated with institutions that subscribe to network licenses.

It is possible that the campus intranet license will be purchased by campuses that have not previously subscribed to the AEA's journals. If the institution's cost of participating in network delivery is much less than the cost entailed in sustaining the print subscription, for example, the avoidance of added shelf space as will be discussed below, then more campuses might sign on. This effect may be small for the AEA because it is the premier publisher in economics, but might be significant for other journal publishers.

PAY-PER-LOOK

The AEA has had minimal revenues from reprints and royalties on copies. Indeed, it pioneered in guaranteeing in each issue of its journals, a limited right to copy for academic purposes without charge.[12] The Association adopted the view that the cost of processing the requests to make copies for class purposes (which it routinely granted without charge), were not worth incurring. By publishing a limited, no-charge right to copy, it saved itself the cost of managing the granting of permissions and saved campuses the cost of seeking them.

With electronic distribution, the campus intranet license will automatically grant permission for the journals to be used in course reserves and in print-on-demand services for classes.

On campuses with too little commitment to instruction in economics to justify a library subscription or a campus intranet license, there may still be occasional interest in use of journal articles. There may be law firms, businesses, consulting enterprises, and public interest groups who occasionally seek information and would value the intensity of exploration found in academic journals. With the ubiquitous Internet, they should be able to search a database on-line for a modest usage fee, identify articles of interest, and then call up such articles in full-image format on a pay-per-look basis. Suppose the Internet reaches a million people who are either on campuses without print library subscriptions today or not on campuses at all, but who would have interest in some occasional use of the academic material. This market represents a new potential source of revenue for the AEA which could be reached by an Internet-based a pay-per-look price.

What rate should the Association set per page to serve the pay-per-look market without unduly cannibalizing the sale of campus intranet licenses? Let's take a one-print library subscription campus rate at $280 per year for access to about 3,500 published pages of journal articles (leaving aside the index and abstracts). One look at each published article page per year at eight cents per page would equal the $280 license. A campus that had a distribution of users that averaged one look at each page would break-even with the campus intranet license with a pay-per-look rate of eight cents per page. This rate is the rate of net revenue to the Association, the database distributor may add a mark-up. For discussion, suppose the database distributor's mark-up is 100 percent. If the Internet users beyond the campus intranet licenses looked at 2 million pages per year at 16 cents per page including fees to the Internet service provider, the Association would recoup nearly a quarter of its lost membership revenue from the intranet licenses from this source.

A critical issue for the emergence of a pay-per-look market is the ability to account for and collect the charges with a low cost per transaction. If accounting and billing costs $10 per hit with hits averaging 20 pages, then the charge might be $14.00 per hit ($10 to the agent, $4 to the AEA). Such a rate compares well with the $30 per exchange of costs incurred in conventional interlibrary loan. Yet such high transactions costs will surely limit the pay-per-look market.

A number of enterprises are offering or plan to offer electronic payment mechanisms on the Internet.[13] In the library world, RLG's WebDOC system may have some of the necessary features. These systems depend on users being registered in advance with the Web-bank. As registered users they have accounts and encrypted "keys" that electronically establish their identity to a computer on the net. To make a transaction, a user need only identify herself to the electronic database vendor's computer using the "key" for authentication. The vendor's computer checks the authentication and debits the readers' account at the Web-bank. In this fashion, secure transactions may occur over the network without human intervention at costs of a few cents per hit. If such Web-banks become a general feature of the Internet, Web-money will be used for a variety of purposes. The incremental cost of using them for access to information should be modest and the pay-per-look market gain importance. Mark-ups per transaction might then be quite modest, with gross charges per page in the vicinity of 10 to 20 cents. This rate compares with the four cent per page cost of the *Britannica* when no per page charge is imposed as mentioned in the opening sentence of this essay.

The core idea here is that individual readers make the decisions about when to look at a document under a pay-per-look regime. The reader must face a budget constraint, that is, have a limited set of funds for use in buying information products or other services. The fund might be subsidized by the reader's institution, but the core choices about when to pay and look are made individually. When the core decision is made by the reader with limited funds, then the price elasticity of demand for such services may be high. With a highly elastic demand, even for profit publishers will find that low prices dominate.

Current article fulfillment rates of $10 to $20 could fall by an order of magnitude. The MIT Press offers to deliver individual articles from its electronic journals for $12. EI Village delivers reprints of articles by fax or other electronic means for fees in this range.

ENHANCED MEMBER SERVICES

A third strategy for responding to the possible revenue shortfall from the loss of memberships at the AEA would be to enhance membership services. One approach, proposed by Hal Varian, would be to offer superior access to the electronic journals to members only.[Varian, 1997] The electronic database of journal articles might be easily adapted to provide a personal notification to each member as articles of interest are posted. The Association's database service for members might then have individual passwords for members and store profiles of member interests so as to send e-mail notices of appropriate new postings. The members' database might also contain ancillary materials, appendices to the published articles with detailed derivations of mathematical results offered in software code (for example, as *Mathematica* notebooks), copies of the numerical data sets used in empirical estimation, or extended bibliographies. The members' database might support monitored discussions of the published essays, allowing members to post questions and comments and an opportunity for authors to respond if they wish. These enhancements generally take advantage of the personal relationship a member may want to have with the published literature, a service not necessarily practical or appropriate for libraries.

Indeed, one divide in the effort to distinguish member from library access to the journal database is whether the enhancement would have value to libraries if offered. Libraries will be asked to pay a premium price for a campus intranet license. They serve many students and faculty who are not currently members of the AEA and who are unlikely to become members in any event; for example, faculty from disciplines other than economics. Deliberately crippling the library version of the electronic journals by offering lower resolution pages, limited searching strategies, a delay in access, or only a subset of the content, will be undesirable for libraries and inconsistent with the Association's goal of promoting discussion of economics. However, there may me some demand for lower quality access at reduced prices. The important point is that for membership to be sustained, it must carry worthwhile value when compared to the service provided by the campus license.

Another approach is simply to develop new products that will have a higher appeal to members than to libraries. Such products could be included in the membership fee, but offered to libraries at an added extra cost. One such product would be systematic access to working papers in economics. Indices, abstracts, and in some cases, the full-text of working papers are available without charge at some sites on the World Wide Web today. The Association might ally itself with one of these sites, give the service an official status, and invest in the features of the working paper service to make it more robust and useful. Although freebie working paper services are useful, an enhanced working paper service for a fee (or as part of membership) might be much better.[14]

To the extent that enhanced services can sustain memberships in the face of readily available campus intranet access to journals, the premium for campus intranet access could be lower.

The AEA might offer a discount membership rate to those who opt to use the on-line version of the journals in lieu of receiving print copies. Such a discounted rate would reflect not only the Association's cost saving with reduced print distribution but also the diminished value of membership given the increased prospect of campus intranet licenses.

To the extent that the pay-per-look market generates new revenue, then the campus intranet rate could also be less. The total of the Association's revenues need only cover its fixed and variable costs. (The variable cost may approach zero with electronic distribution.) If membership revenues dropped by two-thirds and pay-per-look generated one-quarter of the gap, then the premium rate for the campus intranet license need be only one-third to one-half above current rates, say, $200 for a one-print subscription campus to $1,000 for a five-print library subscription campus (net revenue to the Association after the net distributor's mark-up).

OTHER PUBLISHERS

At the other end of the publishing spectrum from the AEA are those producing low volume publications. Some titles have few personal subscriptions and depend primarily on library subscriptions that are already at premium rates. For these titles, replacing the print subscription with an intranet license will simply lower costs. The Johns Hopkins University Press offers its journals electronically at a discount in substitution for the print.

Some titles may have mostly personal subscriptions with no library rate, including popular magazines like the *Economist*. Such publications might simply be offered as personal subscriptions on the Internet with an individual password for each subscriber. The distribution by network would lower distribution costs and so ought to cause the profit maximizing publisher to offer network access to individuals at a discount from the print subscription rate. Such a publication may not be available by campus intranet license.

The *Journal of Statistics Education* (JSE) is distributed via the Internet without charge. It began with an NSF/FIPSE grant to the North Carolina State University in 1993. The JSE receives about 40 manuscripts per year and, after a peer review, publishes about 20 of them.[Dietz, 1996] The published essays are posted on a Website and a table of contents and brief summaries are dispatched by e-mail to a list of about 2,000 interested persons. JSE's costs amount to about $25,000 per year to sustain the clerical work necessary to receive manuscripts, dispatch them to suitable referees, receive referee reports, and return them to the author with the editor's judgment. The JSE also requires a part-time system support person to maintain the server that houses the journal. The JSE has not charged for subscriptions, receives no continuing revenue, and needs about $50,000 per year to survive. Merger with a publisher of other statistics journals may make sense, allowing the JSE to be bundled in a larger member service package. Alternatively, it might begin to charge a subscription fee for individuals and a campus license rate for libraries. Making the transformation from a no-fee to a fee-based publication may prove difficult. A critical issue is how much fixed cost is necessary to maintain reasonable production values in a low volume publication. At present, JSE is seeking a continuing source of finance.

In general, a publisher will consider three potential markets: (1) the campus intranet license/library sale, (2) the individual subscription, and (3) the pay-per-look/individual article sale. These three markets might be served by one title with shared fixed costs. The issue of whether to offer the title in each market and at what price will reflect the incremental cost of making the title available in that market, the elasticity of demand in each market, and the cross price elasticities between markets. For example, the price of the campus license will have an effect on individual subscription sales, and the price of the individual subscriptions will have an effect on the sale of individual articles, and vice versa. The more elastic the demands, the lower the prices, even for for-profit publishers. With higher substitution between the three forms, the closer the prices will be across the three forms.[15]

ECONOMIES OF SCOPE

To this point, the analysis applies essentially to one journal at a time, as though the journal were the only size package that counted. In fact, of course, the choice of size of package for information could change. Two centuries ago, the book was the package of choice. Authors generally wrote books. Libraries bought books. Readers read books. In the last fifty years, the size of package shifted to the journal in most disciplines. Authors write smaller packages, that is, articles, and get their work to market more quickly in journals. The elemental information product has become more granular. Libraries commit to journals and so receive information faster and at lower cost per unit. In deciding what to read, readers depend on the editor's judgment in publishing articles. In short, libraries buy bigger packages, the journals, while authors and readers work with smaller units, the articles.

With electronic distribution, the library will prefer to buy a still larger package, a database of many journals. A single, large transaction is much less expensive for a library to handle than the multiple, small transactions. Managing many journal titles individually is expensive. Similarly, readers may prefer access to packages smaller than journal articles. They are often satisfied with abstracts. The electronic encyclopedia is attractive because it allows one to zip directly to a short, focused package of information with links to more. Authors, then, will be drawn to package their products in small bundles embedded in a large database with links to other elements of the database with related information. Information will become still more granular.

If the database becomes the dominant unit of trade in academic information, then those with better databases may thrive. The JSTOR enterprise appears to have recognized the economies of scope in building a database with a large quantity of related journal titles. JSTOR is a venture spawned by the Mellon Foundation to store archival copies of the full historic backfiles of journals and make them available by network. The core motive is to save libraries the cost of storing old journals. JSTOR plans to offer 100 journal titles within a few years. Some of the professional societies, for example, psychology and chemistry, exploit economies of scope in the print arena by offering dozens of journal titles in their disciplines. Elsevier's dominance in a number of fields is based in part on the exploitation of scope with many titles in related subdisciplines. The emergence of economies of scope in the electronic arena is illustrated by Academic Press's offer to libraries in OhioLink. For ten percent more than the cost of the print subscriptions the library had held, it could buy electronic access to the full suite of Academic Press journals electronically on OhioLink.

To exploit the economies of scope, the electronic journal might begin to include hot links to other materials in the database. The electronic product would then deliver more than the print version. Links to other Web-sites is one of the attractive features of the Web-version of the *Encyclopedia Britannica.* An academic journal database could invite authors to include the electronic addresses of references and links to ancillary files. Higher quality databases will have more such links.

The American Economic Association eschews scope in the print arena, preferring instead to let a hundred flowers bloom and to rely on competition to limit prices. Its collection of three journals does not constitute a critical mass of journal articles for an economics database and so it must depend on integration with other economics journals at the database level. The Johns Hopkins University Press's Muse enterprise suffers similar lack of scope. Although it has 45 journal titles, they are scattered among many disciplines and do not, collectively, reach critical mass in any field.

The emergence of more powerful, network-based working paper services seems likely to lower the cost of the editorial process, as mentioned above. A common, well-managed electronic working-paper service might make the cost of adding a journal title much lower than starting a title from scratch without access to electronic working papers. The enterprise that controls a capable working paper service may well control a significant part of the discipline and reap many of the advantages of scope in academic publishing.

In fact, a capable electronic working paper service could support multiple editors of a common literature. One editor might encourage an author to develop a work for a very sophisticated audience and publish the resulting work in a top academic journal. Another editor might invite the author to develop the same ideas in a less technical form for a wider audience. Both essays might appear in a common database of articles and link to longer versions of the work, to numerical data sets, bibliographies, and other related material. The published essays will then be front-ends to a deeper literature available on the Net.

RENTS

In addition to limiting the number of journals it produces, the American Economic Association differs from many publishers by emphasizing low cost. The price of its journals is less than half the industry average for economics journals, and the differential between library and individual rates is low.[Carpenter and Getz, 1995] If the AEA's goal were to maximize profit, it could charge authors more, charge members and libraries more, make more revenue from its meetings, and launch more products to take advantage of its reputation by extending its scope. The rents available in this marketplace are then left to the authors, members, libraries, and competing publishers. The AEA is not maximizing its institutional rents.

Other non-profit publishers may seek higher revenues, to capture more of the available rents, and use the proceeds to generate more products and association services. Lobbying activities, professional certification and accreditation, more meetings, and more journals are common among professional societies.

Many for-profit publishers seek to maximize the rents they can extract from the marketplace for the benefit of their shareholders. In considering how to package and price electronic products, the for-profit publishers will continue to be concerned with finding and exploiting the available rents. The profit maximizing price for a journal is determined by the price elasticity of demand for the title and the marginal cost of producing it. With convenient network access, there may be an increase in demand that would allow a higher price, other things equal. How the price elasticity of demand might change with network access is unknown. The fall in marginal cost with electronic distribution need not lead to a lower price.

One might then ask how a shift to electronic publishing may affect the size of the rents and their distribution. A shift to the database as the optimal size package with falling marginal costs would seem both to increase the size of potential rents and to make easier their exploitation for profit. Suppose control of a powerful working paper service gives a significant cost advantage to journal publishers. Suppose further that academic institutions find major advantages in subscribing to large databases of information rather than making decisions about individual journal titles. The enterprise that controls the working paper service and the database of journals may then have considerable rent capturing ability. The price elasticities of demand for such large packages may be low and the substitutes poor, and so the mark-ups over costs may be substantial. The possibility of a significant pay-per-look market with high price elasticity of demand might cause the profit maximizing price to be lower. The possibility of self-publication at personal or small scale Websites offers a poor substitute to integration in a database because Web search engines are unlike to point to them appropriately.

LIBRARY

In contemplating how to take advantage of electronic publications, universities and their libraries face two problems. First, they face decisions about scaling back costly conventional operations so as to make resources available for acquiring electronic licenses. Second, the cost savings occur in a variety of ways, each with its own history, culture, and revenue sources. Although many boards of trustees and their presidents might like all of the funds within their institutions to be fungible, in fact they face limitations on their ability to reduce expenditures in one area so as to spend more in another. If donors or legislatures are more willing to provide funds for buildings than for electronic subscriptions, then the dollar cost of a building may not be strictly comparable to the dollar cost of electronic subscriptions. Universities are investing more in campus networks and computer systems and are pruning elsewhere as the campuses become more digital. The following paragraphs consider how conventional operations might be pruned so as to allow more expenditure on electronic information products.

CONVENTIONAL LIBRARY COSTS

It is possible that some universities will view electronic access to quality academic journals as sufficiently attractive to justify increasing their library budget to accommodate the electronic subscriptions when publishers seek premium prices for electronic access. Some universities place particular emphasis on being electronic pioneers and seem willing to commit surprising amounts of resources to such activities. Other universities owe a debt to these pathfinders for sorting out what works. However, for most institutions, the value of the electronic journals will be tested by middle management's willingness to prune other activities so as to acquire more electronic journals. The library director is at the front line for such choices and an understanding of the basic structure of the library's expenditures will help define the library director's choices.

Figure 3 provides a summary picture of the pattern of costs in conventional academic libraries. The top four blocks correspond to the operating budgets of the libraries. Acquisitions account for about a third of the operating budget. To give a complete picture, the bottom

FIGURE 3. Conventional Library Costs

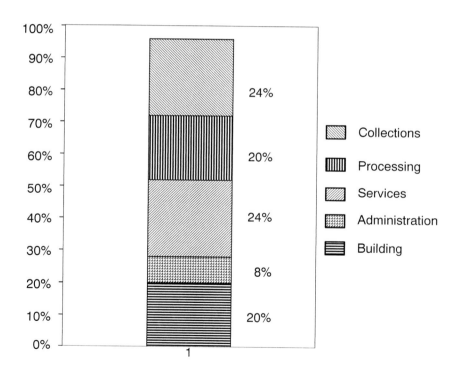

Source: Heuristic characterization based on Association of Research Libraries Annual Statistical Survey on expenditures on materials and operating budgets, and the author's own studies of library space and technical service costs.

section of the figure also accounts for the costs of library buildings. The cost of space is treated as the annual lease value of the space including utilities and janitorial services. The total of the operating budget plus the annualized cost of the building space represents a measure of the total institutional financial commitment to the library.

Library management typically has control only of the operating budget. Let's suppose that, on average, campus intranet licenses to electronic journals come at a premium price, reflecting both the electronic database distributor's costs as well as adjustments in publishers pricing behavior as discussed above. The library, then, confronts a desire to increase its acquisition expenditure, possibly as much as doubling it.

A first choice is to prune expenditures on print so as to commit resources to digital materials. Some publishers offer lower prices for swapping digital for paper and in this case, swapping improves the libraries budget. Some publishers may simply offer to swap digital for print at no change in price. However, many may expect a premium gross price for digital access on the campus intranet. The library manager may seek to trim other acquisition expenditures so as to commit to more digital access. For several decades, academic libraries have been reducing the quantity of materials acquired so as to adjust to increases in prices. The possibility of substantial cuts in the quantity of acquisitions so as to afford a smaller suite of products in electronic access seems unappealing and so may have limited effect.

A second possible budget adjustment is to prune technical service costs. The costs of processing arise from the necessity of tracking the arrival of each issue, claiming those that are overdue, making payments, adjusting catalog records, and periodically binding the volumes. If the electronic journal comes embedded in a database of many journals, the library can make one acquisition decision and one payment. It need have little concern for check-in and the claiming of issues. Testing the reliability of the database will be a concern but presumably large database providers have a substantial incentive to build in considerable redundancy and reliability and will carefully track and claim individual issues, once for all. The library will avoid binding costs. The library will likely have some interest in building references to the electronic database into its catalog. Perhaps the database vendor will provide suitable machine readable records to automate this process.

A third possibility is the library's public service operations. Until a substantial quantity of materials are available and widely used via network, the demand for conventional library hours, reference, and circulation services may change only modestly. In 1996, a third to a half of the references in my students' essays were to World Wide Web sources. However, these sources generally complemented conventional sources rather than being substitutes for them. As front-line journals become commonly accessible by campus networks, the demand for conventional library services may decline. For example, campuses that operate departmental and small branch libraries primarily to provide convenient access to current journals for faculty might be more likely to consolidate such facilities into a master library when a significant number of the relevant journals are available on the Net. These changes are likely to take a number of years to evolve.

A fourth possibility concerns the cost of library buildings. When journals are used digitally by network, the need for added library space declines. Libraries will need less stack space to hold the addition of current volumes. In many larger libraries, lesser used, older volumes are currently held in less expensive, off-site facilities, with new volumes going into the prime space. The marginal stack space, then, is off-site, with costs of perhaps $0.30 per volume per year as a continuing cost for sustaining the perpetual storage of the added volumes.[16] Replacing a 100 year run of a journal with an electronic backfile ought to save about $30 per year in continuing storage costs at a low-cost, remote storage facility. Reductions in the extent of processing and in public services will also reduce requirements for space.

The library building expenses typically do not appear in operating budgets, so saving space has no direct effect on the library budget. The capital costs of buildings are frequently raised philanthropically or paid through a state capital budget, keeping the costs out of the university current accounts. Even utilities and janitorial services may appear in a general university operating budget rather than appearing within the library account. Savings in building costs will accrue to those who fund capital projects and to university general budgets, but often, not to the library operating budget. University presidents and boards may redirect their institutions' capital funds to more productive uses. Of course, the interests of philanthropy and the enthusiasm of state legislators may pose some limit on the ability to make such reallocations. Moreover, library building projects occur relatively infrequently, say every 25 years or so. The savings in capital may not be apparent for some time, or indeed, ever if capital budgets are considered independently of operating budgets. Library buildings, particularly the big ones in the middle of campuses, come to play a symbolic role, an expression of the university's importance, a place of interdisciplinary interaction, a grand presence. Because symbols are important, the master library facility will continue to be important. The marginal savings in building expense will probably be in compact or remote storage facilities and in departmental and smaller branch libraries. Digital access ought then to save the larger campus community some future commitment of capital, but the savings will be visible mostly to the president and board.

A fifth possibility is savings in faculty subscriptions. In law, business, and other schools where faculty have university expense accounts, faculty may be accustomed to paying for personal subscriptions to core journals from the accounts. If the university acquires a campus-wide network license for such journals, the faculty members may rely on the campus license and deploy their expense accounts for other purposes. By adjusting the expense account downward in light of the offering of campus licenses for journals, the university may reclaim some of the cost of the journals. On those campuses and in those departments where faculty members do not have expense accounts and where personal copies of core journals are necessary for scholarly success, the faculty salaries might be adjusted downward over a course of time to reflect the fact that faculty may use the campus license rather than pay for personal subscriptions. Indeed, when the personal subscriptions are not deductible under federal and state income taxes, the cost of subscriptions to the faculty in after tax dollars may be greater than the cost to the university using before tax dollars. As a result a shift to university site licenses for core journals should be financially advantageous for faculty and the university.

In sum, the university may find a number of ways to economize by shifting to digital journals distributed by network. Although direct subscription prices may go up in some cases, the university may trim technical and public services, save space, and offer more perquisites to faculty at some saving in cost.

ELECTRONIC AGENT

Publishers could establish their own digital distribution function by creating a Universal Resource Locator (URL) for each title. The publisher would deal directly with libraries and individual readers. For a number of reasons, the publisher is likely to prefer to work with an agent for electronic distribution. Just as the typesetting and printing is usually performed by contractors, so the design and distribution of electronic products is likely to involve specialized agents. However, the role of electronic distribution agent is becoming more important than that of the printer for two important reasons. The first arises because of economies of scale in managing access to electronic services. The second concerns the potential advantages of integrating individual journals into a wider database of academic information. The electronic agent accepts materials, say journal titles, from publishers and mounts them on electronic services to be accessed by the Internet. The agent captures economies of scale in maintaining the service, in supporting a common payment mechanism, a common search interface and search engine, and may take other steps to integrate articles and journal titles so that the whole is greater than the sum of the parts.

OCLC was an early entrant in the market for electronic distribution of academic journals with *Online Clinical Trials*. *Online Clinical Trials* was priced at \$220 for institutions and \$120 for individuals.[17] OCLC is shifting to a World Wide Web interface in January, 1997 and hopes to offer more than 250 journal titles soon. OCLC's new approach offers publishers the opportunity to sell electronic access to journals by both subscription and pay-per-look.[OCLC, 1996] It charges libraries an access fee based on the number of simultaneous users to be supported and the number of electronic journals to which the library subscribes. Libraries buy subscriptions from publishers. Publishers may package multiple titles together and set whatever rates they choose. The following discussion puts the strategies of OCLC and other electronic agents in a broader context.

STORAGE AND NETWORKS

With electronic documents, there is a basic logistical choice. A storage intensive strategy involves using local storage everywhere. In this case, the network need not be used to read the journal. At the other extreme, the document might be stored once-for-the-world at a single site with network access used each time a journal is read. Between these two extremes, there is a range of choices. With the cost saving of fewer storage sites comes the extra cost of increased reliance on data communication networks.

Data storage is an important cost. Although the unit costs of digital storage have fallen and will continue to fall sharply through time, there is still a considerable advantage to using less storage. Data storage systems involve not simply the storage medium itself, but a range of services to keep the data on-line. A data center typically involves sophisticated personnel, back-up and archiving activities, and the cost of upgrading software and hardware. If ten campuses share a data storage facility, the storage cost per campus should be much less than if each provides its own. Having one storage site for the world might be the lowest storage cost per campus overall.

To use a remote storage facility involves data communication. The more remote the storage, the greater the reliance on data networks. A central problem for data communication is congestion. Data networks typically do not involve traffic-based fees. Indeed, the cost of monitoring traffic so as to impose fees may be cost prohibitive. Monitoring network traffic so as to bill to individuals on the basis of use would require keeping track of the origin of each packet of data and accounting for it by tallying a register that notes source, time, and date. Because even simple mail messages may be broken into numerous packets for network shipment, the quantity of items to be tracked is much more numerous than tracking telephone calls. If every packet must go through the toll plaza, the opportunity for delay and single points of failure may be substantial. Because each packet may follow a different route, tracking backbone use with a tally on each leg would multiply the complexity. Traffic-based fees seem to be impractical for the Internet. Without traffic-based fees, individual users do not face the cost of their access. Just as with urban highways at rush hour, each individual sees only his or her own trip, not the adverse effect of his or her trip in slowing others down. An engineering response to highway congestion is often to build more highways. Yet, the added highways are often congested as well. In data networking, an engineering solution is to invent a faster network. Yet, individuals deciding to use the network will see only their personal costs, and so have little incentive to economize. The demand for bandwidth on networks will surely grow with the pace of faster networks, for example, with personal videophones and other video intensive applications. Without traffic-based pricing, congestion will be endemic in data networks.

Another response to network congestion is to build private networks with controlled access. Building networks dedicated to specific functions seems relatively expensive, but may be necessary to maintain a sufficient level of performance. Campus networks are private, and so access can be controlled. Perhaps investments in networking and technical change can proceed fast enough on individual campuses to allow the campus network to be reliable enough for access to journals and other academic information.

As the telephone companies have launched data network services, they seem likely to introduce time-of-day pricing. Higher rates in prime time and higher rates for faster access speeds are first steps in giving incentives to economize the use of the network and so to reduce congestion. America On Line (AOL) ran into serious difficulty when in late 1996 it shifted from a per hour pricing strategy to a flat monthly rate to match other Internet service providers. AOL was swamped with peak period demand, demand it could not easily manage. The long distance telephone services seem to be moving to simpler pricing regimes, dime-a-minute, for example. The possibility of peak period congestion, however, likely means that some use of peak period pricing in telephones and in network services will remain desirable. In the end, higher education's ability to economize on data storage will depend on the success of the networks in limiting congestion.

Some milestones in the choice of storage and networks are illustrated along the horizontal margin of Figure 4. The rapid growth of the World Wide Web in the last couple of years has represented a shift toward the right along this margin, with fewer storage sites and more dependence on data communication. The World Wide Web allows a common interface to serve many computer platforms, replacing proprietary tools. Adobe's Portable Document Format (PDF) seems to offer an effective vehicle to present documents in original printed format with equations, tables, and graphics, yet allow text searching and hypertext links to other Websites. The software for reading PDF documents is available without charge, compatible with many Web

FIGURE 4. Network Intensity and Database Integration

Database Integration

5	Full Index, Fulfillment, Links to Exrended Literature				**Compre-hensive, Linked**
4	Full Index with Fullfillment				
3	Core Literature, Simple Searching, Fulfillment		**Campus Gigabytes**		**OCLC's E-Library**
2	Journal Group				
1	Journal Alone	**Personal CD**	**CD on Campus Net**		**URL for each Journal**
Storage		Personal Copy	Library	Campus	Consortia	Once for World
Network		None	In Building	Intranet	Regional	World
		1	**2**	**3**	**4**	**5**

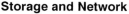

Storage and Network

browsers, and allows local printing. Some of the inconveniences of older network-based tools are disappearing.

The electronic agent may have an advantage over either the publisher or the library in taking advantage of the rightward shift. That is, the electronic agent may acquire rights from publishers and sell access to libraries, while taking responsibility for an optimal choice of storage sites and network access. Storage might end up in a low cost location with the electronic agent responsible for archiving the material and migrating the digital files to future hardware and software environments.

INTEGRATION INTO A DATABASE

The second advantage for an electronic agent is in integrating individual journal titles and other electronic materials into a coherent database. The vertical margin of Figure 4 sketches a range of possibilities. At root, a journal title stands as a relatively isolated vehicle for the distribution of information. In the digital world, each title could be distributed on its own CD or have its own Universal Resource Locator on the Web. Third party index publishers would index the contents and provide pointers to the title and issue, and perhaps to the URL. Indeed, the pointer might go directly to an individual article.

However, relatively few scholars depend on a single journal title for their work. Indeed, looking at the citations shown in a sampling of articles of a given journal reveals that scholars typically use a range of sources. A database that provides coherent access to several related journals, as in the second tier of Figure 4, offers a service that is more than the sum of its parts.

At yet a higher level, an agent might offer a significant core of the literature in a discipline. The core of journals and other materials might allow searching by words and phrases across the full content of the database. The database then offers new ways of establishing linkages.

At a fourth level, the organizing engine for the database might be the standard index to the literature of the discipline, such as *EconLit* in economics. A search of the database might achieve a degree of comprehensiveness for the published literature. A significant fraction of the published essays might be delivered on demand by hitting a "fulfill" button. Fulfillment might mean delivery of an electronic image file via network within a few seconds or delivery of a facsimile within a few minutes or hours.

At a fifth level, the database might include hot-links from citations in one essay to other elements of the database. The database might include the published works from journals with links to ancillary materials, numeric data-sets, computer algorithms, an author's appendices discussing methods and other matters. The database might invite commentary and so formal publications might link to suitably moderated on-line discussions.

The electronic agent may have an advantage over publishers who offer only individual journal titles in integrating materials from a variety of sources into a coherent database. The agent might set standards for inclusion of material that specifies metatags and formats. The agent might manage the index function, indeed, the index might be a basis for forward integration with database distribution as Engineering Information has done. This issue is discussed more fully below.

Integration of diverse materials into a database is likely to come with remote storage and use of networks for access. Integrating the material into a database by achieving higher levels of coherence and interaction among diverse parts may be at lower cost for an electronic agent than for publishers of individual journals or for individual libraries. The agent is able to incur the cost of integration and storage once for the world.

AGENT'S STRATEGY

Given the interest of publishers in licensing their products for campus intranets and the universities' interest in securing such licenses, there is opportunity for enterprises to act as brokers, to package the electronic versions of the journals in databases and make them accessible, under suitable licenses, to campus intranets. The brokers may add a mark-up to reflect their cost of mounting the database. The size of the mark-up will reflect the extent of integration as well as the choice of storage strategy.

SilverPlatter became the most successful vendor of electronic index databases, making them available on compact disks for use on campus intranets with proprietary software. OCLC plays an important role in offering such databases from its master center in Ohio. A number of other vendors have also participated in the index market and are likely to seek to be brokers for the electronic distribution of journals. Ovid is a third vendor, one that supports sophisticated indexing that integrated full-text with standard generalized mark-up language (SGML) and hypertext mark-up language (HTML) tagging.

A core strategy will probably be to mount the database of journals on one or more servers on the World Wide Web, with access limited to persons authorized for use from licensed campuses or through other fee-paid arrangements. This strategy has three important parts, the database server, the Internet communication system, and the campus network.

The advantage of the World Wide Web approach is that the data can be made accessible to many campuses with no server support on any campus. A campus intranet license can be served remotely, saving the university the expense of software, hardware, and system support for the service.

The risk of the Web strategy is with the Internet itself and its inherent congestion. OCLC used a private data communication network so as to achieve a higher level of reliability than the Internet and will do the same to assure high quality TCP/IP (the Internet Protocol) access. Some campuses may prefer to mount database files locally, using CD-ROMs and disk servers on the campus network. Some high intensity campuses may prefer to continue to mount the most used parts of databases locally even at extra cost, as a method of ensuring against deficiencies in Internet services.

The third element after storage and the Internet is the campus network. Campus networks continue to evolve. Among the hundred universities seeking to be top-ten universities, early investment in sophisticated networking may play a strategic role in the quest for rank. On such campuses, network distribution of journals should be well supported and popular. Other campuses will follow with some lag, particularly where funding depends primarily on the public sector. Adoption within ten years might be expected. [Getz et al., 1997]

The electronic agent, then, must choose a strategy with two elements, a storage and network choice and an approach to database integration.

Journal publishers generally start at the bottom left, the closest to print. They could make a CD and offer it as an alternative to print for current subscribers. The AEA offers the *Journal of Economic Literature* on CD instead of print for the same price.

Moves to the upper left seem to be economically infeasible. Integrating more materials together increases local storage costs and so tilts the storage-network balance toward less storage and more network. With more data integration, the agent's strategy will shift to the right.

Moves to the lower right with reduced storage costs and more dependence on networks should involve considerable cost savings but run risks. One risk is of network congestion. A second is of loss of revenues because traditional subscribers drop purchases in favor of shared network access. The viability of these strategies depends on the level of fees that may be earned from network licenses or pay-per-look.

Moves along the diagonal up and to the right involve greater database integration with cost savings from lower storage costs and more dependence on networks. The advantage of moves upward and to the right is the possibility that integration creates services of significantly more value than replicating print journals on the Internet. When database integration creates significantly more value, subscribers will be willing to pay premium prices for using products with remote storage with networks. Of course, network congestion will remain a concern.

A move toward more database integration raises a number of interesting questions. The answers to these questions will determine the size of the mark-up by the electronic agent. How much should information from a variety of sources be integrated into a database with common structure, tags, and linkages? For a large database, more effort at integration and coherence may be more valuable. Just how much effort, particularly how much hand effort, remains an open question. If the electronic agent passively accepts publications from publishers, the level of integration of materials may be relatively low. The publisher may provide an abstract and metatags and might provide Universal Resource Locators for linking to other network sites. The higher level of integration associated with controlled vocabulary indexing, and a more systematic structure for the database than comes from journal titles would seem to require either a higher level of handwork by an indexer or the imposition of standard protocols for defining data elements. Is a higher level of integration of journal material from a variety of sources sufficiently valuable to justify its cost? The index function might be centralized with storage of individual journals distributed around the net. Physical integration of the database is not necessary to logical integration, but will common ownership be necessary to achieve the control and commonality necessary for high levels of integration?

A second question concerns how an agent might generate a net revenue stream from its initial electronic offerings sufficient to allow it to grow. The new regime will not be borne as a whole entity, rather it will evolve in relatively small steps. Each step must generate a surplus to be used to finance the next step. Early steps that generate larger surpluses seem likely to define paths that are more likely to be followed. Experimentation with products and prices is already underway.

Those agents finding early financial success are likely to attract publishers and libraries, and to be imitated by competitors.

JSTOR has captured the full historic run of a significant number of journals, making the promise of 100 titles in suites from major disciplines within three years. However, it does not yet have a program for access to current journals. Its program then is primarily to replace archival storage of materials libraries may or may not have already acquired in print.

OCLC's approach is to sell libraries access services while publishers sell subscriptions to the information. The publisher can avoid the cost of the distribution in print, a saving if the electronic subscriptions generate sufficient revenue. The unbundling of access from subscription sales allows the access to be priced on the basis of simultaneous users, that is akin to the rate of use, while the information is priced on the basis of quantity and quality of material made available. Of course, the information may also be priced on a pay-per-look basis and so earn revenue as it is used. What mix of pay-per-look and subscription sales will ultimately prevail is an open question.

A third question is whether publishers will establish exclusive arrangements with electronic agents, or whether they will offer non-exclusive licenses so as to sustain competition among agents. Some publishers may prefer to be their own electronic agents, retaining control of the distribution channels. If database integration is important, this strategy may be economic only for relatively large publishers with suites of journals in given disciplines. Many publishers may choose to distribute their products through multiple channels both to capture the advantages of more integration with other sources, but also to promote innovation and cost savings among competing distributors.

As the electronic agents gain experience and build their title lists, competition among them should drive down the mark-ups for electronic access. If the store-once and network strategy bears fruit, the cost saving in access should be apparent. If higher levels of database integration prove to be important, the cost savings may be modest. Cost savings here are in terms of units of access. As the cost of access falls, the quantity of information products used may increase. The effect on total expenditure, the product of unit cost and number of units used, is hard to predict. If the demand for information proves to be price elastic, then as unit costs and unit prices fall, expenditures on information will increase.

The electronic agents will gather academic journals from publishers and distribute them in electronic formats to libraries and others. They will offer all available advantages of scale in managing electronic storage, optimize the use of networks for distribution, offer superior search interfaces and engines, and take steps to integrate materials from disparate sources into a coherent whole. The agent will be able to offer campus intranet licenses, personal subscriptions, and pay-per-look access from a common source. The agent may manage sales, accounting, billing, and technical support. Today, agents are experimenting with both technical and pricing strategies. It remains to be seen whether single agents will dominate given content areas, whether major publishers can remain apart, or whether publishers and universities can or should sustain a competitive market among agents.

CONCLUSION

Higher education faces a significant challenge in discovering what academic information will succeed on the Net. In 1996, the MIT Press launched *Studies in Nonlinear Dynamics and Econometrics* (SNDE), one of six titles that the Press distributes by network. The price per year is $40 for individuals and $130 for libraries.[18] MIT's strategy seems to be to launch titles in disciplines where an electronic journal has some extra value, for example, including links to computer code and data sets.[19] The rates for the journals seem to be well below those quoted by OCLC's electronic journal program and lower than at least some new print journals. The cost of launching a new journal electronically seems to be falling. It remains to be seen whether the electronic journals will attract successful editors and valued manuscripts from authors, but the venture shows promise. The number and quality of electronic journals continues to grow. MIT has decided to forgo the use of an electronic agent and so depend only on conventional, independent indexing services for database integration, an incremental approach. Yet, the potential seems greater than an individual journal title reveals.

When Henry Ford launched the first mass produced automobile, he chose a design that carried double the load, went three times farther, and four times faster than the one-horse buggy it replaced, and yet was modestly priced. Successful digital information products for academia seem likely to exploit the inherent advantages of the digital arena, the timeliness, the sophisticated integration of new essays into the existing stock, the links from brief front-end items to more elaborate treatment, the opportunity to interact with the material by asking for "fulfillment," "discussion," and the "underlying data." Network delivery will make possible both the campus intranet license and the sale of information on a pay-per-look basis. It will allow the material to be more readily consulted in circles beyond the academy.

Electronic agents will play significant new roles as intermediaries between publishers and campuses by handling the electronic storage and distribution, and by integrating material into a more coherent whole. Universities and their libraries will make adjustments in operations so as to expend less on conventional activities and more on digital communication.

Of course, there are unknowns. Agents and publishers will experiment to discover optimal pricing strategies. Agents will explore different ways of storing and delivering electronic products and different approaches to integration. Campuses and libraries will consider just what extra dimensions of service are worth their price. The process here is one of bringing order, meaning, and reliability to the emerging world of the Internet, of discovering what sells and what doesn't.

In the end, universities should be drawn to the electronic information services because of their superiority in instruction, their reach beyond the academy, and their power in the creation of new ideas. American higher education is largely shaped by competitive forces, the competition for faculty, students, research funding, public, and philanthropic support. In different ways, the private and public sector, the large institutions and the small, the two-year and four-year institutions share the goal of doing a better, more cost effective job of expanding the human potential. When artfully done, the digital sharing of ideas seems likely to expand that potential significantly.

NOTES

1. Project Gutenberg was a twenty-five year effort led by Michael S. Hart at the University of Illinois to create, store, and make accessible ASCII files of public domain materials from the Constitution, the Bible, Shakespeare, and beyond. A large part of the Project Gutenberg files moved to the Library at the University of Maryland after this essay was written. See http://www.inform.umd.edu/EdRes/ReadingRoom/.

2. Duke's digital papyri are at http://scriptorium.lib.duke.edu/papyrus/ with 1,373 images of Egyptian papyri with a significant database of descriptive textual material.

3. The headquarters publishes *Job Openings in Economics* (JOE) seven times a year with nearly 1,500 job announcements. In 1995, JOE had about 4,000 subscribers and generated about $41,000 of revenue with a base rate of $15 per year ($7.50 for students, $25 for non-members and institutions). The sum of monthly printing and mailing cost was associated with the number of copies produced and the number of pages per copy for 1995 and 1996 as follows (with t-ratios in parenthesis):

Print & Mail = $-$ 1,129.57 + 0.875 # of copies + 76.725 pages per issue
                  ($-$ 2.83)(7.35)   (17.2)

This relationship is estimated from data on each of 14 issues over the two years and has an adjusted R-square of = 0.957. Over this era, JOE averaged 25 pages per issue (ranging from 11 to 51). With seven issues per year, this equation forecasts total printing and mailing costs of $30,019 for 4,000 copies.

JOE became available without charge on a gopher site at Vanderbilt (gopher://www.vanderbilt.edu:70/11/employment/joe) in 1994. The JOE gopher is generating about 25,000 hits per month in 1996 and the subscription list of the printed JOE has dropped to 1,000. The Print & Mail relationship estimated above forecasts a cost of $11,645 for 1,000 copies. The Association will move from a net revenue position of $11,000 ($41,000 - $30,019) in the all print regime to about a zero net ($15,000 - $11,645) with print subscription sales at about a 1,000. Of course, the Association incurs fixed costs in producing JOE that may be similar under both regimes.

4. The headquarters also publishes a Directory of membership biennially. The Directory became available on-line at the University of Texas in 1995 and is getting about 4,600 hits per month. Because the Directory comes with membership, we have no measure of the rate of decline in the demand for the print version.

5. At some point in the future, membership ballots might be solicited and received by the Internet.

6. The AER's reviewing process is double-blind, with authors' names withheld from reviewers and reviewers' names kept from authors. When nearly all working papers are posted on the World Wide Web, the refereeing may become single-blind de facto. Anyone who wants might search the title listing in the working paper file and so identify the author. When working papers are generally accessible on the Net, they would seem to be usable in the editorial process with some saving in cost but with some loss in anonymity.

7. The fixed costs of a print run (but not typography) would be eliminated entirely if print were abandoned completely. The fixed costs of electronic distribution would replace them in part. Presumably, the more sophisticated the electronic files submitted by authors, the lower the fixed cost of production at the publisher.

8. Since 1995, the Association has made the JEL available in CD-ROM format instead of print for the same price. The CD-ROM costs about the same to produce on the margin per subscriber as a printed issue of a large journal. The CD-ROM contains the page images of the published journal and is distributed by mail. Its advantage is not reduced cost, but increased subscriber benefit: It adds the power of electronic searching. Therefore, this version is gaining popularity. More than ten percent of the AEA's members opted for the CD-ROM version of JEL in 1996.

9. The annual meeting contributed a net of about $125,000 in 1995.

10. Assume the current library subscription rate of $140 yields 20 percent of the AEA's gross and that membership plus ads yields $70, about 40 percent. Assume the shift to electronic distribution lowers total expenditures by 20 percent, a saving of about $140 per library subscription. The campus intranet license then needs to generate double its current amount, about $280.

11. The notion of doubling the library subscription rate in setting a rate for the campus intranet license is meant to define the Association's probable revenue goals, but not to define the rate structure. The rate structure will need to be tied to something more substantial like enrollment and total research dollars. Alternatively, the rate could be set on the basis of a forecast of the hit rate. OCLC's electronic journal service sets rates on the basis of the number of simultaneous users. The level of rates would likely be set so as to yield about double the current library print subscriptions unless other revenue is forthcoming as discussed in the following paragraphs.

12. Here is part of the language the AEA prints on the copyright page. "Permission to make digital or hard copies of part or all of this work for personal or classroom use is granted without fee provided that copies are not made or distributed for profit or direct commercial advantage and that copies show this notice on the first page or initial screen of a display along with the full citation, including the name of the author."

13. Sandberg reports an offering from CyberCash, a firm working with Visa and several banks. Cybercash put the cost of a transaction at between eight and 31 cents for purchases between $0.25 and $10. http://www.research.digital.com:80/SRC/millicent/describes the protocols and tools developed by Digital Equipment Corporation to facilitate Web transactions in fractions of cents. "The key innovations of Millicent are its use of brokers and of scrip. Brokers take care of account management, billing, connection maintenance, and establishing accounts with vendors. Scrip is microcurrency that is only valid within the Millicent-enabled world."

14. Getz "Petabytes of Information" lists some features that might be added to the network working paper service. Each Association member might receive a private password and encryption key. When the member submits a paper with the password and key, the service would return a time-stamped digital authentication message. This message and the posting would establish ownership to the working paper at the time of submission. The working paper service might include a more elaborate system of tagging papers, including the author's sense of the target audience, degree of originality, sophistication, empirical content, and revision number. The service might include links to comments.

15. The issue of optimal pricing for three products that share a fixed cost and where cross elasticities are not zero should be explored formally.

16. Getz "Information Storage" suggests that high density off-site storage might yield an annual cost of $0.30 per volume and so, about $3.00 of capital cost.

17. OCLC's Electronic Journals Online (EJO) preceded the Web-based program. With EJO, OCLC charged publishers for mounting their journals, much as printers charge for printing. This approach did not attract many publishers. The OCLC Website (www.OCLC.org) lists several titles. Here is a sample of subscription rates. *The Online Journal of Current Clinic Trials* from Chapman & Hall is distributed by OCLC: Institutional: $220.00, Individual: $120.00, Student (with ID): $ 49.00, Network (unlimited access): $3,000.00. *Online Journal of Knowledge Synthesis for*

Nursing from Sigma Theta Tau International, distributed by OCLC: Individuals, $60.00; Institutions, $250.00.

18. SNDE is one of six electronic journals offered by the MIT Press in 1996 at http://mitpress.mit.edu/jrnls-catalog/snde.html. The library rate includes a license to store the journal on a campus facility and make it available in library reserve services.

19. The MIT Press puts the subscription rate for its electronic journals at $30 for individuals, $125 for libraries, with a $12 fee for downloading an individual article.

REFERENCES

Baker, Shirley. Talk at Washington University, November, 1996.

Burd, Stephen. "President Pushes Tax Breaks to Help Families Afford College," *Chronicle of Higher Education*, January 17, 1997, p. A33.

Carpenter, David and Malcolm Getz. "Evaluation of Library Resources in the Field of Economics: A Case Study," *Collection Management* 20:1/2, 1995, pp. 49-89.E.

Dietz, Jacquelin. "The Future of the Journal of Statistics Education," North Carolina State University, mimeo, 1996.

Engineering Information, www.ei.org.

Fair, Ray. "The Fair Model," http://fairmodel.econ.yale.edu/.

Frost, Robin. "The Electronic Gutenberg Fails to Win Mass Appeal," *Wall Street Journal*, November 21, 1996, p. B6.

The Genome Database, The Johns Hopkins University Bioinformatics Web Server, http://www.bis.med.jhmi.edu/.

Getz, Malcolm. "Information Storage," *Encyclopedia of Library and Information Science*, Vol. 52, Supplement 15, 1993, pp. 201-39. High density off-site storage might yield an annual cost of $0.30 per volume and so, about $3.00 of capital cost.

Getz, Malcolm. "Petabytes of Information," in *Advances in Library Administration and Organization*, XII (JAI Press, 1994) pp. 203-37.

Getz, Malcolm, John J. Siegfried and Kathryn A. Anderson. "Adoption of Innovations in Higher Education," *The Quarterly Review of Economics and Finance*, 37 #3 (Fall, 1997) pp. 605-31.

Los Alamos National Labs, http://xxx.lanl.gov/.

OCLC. "Bringing Your Publications Online With OCLC," (Dublin, Ohio, c. 1996) and OCLC, "A Complete Electronic Journals Solution for Your Library," (Dublin, Ohio, c. 1996).

Sandberg, Jared. "Cash Advances Aid Electronic Commerce," *Wall Street Journal*, September 30, 1996 p. B8, reports an offering from CyberCash, a firm working with Visa and several banks. Cybercash put the cost of a transaction at between eight and 31 cents for purchases between $0.25 and $10.

Varian, Hal. "The AEA's Electronic Publishing Plans: A Progress Report," *Journal of Economic Perspectives* 11(3) Summer 1997 pp. 95-104.

Pricing Models: Past, Present, and Future?

David Stern

INTRODUCTION

This article will attempt to briefly address the major factors leading to change in the academic science, technology and medical (STM) journal market and then focus on a number of possible cost models that may supplement and/or possibly replace the current paper-based distribution systems. A tiered model is proposed that attempts to address the major commercial and noncommercial aspects of the STM information distribution and archiving process. The goal is to create a relatively simple, predictable, reviewable flat-rate budget scheme for quality STM items with market value *and* support for the archiving of nonmarketable information items in relation to both local and global needs. The focus is on a balance between guaranteed publishing revenue (as subscriptions or other packages) and transactional fees through direct billing or aggregator gateways.

Two assumptions underlie this proposal: (1) the tenure and promotion process will accept the validity of the peer-review process whether the item is distributed as a marketable or nonmarketable item, and (2) abstract and indexing (A&I) services will cover both marketable and nonmarketable items.

David Stern is Director of Science Libraries and Information Services, Kline Science Library, Yale University.

[Haworth co-indexing entry note]: "Pricing Models: Past, Present, and Future?" Stern, David. Co-published simultaneously in *The Serials Librarian* (The Haworth Press, Inc.) Vol. 36, No. 1/2, 1999, pp. 301-319; and: *Head in the Clouds, Feet on the Ground: Serials Vision and Common Sense* (ed: Jeffrey S. Bullington, Beatrice L. Caraway, and Beverley Geer) The Haworth Press, Inc., 1999, pp. 301-319. Single or multiple copies of this article are available for a fee from The Haworth Document Delivery Service [1-800-342-9678, 9:00 a.m. - 5:00 p.m. (EST). E-mail address: getinfo@haworthpressinc.com].

Some important points:

- Recognition that not all quality scientific information can be distributed on a commercially successful revenue basis. Some items, even the entire literature from some disciplines, may need to be housed on nonprofit servers. This may be due to a number of factors such as small user bases or little perceived (economic) importance for the field.
- Non-journal material and non-peer-reviewed material will become important items and should be included in both the A&I services and future information packages.
- Differential pricing should exist for various user populations. Large universities should not pay the same amount as small colleges for the same data if the data are used differently. Ultimately usage should determine costs. Some plans now include variable costs measures for CPU time, profit or nonprofit organizational missions, percent contribution to work in the field, etc.
- Libraries are more interested in flat-fee plans and are willing to pay a small premium for this service instead of creating cumbersome tracking mechanisms for frequently used materials.
- Transactional (pay-per-view) and "prepay block" materials may not be commercially viable unless there is a large enough subscription base for first production costs. Those items that do not survive in the market world will migrate to the "Tier 2" nonmarket arena.

The Tier 2 arena will be subsidized by a balance of direct or indirect government, commercial, and society dollars. The balance will be determined by the perceived value of the material to the larger population. (Higher value equals higher public funding.) Logical hosts for these Tier 2 services might include present organizations (e.g., CRL [Center for Research Libraries] and OCLC) and newer options (e.g., the LANL [Los Alamos National Laboratory] preprint server).

Over time, publisher-based cost models will be migrated to discipline-based plans. These plans will be organized around aggregators that will maintain flexible tracking and validation options that closely match local site requirements.

Technology to accomplish these goals is not the problem; cooperation among publishers, A&I services, and faculty will be the most difficult element. All players must recognize the long-term benefits to this model. If some movement toward such a model is not evident soon, the present system will experience a crash in terms of tenure and promotion support. The drain on the higher end of the market from the currently subsidized nonmarketable titles will create impossible subscription costs across the present system.

Many current commercial titles will (and should) fall into the Tier 2 level.

The tiered model provides:
- Two levels of desirable (and budgetable) flat-fee support for identified core materials if the items are marketable. Annual statistical analysis determines the level of payment.
- Two levels of risky revenue support (payment dependent upon specific needs) for non-core materials. Non-core designation is dependent upon local needs.
- One level of subsidized archives for nonmarketable materials.
- New aggregator roles for search, charge, tracking, and validation across publishers, which will generate both costs (hardware and software) and revenue.

WHY IS CHANGE NECESSARY?

I. Complexity. The complexity of the pricing issue is directly related to the new options made available by distribution technology. No longer is there one, and only one, solution to information distribution on a sales basis. The familiar, comfortable, paper paradigm, with its subscription, ownership, and archive options (and static items) is now being enhanced through a variety of alternatives, some offering only convenience by mimicking the paper paradigm and some going far beyond in terms of options. This discussion will *only* address pricing models in relation to academic materials, and is not relevant for trade publications, which have an entirely different mission and socio-economic niche.

II. The power is in value, or added value, to be more precise. The primary value in the traditional paper publication process was in the peer review, editing, typesetting, distribution, and archiving of materials. The added value was in the validation and filtering services provided to researchers by this process. The eventual explosion of paper journals resulted in the development of even more powerful added-value validation and filtering tools, namely, abstracts and indexes. Early in the scientific enterprise we had already seen a problem with the identification of relevant material from among the large amount of material published.

The question of how much of this material (and at what level of quality) to purchase/support was impossible to ask, since there was no alternative means of distributing this data; it was either pay for the paper or lose the data. A good deal of the data was actually lost even though it was printed and distributed. Remember the discovery of Mendelian genetics?

Another important enhancement to the traditional publication process was the addition of images (e.g., charts, tables, or photographs) to the material. These items, as well as advertising materials, were often not indexed and were only discovered through browsing.

As an aside, those systems that still claim to provide full text when they actually serve only ASCII text must change their sales advertising to avoid confusion with those offering real full text as either PDF or other SGML/XML/HTML and image products.

There are real reasons to provide these new distribution tools, reasons beyond the typical marketing of any new electronic toy. That reason is for the utilization of the enhanced capabilities.

From an economic perspective, simple searching of traditional A&I services no longer provides much added value in certain niche populations. The advent of free search systems, such as CARL UnCover, and the development of government-funded search and retrieval databases, such as PubMed (Medline) and the Astrophysics Data System (ADS), make the identification of published articles very easy and often free. In addition, many of the not-for-profit and for-profit publishers even provide free searching of their bibliographic data, some including abstracts, freely on the Internet. It will not be long before a federated site searches all these tools at one time for no charge.

Of course, there are also commercial products that will offer the same service tailored for specific users, and possibly adding new value, be it fancy interfaces or real value. Some new system enhancements include added scope and coverage (Web data and preprints–Ei Electronic Village), personal file cabinets and comments (IoP Co-DAS), seamless bi-directional links between articles and nonbibliographic data (ADS), and document delivery options (Northern Light, Electronic Library).

In many of these new tools the value is not only in the published data itself, but in the added value, the filtering and seamless authorization (electronic commerce) to the data. The data itself are often freely available on preprint servers (or very inexpensively from reprint/document delivery services) if one is willing to search.

III. New paradigm cost issues. If in the future of information access there is great commercial value for portions of current journal articles (e.g., data packages such as images, tables, and data supplementary material), for the finding aids (and the metadata descriptors used for this identification), and for seamless delivery, perhaps we will need new concepts of revenue items and revenue sources.

The traditional idea of subscriptions for undifferentiated materials by journal title is becoming less relevant. Packaging of materials can now be done based upon considerations other than paper distribution. Of course, some of the values of paper journals are still important, for example, evidence of data quality through peer review (a result of editorial boards legitimatized through publisher branding) or the pre-selection of related items. Other traditional values might not be as important in the future (e.g., typesetting, advertising, etc.). The desirable portions of traditional journals can be continued in electronic publications in a variety of ways and possibly with less expense. One example of this approach is seen at the American Physical Society, where they are testing such efficiencies and the incorporation of added-value options in their new *PRST-AB* online journal. The current plan for funding is through author support.

Given these factors, one can assume that eventually journal articles will no longer be the only items of purchase, but will be supplemented and/or replaced by parts of items and/or packages of related materials from a variety of sources (e.g., previously published materials such as Springer handbook materials and Elsevier dictionaries, which are now available electronically by title or segment). In addition, library missions (and library relationships with journal publishers) may change dramatically as archives of full journal sets are no longer required at all sites. But of course some archival mechanism(s) will still be required.

IV. Archival concerns. Possible archival solutions might include a mix of the following options:

- Geographic clearinghouses (Internet carrying capacity limitations may cause bottlenecks)
- Discipline-based centers of excellence (discounts for those capable of and interested in housing large data files)
- Consortial economies of scale (e.g., OhioLink, HighWire, OCLC, CRL)
- Society-based clearinghouses (e.g., APS PROLA)
- Government-funded clearinghouses for direct overhead support (e.g., LANL)

Regardless of the archival solution, there will need to be some budget for hardware, software, and personnel support. The scalability and federation of these clearinghouses will also require technological research and development, with their associated costs.

V. Gateway services for seamless access. Gateways, and their associated costs, will be an integral part of the new seamless information search and delivery system. Regardless of where the citation was located, users will still require gateways for validation, transaction logging and cost-recovery tracking, and cross-linkage of services. The Coalition for Networked Information (CNI), is currently involved in the investigation of authentication (electronic commerce) services. Under the auspices of the CNI, Clifford Lynch recently edited a "White Paper on Authentication and Access Management Issues in Cross-organizational Use of Networked Information Resources" (available at http://www.cni.org/projects/authentication/).

VI. Revenue sources over time. Where will these archiving and access funds come from? Will they be in the form of guaranteed subscribers and/or transactional buyers? They obviously cannot be supported entirely from library subsidies, as this revenue source has been static at best and often shrinking in terms of buying power in recent years. And what changes are coming that will affect the final costs (e.g., levels of editorial effort, continued duplication of paper and online, archiving requirements, additional integrated media support)?

VII. Other considerations. An area that needs further analysis and design is validation and logging by "type of rights" (unlimited access, prepaid blocks of accesses, subsidized access, etc.).

Another area of design and cost modeling issues to be considered is that of end user options. Up until now most models have only addressed individual users at networked workstations. IP validation provides a solution for group access but not for enhanced data utility scenarios (saved strategies, personal preferences) which often require cookies or personalized user spaces. There are multiple needs/requirements for individual end users that must be considered. Individuals may be happy with generic options, but some users desire advanced options. Customization options may use sophisticated personal commenting and virtual file cabinet capabilities. Data manipulation requirements (rather than simple delivery of PDF images) may utilize the enhanced capabilities of SGML or XML data files. There are an entirely different set of concerns for groups; for example, some populations might include laboratory or reading group collaborations and classes using reserve materials.

There are also many issues of access for legitimate researchers away from home, for instance, in the case of scholars requiring access to institutionally subscribed data from off-site while on sabbatical, or scholars expecting traditional reciprocal library privileges.

HISTORY OF THE REACTIONS
TO THIS ESCALATING SITUATION

It would be fair to say that libraries remained quiet for too long while this price escalation occurred. Book budgets were decimated in STM areas in order to protect serial subscriptions. Only when the situation was so desperate that researchers were impacted by journal cancellations were there loud concerns expressed by those in control of budgets. These first reactions were little more than complaints and pointing the entire blame at commercial publishers. The words "differential pricing" and "price gouging" were thrown about with very little supporting data. Nonprofit publishers were seen as the good guys, charging far less for equal-value materials.

The next stage of analysis was one of gathering data, reviewing past histories, and engaging in discussion (even collaborating in some cases). This resulted in constructive criticism, a shared understanding of the issues, follow-up cooperation (such as this meeting of publishers, services, and librarians), the development of alternative actions and/or scenarios–and lawsuits.

Some publishers, services, and librarians still feel that natural selection alone will weed out the bad and leave the entire pool of money for the quality journals, with no further action necessary. These people simply don't understand the factors involved. The costs of present paper-based editing, printing, and distribution continue to rise beyond any reasonable budget expectations; maintaining the present system will only stall the inevitable. Two additional factors responsible for an ever increasing amount of publication include (1) a higher number of researchers producing a higher level of novel ideas, and (2) an increase in quality and quantity of publications due to new technology, which produces more and more data.

However, in addition to these factors, in the real world, publication is not only for the distribution of quality data; it also serves as a means to attain promotion and tenure. Authors must publish and edit journals, regardless of their quality, in order to demonstrate their expertise. Until this factor is removed from the publication process, or until a better means of evaluating quality and quantity within this system is discovered, we will still see the problematic desire for more and more publication regardless of all other factors.

Of course, regardless of these factors, if the process is a commercial enterprise there will always be the need for a profit. Many nonprofit society publishers also supplement their revenue sources (e.g., user dues and endowments) with surplus subscription dollars. The idea of using a relatively flat (zero base) fixed library subscription as the source for long-term profit revenue seems a bit foolish given the tight budgets of the 90s.

So what can be done to provide some form of guaranteed revenue stream for quality materials, given the new technologies and present and/or future user behaviors? The first significant reaction was the coordination of libraries in order to force conversations on the issue of using these new technologies to provide innovative information distribution systems *with savings or added value.* The Association of Research Libraries (ARL) and other academic communities produced the following manifesto in the March 1998 issue of *Policy Perspectives*, the publication of the Pew Higher Education Roundtable (available at http://www.irhe.upenn.edu/pp/pp-main.html):

> Academic Community Sets Agenda to Reclaim Scholarly Publishing. Research universities have it within their power to work with each other and scholarly societies to transform scholarly communication into "a system of electronically mediated publications that will provide enhanced access to scholarly informa-

tion and relief from the escalating prices of commercial publishers." So conclude the participants–university presidents, provosts, faculty, librarians, counsels, and representatives of scholarly societies and university presses–in a special Roundtable on Managing Intellectual Property in Higher Education. The findings of this group are reported in the essay, "To Publish and Perish," featured in the March 1998 issue of Policy Perspectives, the publication of the Pew Higher Education Roundtable.

Noting that the rising cost of scholarly publications is not a 'library problem,' but a symptom of the deeper conflict between the sociology and economics of academic publishing, the essay contrasts the expectation of an open exchange of information within the academy to the pricing and copyright practices of commercial publishers that control many of the major scholarly publishing venues. In an effort to regain some control over the research and scholarship generated by the academic community, the Roundtable participants proposed a set of five strategies to address the problem. They recommended that:

- promotion and tenure committees disentangle the notions of quality and quantity in the work of the faculty;
- libraries leverage their resources by creating a more coherent market for scholarly publications;
- universities, led by their national associations, help faculty understand the implications of signing away their intellectual property rights;
- universities and scholarly societies invest in electronic forms of peer-reviewed scholarly communication; and
- universities and scholarly societies decouple publication and faculty peer-reviewed evaluation of the merit of scholarly work.

The participants stated that "The outcome we seek is a set of specific arrangements–linking institutions, their faculty, and their scholarly organizations–that protects the rights of faculty and secures for their appointing institutions a more assured ability to provide access to research and scholarly information." While the challenges are not insignificant, the group concluded that the risks of doing nothing substantially outweigh the difficulty of doing something–and doing it now! A moment of opportunity is at hand, occasioned by the potential for peer-reviewed electronic publishing and a sense of desperation spawned by runaway acquisition costs. Missing this opportunity will mean more rapidly accelerating costs, greater commercial control, and, in the end, less access to scholarly communications.

Some examples of real action include (1) consortial activities, as seen by recent Consortia of Consortia price and service parameter negotiations with Nexis, (2) the creation of university policies, as seen in the recent Purdue reaction to Elsevier, and (3) leverage in public forums, as seen in the fast and effective reaction that played a part in the nonmerger of Elsevier/Kluwer.

There are a number of real world experiments underway, some of which are proprietary and subject-specific and may not scale up to a workable system; but perhaps they will eventually use open standards to seamlessly link to any final solutions that are developed. Some use simple paper-based scenarios, providing convenience but no added value–a short-term solution with little hope of fitting into the commercial world solution, in which one selects services based upon added value. Some are initiated by either libraries or user groups, in some cases working with societies or commercial publishers. At least the correct user groups are now involved in discussions of all aspects of the future systems.

Below are listed a few examples of services with highlighted characteristics:

- The Los Alamos National Lab (LANL) e-print server, created and maintained by users (the physicist, Paul Ginsparg, with NSF funding), was one of the first novel and innovative approaches to e-prints. Using familiar technology and existing LANL hardware, his relatively inexpensive and uncomplicated platform allowed for easy searching, listserv distribution, and archiving. The solution developed for high-energy physicists is probably scalable for multiple disciplines and is now being used for other disciplines. It has been cloned in other locations for other uses. This e-print server approach needs to be seamlessly linked to the standard A&I tools for maximum effect.
- The American Mathematical Society preprint server, also developed by the appropriate content creators, uses state-of-the-art technology and has the advantage of being supported by the prin-

cipal academic and professional society in the discipline. This should make the seamless link to A&I services and archives easier, given the producer position of the AMS.

- The American Physical Society's *Physical Review Special Topics-Accelerators and Beams* (*PR-STAB*) is also providing e-prints directly from the society responsible for peer review and publishing of the final manuscripts. The proposed funding is innovative in that dollars will come directly from authors, much in the style of page charges. The society is testing the technical feasibility of electronic editing, composition, and archiving, particularly in terms of faster distribution and lower production costs.
- Other university-based prototypes, such as HighWire, JSTOR, and Project Muse, involve collaborations between appropriate creators and libraries as partners for this investigation. This collaboration should guarantee awareness of the appropriate archival aspects of the information network; it also seeks to develop reasonable long-term economic models for the support of peer review and user/library interests.

COST MODELS

What should revenue be paying for? Revenue should pay for selected present values plus added value. The present values in the publishing process include

- Editorial work, a large component of present costs, which is often donated on a volunteer basis.
- Composition costs, which are a significant component of the final production cost. Can these costs be lowered by changing standards such as typology without seriously influencing the quality of the content? Many readers are no longer interested in paying more for glossy paper; maintaining publisher "look and feel" may not be as important to readers as was once thought.
- Printed products. Some initial distributed print copies will continue to be necessary until all users are connected to the enhanced versions available on the Internet. Eventually printed products may be limited to enhanced abstracts with linked URLs provided for access to the full text.
- Distribution of materials. Distributed print copies will continue to be necessary until all users are connected to the enhanced ver-

sions available on the Internet. These costs will be lowered after paper duplication is reduced, if electronic transmission proves to be less expensive.

- Archiving, which is easier for paper material at this time, due in part to the stability of static paper documents. In addition to providing enhanced linkage possibilities, electronic archiving may prove less expensive through economies of scale, but we must consider the issues of long-term stability and periodic conversion costs.

The added-value factors introduced through electronic publishing include

- Hyperlinks, providing for convenient access, new approaches to information storage and retrieval, and new behaviors that may generate new revenue through greater access to older materials.
- Integrated media blending, a very important paradigm shift in presenting visualization options. This powerful opportunity may present new costs for network support of the required bandwidth until better compression techniques are available.
- Convenience, as seen through timeless and lagless distribution. Ease of duplication.
- Improved accountability for tenure process support. Present quantitative and qualitative criteria can be supported through distribution mechanisms that track readership. This same data could be used to analyze traditional subscription renewals. A key question that needs further attention and experimentation is whether or not some form of society-based, peer-reviewed, e-print system can provide a validation and distribution mechanism for certain academic disciplines?

POSSIBLE SERVICE FUNDING MODELS

The following is a continuum of funding models, showing possible revenue bases between the two extremes of direct or indirect public support and commercial operations. In a real world scenario, revenue can be provided by a blend of the general population and/or a vested user support base.

- Direct support from vested user population or government
  –American Physical Society (Bob Kelly) proposes direct government funding

–NSF LANL prototype for direct government funding through NSF

–DLI prototype for direct government funding through NSF and other agencies

–ADS/NASA prototype for direct government funding through NASA

- Indirect support channeled through academic departments and libraries

–Optics Express (overhead provided from author grants or page charges)

–Other university-based e-journals (subsidized editorial and server support); e.g., HighWire (exploring a commercial model and archive solution) and Project MUSE or JSTOR

- Society-based support (through member dues and overhead support, e.g., "page charges")

–Bob Apfel's (Yale University) Peer Review Inc (proposed validation of the editorial process)

–APS PR Special Topics-Accelerators and Beams

–APS PROLA (pay for the APS archives if they are required/desired in relation to package plans and local needs)

–*JHEP Journal of High Energy Physics* (This is peer reviewed and is free for now. The plan for revenue in the future is that those who pay for paper or CD-ROM archive provide the support for the editorial and distribution costs. The question remains as to why revenue should be based on paper? Is there a better long-term strategy?)

–*Advances in Theoretical and Mathematical Physics* (All items in this compilation are previously released as free LANL preprints. Is this peer review worthy of commercial support? Will it eventually conflict with later APS or other validation and/or commercial sale approaches?)

- Taxpayer support (Continues to increase university library expenditures. This is treating the symptom, not the cause of publication cost concerns.)
- The tiered model and the PEAK test (Provides some guaranteed revenue in relation to quality. Costs are related to an accountable simultaneous user basis (as opposed to current FTE figures). Represents a move away from the artificially created, paper-based, "journal title" approach to information packets. Revenue

is based upon the viability and marketability of individually selected materials (i.e., articles).[1]
- Chadwyck-Healy approach (Have libraries cover the R&D risk,
  and charge for gateway and server services.)
- Aggregators (Charge for added-value costs such as interfaces and
  creation of packages for specific populations.)
  –Northern Light
  –Electronic Library
  –One new approach is the Elsevier journal, *Combinatorial Chemis-
  try-An Online Journal*, which is attempting to serve as an aggregator for information in both Elsevier's and other publishers'
  journals.
- Publisher control (Maintains the status quo. How long can this
  inflated revenue drain into commercial profit continue? The
  OCLC gateway archive is an attempt to create a collaborative
  publisher/nonprofit operation for distribution and archiving in
  which users are charged per simultaneous user plus a cost-per-
  title subscription. Other publishers are attempting to arrange subscriptions by title and/or by "all titles" package plans. These all-
  or-nothing plans force libraries to subsidize unwanted titles and
  remove the title-by-title accountability that is required in these
  difficult fiscal times.)

Two points to stress: (1) There is no such thing as a "free-with-pa-
per" subscription. There are hidden costs for all electronic titles. Perhaps these plans should be stated as "electronic-costs-imbedded-with-
in-paper" subscriptions. (2) Libraries want to avoid double paying for
added-value options (i.e., links to A&I services that they already access, such as PubMed). Perhaps these features should be offered as
additional options for a fee, for those that need such services.

THE TIERED MODEL

This tiered journal cost model[2] (see Figure 1) attempts to provide a
price model that accomplishes two objectives: (1) preserving some
stable base for quality journal publications during this transition period from paper to electronic delivery, and (2) providing a system for
fiscal accountability through purchasing customized packages of
scientific (non-trade) products in relation to identified (and, over time,

FIGURE 1. The Tiered Model

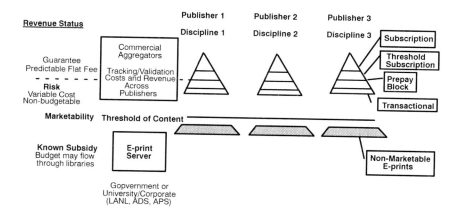

Requires complete A & I coverage for acceptance within the promotion and tenure process. Journal, non-journal, non-peer-reviewed materials eventually included.

further refined) local and/or consortial needs. One possible approach for creating a fiscally accountable, annual, electronic journal-pricing model might include the following tiered approach:

- First tier: (Commercial Materials)
  –Subscriptions for *unlimited access* to a selection of frequently used journal titles.
  –Threshold subscriptions for *unlimited access* to a *selection of lesser-used journal titles at reduced prices*, with annual statistical usage reviews for possible movement to a standard subscription, or downward to a prepay block.
  –Prepay blocks: flat-fee purchasing of a *pre-selected number of articles* from a *previously identified list of less frequently* used journal titles (with the ability to add additional blocks of accesses when necessary).
  –Transactional (commercial pay-per-view) delivery for infrequently used journals.
- Second tier:
  –Non-marketable STM items will be archived *in noncommercial e-print servers.*

–These items should be searchable through standard A&I services, and the support of such servers should be paid for by a combination of government, university, and commercial populations with interests in the long-term survival of discipline-specific materials (e.g., LANL, ADS, APS). *Additional funding might be required for peer review and editorial/composition work* as opposed to simple author-provided materials. Any retrieval revenues that might be generated should be shared between the archival sites and the A&I services.

This approach provides some degree of security for publishers of high quality material, provides accountability for purchasing (and supporting) only the best of lesser-used materials, and provides little commercial subsidizing of (locally) unnecessary or lower quality information, which is better housed in a central clearinghouse.

This approach could also be used by consortia of both users (i.e., subject-based collectors) and producers (i.e., subject clusters of primary material publishers) for coordinated purchasing of packages across publishers through aggregators. The required validation and tracking mechanisms could be built into the individual full-text servers, but would scale much better if built into federated gateways (e.g., Blackwell's Electronic Journal Navigator) as we work toward developing the new open standards, seamless information search and retrieval systems (see Figure 2).

Aggregators may be involved in all aspects of the information storage, retrieval, and archiving mechanism, or they may find a partial niche. Not all aggregators share the same missions or intentions. I would classify existing aggregators in two categories:

- Full service aggregators, who perform all tasks involved in maintaining an archival repository, i.e., validation, transaction logs for cost recovery, and archiving of materials (e.g., HighWire, Ovid, Northern Light).
- Partial service aggregators, who perform only some of the above functions.

Blackwell's is a remote aggregator, providing only validation and log transaction. It is not an archival site. ADS provides local mounting, but has no plan to serve as the long-term archive for publisher backfile material. It has no costs or validation mechanisms and no

FIGURE 2. The Future Scenario

Phase I

1-5 Years?

Phase II

5+ Years?

HighWire	**APS/AIP**	Elsevier	**Springer**	**Physics**
Subscription	Subscription	Subscription	Subscription	Subscription
Threshold Subscription	Threshold Subscription	Threshold Subscription	Threshold Subscription	Threshold Subscription
Prepay Block	Prepay Block	Prepay Block	Prepay Block	Prepay Block
Transactional	Transactional	Transactional	Transactional	Transactional

Through Aggregators
Through Consortia
Customized for Sites

long-term funding. LANL provides local mounting but has no ability to serve as the long-term archive, due to no long-term funding. It provides no costs or validation mechanisms. Document delivery services have no archival mission and often no subscription base (use universities).

Aggregators will play a large role in the development of practical integrated systems, particularly across publishers. But that is another article.

ADDITIONAL REVENUE SOURCE

Paper "enhanced abstracts" will provide *an additional revenue source* for those that want to browse or for those that want some level of paper coverage. First copy costs will still be necessary for many years, and the technology will still be in place. Of course, these paper products will not serve as an official archive, as they will not include many of the integrated media enhancements that the electronic publishing world can accommodate. The enhanced abstracts can provide some level of browsing without the full costs of check-in, shelving and binding. This may be a long-term option, depending upon the behavior of readers.

QUESTIONS TO CONTEMPLATE

Commercial ventures should support better editing and composition. If not, why pay? Can added-value features be introduced faster through commercial development? If not, why pay? Will A&I services increase their scope to include electronic, peer-reviewed material? This is essential for the promotion and tenure process to function. Will A&I services increase their scope to include non-peer-reviewed material? If not, other services will appear to federate searching across various databanks. (This is only important because the academic community has a real interest in the continuation of some form of A&I services in the future, and the stronger the product the better the search engines.)

CONCLUSION

There will probably be a blend of the previously described cost models, depending upon a combination of desired features, available start-up capital funds for new players, and the short-term versus the long-term vision of those designing and paying for the services. Some important considerations will be:

- Serious reevaluation of the current needs/criteria of the tenure process
- Serious reevaluation of the various requirements of an information distribution system
- Analysis of the continuing application of copyright revenue concepts to academic information
- The balance of academic subsidies for corporate research (e.g., free editing, in-house use)

- Taxpayer subsidy for research versus vested-interest user group direct support
- Faculty/administrative/library leverage in relation to use statistics and products/packages

It is now time to start designing the infrastructure to support these models.

NOTES

1. Vincent Kiernan, "Paying by the Article: Libraries Test a New Model for Scholarly Journals," *The Chronicle of Higher Education*, August 14, 1998. This article describes the PEAK Project (Pricing Electronic Access to Knowledge). The University of Michigan Libraries, with the cooperation of Elsevier, is looking at three alternatives: (1) per-article pricing, i.e., individual users purchase unlimited access to a specific article for a fixed price, (2) traditional subscriptions, and (3) generalized subscription, i.e., institutional purchase at the beginning of the year for unlimited access to sets of 120 articles selected after-the-fact by the users. Individual users can purchase smaller bundles.

2. Modified from the article by David Stern, "Three-Tiered Journal Cost Model," *Newsletter on Serials Pricing Issues*, no. 187 (August 12, 1997):187.2. Available: http://www.lib.unc.edu/prices/1997/PRIC187.HTML. September 23, 1998.

USING TEAMS TO EVALUATE AND IMPLEMENT NEW SERVICES FOR ELECTRONIC SERIALS

The Team Approach in Building Electronic Collections and Services

William Kara

SUMMARY. Teams can be effective tools to evaluate electronic collections and implement new services. With rapidly changing technologies and the availability of new options, teams provide a way to share information, learn new skills, and develop a greater appreciation for the work, concerns, and needs of staff throughout the library. This communication and involvement can be critical to implementing new library services. *[Article copies available for a fee from The Haworth Document Delivery Service: 1-800-342-9678. E-mail address: getinfo@haworthpressinc.com]*

William Kara is Acquisitions Librarian/Acting Head of Technical Services, Albert R. Mann Library, Cornell University.

[Haworth co-indexing entry note]: "The Team Approach in Building Electronic Collections and Services." Kara, William. Co-published simultaneously in *The Serials Librarian* (The Haworth Press, Inc.) Vol. 36, No. 3/4, 1999, pp. 321-335; and: *Head in the Clouds, Feet on the Ground: Serials Vision and Common Sense* (ed: Jeffrey S. Bullington, Beatrice L. Caraway, and Beverley Geer) The Haworth Press, Inc., 1999, pp. 321-335. Single or multiple copies of this article are available for a fee from The Haworth Document Delivery Service [1-800-342-9678, 9:00 a.m. - 5:00 p.m. (EST). E-mail address: getinfo@haworthpressinc.com].

Libraries differ in many different ways–in their mission, their size, and their history; but regardless of what type library they're in, one thing that all librarians have needed to deal with is change. In a relatively few years resources in a variety of electronic formats have been increasingly available and essential for any modern library. There are many library services that are still evolving due to the continuing rapid changes in technology and electronic collections available. This paper examines how a library can get to the point of offering and maintaining access to an electronic collection, particularly using a team approach to investigate and implement a new service. It will address project teams rather than investigate using the team management approach to organizing the structure of library operations. Although a more permanent team management structure shares many of the strengths of using teams for an investigation or implementation project, the teams for these initiatives usually have a much more defined objective.[1] This paper is divided into three sections, covering the purpose of teams and how they fit into the library organization, a brief discussion of contemporary management theory about teams, and use of teams at Cornell to illustrate how teams can be used.

THE PURPOSE OF TEAMS

Although not written specifically for libraries or corporations, standard definitions of "team" and "teamwork" help to illustrate these basic concepts very well. *Webster's Third New International Dictionary* defines "team" as "a number of persons associated together in work or activity" and "a group of specialists or scientists functioning as a collaborative unit." The emphasis on collaboration or teamwork is an important element. *Webster's* definition of "teamwork" is "work done by a number of associates with usually each doing a clearly defined portion but all subordinating personal prominence to the efficiency of the whole."[2] Although these are very basic definitions they can also be applied to teams in a library environment. A team that utilizes the skills and contributions of all its members can more effectively tackle complex assignments and be a means of enhancing communication and collaboration within the organization. Teams can also serve as a mechanism for sharing ideas and building skills and awareness.

Project teams formed to investigate and implement new services for electronic resources have been used effectively at the Albert R. Mann Library. The Albert R. Mann Library at Cornell University is the second largest library in the Cornell University Library system and serves the Colleges of Agriculture and Human Ecology and the Divisions of the Biological and Nutritional Sciences. The library has been an innovator in providing access to electronic resources to the faculty, staff, and students in the Cornell community. In the early 90s the library developed the Mann Library Gateway (http://www.mannlib. cornell.edu), which is a single point of access to the bibliographic, numeric and full-text titles selected by the bibliographers at Mann Library. By the end of 1997, before it was integrated in the new Cornell University Library (CUL) Gateway, it provided access to approximately 1,000 titles. The new CUL Gateway now includes 2,000 individually listed titles.

The Mann Library Gateway was developed before many commercial packages were available. In addition to mounting several bibliographic files locally on magnetic tape, it forged partnerships with commercial enterprises and public agencies to provide the Cornell community with titles essential for its teaching and research missions. As the Acquisitions Librarian at Mann I had the opportunity to be involved in the development of this online collection. Although this collection grew gradually with the addition of individual titles, much of the growth was in large spurts, adding numerous titles at one time. Advances in technology or the opportunity to provide access to larger collections of titles often involved reexamining the gateway structure and workflow and user support issues. It was at these times that teams would be formed to more fully analyze the possibilities and implement new services.

During the last sixteen years I've worked in technical services, particularly in acquisitions, and I am familiar with the changes that technology brought to processing monographs and serials. Procedures for handling print items became well established. In the early 90s, however, acquiring electronic resources was something new. There were not well-established procedures and policies for acquiring and processing resources in varied electronic formats. Additionally, adding electronic resources to the collection would have an impact on every department in the library. Electronic resources brought new challenges and required many decisions on how they would be handled and supported. Working with my colleagues was an essential part of my education about electronic resources. Working as part of both formal and informal teams not only helped reinforce my appreciation and awareness of issues facing others in the library, but helped them to understand the complexities that acquisitions and technical services faced when dealing with electronic resources. These teams with members from the different units also served as a hub, and each team member could go back to their own units to discuss details and share information. The team facilitated awareness and cooperation beyond the relatively small membership of the team.

Libraries had been dealing with change long before the pace of technological innovation quickened during the last two decades. Whether through reorganization or reengineering, libraries have tackled new challenges differently. All libraries have needed to face the new challenges and opportunities that electronic publications and services offer. Nothing remains the same for long. Some libraries have concentrated expertise about new technology in specialized staff and units, and technical specialists are certainly an essential part of any modern library organization.

The addition of electronic resources and services to a collection, however, also requires the work and attention of staff in many other departments throughout the library. In providing access to a large collection of electronic resources–whether bibliographic, full-text, or numeric–many questions need to be addressed: What will be acquired and how? How will the resources be cataloged and organized for access? What are the technical requirements? What will the demands be on the public services staff?

This is far from a complete list, but it identifies the potential complexity involved in offering a new service. Each of the questions above would generate many more questions that would need to be answered before the implementation of a new service. Library staff often have expertise in a core area, but it's unlikely that anyone would have the experience, skills, or the authority to handle all details effectively. Many decisions cut across departmental lines, and how staff in different departments and at different levels cooperate, coordinate, and communicate their activities will dramatically affect the process and affect the success of implementing a new service.

One of the mechanisms that a library could use to manage this complexity is to form a team, comprised of selected staff from throughout the library, who provide different perspectives and expertise. This diversity of talent and experience is critical. With the right members, teams can be very useful for sorting through the issues that need to be examined when making significant changes to our library services. They can be useful in getting the job done and getting it done more thoroughly.

A team is similar to a committee but often differs in its mission. It is certainly a forum to discuss ideas and projects, but an investigation or implementation team usually has a more defined goal. Depending on the assignment to the team, teams can also be involved in different stages of a project and need to investigate various aspects of any new service before, during, and even after implementation. This involvement and continuity is important; it not only instills a sense of ownership in the project, but team members have been involved with so many details from the beginning that they already know much about the project and its goals. At some point, however, the investigation or implementation team would need to involve staff with other expertise, or when it is no longer a "project," it should be fully integrated into the more routine operations of the library.

Library organizations are certainly familiar with committees. Committees come in all sizes and structures and serve many purposes. It is often the case that many librarians approach what could be termed as "committee overload." The formation of yet another committee might receive less than positive responses, such as, "Oh no, not another committee. Not more meetings!" There is also the situation when a quick answer is needed and one is told to "run it by Susan," who then tells you to "run it by Joe," who will then add it to the agenda for a committee meeting two weeks from now. The quick answer or decision wanted by you or your staff is now on the agenda at a future meeting.

At the same time that committees can add another bureaucratic element to the process and even slow the pace of decision-making, nearly all professionals have also all had the experience of decisions being made without the involvement or participation of staff who will be directly affected by the result. A decision made without the input of appropriate staff could also get negative reactions: "Didn't she realize what impact this would have on public services?" "Are they nuts? We can't do that by then."

Is there a happy medium between too much involvement and not enough? Not always, but good communication and the involvement of staff with appropriate skills and experience can make an organization more efficient and enable it to tackle changes effectively. Project teams can be an effective means of involving appropriate staff.

Whether a group is designated a team, committee, or task force, the mission and goals of the group are critical to the role it will play within the organization and its effectiveness in accomplishing its goals. The name of the group should indicate some sense of the group's purpose. For example, a group in the Cornell University Library system was just renamed the Database Review Committee (formerly, the Database Review Task Force), reflecting the need for a more permanent, continuing review of electronic products and access in a fast-developing market. Most libraries would have a need for more formal committees and staff to deal with the ongoing selection and support of digital resources, but assigning staff to a team to deal with a project gives the organization more flexibility in dealing with particular issues. It also gives an opportunity for a wider range of staff to be involved in developing the digital library. At the Albert R. Mann Library–as in many organizations–committees, groups, or teams can be formal or informal; ongoing or temporary; can look at issues theoretically or practically; and can include a myriad of styles, structures, or intentions. There's no magic formula, but a team must include or have access to a variety of skills, which differ from project to project.

MANAGEMENT LITERATURE ON TEAMS

The management or leadership style also varies among and within organizations. Library management can be fairly authoritarian; consultative, where the director consults with key staff or other administrators before making significant decisions; or participatory, where much more involvement from staff is encouraged and expected.[3] Different management styles and structures certainly have their strengths and weaknesses, but any management style that fails to fully utilize and develop its staff misses an opportunity. At many institutions (Mann Library included) professional staff are hired after a long review, whose purpose is to identify potential as well as existing skills and experience.

One of the ways staff, whether new or long-term, can develop skills is through involvement. At Mann Library a decision was made early in the evolution towards the electronic library that for the library to move forward all units in the library needed to participate in the changes.

Staff would not be sidelined, and technical skills would not be compartmentalized or isolated in relatively few staff or units. This is not to say that technical skills don't vary considerably–they do–but there's a minimum level of awareness and involvement expected of all staff, particularly the professional librarians. Even technical and computer staff are hired with the potential or experience to think of the broader role technology plays in libraries. The culture of the library is that of a "learning organization," and teams fit well within that framework.

Libraries are organizations that provide a service, and many aspects of library management are akin to working in business. Current trends in management theory and practice include the concept of a "learning organization." Although these might be the 90s buzzwords, similar to TQM (Total Quality Management) that came along a few years before, there's much logic in many points. Every organization, however, is different, and each needs to examine what changes, if any, would benefit them in helping them better fulfill their mission.

Current management theory has increasingly stressed involvement of staff and using their full potential. The top-down approach and strict pyramidal structure where decisions and ideas come from the boss to the staff have been increasingly rejected as ineffective, especially in organizations that deal with complex variables. This is particularly true in organizations that have a need to discuss and develop ideas to better serve their patrons. Buzzwords and theories come and go and are usually built on earlier ideas and what worked well in practice.

One of the leading proponents of learning organizations is Peter Senge. In his books *The Fifth Discipline: The Art and Practice of the Learning Organization*[4] and *The Fifth Discipline Fieldbook: Strategies and Tools for Building a Learning Organization*,[5] he and others describe the skills needed in contemporary organizations. These two books contain over a thousand pages of his and others' ideas and how to put them into practice. Teams and team learning are not only central to his ideas, but are also an essential component in successfully developing a learning organization.

In *The Fifth Discipline Fieldbook*, Senge summarizes the five disciplines, which are core to learning organizations, as follows:

> *Personal Mastery*–learning to expand our personal capacity to create the results we most desire, and creating an organizational environment which encourages all its members to develop themselves towards the goals and purposes they choose.

Mental Models-reflecting upon, continually clarifying, and improving our internal pictures of the world, and seeing how they shape our actions and decisions.

Shared Vision-building a sense of commitment in a group, by developing shared images of the future we seek to create, and the principles and guiding practices by which we hope to get there.

Team Learning-transforming conversational and collective thinking skills, so that groups of people can reliably develop intelligence and ability greater than the sum of individual members' talents.

Systems Thinking-a way of thinking about, and a language for describing and understanding, the forces and interrelationships that shape the behavior of systems.[6]

Senge's work and other literature on learning organizations is the 90s idea of management and transforming corporate culture. Although much of management literature is written more from the corporate standpoint, much is applicable to the library environment. In the above five disciplines there is an emphasis in building skills that permit individuals and organizations to move forward, to think creatively and differently, and to develop a vision of the future and examine how that vision could be realized. Team learning is essential to this process. Rather than individuals working separately with little communication, teams permit the free flow of ideas among the members. By examining projects holistically and understanding the larger system, teams-although given a specific assignment-should be able to better sort the many details and issues in a complex project. In the *Fieldbook* there is also an emphasis on the need to start afresh and question assumptions, which is something librarians have needed to do for electronic resources where new procedures and policies need to be developed. Senge also writes about avoiding the "quick fix," which might be the easiest solution at the time but often lets a problem resurface later or even cause additional problems. By having a project team carefully analyze many details and issues, the system can more completely manage changes rather than react to individual new titles on an ad hoc basis. By systematically analyzing workflow and policy issues the organization can take a more holistic view of the electronic collection and how it should be developed. In learning organizations teams are an important element in the structure. A collaborative team approach should engender open discussions of the issues. The importance of the composition of the team is also critical and must include participation and representation from all units that would need to implement and support a new service.

The concept of a learning organization isn't confined to corporate literature. A recent article by Rena Fowler in *College and Research Libraries* addresses the need for libraries to invest in their organizations to accommodate technological innovation. She also strongly endorses the concept of "planned change" and that "through the team or group may be examined the presence of shared vision, team learning, and continuous or lifelong learning."[7]

EXAMPLES OF INVESTIGATION AND IMPLEMENTATION TEAMS AT MANN LIBRARY

Leadership is also essential in moving an organization forward. If the shared vision isn't shared by the director, a crucial link is broken. The organizational structure and will need to be there to lead the organization through change, to encourage participation and innovation, and to create both formal teams and an informal, effective team environment. The absence of effective leadership can be a severe obstacle to adapting to change. A library should not merely react to changes around it, but should proactively investigate opportunities and develop the structure and skills to better meet new challenges.

Fortunately, throughout this evolutionary period, having a strong leader was not a problem in Mann Library. The director, Jan Olsen, had the vision to see what changes and opportunities technology would bring to libraries and information management. The director and other senior administrators worked closely together and were able to articulate a vision for the library, engender enthusiasm and cooperation among the staff, and develop the organizational structures to support the development of a digital library.

In the early 90s the director formed the Electronic Resources Council (ERC), which served as a discussion forum and decision-making body for significant new initiatives involving electronic resources. This group mirrors teams, but is a standing committee. It contains representation from all involved units, it is a forum to exchange and discuss ideas and information, and it serves as a mechanism to identify the needs and concerns of different units. The ERC primarily comprises administrative and supervisory staff, but regularly invites staff with particular expertise or assignments to join in discussions.

One of the ERC's goals was to get the council's members out of the loop for all decisions. In order to do this, the ERC needed to grapple with and understand the issues and put policies and procedures into place that would integrate the processing of electronic resources into the workflow of the different divisions. Mainstreaming was a goal, and a fairly successful goal. Adding pointers to selected publicly accessible Internet sites, establishing subscriptions to individual electronic titles, and adding new CD-ROMs to the LAN all eventually became fairly mainstreamed. With electronic access still undergoing considerable changes, there were new issues that arose along the way, but, in general, collection development hashed out the selection policy and technical services developed the skills to catalog and add titles to the gateway. The information technology section and public services became adept and flexible in handling a wide variety of electronic titles. Many items were effectively mainstreamed into procedures in each division. Originally the ERC met more frequently, hitting new issues or rehashing earlier ones. More recently, however, it only becomes involved when there are larger new iniatives to discuss or when new technology is involved. For example, within the last two years GIS, Geographic Information Systems, raised a number of issues regarding what will be collected and how it would be supported by the library.

When there were issues involving larger initiatives to discuss or decide, the director, the Administrative Council, and the ERC would often form an investigation or implementation team. These teams have proven to be very useful in sorting through the numerous details involved in any larger project. I'm going to use examples of several teams, not going into detail about their investigation, but more on what role they and their members played. I'll use examples from Mann Library and from the Cornell University Library system to identify some teams and their work.

One of the first teams I was involved with for investigating and implementing a new service started basic discussions at the end of 1992 and by the end of 1993 provided a new service to the Cornell user community. The library worked closely with Dialog Information

Services to provide access to over 100 databases and full-text resources to the Cornell community via the Mann Library Gateway. Although aggregations or collections of electronic resources are common now, this was particularly innovative at the time. The library had already mounted locally on magnetic tape several major databases that were core to our collection. These were heavily used and directly available to the user, but were only the tip of the iceberg of what databases were available through mediated searching with the reference staff. Contact was made with Dialog and there was interest on both sides in pursuing an experimental service. In the library the Dialog Team started out as an investigation team, which then became an implementation team. Some seriously considered services or projects never reach the implementation stage.

In the library, the Dialog team comprised the head of collection development, who looked at developing the collection in all formats and who also managed the acquisitions funds, the bibliographic files selector (who was also a public services librarian) and the acquisitions librarian (who handled contracts for the library). In addition, a staff member in the information technology section was assigned to look into the technical questions. Although he wasn't involved in the selection of files or the financial and contract discussions, he needed to ensure that what we were talking about was doable. Could we handle the scripting and security issues and control the passwords and accounts? Another important member of this team was Anne Caputo (manager of academic programs at Dialog Information Services), who was both our advocate and our primary contact. Usually I wouldn't consider a vendor representative to be an integral part of the investigation team, but Anne's role and support were pivotal to this project. We were not dealing with an off-the-shelf product, but developing an innovative service. Anne was contacted frequently, sometimes in conference calls, and she also visited Cornell for very open discussions of issues.

The team met frequently, gathering information, prioritizing what files would be appropriate for the service, contacting Anne regarding limitations and getting test passwords to explore possibilities. The bibliographic files selector fully involved the public services staff in discussions about the list of titles. The programmer assigned to the team also had experience with interface design, but back in 1993 systems looked much more primitive than they do now, and we certainly couldn't rewrite Dialog's programming. I worked on contractual details with the team and with Dialog, and in technical services we discussed how over 100 titles would be listed and organized for the Mann Library Gateway. Adding a large number of new titles would require some reorganization and refinement of our subject structure for the gateway. The team met with the ERC to give updates and met with the director to make final decisions. We had an ideal vision of what type of service we'd like to provide, but reality reined us in. There were technological limitations, financial issues, and contractual details to consider and deal with. Before implementation there needed to be programming completed in the library and at Dialog, subject terms needed to be evaluated to better organize the significantly expanded Gateway, there was publicity to do, staff instruction, and user guides to write. It did become a service, a heavily used service, for four years. During those years much changed. The Mann Library Gateway moved from telnet to Web. There are now numerous products and services available commercially to choose from. Users, who were thrilled in 1993, within a few short years wanted more and expected much more user-friendly systems. This is no surprise; technology has changed rapidly. Despite all the planning and preparation, however, even the best laid plans sometimes hit a snag. Back in 1993 our accounts were turned on by Dialog in July as agreed. As a university governed by the cycle of the academic calendar, one of our cardinal rules–which we break often enough, but try not to–is to bring up major changes during the summer and not in the middle of the fall or spring semesters. However, due to other projects taking priority in a short-staffed information technology section, this service wasn't implemented until early October.

This was my first experience with a team involving electronic resources, and it was a very positive experience. Not only did it foster communication before, during and after implementation of the Dialog project, but it built long-term avenues of communication with my colleagues in other departments. It also developed my skills and awareness of a variety of issues and developed an awareness in the library of how tricky some contractual issues could be. Sometimes it is not very obvious why there are delays in implementing a new service, but there are many potential pitfalls. This project and the ongoing support for it developed a better understanding of the complex variables that need to be considered. Some of the sticking points were confidential contractual issues, but I appreciated being able to discuss and share these points with members of the team.

With a large collection of bibliographic files in place, the library also wanted to further develop its full-text collections. Pointers to individual full-text titles were already being added to the Gateway, but we now wanted to add a critical mass of full-text titles in our core subject areas. Another team was formed, with similar composition to the Dialog team, but with a full-text selector instead of a bibliographic files selector, and the information technology section member had a more active role in discussions, especially since the retrieval and display of full-text were still undergoing significant changes. This was in 1995, before the explosion of aggregators offering online collections. This was an opportunity for all the members of this full-text team to dig into a variety of issues, many not particularly related to our primary responsibilities. However, there was no implementation following our investigation. There were a few contractual and price issues where the library drew a line in the sand and wouldn't cross. Even though we were anxious to provide more full-text, and have since done so, there were principles that we thought were a bad precedent. The team, the ERC, and the director all concurred. As the staff member primarily responsible for contracts, I've particularly appreciated this type of support.

The last example is of a campus-wide task force formed to investigate which databases and electronic resources that the entire library system should offer. For a major research university this is an enormous undertaking and involves significant expenditures and planning. Staff who were not previously intensely involved in these decisions now became involved. The Database Review Task Force (DRTF) did a nice job sorting through the mass of possibilities. It was formed in early 1997 and included collection development and public services staff. Additionally, the central acquisitions librarian participated to assist in contract negotiations. The DRTF, however, did not include a spokesperson for cataloging issues. Although as a system the procedures for cataloging and providing access to large bibliographic databases were well established, among the resources selected for remote access in 1997 were two UMI ProQuest Direct databases. These collections provided access to several years of the full-text for nearly thirteen hundred journals. As a result of not considering the cataloging and access issues thoroughly beforehand, these collections were available through the CUL Gateway without the individual titles listed in any way. Users who were looking for the full-text of a particular journal needed to know to check the UMI ProQuest Direct link or needed to be directed there by library staff. To provide enhanced access to these collections through the OPAC and the gateway would be no small undertaking, and it would be several months after the start of these subscriptions before the cataloging issues were discussed campuswide. Teams can be very effective in sorting through the issues, and in this case, very effective in selecting resources for the whole system; however, in this case the team failed to adequately address all the basic issues. Cataloging is a core library activity, and catalogers need to be full participants in the development of the digital library. There is a campuswide ERC that took up this challenge and now these access issues are being more proactively targeted. Understanding the complexities in offering a complete service is a learning experience for any organization.

CONCLUSION

Project teams can fit well within the organizational structure of many libraries. They're not meant to replace the existing structure, but when the project needs the skills and experience of staff in different units for a specific goal, they can more comprehensively investigate and work with numerous details and issues. Effective teams also have a lasting legacy; they build skills and awareness and open up lines of communication that exist well beyond the project.

One of the goals of Mann Library and the ERC is to develop the skills necessary for staff to handle various electronic formats. By tackling different issues holistically, we've found that many items were suitable for "mainstreaming" and no longer needed special handling by a team or committee. There are now procedures and structures in place to handle many electronic titles. Teams certainly don't need to be formed everytime something new comes up, but such teams can fill a real need in any organization undergoing significant changes in its collections and services.

NOTES

1. For more information on team management as a way to structure a library organization, see Robert Bluck's *Team Management* (London: Library Association Publishing, 1996).

2. *Webster's Third New International Dictionary* (Springfield, Mass.: G. & C. Merriam Co., 1961), 2346-2347.

3. For more information on the types of organizations, see Robert D. Stueart and Barbara B. Moran's *Library and Information Center Management*, 4th ed. (Englewood, Colorado: Libraries Unlimited, Inc., 1993).

4. Peter M. Senge, *The Fifth Discipline: The Art and Practice of the Learning Organization* (New York: Doubleday/Currency, 1990).

5. Peter M. Senge et al., *The Fifth Discipline Fieldbook: Strategies and Tools for Building a Learning Organization* (New York: Currency, Doubleday, 1994).

6. Ibid., 6.

7. Rena Fowler, "The University Library as Learning Organization for Innovation: An Exploratory Study," *College & Research Libraries* 59 (May 1998): 220-231.

Using Teams to Evaluate
and Implement New Services
for Electronic Serials

Nancy Gibbs

As I hear Bill talk about teams and current management philosophy, I look at the teams we have established at the North Carolina State University (NCSU) Libraries to deal with electronic resources and think sometimes we did it good and sometimes we did it bad! But we did it! We learned from our experiences, and perhaps that is what counts. I don't have any panaceas for handling electronic serials, but perhaps my experiences will offer direction and affirmation for the processes you employ at your institution.

My institution has asked several different groups, matrices, task forces, and teams to review the issues surrounding electronic serials:

- What and how to purchase
- What and how to catalog
- What and how to access
- What and how to display
- What and when to index

I suspect these same issues have been discussed at your institutions. I certainly hope so. I hope you will share your situations and experiences during the discussion later in this program.

Nancy Gibbs is Acting Head, Acquisitions Department, North Carolina State University Libraries.

[Haworth co-indexing entry note]: "Using Teams to Evaluate and Implement New Services for Electronic Serials." Gibbs, Nancy. Co-published simultaneously in *The Serials Librarian* (The Haworth Press, Inc.) Vol. 36, No. 3/4, 1999, pp. 337-345; and: *Head in the Clouds, Feet on the Ground: Serials Vision and Common Sense* (ed: Jeffrey S. Bullington, Beatrice L. Caraway, and Beverley Geer) The Haworth Press, Inc., 1999, pp. 337-345. Single or multiple copies of this article are available for a fee from The Haworth Document Delivery Service [1-800-342-9678, 9:00 a.m. - 5:00 p.m. (EST). E-mail address: getinfo@haworthpressinc.com].

The teams at my institution are generational. The first generation team organized for electronic resources/serials was a rather unstructured group with a representative from acquisitions, systems, and collection management. We were not even a formally appointed team but rather a novice few librarians trying to solve the problems of a few electronic serials and databases to which we initially subscribed. In the beginning the titles we acquired presented few problems. We had the equipment or it came with the product; we had the knowledge to mount the titles; and we were fairly successful in completing these tasks. I think our first attempts at electronic resources gave us the false hope we could handle these new serials without too much assistance beyond our small team. But very soon other titles presented all sorts of problems.

The patrons wanting the subscription and those implementing the subscription were as uninformed as the staff who were taking the orders for the subscription at the publishers or vendors. We wrestled with access, as different titles had formats we were not ready to handle. I remember one specific title where there was much talking back and forth about the software to launch the title on the desktop. Did we have it in the building? Did the faculty who were interested in this title have this software on their desktop? If not, what role did the library's systems department play in assisting faculty in their offices? Did public services need to visit faculty offices?

As you can see, thoughts of bringing public services into this arena came after a title was subscribed to and began to be received by the libraries, rather than at the beginning of the acquisitions process. Contacts by collection management with the faculty to publicize these titles also came later, as did training of public services desk staff in how to provide service to a particular title.

Obviously we were thinking there were just a few titles we would be dealing with at any given moment, so we could take our time and evaluate our processes later. We would also worry after the fact about training and notifying public services staff and assisting users with accessing the electronic title.

This was probably the first and last time we have had the false luxury of time. We realized very quickly we did most things backwards and should have had more key players thinking through these issues early on. On the other hand, this initial foray with electronic resources and serials probably was a good experience for us to have as we learned we had to resolve critical issues quickly if the offers and wants of our patrons meant anything.

About this same time the electronic world was picking up speed and moving at a heightened pace. Publishers and vendors were sending messages to faculty on an almost daily basis that they could get this and that title electronically if they would just contact their library. Faculty heard from their colleagues what was available at other institutions, or they received flyers inside their print journals advertising electronic access. We knew we needed to move forward quickly and with a more sophisticated team structure. Thus was born the second generation electronic serials team consisting of members from cataloging, acquisitions, systems, collection management, and public services. This team was appointed by a member of the libraries' administrative council, giving it more structure but also more accountability. In an effort to have a more robust team, we acquired one or two public services librarians, a major role by cataloging, and a more specialized role from a specific staff member in the systems department.

Our team knew we had to have more and better skills if we were to make electronic serials services efficiently and effectively available to our patrons. The second generation team also knew immediately it needed to have a more formal structure for reviewing, acquiring, accessing, training, and publicizing the use of the new electronic serials. Even though collection management and public services staff were continuing to be bombarded by faculty about offers for specific electronic titles, the team members took some time to build a vision of where we wanted to go and how we wanted to get there. We spent some critical time thinking through this vision.

The issues we were now facing were different and more complex than in the past: understanding what we were buying; how we were buying it; how we were accessing these resources; how we were training staff for this new venture; and how we were alerting staff and patrons to these new services. We sat down with our original few team members and made major adjustments to our team, our workflow and processes, our reporting of new titles, our training of staff, and our mounting of these titles on the libraries' Webpages and in our OPAC.

First we put into place a formal structure for deciding what we would acquire, how we would access it, and how we would publicize it.

Acquisitions would place all electronic subscriptions as we do for all print subscriptions and would handle all license agreements.

Paid electronic-access-only titles would be accessible from the libraries' Webpage, subscribed to by acquisitions, and cataloged in the OPAC. Collection management would need to review all purchasing decisions and would work directly with faculty for input and announcements of purchase. Public services would have time to review the title before it was "live" for the public.

Electronic titles purchased from a publishing or association aggregator such as Project Muse, JSTOR, and IOP would be accessible on the libraries' Webpage, subscribed to by acquisitions and cataloged in the OPAC. Collection management would need to review purchasing decisions. The libraries would mount a large-scale publicity campaign to notify faculty and students regarding our participation. Public services would have time to review the title before it was "live" for the public.

Free electronic versions of currently subscribed print titles would be accessible from the libraries' Webpage, subscribed to by acquisitions and cataloged in the OPAC. Collection management would not need to be consulted before subscription could be activated. Public services would have time to review the title before it was "live" for the public.

Free electronic versions of non-subscribed print titles would be accessible from the libraries' Webpage, subscribed to by acquisitions, but not cataloged in the OPAC. Collection management would need to be consulted before these electronic subscriptions could be activated. Public services would probably not have time to review the title before it was "live" for the public.

With these guidelines we set into place a formal structure for acquiring the titles and handling bibliographic access for the patron. We formalized an internal structure for notifying staff of new titles we subscribed to or those which were in negotiation. We undertook a major training effort for staff members and student assistants to be alert for offers for new electronic serials and resources.

The second generation team learned a great deal of personal mastery and vision sharing, especially for each others' issues and concerns.

LICENSING ISSUES

We were being asked to sign license agreements for most of our titles. This meant we had to bring in the experts from outside the libraries as all our licenses are sent to the campus legal and purchasing departments for review and signature. Legal affairs had to understand our needs for asking for a specific license to be signed, and we had to come up to speed with what the university is actually allowed to sign. This was a totally new experience for both sides!

Everyone learned to appreciate the amount of time and work it took to acquire and license any electronic serial. Because the signature process involves campus personnel, we all needed to understand the timelines and adjust those timelines when making promises of accessibility to patrons.

SYSTEMS CONSTRAINTS

All of us learned how difficult it is to mount so many titles quickly on the libraries' Webpages and provide access to all users. We learned the complexities of the many different browsers for the journals out there: Catchword, Portable Document Format (PDF), Adobe Acrobat, etc. We learned about embedded scripts in logon messages. We learned to wrestle with publishers over the issue of IP addresses versus password access to a title. And we haven't finalized the issue of verification of off-campus users. We still are not successfully offering the distance learner a solid connection to the university's host machines if a patron accesses the title from a distant North Carolina county but works for the university.

CATALOGING

Cataloging taught us all the questions of providing the Uniform Resource Locator (URL) in the 856 field and the holdings statement and whether we give the URL for the publisher's Webpage, or try to direct the patron right to the actual electronic title and perhaps eliminate a page or two of publisher advertising. Cataloging taught us about the issues of access to our catalog: some of our uses come from a telnet client and some come from a Web client. The access is different for each, yet we wanted to give each user the best possible service. Cataloging continues to ask questions about displaying virtual holdings in our catalog, and we have not resolved this issue completely.

PUBLIC SERVICES

Public services learned to appreciate our timelines and taught us to appreciate the amount of time and work it takes to become familiar with the many different resources to which we subscribe. They also continue to ask about virtual holdings.

By communicating all of these issues in team meetings, each member was able to understand the issues of other departments and to provide some insights into solving some of these problems. We formalized each step in the process with concrete procedures that have begun to stand us in good stead as we continue to increase the number of titles we access. Our team meets regularly! We keep written minutes of decisions made and ideas discussed. We communicate with the library administration through our assistant director and we receive questions and welcome comments from all library staff members. We communicate with the key players!

Right now the team is grappling with thoughts of allowing an outside serial vendor to take over a number of these processes for us. There are serial vendors who provide some of the same services we inside the library scuffle with: licensing agreements, keeping URLs current for disparate titles, verification of users, simplification of payments, notification of new titles, tracking of titles, and user statistics, to name but a few. Is it more cost effective to allow a vendor to do this for us for a price? Is this something the library wants to continue doing in-house? In some instances libraries have already invested heavily in infrastructure, and it could make sense to keep going along the same avenue. In other instances this is a very time consuming process to complete. Would the cost to systems and staff be time better spent elsewhere? Should we pay a vendor a flat service fee or a fee per title to do this work for us? We have not resolved these questions but are planning a small pilot project this summer to test the vendor waters.

As you can see, the second generation team has come a long way with understanding, accessing, and servicing electronic serials. The issues have become much more complex, and the skills needed to serve on this team have had to grow accordingly. The systems expertise needed to understand some of these complex issues is phenomenal! Dealing with faculty is sometimes political! Coordinating training for public services staff to have access to a title before it is mounted on the Webpages takes negotiating skills. Keeping track of what we have access to, what we are paying for, and what has been through the legal process requires juggling skills. I see no end in sight! Rather I see a continued effort by everyone on the team to keep current with what is coming down the electronic highway.

The third generation team I would like to discuss this morning is one that is unique to my institution, but I suspect could be replicated in many institutions. This is called the "e-pubs team." This is the team that is dealing with those electronic serials that are being created and produced on our own campuses. The NCSU Libraries has always had a great interest in what is produced on the campuses and in most instances has tried to preserve those endeavors. In some institutions there is a mandate and an archive that is required by law or legend to preserve anything produced on the campus. That mandate now includes electronic serials as well as print serials. This is true whether the serial is the local student newspaper, an economics faculty member's venture, or the latest title produced by the university's extension service. Currently on my campus, there are over fifty serial publications and forty electronic serials. These have titles such as *Blue Mold*, *Meridien*, and *The Technician*. Some are basic journals or newspapers, while others have incorporated many bells and whistles, video, graphic, and audio feeds, and links to other Webpages into their production package.

These titles have presented the e-pubs team with a whole different set of issues to consider.

The large issue of the life cycle of a publication or an issue is something we are considering as I speak. At what point is the title part of a university publication? Are the different iterations of a graduate-student-produced education journal as important as the final product? When do the archives/library functions become important? Do we try to mirror the site so that any changes made before publication are recorded for campus posterity? Do we depend upon the campus publisher to give us a year's worth of the title each year, or do we receive each issue as published?

Do we ftp each new issue onto the libraries' Webpage when it appears or do we point the patron to the student publisher's website and let the patron decide when a new issue is available? Do we monitor the site continually so notification by the publisher is not necessary? Do we assume a serial will have a regular publishing pattern and not experience the vagaries of the university's class calendar?

These and many other issues are being discussed now. My institution has set up the e-pubs team to look into all of this. The key players are those associated with the university archives and special collections department as well as those that acquire, mount, and assist patrons with electronic serials. I should say at this point that the work of another NASIG member has been helpful in getting a handle on this issue. My personal thanks to Ellen Duranceau of MIT for the report[1] she published on this topic. Our e-pubs team has read that report from cover to cover and continues to refer to it as we meet some of these new challenges. For the moment, the e-pubs team is commencing a pilot project to acquire and access three electronic serials titles produced on our campus. We hope to investigate acquiring each title by one of the ways mentioned above (mirroring, ftp, or pointing to the publisher Website). We will track how this works, note what works well and what is problematic, and make recommendations in nine months to the library administration for a way to proceed with the forty or more university electronic publications.

Once again the e-pubs team had a large learning curve to overcome when discussing technology. These technology questions appear to be very different from those of the previous teams. These are much more hardware related, including discussions of servers and capacity and burning CD-ROMS for archival purposes. The issue of campus agreements between computing departments and individuals will be of interest and, of course, our work with a new breed of student and faculty publishers will present a whole range of concerns. Working with so many diverse groups on campus in each of these ventures will prove interesting and, I am sure, frustrating at times. But the skills we learn will serve us well when the next electronic resource comes our way.

To sum up what I have learned being a part of the team environment in my institution is not difficult but takes honesty. It has not been an easy path, and sometimes we have not proceeded in the true team mentality. I have found it takes a lot of effort to be a contributing member to these types of teams. You must be willing to communicate needs, objectives, and failures to the group. You must be accountable. You must to be willing to say, "I don't understand what you are talking about," when the system talk gets deep and involved. You must be willing to share your knowledge and your ignorance. You must be willing to be patient while someone else gets up to speed in a discussion which you know all about. You must be willing to understand that the team can move slowly when you are ready to forge ahead. You must be willing to do outside research and reading on your own to keep your knowledge skills current. You must be willing to always learn something new.

NOTES

1. Ellen Duranceau, *Electronic Journals in the MIT Libraries: Report of the 1995 Ejournal Subgroup.* Available: http://macfadden.mit.edu:9500/ejreport.htm1.

WHEN DISASTER STRIKES: FIRST STEPS IN DISASTER PREPAREDNESS

When Disaster Strikes: First Steps in Disaster Preparedness

Julie A. Page

SUMMARY. Learn what you can do to help better prepare your library for the inevitable disaster. The steps your institution takes now can make the difference between prompt, effective action or unnecessary collection and equipment loss. Institutional and regional disaster preparedness are achievable goals in which all library staff play an important role. Suggestions are given for getting involved in your library's disaster planning and suggestions for disaster planning resources. *[Article copies available for a fee from The Haworth Document Delivery Service: 1-800-342-9678. E-mail address: getinfo@haworthpressinc.com]*

INTRODUCTION

When I was first asked to speak at NASIG, I had to consider seriously how disaster preparedness *fit in* with this conference and

Julie A. Page is Preservation Librarian at the University of California at San Diego.

[Haworth co-indexing entry note]: "When Disaster Strikes: First Steps in Disaster Preparedness." Page, Julie A. Co-published simultaneously in *The Serials Librarian* (The Haworth Press, Inc.) Vol. 36, No. 3/4, 1999, pp. 347-361; and: *Head in the Clouds, Feet on the Ground: Serials Vision and Common Sense* (ed: Jeffrey S. Bullington, Beatrice L. Caraway, and Beverley Geer) The Haworth Press, Inc., 1999, pp. 347-361. Single or multiple copies of this article are available for a fee from The Haworth Document Delivery Service [1-800-342-9678, 9:00 a.m. - 5:00 p.m. (EST). E-mail address: getinfo@haworthpressinc.com].

your day-to-day library jobs. I have strong feelings about the preservation of library collections and its relationship to virtually every job in the library from administration and finances to technical and public services. At UCSD I present a general preservation training session, which is required for all library staff, where I reinforce the importance of their role in the library's preservation program.

Disaster preparedness is an important component of a comprehensive preservation program. It is also related to our personal lives and our family planning for emergencies. The more I thought about disaster preparedness, the more I realized that it also is tied to everyone's library job. It can be the point at which staff begins to understand the broader needs for preservation in their institution. If you don't have a preservation program or some sort of organized preservation effort in your library, disaster preparedness planning is a great place to start.

Disaster preparedness is not simply having a plan or manual, but rather it is a combination of writing documents, raising awareness, conducting drills, rewriting or clarifying procedures based on those drills, and providing ongoing training. You conduct this preparation process within your library, your larger institution, and in some instances, within your community, such as for public libraries. At the end of the program we will discuss very specific roles you can take in your library's disaster planning.

I use the terms "disaster planning," "emergency preparedness" and other combinations somewhat interchangeably to encompass the broad aspects of planning and preparedness. The Library of Congress provides a very practical explanation of these terms in its *Emergency Preparedness for Library of Congress Collections*: "a disaster [is] an emergency which is out-of-control, so what we prepare for are emergencies and if our planning is successful we will not have disasters."[1]

Why do library emergencies have such potential for becoming disasters? "Perhaps because events that involve water and paper or leather quickly become disasters, whether fire or other circumstances are present or not. Also libraries and archives have a large number of organic materials stored in one square meter, so there is a large quantity of material that can be affected by one incident . . . and each item must be individually handled, often in an extremely fragile condition, and handled rapidly."[2]

OBJECTIVES

The objectives for today's program are

- To raise your awareness of the role that all library staff have in disaster prevention and preparedness
- To provide you with the key steps and sources of information to help you initiate or refine disaster preparedness in your library or region
- To give you a first hand account of the Colorado State University disaster and "lessons learned"

It is not the purpose of this program to teach you how to write a disaster plan or how to salvage water-damaged materials. Instead, you will leave here with suggestions for the issues that need to be addressed and how you might approach the key people in your library about disaster planning.

WHAT CONSTITUTES A LIBRARY DISASTER?

We know about the big ones, the natural disasters such as earthquakes, fires, hurricanes, tornadoes, and floods. Many of us look at our library's risk for these as being low, depending on our physical location and library facility. If these were the only disasters we had to worry about, things would be much simpler. However, we have the additional category of what I call *human disasters*, the human-caused or man-made disasters.

No matter how low your library's risk for a natural disaster, all libraries run the rather considerable risk of facing recovery from a human disaster. It may be the result of vandalism, carelessness, or an accident. Libraries that take disaster preparedness seriously prepare for the natural disasters but more often use that preparation to handle the human disasters.

Your role as a library staff member can be critical to the prompt and effective response to both kinds of disasters. Increased awareness of potential problems, such as overloaded electrical outlets, unusual odors, leaking ceilings or pipes, and excessively high water pressure. Also critical is attention to unusual behavior of library users that might lead to vandalism such as tampering with fire sprinklers or setting books on fire. What all these situations have in common is that if disaster strikes, time becomes a critical factor. The better prepared the library is, and the more efficiently it responds, the more likely the recovery will be successful and the costs will be kept down.

I have learned one thing time and time again. Do not assume that someone else will follow through on a potential problem. Ask questions and get the facts, and follow up on anything that you feel might be important, such as a dripping sound or a strange smell. Don't take a "just-wait-and-see" approach. Take action!

What would your reaction be right now if you heard that a disaster–flood, fire, earthquake–had affected your library? Would you be able to say that knowledgeable staff and administration would be able to implement a coordinated and effective disaster response plan? Or would your heart jump into your throat as you realized the library was unprepared and without a plan or trained personnel?

If you feel any hesitation or realize you don't even know the level of your library's preparedness, the following information will help to define the issues and prepare you to ask questions and bring about increased awareness and staff preparedness.

WHAT HINDERS DISASTER PREPAREDNESS?

Why do libraries continue to be unprepared for the inevitable disaster? The statistics show that each one of us will experience at least one library disaster in our careers. As we approach the year 2000 there are still a significant number of libraries that have made no disaster preparations or only minimal attempts.

AMIGOS Bibliographic Services, Inc. has conducted periodic preservation surveys of their members since 1991.[3] The 1998 survey indicated that 53 percent of the libraries responding did not have a disaster plan for the recovery of fire-or water-damaged materials. Even though this is an improvement from the 1991 survey (75 percent had no disaster plan), there is still a large number of libraries that have not taken this important step of planning and documenting procedures.

Another sobering statistic from the same 1998 survey is that 38 percent of the libraries reported they had had a disaster at their library. The percentage of libraries experiencing disasters has remained relatively high over the course of the AMIGOS surveys. In one of their surveys, one-third of the responding libraries reported experiencing a disaster in the last two years.

Several issues can put a damper on effective disaster preparedness and planning. First, planning and preparedness can be overwhelming. Disaster preparedness takes time, commitment, some expertise, and a cross between being diplomatic and bullheaded! However, if you think planning and preparedness are overwhelming, just think about being in the middle of a disaster *without* them. Now that defines overwhelming!

Administrative support is sometimes lacking. First and foremost is to get administrative support. If directors and top administrators are not supportive, disaster planning will not happen. Present your case for why the library needs to spend valuable staff time on disaster preparedness. Stress resumption of services, value of collections, and potential losses if the library is not prepared. Finding a couple of like-minded staff members, who would be willing to divide up the responsibility for initial planning, can help your case. Set a timeline that is not overly ambitious but results in the highest priority tasks being accomplished first. Successful completion of these will result in your next steps, such as the need for financial support, being more favorably received. At this point you can also propose some orientation for the staff at large, with the goal of getting them to buy into the planning process. It has been my experience that people in general find talking about disasters fascinating, and the questions and issues they pose can really get the ball rolling.

There is no assigned responsibility. Assigning responsibility for disaster preparedness so that it becomes part of someone's job is a critical step. Even better is to have the responsibility shared, with a team of people taking on aspects of the process most directly related to their jobs. Representatives from facilities, business services, preservation and access services who maintain close coordination with administration, personnel and systems staff make for a well-balanced and informed team.

Often financial or personnel resources must be found. Fiscal concerns, as well as lack of personnel time, can be addressed by proceeding at a manageable pace, tackling the most important preparation issues first. Gradually building up a store of disaster supplies by purchasing several hundred dollars of the most important supplies is at least a start. For about $500, a couple of disaster supply cans can be equipped.[4] Money will still be left for extra rolls of plastic, a hundred cardboard boxes, sealing tape, and freezer paper. For that $500 investment, you could have supplies on hand to salvage about 1000 books. For every additional $500, you can salvage an additional proportion of books or provide your staff with other disaster supplies such as hardhats, megaphones, and flashlights.

Disaster planning is not an institutional priority. The key to this is getting administrative support and making disaster planning become a priority, with a commitment to both personnel and financial support.

Finally, most people have the "it-can't-happen-to-us" mentality. I hope that after this program you will have the necessary information to go back to your institution and dispel the myth and conquer the issue of making disaster preparedness a priority. Certainly the AMIGOS statistics support that it can happen to any of us, at any time.

KEY STEPS IN DISASTER PREPAREDNESS: PREVENTION

The efforts put toward *prevention* should be as great as the resources allow. All the time, money and close attention to potential problems will pay off in the end. I don't know anyone who has been through a disaster who has said that their prevention efforts were not worthwhile. They may say they didn't do enough, but that is a different issue.[5]

First, assign responsibility. Appoint disaster coordinator(s) and a committee or team with assigned responsibility for disaster preparedness. By dividing up responsibility, perhaps by job responsibilities, this can become a manageable task. An example: access services and personnel staff handling people issues, facilities staff handling building issues, preservation and reference staff handling collection issues. Assemble a small group that can work effectively together. Make it a part of job descriptions and reward those who take on these important tasks.

Next, coordinate with agencies and institutional personnel. Find out who the significant "players" are in your institution, campus, and city. What procedures already exist? Is a plan in place on which you can model a library plan? Is an institutional plan in place? At UCSD the campus plan has specific roles that are to be assumed by key personnel, and the library has developed its emergency plan around these same roles (e.g., first aid coordinator, communications coordinator) with the addition of a collections coordinator. If you are a public library, you may be an evacuation site for the community. The library staff may be expected to assist with people issues, and the priority for collection salvage may be very low.

How does the library "rank" in the priority scheme of the police and fire departments? You may be surprised at how low, but it doesn't have to stay that way. Obviously emergency personnel respond first to life-threatening and people-related emergencies. After this category, you can make a difference in how they perceive the library. The monetary value of library collections is dramatic. It can impress physical plant and police personnel and cause them to stop and think about their response plan for library disasters. Most ARL library collections have an insured value of at least several hundred million dollars. This does not even address the research and historical value of the collections, which is inestimable.

Impressing on fire personnel the devastating damage to books that can be done by high pressure hoses, or on city maintenance crews how critical the time factor is for dealing with wet books, can make a difference. Get to know the risk management personnel and meet with them before a disaster strikes. If there is a safety coordinator, find out how they can help the library get organized.

Next, assess potential sources of emergencies and identify hazards. What disasters are most likely to befall your library? In areas of California, it may be an earthquake, or, if at the base of a mountain, it may be flood. Conduct a risk analysis in order of likelihood. Then use the results to prioritize what needs to be done as far as prevention and focus your plan to handle the most likely disaster events.

Identify the hazards in your library facilities. Conduct a building survey and walk-through with physical plant, fire, and police personnel. Is your roof in poor repair? Can you effectively lobby for improvements as part of your prevention planning? The recent threat from El Nino was enough for UCSD physical plant to move ahead with library roof improvements that had been requested for years. Do you have fire sprinklers? You have a potential risk from their being tampered with. Do enough people know where to turn off the water to the sprinklers in the event there is no fire? Do you have asbestos in the building? Know the hazards that could be harmful to staff and that could halt recovery efforts, potentially resulting in complete collection loss if access to the building is forbidden.

What are the potential nonstructural hazards if earthquake potential is high in your area. Do you have braced shelving and file cabinets? Are hallways used as storage areas, filled with old equipment and furniture? Are fire exits blocked or fire doors propped open, when they should be closed at all times? Are any materials stored on the floor where water could cause severe damage?

Are you undergoing construction or remodeling? Even though this isn't a permanent hazard, it is a very real one. Many major library disasters have happened during construction in and around libraries–the temporary wall that gives way during heavy rains; normally effective drainage that is blocked and carries mud and water into a building; or roof repair that is not properly cleaned up, with debris washing into drains that become plugged and then back up. A heightened level of awareness during these times can avert a disaster.

Next, assess collection assets and set priorities. Priority for packout and salvage should be given to those records and collections that have information needed to establish or continue operations after a disaster (e.g., bibliographic records, staff and personnel records). If you already have key records duplicated and stored off-site you will be able to more quickly focus attention on library collections.

When it comes to prioritizing collections, it is more challenging and time consuming. Use existing collection development policies if available, categorizing materials into high, medium, and low priority for salvage. Assign high priority for those materials most frequently used, vital records without backups, irreplaceable and most important materials, and materials critical to ongoing operations. Assign medium priority for important materials that could be replaced, but whose replacement costs would exceed the cost of salvage. Give low priority to materials that can be replaced, even if they have a high monetary value but are low in other measures. Make decisions based on stack sections, not book by book or shelf by shelf.

Format of the materials may change a collection's priority (e.g., leather-bound books, nonprint materials, clay-coated paper stock). The priority list should guide the order of the salvage operation. Accessibility to the materials for salvage will not be known until the disaster happens. Your high priority items may not be accessible immediately, and you will have to focus the first salvage phases on lower priority materials.

If you have trouble figuring out the best approach for recording collection priorities, look at other library disaster plans. I have seen the effective use of the database approach using building, floor and call number as well as the one-page ranking of key collections. The main thing is to get something down on paper that has been discussed by an appropriate group with input from key people.

Next, assess prevention and protection needs. Work with your facilities and campus or city staff to assess your disaster prevention needs. For example, if you have book returns from the outside into the building, what can you do to protect your library from an incendiary device being dropped inside? This can be as simple as closing them when the library is not open. Or you may want to improve smoke detectors or sprinklers in the book return area.

Are emergency maps with locations of exits, fire pulls, and fire extinguishers clear and mounted throughout the building, in both public and staff areas? Computer-produced floor plans can save considerable time in preparing and updating maps.

Next, consider fiscal implications. What prevention steps can be taken at no cost, for example, closing the book return, or at low cost, such as improving signage? What can you do with the moneys you have available? Can earthquake bracing of book stacks be phased in over several years? What needs additional funding, for instance, a new roof? There will also be staff time implications for the disaster team members.

Finally, implement when possible. A plan should be formulated with goals that are fiscally responsible, achievable over a manageable period of time, and sensible based on the risk analysis process. Periodic review of the goals and steady progress with reevaluation and reassessment will help keep the process moving forward.

KEY STEPS IN DISASTER PREPAREDNESS: PREPARATION, RESPONSE, RECOVERY

The *preparation* process includes the actions we take for *when* or *just in case* disaster strikes. It provides the framework for *response.* Response is the implementation of the parts of the plan that are needed to meet the institution's needs in the event of a disaster. *Recovery* is what you do to get back to delivering materials and services. I like to consider these processes linked together with a set of actions.

First, identify insurance and emergency funds. What are the steps required of your insurance coverage? If you take pictures and document the disaster, can you start salvage operations? You can't just sit and watch wet books for a couple of days. Planning ahead with the insurance company will often allow you to start recovery operations immediately. Find out the emergency funds that may be available for supplies and services. There is the likelihood that staff will need to write personal checks or use their credit cards for supplies or vendors. Is any prior authorization needed so staff are assured that they will be reimbursed? What kind of accounting procedures need to be in place?

Prepare a telephone tree. An emergency responder home phone list should be prepared for the key members of your disaster response team, administrators, and first response staff. Cell phone numbers should be included when available.

An up-to-date home telephone list of all staff is very important. It may be necessary to organize staff to come to work in shifts. If they are at home at the time of the disaster, you may want to stop them from reporting to work until a later time. Phone trees should include student workers and volunteers. In the event of something sudden such as an earthquake, the phone list may be the only way of verifying that someone is at home and not trapped in your building.

Identify sources of supplies, services and experts. Supply sources and services can be very effectively worked on regionally. Several libraries can work together by dividing up a list of resources that would be needed for collection salvage (e.g., boxes, plastic sheeting, vacuum freeze drying) and calling local vendors to determine costs and availability of supplies. Regional preservation networks have vendor and supply lists published or available electronically on the Web. The names and phone numbers of preservation experts in your area can come in very handy. Simply being able to review a situation with someone knowledgeable can be reassuring in a time of crisis.

Purchase and distribute in-house supplies. Having a reliable source of in-house disaster supplies can mean the difference between being able to start a salvage operation of your high-priority materials versus having to wait to obtain the supplies from outside your institution. As I stated earlier, for a small investment, you buy a great deal of peace of mind. There is a real sense of reassurance knowing that in the library there are supplies to pack out over 5,000 books. By the time these supplies have been used, additional regional and vendor supplies can be obtained. In addition, immediate-response supply cans can be distributed throughout the libraries for use by library staff. Of course, you also need to set up a mechanism to monitor and replace these supplies.

Document and post emergency procedures. As procedures are developed for inclusion in a disaster plan, decide which information needs to be posted and readily available to all staff. Emergency exit maps should be specific to each department or room. A ready reference-type guide to the most common emergencies can be posted near telephones or on departmental bulletin boards. Staff should start thinking about their personal safety in their work areas. What are the non-structural elements that may be of danger, especially in earthquake-prone regions? What is going to fall and hit them on the head or trap them in an office?

Write an adequately detailed disaster plan. A detailed plan does not mean a long plan. Start simple with the basics, using examples and guidelines available on the *CoOL Conservation OnLine* Website.[6] See what you can use, printing and hole punching liberally when permitted. I am a great proponent of using what others have already written whenever possible. The fill-in-the-blank templates can be real time savers for the pieces of the plan that need to be customized for your institution with building locations, names, and phone numbers. Make the plan easy to update. Do not make it such a complex plan that it doesn't get completed or is too long to be easily duplicated and distributed. Your goal should be to get clear and reliable information widely distributed and kept up-to-date.

Finally, train staff. Make it clear that all staff share a responsibility for disaster preparedness. Open meetings where the process is presented, along with e-mail or library newsletter articles, can be useful communication tools. Consider devoting a short part of several staff or departmental meetings to institutional and personal preparedness. If you have a staff training department in the library, work with them to develop a training session.

KEY STEPS IN DISASTER PREPAREDNESS: FOLLOW-THROUGH

Follow-through includes the plan distribution and those parts of the process that are ongoing to assure that disaster preparedness remains a priority for the library.

First, distribute written documentation and plans. You want to have commitment and support from all the players and decision makers and their clear buy-in for the plans and procedures. Survey all the appropriate people, including library staff and campus or city services, especially risk management staff. Hopefully you will have already made revisions based on previous drafts and feedback, but be prepared for more. It is advisable to have your disaster plans in electronic form and on your Website, but make sure that key staff have printed copies at work and at home in case computers are not useable.

Educate staff and fire and security personnel. Review the parts of the plan that affect their departments and reach agreement on what you can expect from them. Keep in mind that fast reaction by staff and emergency personnel can mean the difference in having an emergency instead of a disaster, and saving thousands of dollars in damage.

The UCSD Libraries conduct a general emergency preparedness training session that is required of all staff. In addition, specific training is held regularly for the Disaster Recovery Team for collections salvage and for the access services staff, who usually handle the first response for emergencies. Don't forget new staff. What provisions are made to train them? Is part of new employee orientation a review of the library's emergency procedures? It should be included in both the librarywide and departmental training.

Make provisions for key disaster preparedness staff to stay informed about developments in the field through reading the literature, attending advanced and hands-on disaster training programs, and participating as a trainer at workshops and conferences such as this one.

Test and evaluate the plan. When people understand their role and functions during a disaster, things seem to fall into place much faster. I am especially fond of using tabletop drills to test and refine procedures. The drill includes a realistic disaster scenario, where groups of eight to ten people, with a facilitator, are guided through an exercise. By developing questions for them to discuss and come to agreement on, everyone participates and has a true hands-on use of the disaster plans and documentation. The drill can also include role playing or participants assuming their real disaster roles. The result is a more aware, better-trained staff and a testing of the plan for weaknesses and lack of clarity. Staff are also quick to give evaluation and tell you what is effective or what aspects need more training.

During a drill you may also discover that some people cannot handle their assigned responsibilities. The time to find this out is before a disaster rather than when decision making under stress is the norm. This allows for reassigning jobs and even discovering alternate staff to take a leadership roll during disaster drills.

Finally, review, revise and update the plan at least annually. The disaster plan is not cast in stone and should not just sit on a shelf and gather dust. It needs to be looked at regularly and used for minor emergencies. The plan contains a variety of components, some of which need frequent updating (e.g., phone trees) and testing. If the plan becomes outdated, it is more likely to be ignored in a disaster. The drills and testing of the plan will help provide input for revisions. One approach is to set a regular month each year during which the plan is reviewed, training is held for new employees, and phone numbers are verified. My rule is, if you literally have to dust off a notebook in which you have your plan, then it has been sitting there too long!

NEXT STEPS

As a library staff member, you have a role in your library's disaster preparedness and planning. You can make a difference by asking the questions, "Where's the plan, and what have we done to prepare?" If you discover there is no plan, look for ways to *kick start* disaster preparedness at your institution. Do not assume that someone else is going to do it. The following steps can provide you with a place to start:

- *Contact a regional network, such as AMIGOS or SOLINET.* Additional information is available on the Regional Alliance for Preservation Webpage.[7] They can help you get started, provide planning information and training and put you in touch with local library networks and libraries of similar size who can provide assistance.
- *Find out the plan for your larger institution.* Who are the appropriate people for the library to be working with on your campus or in your city? Who would be the other key players in a disaster?
- *Bring in a speaker to talk about disaster preparedness, similar to what has been covered in this talk.* Include people who are responsible for disaster planning for the larger institution or municipality. Invite all library staff to attend.

If you discover there is a disaster plan at your library, take a look at it and see if it needs revitalizing. Again, don't assume someone else is going to do it. The following ideas will lead to better preparedness:

- *Suggest that a small group review the plan and update it where necessary.* Are the names and phone numbers correct? Floor plans still accurate? Procedures and priorities for salvage relevant? Divide up the work so no one is overwhelmed or slows the momentum.
- *Offer to help with a tabletop drill to review the plan.* Keep the initial group small and unthreatening if the plan still needs considerable work. Let it evolve to a final revision before involving those who may be too critical or may stifle enthusiasm.

Whether you have a disaster plan or not, perhaps you are interested enough to write up your thoughts about disaster preparedness and send them out on a library listserv or in your library's newsletter. If the more informal approach appeals to you, take one of the key disaster people to lunch, and let them know about your interest. Above all, be constructive in whatever approach feels right to you. Not everyone on the staff needs to know how to catalog or acquire a book or access an electronic journal, but all library staff need to know at least the basics of disaster planning and preparedness, and each has a role to play both at work and at home.

NOTES

1. Ann Seibert, "What is an Emergency? What is a Disaster?" in *Emergency Preparedness for Library of Congress Collections* (Washington, DC: Library of Congress, 1996). Available: http://lcweb.loc.gov/preserv/seibert/whatsa.html. September 21, 1998.

2. Ibid.

3. Surveys were conducted in 1991, 1995, and 1998 by the AMIGOS Preservation Service. For additional information and analysis, contact AMIGOS at 1-800-843-8482.

4. A list of basic disaster supplies compiled by the UCSD Libraries Preservation Department is available on the Web at http://orpheus.ucsd.edu/preservation/drtcan.html. September 21, 1998.

5. Some of the information included in the "Key Steps in Disaster Preparedness" section of this paper are based on training materials developed by Sheryl Davis, University of California, Riverside and are used with her permission.

6. *CoOL Conservation OnLine.* Available: http://palimpsest.stanford.edu. September 21, 1998.

7. *RAP Regional Alliance for Preservation.* Available: http://www.solinet.net/RAP. September 21, 1998.

SELECTED LIST OF DISASTER RESOURCES

Disaster Wheel: National Task Force on Emergency Response, *Emergency Response and Salvage Wheel.* A user-friendly slide chart providing quick access to essential information on protecting and salvaging collections. Authoritative, hands-on advice developed by conservation professionals for staff at museums, libraries and archives. Nonprofit/government rate: $5.95 each. Quantity discount available. For order information and picture: http://www.nic.org/Emergency/wheel.html or call 1-888-979-2233.

Websites: *CoOL Conservation OnLine* at: http://palimpsest.stanford.edu. September 21, 1992. "A project of the Preservation Dept. of Stanford University Libraries is a full text library of conservation information . . . of interest to those involved with the conservation of library, archives, and museum materials." (From *CoOL* page, par. 1.) "Disaster Preparedness and Response" is one of the conservation topics that includes a wealth of information linking to organizations (e.g., LC, NEDCC, SOLINET), disaster plans, and a broad spectrum of other disaster and emergency resources. *CoOL* is the best place to start because it is so comprehensive. "Disaster Preparedness and Response" is continually being added to and updated by Walter Henry. Many resources can be linked to or printed directly from *CoOL* for use in your own disaster plans. Scan the disaster plans of other institutions similar to your own.

RAP Regional Alliance for Preservation. Available: http://www.solinet.net/RAP. September 21, 1998. "A cooperative project to share preservation training resources" (From *RAP* page, par. 1.) Five field services (AMIGOS, CCAHA, NEDCC, SOLINET, UMCA) with information about each one, their training schedules, contacting them and other organizations.

San Diego/Imperial County Libraries Disaster Response Network. Available: http:// orpheus.ucsd.edu/sildrn. September 21, 1998. Regional disaster network in California. It is linked from *CoOL* as are several of the other California network pages (IELDRN, BAPNet). Gives an idea of specific regional information that can be delivered via the Web as well as including general library disaster response and recovery resources.

Colorado State University Flood Recovery. Available: http://www.colostate.edu/ floodrecovery. September 21, 1998. "Lessons of Recovery" from the July 28, 1997 CSU Ft. Collins flooding. Library disasters can be immediately documented and made visually "public" via the Web. This can be especially beneficial for disseminating news bulletins, keeping the public and university community updated, and requesting assistance. Stanford University very effectively used this same approach in February 1998 following their library flooding.

When Disaster Strikes:
A Case Study:
Colorado State University Libraries,
July 28, 1997

Diane B. Lunde

INTRODUCTION

This part of the presentation on "When Disaster Strikes" spotlights the water disaster at Colorado State University Libraries last July 28, 1997. I will cover the disaster itself, the libraries' recovery effort which still continues today, and relate our experiences to the presentation by Julie Page.

THE DISASTER OF JULY 28, 1997

Monday, July 28, 1997, was my first day back to work after a three-week vacation. I spent the day going through my mail, my numerous e-mail messages, and talking to my staff to see what had happened during my absence. When I left work for the day, projects for the coming week were sorted on my desk. But because of the disaster, I was not able to work at my desk again until one month later!

The previous rainy days had not prepared us for the deluge that hit

Diane B. Lunde is Preservation Librarian, Colorado State University Libraries.

[Haworth co-indexing entry note]: "When Disaster Strikes: A Case Study: Colorado State University Libraries, July 28, 1997." Lunde, Diane B. Co-published simultaneously in *The Serials Librarian* (The Haworth Press, Inc.) Vol. 36, No. 3/4, 1999, pp. 363-382; and: *Head in the Clouds, Feet on the Ground: Serials Vision and Common Sense* (ed: Jeffrey S. Bullington, Beatrice L. Caraway, and Beverley Geer) The Haworth Press, Inc., 1999, pp. 363-382. Single or multiple copies of this article are available for a fee from The Haworth Document Delivery Service [1-800-342-9678, 9:00 a.m. - 5:00 p.m. (EST). E-mail address: getinfo@haworthpressinc.com].

the western part of Fort Collins that night. Some areas of the city along the foothills got up to ten inches of rain in a short time span, while the eastern part of the city got only a couple of inches. I live in southwestern Fort Collins where we had up to seven inches that formed large puddles in the back yard. The dogs would not even stick their heads out the door–it was just *too* wet!! I heard sirens after dark, but really did not think much about it, as I live next to a major thoroughfare.

My concerns about the Colorado State University library building were related to the numerous regular leaky spots we still had due to continuing construction. There had been enough of them over the past two to three years that I had a folder earmarked "construction accidents."

About 9:00 P.M., Carmel Bush, the assistant dean for technical services, called me. Staff at the libraries had phoned her because there was water in the building. She decided to go in to take a look and would call me *if* I was needed to deal with wet materials. Carmel's call at about 10:45 P.M. relayed the real disaster–the water had punched a hole in the new west-basement wall and had filled the basement up past the ceiling tiles. We were very lucky that no one was injured, as few patrons were in the building and staff working in the basement made a very hasty retreat when they heard the wall "groan."

My assignment was to contact my staff to tell them not to come in to work the next morning and to start contacting potential disaster recovery vendors. I had the libraries' *Disaster Plan Quick Reference Guide* at home, but my disaster manual was in my office on the second floor of the library (safe, I hoped!). The quick reference guide was for libraries' staff use as an immediate response tool, with instructions for action in case of a fire alarm, tornado, etc. In the case of this disaster, we were already beyond the scope of the guide.

Lesson Number One: Always have a copy of your Disaster Manual and related phone numbers at home. I had to call friends in Denver to finally obtain telephone numbers of disaster recovery vendors. Arrangements were made for the vendors to come to the libraries at 10:00 A.M. the next morning.

The disaster team was at the libraries by 7:00 A.M. the next morning. I had stopped to buy two one-use only cameras to record initial impressions. The view that presented itself was awesome! The lagoon area behind the Lory Student Center to the north of the libraries was under several feet of water and the terrace down to the library basement was completely filled with water.

The university has produced a very fine video of the disaster,[1] but because of the program time restraints, I will show illustrations of the library disaster.

Illustration One: The reflection in the water would have been beautiful if not for the scope of the disaster. You can see the tide lines above the water level. From the outside, one could see the water in the basement up to the level of the upper stack shelves, with UFOs (unidentified floating objects) in the water. When looking down at the basement from inside the library, all we could see were dark pools of water in the stairwells, as there was no lighting.

Illustration Two: This picture shows the actual hole that the floodwaters punched in the wall. The area between two windows gave way to the floodwaters. The hole became visible over the next few days as water was pumped out of the basement.

Illustration Three: When the water was finally pumped out of the basement and disaster staff were allowed downstairs, the scope of the disaster was overpowering. The force of the water had tumbled stack ranges over, spilling materials on the floor. Books were mixed in with debris and fallen ceiling tiles. Luckily, the new computer cables were in cable trays in the ceiling, or otherwise they would have also been down.

Illustration Four: Half of the basement was movable shelving that contained all our bound journals and monographs in the LC classifications Q-V. Because most of the aisles were "closed," many of the materials had remained on the shelves and arched upwards as they swelled. As there was no electricity, and some shelves were off their tracks, the now immovable shelving had to be taken apart to remove the materials.

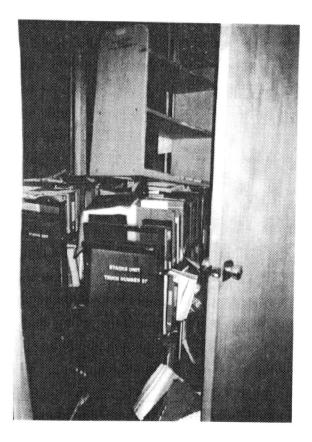

Illustration Five: In the shelving work room, the force of the water took one book truck and placed it on top of another book truck.

Illustration Six: The newspaper area was very close to the hole in the wall. This picture was taken later in the pack-out. If you look carefully, you can see the mold already on the materials which were stacked by the workers after being removed from the floor.

This fact sheet (Table 1) lists the damage to the campus and library building. There were thirty buildings damaged on campus, including Lory Student Center, which lost the entire supply of textbooks for fall semester. One call I received that first week was from the student newspaper office, which lost everything in the disaster. Yes, our archival copy of the complete run of the *Collegian* was safe on the second floor!

TABLE 1. COLORADO STATE UNIVERSITY
DISASTER, JULY 28,1997

THE CAMPUS

> 30 buildings, including Police Department and Lory Student Center (student newspaper offices and bookstore with all fall semester text books), and over 200 faculty, staff and graduate offices

THE LIBRARIES BASEMENT

> VOLUMES: Estimated 425,750 volumes representing all bound periodicals, all monographs in LC classification HG-N, Q-Z, Current Awareness collection, Curriculum materials, Oversized collection and current newspapers

> SHELVING: 40,000 linear feet of movable shelving and 41,000 linear feet of standard shelving

> OFFICES: Staff offices and contents of the Bindery Section and Gifts & Exchange; Electronic Information Lab; 5 group study rooms; 2 photocopy rooms

> EQUIPMENT & FURNITURE: 30 PCS (EIL/offices/public terminals); public furniture (486 chairs, 36 tables, 19 carrels and 11 couches; 30 book trucks; Preservation supply cabinet

> MISCELLANEOUS: Stored equipment, furniture, records, and supplies; 3 elevators; telecommunication closet; several mechanical rooms and equipment

Library statistics prepared by Halcyon Enssle, Library Building Proctor

The number of books in the libraries' basement was calculated from the number of linear feet of shelving and the average number of volumes per linear foot. The number was later compared in the online public catalog against the number of item records for materials located in the basement.

Note that the preservation disaster supply cabinet was in the basement. Its replacement will be housed on the second floor!

DISASTER RECOVERY

As I mentioned, the libraries' disaster team met at 7:00 A.M. on Tuesday morning in the lobby of the library. Our main concerns were

- recovery of the library materials in the basement
- stabilization of the environment and prevention of any damage to the first through the fourth floors due to mold, etc.

- restoration of the building itself, including the HVAC and electricity
- restoration of libraries' services, including reference, interlibrary loan, and circulation
- moving the main computer out of the building for its own protection and to restore remote access to the online computer
- security of the building and its contents
- status of the staff, because the libraries would not be operational for the immediate future

As my part of the disaster team, I worked with the recovery of the library materials and planning for the processing plant to be set up to deal with the materials when they returned to the libraries.

I need not have worried about finding a vendor! Not only did the vendors I had contacted show up at the libraries, but other vendors did also. We discovered that the disaster recovery business is very competitive, and given a major disaster, all vendors show up looking for business. By the end of that first day, the university had hired Boss & Associates to oversee the recovery efforts of the whole campus. Only one of the vendors that I contacted was hired, in this case to handle the stabilization of the building environment.

Lesson Two: Before a disaster, know who all the major players are in case of a major disaster. For previous small disasters in the libraries, staff from the libraries and/or university facilities handled the emergency, with occasional help from the construction company if the problem was construction related. Because of the scope of this disaster, the University was in charge of recovery effort. Vendor relations were handled by the university administration. Do not underestimate the role of the insurance companies–they have the checkbook!

Illustration Seven: If you work for an educational institution, take a look at the University Emergency Operations Plan located at the CSU Website at http://www.colostate.edu/floodrecovery/. It will give you an idea of what such a plan looks like. The Website also contains other information on the campus disaster, including information about the libraries.

ILLUSTRATION 7

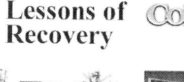

Lessons of Recovery

CSU Home

On July 28, 1997, Colorado State University was hit by a devastating flood that swept through campus and caused $100 million in damages to buildings and property. But thanks to the hard work and perseverance of the university community, recovery efforts have been remarkable - days after the flood, summer session classes resumed as normal, and, not quite one month later, fall semester 1997 began for more than 22,000 students.

In dealing with this natural disaster, we have learned a great deal. This webpage is dedicated to sharing information with our colleagues in higher education about dealing with such a disaster. We consider this webpage an ongoing effort, and we will continue to add information from key participants in our continuing recovery process. Ultimately, we hope this will become a comprehensive resource. For now, this information will help outline the challenges we faced and continue to face, and to show some of our responses.

A look at the following pages will not only show you why Colorado State University is recovering, but will also demonstrate our commitment to coming back stronger and better than ever.

Lessons from an Extreme Event-A Scholarly Review	Tips From a Disaster Recovery Expert
1997 Fall Address President Albert C. Yates	Public Relations Response to Crisis
Images from the Flood	Recovery: The Stories and People of Colorado State University
A Scientific Look at the Storm	University Emergency Operations Plan
Critical Flood-Damaged Journals Identified by CSU Faculty	Cooperative Extension Flood Recovery Tips
Lessons of Recovery! Issues of Comment (Staff and Faculty Newsletter)	
Opening Buildings More Complicated Than Swinging Doors Open	University specialist in grief talks about coping
Related Links	News Releases

Table Two: The disaster timeline outlines the major activities from Day 1 (July 28, 1997) to the present (June 21, 1998). As Day 2 ended, facilities staff were pumping water out of the basement, a vendor had set up to stabilize the environment, and the libraries' main computer was moved off-site.

TABLE 2. COLORADO STATE UNIVERSITY
DISASTER AND RECOVERY TIME LINE

DAY 1: JULY 28, 1997
* Evening: Storm stalls over western Fort Collins, sending flood waters across town.
* 9:00 p.m. (Approx.) Phone call from Libraries staff to Carmel Bush concerning water in the building.
* 10:00 p.m. (approx.) Water punches hole in basement wall and floods basement up past the ceiling. (Est. of 658,750 cu.ft. = 4,928,109 gallons = 41,106,000 lbs.).
* 10:45 p.m. (approx.) Notification to Preservation Librarian to start contacting vendors to deal with flooded basement.
DAY 2: JULY 29, 1997
* 7:00 a.m. Disaster team gathers in main foyer of library. Water can be seen just over the top of the book stacks in the basement. There is no electricity, HVAC, or telecommunications.
* 10:00 a.m. Appearance at the library of the first vendors for environmental control and recovery of the damaged collection.
* Facilities staff begin to pump water out of the basement.
* Library computer moved out of Libraries to other quarters.
* Boss & Associates hired by CSU as disaster recovery consultant.
DAY 3: JULY 30, 1997
* Most of the water is pumped out of the basement.
* First staff members allowed into basement to make assessment.
* Establishment of library command center in Clark Building.
* Establishment of off-site services for Reference, Circulation and Interlibrary Loan.
* All staff meeting in the courtyard in afternoon.
DAY 4: JULY 31, 1997
* Begin of packout of Libraries materials from the basement.
DAY 18: AUGUST 14, 1997
* Finish of packout of Libraries materials.
DAY 25: AUGUST 22, 1997
* Staff allowed in building for "normal" operations.
* Still not working: PAC access in building, elevators.
DAY 29: AUGUST 25, 1997
*First day of the fall semester–Libraries back in operation.
NOVEMBER 25, 1997
*Beginning day of Processing Plant Center, receiving gifts to replace damaged materials.
JUNE 22,1998 (scheduled)
*Shift of materials back to the basement, including gift and newly purchased volumes and those volumes that were checked out at the time of the flood and returned later.
AUGUST 1, 1998 (scheduled)
* Receipt of first damaged materials back from treatment.
AUGUST 7, 1998 (scheduled)
*Date for damaged materials to go back to the shelves.

Illustration Eight: This picture shows the drying tubes that ran throughout the building. As the tubes were knee high, they made getting around the building interesting.

By Day 3, a command post was set up in a classroom building next door, library services were being set up off-site, and an all-staff meeting was held in the courtyard that afternoon. Some staff would be working at the off-site locations, technical services staff would be working in the library storage facilities on a bar coding project, and other staff would be "on call" at home.

Illustration Nine: On Day 4, the pack-out began in the movable shelving. It would take fourteen days to finish, with over 7,000 pallets of materials packed out. A conveyor belt was installed up from the basement and out a side door, where the boxes were put on pallets, loaded on to refrigerated trucks, and taken first to a commercial freezer in Laramie, Wyoming, and later to Texas.

By the first day of school, less than one month after the disaster, the libraries were open for business. Not *open as usual*, but due to intense activity by all concerned, *open* for the students and faculty to use.

CONSERVATION TREATMENT OF LIBRARY MATERIALS

A major part of the planning done by libraries' staff was for the recovery process of the materials damaged in the flood. All the materials were to be freeze dried by Disaster Recovery Services (DRS) in Texas. Procedures had to be worked out for the exact processing of the materials.

Illustration Ten: During an August visit to Texas by Bill Boss, Ann Siebert of the Library of Congress, several others, and myself, the protocol for the processing was determined. Each volume would be thawed-out, washed to remove the dirt, and then reshaped if necessary. Books would be refrozen and then freeze dried before being returned to Fort Collins. Illustration Ten shows Ann Siebert and Larry Wood, DRS, conferring over a damaged volume.

Illustration Eleven shows library materials being wheeled into the freeze dryer which is a large chamber almost the size of a freight car.

Illustration Twelve: In October 1997, the libraries got its first view of the dried materials as a group of more than 100 volumes was sent to Fort Collins from Texas. This picture shows the numerous people who were interested in the condition of the materials, including (left to right) Diane Lunde, Jack Peterson representing an insurance firm, Kirk Lively and Larry Wood of DRS, Bill Boss, and Rankin Alm, an insurance consultant. Partially based on this sample, staff estimated that 20 percent of the materials would be a total loss and 80 percent would be salvageable.

Procedures were needed for the processing of the materials back into the collection. A processing plant was established in the now clean, but gutted-out basement to be operated by Mr. Boss and non-library staff. A database was created to track materials through the plant, from inspection, page repair, page replacement, binding, and then back to the stacks.

From the very beginning, the libraries received offers of gift materials to replace damaged materials. When the Processing Plant became operational on November 25, 1997, it began with processing gifts resulting from a now very active gift solicitation program.

As of mid-June 1998, the Plant has processed over 40,000 gift volumes for the stacks, with the goal of 80,000 volumes on the shelf by September 1, 1998. On June 22, 1998, the first books will be returned to the movable shelving in the basement, with complete renovation of the basement to be finished in time for spring semester 1999. The first materials from DRS are scheduled to arrive around August 1, 1998, one year after the disaster! Processing of the DRS materials could take from one and one-half years to two years to be completed.

Lessons Learned/Points to Ponder:

- Did we have a disaster plan? Yes.
- Did we have a disaster response team? Yes. (See Table 3.)

Did we have experience with disaster response/recovery? Yes. During the small disasters over the previous three to four years of building construction, libraries' staff had responded to frozen water pipes, leaks in the ceiling, especially at the seam between the old and the new building, water in the journal reading room when new sprinkler valves went off, water from a hole in the roof where they constructed the bridge linking the new third floors over the old second floor, and water that sat unnoticed in map cabinets for several months. Also, the libraries' staff had seen the results of "human disasters" or vandalism, such as the patron who put new books in the toilets or tore paperbacks in half.

Colorado State University Libraries had operated a Wei T'o Book Dryer for ten years and had seen firsthand the results of water damage to such varied materials as church music, business records, children's books and library materials. Staff knew how freeze drying worked and what results can be achieved.

Did we have recent training in disaster recovery? Yes, especially the preservation librarian. The 1997 Colorado Preservation Alliance annual meeting was a two-day seminar on disaster preparedness and recovery. For the hands-on workshop, I was the one who demonstrated washing dirty books!

TABLE 3. COLORADO STATE UNIVERSITY LIBRARIES DISASTER TEAM ORGANIZATIONAL CHART

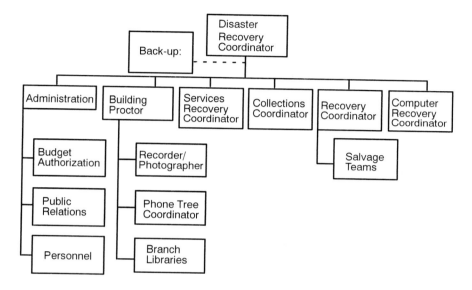

Table Three: Libraries Disaster Team Organizational Chart. The organization of the disaster team played an important role in the recovery effort. The staff members knew their roles and stepped right into them from the very beginning. The one position that was not needed was that of recovery/salvage, as the work was done by the vendors.

Were we ready for a disaster of this magnitude? Not really! But I do not think anyone ever thinks such a disaster can really happen. This is probably the largest library water disaster in the United States to date.

What made it work? There are numerous factors that influenced the libraries' disaster recovery effort, including

- the leadership of Camila Alire, new dean of the libraries, who was on the second day of her second week on the job the day of the disaster. Although the disaster team organization chart had the preservation librarian as the head, it was essential that the dean assume the lead position, especially in regards to the many meetings and planning sessions with the university administration;

- the feeling that the libraries' staff were in this together;
- the fact that no one panicked, although staff seemed to be working on pure adrenaline the first week or so. The members of the disaster team dug right in and found solutions, often creative ones, for the problems that they faced; and
- the experience of the staff of working together on many projects. We were used to each others foibles, which goes a long way in planning sessions that last until 3 A.M.

CONCLUSION

The disaster at the Colorado State University Libraries has greatly influenced the past year, in both the kind of work that has been done and the staff who have done it. It has been a tremendous learning experience! There still is a long way to go to get the damaged collections back on the shelf for patron use, and some materials will never be replaced. Although Colorado State University Libraries has come a long way, there are still many challenges ahead!

My fervent wish for all librarians and their libraries is that they *never* have a disaster. But just in case, please use the very sound information on disaster preparedness presented by Julie Page to "plan ahead." And remember that a disaster is always a "nasty surprise," but if you plan for the unexpected, it can be survived.

NOTES

1. *After the Flood: Colorado State University*, Public and Media Relations Department, Colorado State University, 10 min., 1997, videocassette.

What If Gutenberg Had a T-1 Connection?

Joseph Janes
Lorrie LeJeune

SUMMARY. The emerging information environment (incorporating print, digital and networked resources) opens up enormous potential for publishing and access to information but raises lots of questions such as, When does a book with a continually-revised Web presence stop having editions and become a serial? Or, How is the editorial process different in a digital work? There are dynamic processes involved, and publishers and librarians needs to figure them out together. *[Article copies available for a fee from The Haworth Document Delivery Service: 1-800-342-9678. E-mail address: getinfo@haworthpressinc.com]*

Joseph Janes is Director of the Internet Public Library, School of Information, University of Michigan.

Lorrie LeJeune is Product Marketing Manager, Technical Publishing, O'Reilly & Associates.

[Haworth co-indexing entry note]: "What If Gutenberg Had a T-1 Connection?" Janes, Joseph, and Lorrie LeJeune. Co-published simultaneously in *The Serials Librarian* (The Haworth Press, Inc.) Vol. 36, No. 3/4, 1999, pp. 383-398; and: *Head in the Clouds, Feet on the Ground: Serials Vision and Common Sense* (ed: Jeffrey S. Bullington, Beatrice L. Caraway, and Beverley Geer) The Haworth Press, Inc., 1999, pp. 383-398. Single or multiple copies of this article are available for a fee from The Haworth Document Delivery Service [1-800-342-9678, 9:00 a.m. - 5:00 p.m. (EST). E-mail address: getinfo@haworthpressinc.com].

WHAT IF GUTENBERG REALLY DID HAVE
A T-1 CONNECTION?

Let's imagine for a moment a parallel universe where digital had come before analog. In this universe Johannes Gutenberg, instead of inventing moveable type, created HTTPD, HTML, and a Web server that ran on his new Pentium Pro. Being a man of his time, he promptly built a Website on which he posted an HTML-coded version of the Latin Bible. In our universe, the Gutenberg Bible revolutionized the dissemination of information. In our parallel universe the Gutenberg Website caused an information revolution of a different sort. Since the Web was free, every scholarly theologian felt obligated to log on and study this new biblical marvel. Martin Luther downloaded the New Testament and made a German translation, which he promptly posted on his Website. John Calvin made a few stylistic edits to Luther's translation and reposted it. And William Caxton, having designed a new typeface and illustrations just for the occasion, issued an English translation in print! Librarians of that alternative day were hard pressed to keep up with this barrage of Web publishing, much as they are in our world today.

The world of information management is truly at a crossroads. It has become a hybrid world, a mixture of old (print) and new (CD-ROMs, e-mail, the World Wide Web). It is the new part, the virtual part, that presents the most excitement and the most challenge, since intellectual content is detached from any physical carrier medium. Librarians, publishers, authors, and readers alike are struggling to make sense of the glut of information the Web and other digital technologies have unleashed. In a sense, the long, rich histories of publishing and libraries hamper us. As librarians we have difficulty thinking about how to organize and archive digitally based information because we have so many years of experience organizing printed information. As publishers we struggle to make the shift from developing print-based content to developing multimedia and Web-based content. All those years of thinking between clothbound covers has made it hard for us to think of content in any other form, let alone a new form that is actively evolving.

But suppose for a moment we cast off the burden of history and think about information as if it had always existed in multiple forms. How might we answer such questions as, Who owns what and for how long? How do we catalog hyperdocuments and multimedia, never mind manage them? How will we access this content ten or a hundred years from now?

But before we put history aside and examine those questions, let's take a quick look at the past to put our current situation in proper perspective.

HISTORY:
PREVIOUS LIBRARIANSHIP REACTS
TO NEW TECHNOLOGY

The libraries of antiquity were concerned with many of the same issues as the libraries of today: collection development and acquisition (including some interesting ideas, such as confiscating all books of people entering the city and reimbursing them with cheaper copies), organization by subject, and arrangement for access.[1] In addition, librarians were scholars, keeping varying nonstandard texts straight, investigating and completing incomplete copies, and developing contents indicators for nameless scrolls.

Medieval librarians, often monks overseeing small collections in monasteries, were quite concerned with selection. The primary issue here was in deciding what works were worth copying (a new Bible would take at least 1600 hours to produce) and identifying spurious and fictitious titles. Preservation, in unheated, vermin-ridden and often damp conditions, was also a concern. By the twelfth century, some libraries were limiting loans to "outsiders," those outside the monastery, due to increasing demand.

We'd like to take a moment to point out that publishing, as the field we think of today, did not exist in this pre-Gutenberg era or for at least 200 years after. Early publishers did not solicit and develop new content, but were invariably printers who produced (and reproduced) existing religious and scientific works mainly for the scholarly (library) audience. The largely illiterate public of the day could not conceive of "popular" publications let alone pay for them.

Renaissance librarianship gave rise to precise bibliography, including the *Bibliotheca Universalis*, compiled by Gesner in the 1540s, a comprehensive list of over 10,000 titles by 3,000 authors with birth and death dates, an index, and much we would now know as descriptive cataloging. Bibliography was of increasing importance for both national prestige and profit; booksellers and publishers needed precise lists of their offerings to take to book fairs and for other sales. In addition, during this period, the acts of reproduction and distribution are splitting from that of composition as the industry becomes increasingly specialized.

The seventeenth century saw continual increase in the amount and complexity of meta-information, both from the publishing world and from scientists, who needed it to help in finding interesting new information increasingly found in books. The first book review journal, the *Journal des Sçavans*, begins publishing weekly in 1665. Naude, writing in the 1650s, declares that libraries should be publicly available for the curious, that catalogs should be arranged both by subject and alphabet, and that all schools of thought should be kept at arm's length, so readers could evaluate and make up their own minds.

A number of cataloging and classification advances occurred in the nineteenth century: card catalogs replaced printed, book catalogs because too many items needed to be added too quickly, and several cataloging codes (including those of Panizzi, Cutter, and Harris) were developed, as was the Dewey Decimal Classification. Subject cataloging was slower to grow, compared to organization by author, title or keyword-from-title in some quarters, since many librarians believed that most users came to libraries in search of a known item. Many cataloging systems are inspired by particular philosophies (those of Bacon, Hegel, or Utilitarianism), and several ideas for standardized, shared cataloging fail for various technological and economic reasons.

Reference work as we know it today is a creature of the late nineteenth and early twentieth centuries; a reaction to increasing volume and use of materials and a recognition of the difficulty on the part of users in making sense of steadily more complicated classification and organization mechanisms. Reference is developed first in public and special libraries, later in the academic world, and by mid-twentieth century is established as a separate unit, increasingly specialized, and taking on new functions such as instruction and reader's advisory.

Documentation arises early in the twentieth century around problems of retrieval of data; a questioning of its effectiveness in the 1930s leads to a borrowing of technique and ideas from statistics and the social sciences. Of course, automation enters the scene after World War II, and information science emerges therefrom.

As Jesse Shera wrote of librarianship, "it developed over the years, decades and even centuries a substantial body of procedures and techniques as a result of certain assumptions about man's use of recorded knowledge. This ad hoc technology was refined by trial and error and tested over years of experience."[2]

We see that librarianship and (by default) publishing have taken centuries to evolve into the well-defined fields we know today. But all that is changing, and changing fast. The changes happening in the library and information technology world in the last fifteen years are probably equal to those that happened in the previous 400 years. We anticipate that speed of change to continue accelerating for some time to come.

So now we come to the issues we touched on in the introduction. It will be some time before we identify concrete procedures for managing digital information, but for the time being, let us raise some questions and pose some theories.

FROM A LIBRARY PERSPECTIVE: WHO OWNS WHAT AND FOR HOW LONG?

The idea of "ownership" of information, especially in the context of library service, has broadened dramatically with the coming of new media and modes of delivery. What follows is not a complete taxonomy of issues or possible features of each; rather, it is a list of some important aspects of "ownership," enumeration of some features, and questions raised.

MODES OF PAYMENT

There are a number of possible payment models, several of which are familiar, others are less so:

- Pay once–and then you own it forever to do with as you wish, subject to the laws of copyright
- Standard subscription model–as with journals, magazines, and newspapers in print as well as some CD-ROM products and other services
- Never pay–for free materials, donations, gifts, and, of course, freely available Web resources (ignoring the cost of computers, software, connectivity, staff, paper, wiring, etc.)

- By the "drink"–as with some currently available services, where you pay only for the number of documents retrieved, printed out, or for time connected; we are used to this of course with DIA-LOG and other online search services
- Volume discounts–really a variation on a common theme; large customers get a break to encourage them to use more
- Auctions–which are a more radical departure; some digital library researchers have discussed the notion of intelligent software agents continually negotiating the price of information resources based on use, popularity, time of day, status of user, etc.

This multiplicity of payment schemes leads to some important questions: If the costs of information resources are continually fluctuating or are based solely or partly on usage, how does a library plan or budget? Will users accept or even understand some of these more complicated payment models? Should we continue to hide payment models from them or make them more obvious? In what circumstances should patrons share in the costs, especially when they are usage driven? When are caps or limits on use or expenditures appropriate? Can we continue to guarantee equality of access when we do not necessarily know how much we are spending on information at any given moment?

MODES OF ACCESS

Possible scenarios:

- One user at a time–as is the case with most analog resources (although multiple-volume or multiple-part works can support several people if they want access to different parts)
- Membership–as long as the user is authorized by virtue of membership in an appropriate community and can prove it somehow, the user can access the resource
- Time-limited access–which could be implemented in several ways: a fixed amount of time per user per session, no time limit as long as nobody's waiting, available only when the library is open (as with reference and reserves now), twenty-four hours a day/seven days a week

- First in line–until the licenses run out. The first fifteen people are allowed to use the resource but the sixteenth has to wait until somebody is finished
- By priority–rank, pay grade, length of service, etc; for example, staff and students may have access, but a faculty member takes precedence

Each of these scenarios limits access in some way. Some–such as limiting the resource to in-building use or to a particular community of users–are familiar to us and therefore do not seem problematic. Others, such as ranking by priority or limiting by time, seem more intrusive or violate our notions of the values of librarianship. Questions of user acceptance and equality of access are raised here as well, as are questions of authentication, which is especially problematic in a public library.

Most of these scenarios require a new way of thinking, particularly about use of library materials outside the time and space constraints of the library. We are accustomed to people coming to the library, borrowing or copying materials and taking them away, but the idea that they could "use" resources of the library without setting foot in a physical space is a departure. How do we take that kind of usage into consideration, especially in places where funding or support is based on foot traffic or circulation?

CONSUMPTION, DUPLICATION, AND PLASTICITY

Possible forms a resource may take:

- Analog–offprints, or print on paper, audio on disc, video on tape, microfilm, etc.
- Digital–on screen, or over a speaker
- Analog/Digital hybrid–downloading material from an online site and presumably taking something away in either analog or digital form

We all know the cannot-curl-up-in-bed-with-a-computer argument against reading large volumes of text on screen, but there are distinct advantages to interacting with digital versions of resources. These include enhanced searching, hypertext, and other unique opportunities provided by new media and genres.

In addition, the ability to make innumerable perfect copies of an intellectual work and to alter it in imperceptible ways raises questions both about intellectual property rights for creators and about new modes of scholarship and creativity. The copyright warning signs we now post next to photocopy machines merely hint at what may lie ahead.

LIMITATIONS, PROBLEMS, AND OTHER BARRIERS TO ACCESS

As if there were not already enough problems, here are some new ones:

- License agreements–with publishers and vendors which restrict access by clientele, time, simultaneous users, etc., as described in the section above
- Authentication–a situation we are used to in academic circles and the corporate world, but something of a departure in certain public and school libraries
- Technical problems–including unreliable servers (both local and remote), printers with "bad attitudes," client/server incompatibilities, and so on
- Bad search engines, bad command languages, bad harvest/spider programs

To be sure, digital resources allow for enhanced access and availability, but they carry their own problems as well. Strangely enough, the need to meet the Americans with Disabilities Act (ADA) requirements for Websites and other digital resources (compliance may include minimizing graphics and adding text-only versions of content) creates more complications in terms of access.

SUPPORT AND STAFFING

If our resources are available twenty-four hours a day, people will probably expect help and support to be available as well. We've never had to deal with a need for access on nights and weekends or for nonstandard kinds of support because fixing a printer jam is not the same as explaining how to use Britannica on the Web, right?

We are not used to thinking about people "using" the library at 3:00 A.M. on a Sunday, but if they are, should they expect less service or fewer kinds of service than people in the building at 2:00 P.M. on Tuesday? Furthermore, the diversity of skills and experience required on the part of staff will broaden, requiring more extensive training for current staff as well as hiring a wider range of new people, both technical-and information-oriented.

DURATION AND DURABILITY OF INFORMATION

At the end of a subscription for a printed resource you still have a physical archive of the resource for the period you subscribed. In the case of an electronic subscription or license, does everything–back issues included–vanish when the subscription ends? It does if the license only allowed Web access. How long a resource lasts, both physically (book bindings and paper quality, for example) and institutionally (stability of a journal publisher), is a major issue for both publishers and libraries in the online world. It is clear that the Web is permanently impermanent; truly valuable Websites go away and old stuff, which may be totally worthless, stays forever. At first blush, this may seem a new problem, but it is not unrelated to questions about durability that librarians have pondered for years. It is harder to plan for the future right now since we do not yet have the experience to predict which resources will vanish or degrade quickly. Also, if all you have when a subscription ends is a happy memory and some coffee-stained print-outs, there is much more pressure to renew just to have access to backfiles and the resource as a whole. Publishers, of course, stand to gain from this scenario, but it is not clear that libraries or users do.

FROM A PUBLISHING PERSPECTIVE: A CASE STUDY IN ONLINE PUBLISHING

Libraries are not the only ones pondering all these new scenarios. Publishers are struggling as much as their library counterparts to come up with new strategies for developing online and electronic content, setting fair subscription rates, defining the boundaries of nonprinted content, and dealing with information storage and retrieval. Let's look at some of the same questions we examined earlier in this discussion but from a publisher's point of view and in the context of a real online product: *The Java Deluxe Library on CD-ROM* from O'Reilly & Associates.

O'Reilly & Associates is one of the premier publishers of technical books and software about UNIX, the Web, and Windows. The technical expertise of our editorial and production staff is unparalleled in the computer publishing industry, and we pride ourselves at having taken the science of developing books about computers and technology into the realm of art. We had no idea how much more there was to learn.

The Java programming language is a hot topic in the world of software development. There are currently over 1,000 books and countless Web-based resources dedicated to it. The *Java Deluxe Library* arose in response to Java readers groaning over the sheer (literally toe-crushing) weight of basic Java documentation. Sensing a marketing opportunity, we designed a new HTML-based product that combined five of our core Java reference books (4,000+ pages) in digital form with a master index and presented it all on CD-ROM. To make it even more palatable, we included a printed copy of our best-selling *Java in a Nutshell* in the package. *Java Deluxe* is still available in bookstores on CD-ROM, as well as by subscription over the Web.

MODES OF PAYMENT AND MODES OF ACCESS

Since *Java Deluxe* is sold mainly on CD-ROM, the traditional unit-based payment model still applies. Pricing the product, however, was trickier than we thought it would be, and it brought us face to face with an online publishing conundrum: consumers are unwilling to pay as much for a CD-ROM or online product as they will pay for the same information in print. The reason is that most people associate CD-ROMs with music and entertainment, and since the average music or entertainment CD-ROM rarely exceeds $50, consumers set their baseline of perceived value accordingly. But the cost of developing and distributing entertainment on CD-ROM is astronomical; why haven't publishers of products like *Myst* gone broke?[3] The answer is in the economy of scale. A game like *Myst* may cost several million dollars to bring to market, but the developers are banking on sales in the tens of millions. This allows them to set a very low unit price. A product like *Java Deluxe* is not as expensive to develop, compared to a multimedia extravaganza like *Myst*, but it is a very specialized product aimed at a smaller, more specialized audience. Sales will obviously be lower and the unit cost higher. The same economies of scale hold for publishers of mass market paperbacks and best-sellers. If sales are expected to be very high, the cost of a single unit can be very low, and the cost of developing the content need not be factored as heavily into the pricing equation.

This is a simplistic example, but it makes a point: sales of scholarly and specialty content are never as high as in the mass market, so the cost of content development becomes a major influence on the final price. Unfortunately, thanks to the apparent "inexpensiveness" of mass market content, buyers assume that specialty publishers are guilty of overpricing. In reality, this is not the case. As most publishers will attest, a product that has specialized or complex content–no matter how high the price appears to be–usually has the smallest profit margin on the list. Pricing must reflect the cost of development or the developer will be out of business.

Returning to our previous discussion, the five volumes that make up *Java Deluxe* cost a total of $170 if purchased in print. Our market research indicated that $60 was the maximum we could charge for the CD-ROM set, so we set the price at $59.95 and hoped that sales of the printed books would not suffer. Our readers were getting quite a bargain. But to our astonishment book sales did not decline even as the CD-ROMs flew off the shelves. It went against all our initial assumptions, but we were not inclined to argue!

To further enhance the value of this product to our readers (and to conduct some experiments in online publishing), we decided to offer *Java Deluxe* over the Web on a subscription basis. Pricing considerations went from being merely tricky to downright confusing. We discovered that access restrictions are a nightmare to program on the Web–there are too many easy ways for users to slip around them–so we decided not to use pay-by-the-drink, volume discounts, or any of the other popular online models. In the end, we opted for a flat fee, one-year subscription model. We do not yet have an educational or institutional site license policy, mainly because we do not have enough data on which to build one. We've negotiated licenses on an individual basis with several university libraries, but none of those license agreements was based on hard facts. As Mary Ellen Bates says, "Negotiating electronic subscriptions takes work and requires a different approach than is traditionally used by vendors."[4] We found this statement to be absolutely true.

CONSUMPTION, DUPLICATION AND PLASTICITY

Java Deluxe showed us that rather than undermine it, content in an electronically accessible form actually enhances print. We learned that readers want both components, and they're willing to pay for both. We think that a combination of print- and CD-ROM-based information represents a new kind of reading environment for the user. In fact, when asked why he was willing to buy both the CD-ROM product and all five books in print, a reader had this to say: "I like to read the books and I use them as references when I write code. But sometimes it's hard to find a specific bit of information buried in all those pages. So I bought the CD and I use it as an index. I can search for something and either read it on screen, which is helpful if I want to cut-and-paste a line of code, or I make a note of which book it's in and where, and then I can read it at home later."

This kind of usage is not what we envisioned, but it certainly is a clever and truly hybrid approach to efficient use of content!

LIMITATIONS, PROBLEMS, AND OTHER BARRIERS TO ACCESS

We've already brought up issues surrounding access restrictions, authentication, and technical problems for libraries. On the publishing side, these issues are nearly identical. As we mentioned in the previous section, access restrictions are difficult to program on the Web. In the process of making *Java Deluxe* easily accessible to our readers on the Web, we encountered a number of startlingly simple ways in which users could circumvent our restrictions. Some of these included opening a new account each day with a false credit card number, creating and juggling multiple accounts, and downloading the files.

Authentication requires a time delay for checking a password or verifying a credit card number. We found that people frequently lost their passwords and needed to be issued new ones, or the ones that they were given did not work. And in the realm of "technical difficulties," we were stunned by how much time we spent debugging file errors and rebooting the servers. We've also had a number of instances of readers posting the entire *Java Deluxe* resource on their Websites, blatantly ignoring our copyright and duplication restrictions. While we make every attempt to discourage this practice, it is still difficult to know just how many electronic copies are floating around on the Web free for the taking. When added up, all these little problems proved to us that offering a Web-based resource (which did not bring in nearly as much revenue as we'd hoped) required much more in the way of staffing, time, and financial resources than we had originally planned.

SUPPORT, STAFFING, AND DURABILITY OF INFORMATION

At first we thought we would be offering our *Java Deluxe* customers a unique opportunity to read the freshest content via the Web and we had grand plans to "update frequently." Journals, by their nature, are updated frequently and serials publishers are staffed to release an issue or "update" on a weekly, monthly, or quarterly basis. Books and their publishers, however, are not set up for that kind of updating. At O'Reilly, we discovered that we did not have enough staff to manage monthly updates for one product–let alone any others. We've since restructured to allow for development and management of more online products, but we have not significantly added to our staff. This is mainly because we are not sure that online products will bring in sufficient revenue to support our efforts. The level of staffing needed for this new 24-hour information environment is much larger than we initially thought, and it seems that if we are to achieve it–and keep the accountants happy–the price of information will have to go up. This is one reason why our books are not going to disappear or go "totally digital" anytime soon.

Many people think that, like games and entertainment on CD-ROM, digitally based information should be less expensive than print. And why not? Digital information incurs no printing, binding, or shipping costs, and for all practical purposes, incurs no warehousing costs. What most people do not realize is that these activities account for only 30 percent of the cost of a book. The remaining 70 percent is incurred in development–acquisition, review, editing, marketing, and prepress. And those processes are still necessary no matter what the delivery medium, as anyone who has ever read the first draft of a manuscript will attest. So in the real world (the one where income must equal or exceed expenditure), the price of high-quality information may be reduced a bit by online delivery, but it will rarely be cheap and it will never be free.

CONCLUSION: CHANGING ROLES

We are all, librarians and publishers alike, accustomed to each having our own special places in the life cycle of information–arcs on that circle, if you will. Publishers have been concerned with information from its creation through its editing and refinement, publication, marketing and selling. Librarians have been concerned with selecting, buying, describing, organizing, and providing access to information.

Increasingly, however, those complementary but largely separate arcs are merging and blurring, as libraries and librarians are more involved in creating, evaluating, and acquiring information and as publishers become more interested in organization and access. It would seem logical, then, to imagine a world in which these two historically and economically separate groups begin to work together more closely to realize their joint goals of spreading knowledge and producing better quality information for the people whom they serve.

If we are able to identify modes of cooperation, publishing solutions could be more sensible and cost effective, and library responses could be more effective. Librarians, as avatars for the greater reading public, could be valuable partners for publishers, and publishers could help librarians better cope with the growing mass of information available through so many new channels.

But can we do it? Is it feasible to think that these two professions, so long seeing themselves as different if not actually at odds, could collaborate effectively? Many models for the distribution of information are possible, but only a few will benefit authors, publishers, libraries and users.

Much of the separation between the two fields is based on tradition, and in fact tradition is a central question here. As a new information environment unfolds before us, how much of traditional practice–in publishing and in librarianship–can we draw on? There are perils in adopting too much as well as too little. In staying too close to familiar practices of acquisition, pricing or cataloging, we run the risk of becoming stuck in an inappropriate past–"fighting the last war," in military terms, and missing out on new and exciting ways of using information. By abandoning too much of what we have learned, however, we are in danger of drifting, anchorless, in an ocean of information that grows ever larger and harder to navigate.

It would seem that we need appropriate metaphors–new and old–to help us think clearly about the new environment. Electronic journals and books are not "just like" their familiar print counterparts, and thinking that they are may get in the way of our progress in dealing with them. As is always the case, these metaphors will emerge from practice, trial and error, and what seems natural to all concerned.

The bottom line is control over information–who has it, when, how, and for how much money. The familiar paradigms arose from a particular set of economic and historical circumstances. The first publishers were businessmen out to make a buck (or a florin, or whatever); while they were not unconcerned with high-minded notions of disseminating knowledge, they were largely in it for the money. There was little of "librarianship" as a recognizable profession, and the physical containers in which information sat lent themselves to a straightforward business transaction model.

The world has changed. Removing the physical container from its central role leads to all the issues we have discussed: varying potential payment and access schemes, perfect duplication and infinite plasticity, control mechanisms, concerns about support and durability.

Information containers and ownership–things we have always thought of as stable–are not stable anymore. Librarians with significant investment in Web-based information systems or multiple subscription models could wake up on any given morning with a substantially different collection than they had the night before. Publishers who make information available over the Web look more than a little like the subscription libraries of the nineteenth century, where members paid annual fees to be able to use their materials, but this is new territory for them, too.

These are not old issues, or at the very least they have not been questioned in this way before, because the answers were taken for granted. The digital environment allows the old ways to be broken apart, reexamined, and changed forever, in ways beneficial to us all–if we are willing to take some risks.

The worst possible scenario–where both professions cannot acknowledge that each is necessary to the other–is, sadly, not the least likely. All parties involved are understandably frightened of an unknown future, but paradoxically, of opposite outcomes. Librarians with limited and sometimes shrinking budgets worry that they will wind up paying too much for information, and publishers fear that they will be forced to sell information at no profit, which they must have in order to survive. Even though we have different parts to play, we must recognize that we are in the same business, and neither of us can survive for long without the other. Common sense, communication and cooperation could well lead us forward toward a jointly beneficial future. It behooves us to work toward this goal.

NOTES

1. Much of this historical discussion is summarized from Sidney L. Jackson's *Libraries and Librarianship in the West: A Brief History* (New York: McGraw-Hill, 1974).

2. Jesse H. Shera, *Introduction to Library Science: Basic Elements of Library Service* (Littleton, CO: Libraries Unlimited, 1976), p. 107.

3. *Myst*, created by Robyn and Rand Miller, is the bestselling computer game of all time.

4. Mary Ellen Bates, "How to Implement Electronic Subscriptions," *Online* (May/June, 1998): 81.

WORKSHOPS

What Happened to the Serials Cataloger: Copy Cataloging of Serials

Sharon Wiles-Young
Linda Novak

Workshop Leaders

Linda Smith-Griffin

Recorder

SUMMARY. As many academic libraries continue to redefine positions in response to budget cuts, downsizing, outsourcing, technology and the incorporation of electronic resources, the effects on managers and team leaders in bibliographic access services are overwhelmingly shifting from day-to-day hands-on experience to primarily administrative. At Lehigh University the only serials cataloger was reassigned to a team leader's position, which left no other professional serials catalog librarian in the department at a time when the library began canceling print subscriptions and acquiring electronic journals. This paper will discuss the changing roles, responsibilities and challenges the team leader experienced and its effect on the copy cataloging of serials. *[Article copies available for a fee from The Haworth Document Delivery Service: 1-800-342-9678. E-mail address: getinfo@haworthpressinc.com]*

Sharon Wiles-Young is Team Leader, Information Organization Services, Linderman Library, Lehigh University.

Linda Novak is Acquisitions/Cataloging Senior Assistant, Linderman Library, Lehigh University.

Linda Smith-Griffin is Catalog Librarian, Louisiana State University Libraries.

[Haworth co-indexing entry note]: "What Happened to the Serials Cataloger: Copy Cataloging of Serials." Smith-Griffin, Linda. Co-published simultaneously in *The Serials Librarian* (The Haworth Press, Inc.) Vol. 36, No. 3/4, 1999, pp. 401-405; and: *Head in the Clouds, Feet on the Ground: Serials Vision and Common Sense* (ed: Jeffrey S. Bullington, Beatrice L. Caraway, and Beverley Geer) The Haworth Press, Inc., 1999, pp. 401-405. Single or multiple copies of this article are available for a fee from The Haworth Document Delivery Service [1-800-342-9678, 9:00 a.m. - 5:00 p.m. (EST). E-mail address: getinfo@ haworthpressinc.com].

Lehigh University, located in Bethlehem, Pennsylvania, is a small coeducational, nondenominational, private institution with approximately 4,000 undergraduate students and 2,000 graduate students. In 1994/1995, the University was engaged in a system-wide strategic planning process. This planning led to a recommendation to merge computing services and the libraries. The vice-provost of information resources led the reorganization process with the input of several teams comprising librarians, media, telecommunications, and the computing staff. By June 1996 the new organizational structure was implemented and a team-based, flatter organizational model was created with large-scale department mergers. In addition to the libraries and computing services, the merger involved media services, administrative computing and telecommunications. This resulted in significant changes within the roles and responsibilities of department managers and staff.

Prior to the merger, the library's technical services department was organized by format and followed the organizational structure of a traditional technical services department–acquisitions, cataloging and serials. The reorganization merged technical services with government documents, library systems, and information resource Web managers to form the information organization services under one team leader, the former head of serials cataloging and the department's only professional serials cataloger. In the team leader's former position she was responsible for the management, decision making, workflow, and training of four staff members whose principal duties and responsibilities were toward serials cataloging, and now the department consisted of sixteen staff members, twelve non-exempt staff (non-librarians) and four exempt (librarians), some joining the team from other areas of the library and the university. Similar changes were occurring in the public service areas as well.

Almost immediately, the team leader became overwhelmed with the new responsibilities and challenges the reorganization imposed:

- Rewriting job descriptions
- Cross training staff
- Training new staff with no library or cataloging experience
- Writing manuals and department policies
- Managing database system upgrades
- Working with a new periodical vendor
- Establishing a new approval plan

- Outsourcing
- Providing access to electronic journals
- Negotiating contracts and licenses
- Monitoring vendor performance
- Managing a growing serials backlog
- Allocating resources
- Strategic planning
- Developing department goals and priorities
- Serving on committees
- Shifting to client centered services
- Motivating staff in time of change

The team leader's role became more that of an administrator and dealt less with the day-to-day hands-on work which she had been accustomed to in her former position. Feeling overcome by this major paradigm shift, she conducted a literature review on the changing roles of librarians and department heads in academic libraries. From the review she found that the role of the department head is changing significantly due to societal, economic and technological changes, and that the traditional department head responsibilities will have to be accomplished with a different approach.[1]

STAFF REACTION TO THE CHANGE

The university system-wide reorganization created many uncertainties among the staff in the information organization services team, formerly technical services. Linda Novak, acquisitions/cataloging senior assistant, nonexempt staff, shared the experiences and challenges she encountered within the new organizational structure.

With twenty-five years of work experience in the former serials cataloging unit, Novak acquired considerable knowledge and expertise that proved invaluable in helping her adjust to changes brought on by the university's system-wide reorganization. Prior to the changes, Novak performed copy cataloging of serials and worked very closely with the head of serials cataloging. Currently her workflow consists of tasks previously performed only by the professional librarian such as complex serials cataloging, original cataloging, cataloging electronic journals, and using resource tools and manuals for serials cataloging (*AACR2, CONSER Cataloging Manual, CONSER Editing Guide* and others).

Novak welcomed the opportunity to take her work to another level, but in spite of the new opportunities, several workflow issues needed to be addressed:

- The absence of the team leader and resultant lack of consistent training
- Blurring the lines; not sure at which level she should be cataloging
- Not sure what her priorities should be
- Need a balance and better workflow
- Pay equity

The issues Novak calls attention to are consistent with the results of a recent study conducted on the changing roles of paraprofessionals in ARL libraries. Mohr and Schuneman note several factors that have caused the blurring of responsibilities among librarians and paraprofessionals: cost savings, automation, delegation of tasks, and the increased availability of copy for copy cataloging.[2] Oberg further explores the perceptions and realities of the emergence of the paraprofessional in academic libraries.[3]

In conclusion, Wiles-Young and Novak agree on the following as they relate to the reorganization:

- The new roles in the new organization have not fully evolved.
- The team leader's responsibilities have not been fully transitioned to the economics of the staff.
- There is a need for more training and rebalancing of duties; a need to revisit job descriptions; a need to review workflows and try to make them as efficient as possible using new technologies.
- When planning new projects, staff considerations must be made in order to evaluate what processes can be automated and what processes will fall to staff.
- As more electronic access is given, technical services staff must prepare to embrace change by cataloging more electronic resources.
- More professionals are needed to plan the training and to keep the print cataloging organized.
- In the absence of additional professionals they must use current staff and technologies as efficiently as possible.

Following the presentation the audience engaged the presenters in an interesting discussion on many issues relating to serials cataloging.

Several participants were interested in knowing how the team leader remains current on issues concerning the day-to-day cataloging of serials if most of her time is spent in an administrative capacity. Wiles-Young, team leader, replied that it is getting increasingly difficult, and as time progresses, she is very concerned about how effective she will be in the future as a trainer. Another issue that drew much discussion and feedback from the participants was training for serials catalogers. Many in the audience expressed concern that he/she is the only serials cataloger in his/her department and sometimes felt uncertain about some of the decision making and would like to know about the availability of continuing education. One participant suggested the use of the SERIALIST listserv for immediate help. Another suggestion was to have CONSER develop a serials interactive training classroom on the Internet. That suggestion received applause. Jean Hirons, CONSER Coordinator, was in the audience and she gave the group an update on what CONSER is doing to address the issue of training for serials catalogers. Another participant shared with the group her recent participation in a one-week serials training pilot project at the University of Texas, Austin, a CONSER library.

The issue of outsourcing was another topic that received much audience feedback. Many of the participants voiced concerns over what will happen to the serials cataloger when large-scale outsourcing of serials takes place. Other issues discussed were shelf-ready serials, title changes within electronic journals, staff morale, motivating staff in times of change and blurring of the lines between work performed by librarians and paraprofessionals.

NOTES

1. Alex Bloss and Don Lanier, "The Library Department Head in the Context of Matrix Management and Reengineering," *College and Research Libraries* 58 (1997): 499-508.

2. Deborah A. Mohr and Anita Schuneman, "Changing Roles: Original Cataloging by Paraprofessionals in ARL Libraries," *Library Resources & Technical Services* 41 (1997): 205-217.

3. Larry Oberg, "The Emergence of the Paraprofessional in Academic Libraries: Perceptions and Realities," *College & Research Libraries* 53 (1992): 99-112.

With Feet Planted Firmly in Mid-Air:
Staff Training
for Automation System Migration

Rick Ralston
Margaret A. Rioux

Workshop Leaders

Kathryn D. Ellis

Recorder

SUMMARY. Migrating from one automated system to another has become a common experience in libraries. Such a migration is as great a change for serials staff as implementing the library's first automated system. It involves conversion or re-entry of data, alterations in workflow, changes in system "philosophy," and a lot of relearning. Much of the success of the process depends on staff training. This workshop offered practical ideas and suggestions for training serials staff to deal with a new system and the transition process. The emphasis was on practical steps to help with the migration process from initial planning through implementation and on to daily operations under the new system. *[Article copies available for a fee from The Haworth Document Delivery Service: 1-800-342-9678. E-mail address: getinfo@haworthpressinc.com]*

Rick Ralston is Automated Processing Manager, Ruth Lilly Medical Library, Indiana University School of Medicine.

Margaret A. Rioux is Information Systems Librarian, MBL/WHOI Library, Woods Hole Oceanographic Institution.

Kathryn D. Ellis is Systems Librarian for Acquisitions and Processing, University of Tennessee, Knoxville Libraries.

[Haworth co-indexing entry note]: "With Feet Planted Firmly in Mid-Air: Staff Training for Automation System Migration." Ellis, Kathryn D. Co-published simultaneously in *The Serials Librarian* (The Haworth Press, Inc.) Vol. 36, No. 3/4, 1999, pp. 407-413; and: *Head in the Clouds, Feet on the Ground: Serials Vision and Common Sense* (ed: Jeffrey S. Bullington, Beatrice L. Caraway, and Beverley Geer) The Haworth Press, Inc., 1999, pp. 407-413. Single or multiple copies of this article are available for a fee from The Haworth Document Delivery Service [1-800-342-9678, 9:00 a.m. - 5:00 p.m. (EST). E-mail address: getinfo@haworthpressinc.com].

Rick Ralston and Maggie Rioux have each experienced a migration from one automated library system to another. They presented background on their libraries and the migration, then gave suggestions for how to train serials staff before, during, and after the migration. They provided an annotated bibliography of "Information Resources to Help Keep Your Feet Planted Firmly in Mid-Air" as well as a list of "False Assumptions About Training."[1] A lively discussion followed, with suggestions and comments from librarians in the audience.

Rick Ralston described his experience at the Ruth Lilly Medical Library of the Indiana University School of Medicine. In 1994/1995 the Indiana University Library System entered into a partnership with Ameritech Library Services and the University of Chicago to help develop Ameritech's Horizon, originally designed for smaller libraries, into a system for research libraries. The Ruth Lilly Medical Library migration from NOTIS to Horizon, set for December 1997, was delayed, but the university library on the Indiana University-Purdue University Indianapolis (IUPUI) campus migrated in July 1997. Rick used their experiences as well as his own as the basis for his presentation, in which he identified four stages of system migration training: mental preparation, physical preparation, formal training, and follow-up.

Mental preparation of staff is very important. First, keep staff informed during planning stages with progress reports and explanations of why the migration is necessary. Understanding why change is necessary can ease the transition for people who are uneasy. Next, provide opportunities for staff input during all stages of the process. This helps them feel they have some say in what the new system will be like. Third, early in the process prepare people for the likelihood of organizational change, letting them know their jobs are secure even though some things will be different. Fourth, focus on the big picture, not just daily tasks, some of which may be harder in the new system. The new system will have many new, good features for users, and it is helpful for staff to recall that one library goal is to provide users the best possible service. Finally, be positive, yet realistic. Staff easily become discouraged and negative, especially when a project takes longer than expected. It is much harder to remain encouraged, but it is the job of leaders to help staff in that task. Given two ways to say the same thing, try to choose the positive approach while still being realistic.

In the area of physical preparation, complete necessary hardware upgrades early, if possible, so staff can focus on one thing at a time. Provide training on companion software, such as new interfaces, operating systems, or spreadsheets, that will be used with the new system. Involve staff in the data conversion process. They know the current system better than anyone and their input is crucial to a smooth conversion of data. Finally, load software well in advance of implementation to give staff time to evaluate it before going live.

Formal training should be conducted close to the implementation date. Train again if there are implementation delays. Training too early can result in low staff motivation for learning as well as people forgetting much of what they learned. Next, realize that training cannot occur in a single day–there is just too much to absorb. Allow time for practice and working with the system to help training sink in. Third, the trainer should identify with the trainees, so it is helpful if he or she has experience working in a library as well as with the new system. It is ideal if the trainer has migrated from the same old system to the same new system. Finally, provide for different learning styles. Some staff prefer to learn by themselves, following a book and trying things out on the system. The library may want to develop a workbook if the system vendor does not provide one. Guided hands-on training, going through steps at the same time that the trainer is demonstrating, can be very effective for some situations. One-on-one training is helpful for those who do not want to ask questions in large groups and can be provided by library staff to one another. At the beginning, lectures and demonstrations can provide an overview of the new system. Training should include a combination of styles to effectively reach all staff.

Follow-up after formal training is an important step which is frequently overlooked in early planning stages. First, create a local procedure manual for the new system. A manual is helpful throughout the life of the system, but especially important in the beginning when nobody knows anything about the system. The manual will be used later for reference and for training new employees. At the IUPUI library, the staff in each job wrote out the procedures to include in the manual. Next, provide cross training in different areas of the system. This helps provide redundancy in staff skills, so that if someone leaves other people know how to accomplish the work he or she was doing. Finally, provide mechanisms for and encourage staff communication about the system. Have periodic meetings with affected staff, giving them opportunities to discuss issues and procedures. Consider establishing a listserv for the library or department where staff can ask questions and provide answers among themselves. Designate people to collect and share "tips and tricks." Test software and hardware upgrades and share results with others in the organization. These and other techniques will help all staff stay abreast of changes as the system and library procedures evolve.

Maggie Rioux discussed the migration of the Marine Biological Laboratory/Woods Hole Oceanographic Institution (MBL/WHOI) Library from DRA to Endeavor's Voyager system during fall 1995. Maggie compared system migration training to driver training, in which people learn some things in formal classes, but do not really become proficient until they are on the road. This model includes several stages: the anticipation stage, driver's ed class, learner's permit, hitting the road on one's own, and living happily ever after with the new system.

The anticipation stage entails planning for training and looking forward to the big day. First, start the process early by involving staff in decisions about the new system. At MBL/WHOI, all staff were involved in vendor demonstrations and were consulted during the decision-making process. Staff were even more involved in figuring out how to set up the new system and in deciding what migration procedures would work best. Second, expect stress during the migration and plan how to ease it. The change to a new system may be even more stressful than the one from a manual to an automated environment, because the magnitude of this change is usually underestimated. Stress is especially great for serials staff because there is no standard way of automating serials, and whatever the new system, it will be very different from the old. One suggestion from MBL/WHOI is to have everyone write a list of things he or she really hates about the current system, then save these lists to look at later, when frustrated by the new system.

Formal training comprises the driver's ed class stage. Training may be conducted by vendor staff or by trained library staff. In-house trainers should be chosen for their ability to learn, to teach, and their enthusiasm for the new system. Training should be tailored to the library's situation, with documentation of local procedures as needed. All staff need an overview of all modules in the system, in order to understand how the whole system works and fits together. Staff also need to know procedures for customization, so they will understand what they can ask for in future. Maggie suggested setting up a training area away from regular library activities. Install client software on training machines and conduct sessions with small groups. Include training for things besides the modules, such as a new operating system, the mouse, or the MARC holdings format.

The learner's permit stage consists of practice before roll-out. Staff need time to try out the system before going live, to remember what they learned in formal training. Provide staff access to a training database. Have trainers provide informal follow-up with their trainees. Keep this stage brief–formal training should be only a short time before work begins in the live database. At MBL/WHOI, client modules were installed on staff workstations as soon as hardware permitted. The trainer followed up with one-on-one sessions about the modules that staff would use most. Staff talked about change-over procedures as much as possible. Maggie suggested making practice time a formal assignment for staff and giving them exercises to guide their practice. Assign staff to mentor each other, and encourage staff to work together to anticipate and solve problems before roll-out. Listen to ideas and questions of staff and try to adjust procedures to eliminate potential problems.

The next stage, hitting the road on one's own, begins when the new system goes live. Expect to spend a lot of time at the beginning solving crises. Continue mentoring programs and in-house training. Make sure supervisors work with the system regularly so they understand how the system works. At MBL/WHOI, Maggie spent time with each staff member, working through problems. She encouraged staff to call when they had problems or questions, something they continue to do. Maggie found that staff tend to forget what they learned and practiced, so trainers must be very patient. Keep listening to staff ideas, making changes when possible or explaining why they cannot be made.

Living happily ever after with the new system is the final stage, in which staff learn that nothing is perfect, not even the new system. Keep communication channels open and encourage staff to discuss problems. Some may be solved by configuration changes, others may be submitted as software requests to the system vendor. Help empower staff by adjusting the system in response to their comments, when possible. Develop training mechanisms for when new staff are hired or software upgrades occur. When staff begin feeling frustrated by features of the new system, have them bring out the lists they made of things they hated about the old system and see how many items are not there anymore. At MBL/WHOI, Maggie continues to communicate with staff on a regular basis. She provides feedback about local changes and information about expected improvements in future releases.

After the presentations the audience, many of whom seemed to face migrations in the future, participated in a lively discussion. One topic of interest was problems to be expected during migration. Maggie stated that some data will certainly be lost during migration, which led to a discussion of what kinds of old data to keep, for how long, and how to decide finally to discard it. Some suggested using humor or celebrations to deal with the stress of migration. A question about the role of subscription vendors in system migration led to a tangential discussion of prediction patterns, claiming, automated conversion of serial records, and holdings formats.

In reply to a question about the time period between formal training and migration, both speakers felt that about a month before going live was ideal. The Association of Research Libraries Office of Management Services was suggested as a source for "train the trainer" sessions. A training database containing the library's own data is best both for training the staff and for testing customization procedures. When asked about assessment of staff skills, Maggie said they had no time for formal assessment but did some informally. To the question of how job descriptions and workflow changed, Rick said they made some organizational changes ahead of time, to allow staff to figure out new work flows. The session ended with a discussion of job levels in state classification systems, how jobs generally become more complex, and that reward structures are not designed for the kind of work we now do in libraries.

NOTES

1. Sheila D. Creth, *Effective On-the-Job Training: Developing Library Human Resources* (Chicago: American Library Association, 1986), 12.

ANNOTATED BIBLIOGRAPHY

Clark, Cynthia. "ALCTS Heads of Technical Services of Medium-Sized Academic Libraries Discussion Group, Midwinter Conference, February 1997, Washington, DC. *Serials Review* 23, no. 3 (fall 1997), 73-75. General system migration experiences at the University of Virginia, Kansas State, and UNC-Charlotte. A few good reminders about training.

Creth, Sheila D. *Effective On-the-Job Training: Developing Library Human Resources.* Chicago: American Library Association, 1986. Deals with general training, but still applicable to system migration. The exercises are thought-provoking. Note especially "False Assumptions about Training" on page 12.

Glogoff, Stuart, and James P. Flynn. "Developing a Systematic In-House Training Program for Integrated Library Systems." *College & Research Libraries* 48, no. 6 (November 1987), 528-536. Includes lots of ideas that should be taken into account when developing a system migration training program.

Gyeszly, Suzanne D., and John B. Harer. "Replacement of Automated Systems: Organizational and Staff Training Considerations." *Journal of Library Administration* 14, no. 1 (1991), 87-105. Report of a questionnaire study of fifty-one libraries. The results may or may not be useful to libraries that are not large and that are not converting to or from NOTIS.

Hallmark, Julie, and C. Rebecca Garcia. "System Migration: Experiences from the Field." *Information Technology and Libraries* 11 (December 1992), 345-358. Report of a study of thirty-three libraries. Includes a section on training with some tips that may prove useful.

Hallmark, Julie, and C. Rebecca Garcia. "Training for Automated Systems in Libraries." *Information Technology and Libraries* 15, no. 3 (September 1996), 157-163, 166-167. Report of a series of interviews. Note especially the sections on "Problems and Pitfalls" and "Ingredients for Successful Training."

Kirkpatrick, Teresa E. "The Training of Academic Library Staff on Information Technology within the Libraries of the Minnesota State Colleges and Universities System." *College & Research Libraries* 59, no. 1 (January 1998), 51-59. Deals with general technology/computer training, not with ILS migration.

LaRue, James. "Raising the Staff I.Q." In "The Body Electric: Issues in Technology." *Wilson Library Bulletin* 69, no. 10 (June 1995), 79-80. Thoughts on technostress.

Saunders, Laverna M., and Myoung-ja Lee Kwon. "The Management of Change: Minimizing the Negative Impact on Staff and Patrons." In *Library Systems Migration: Changing Automated Systems in Libraries and Information Centers*, Gary M. Pitkin, ed. Westport, Conn.: Meckler, 1991. More theoretical than practical; deals heavily with minimizing stress for patrons rather than acquisitions and serials staff.

Smith, Kitty. "Toward the New Millennium: The Human Side of Library Automation." *Information Technology and Libraries* 12 (June 1996), 209-216. Excellent background article on the "role and impact of automation on a traditional (and frequently bureaucratic) institution."

Weill, Michelle M., and Larry D. Rosen. *TechnoStress: Coping with Technology @work @home@play.* New York: Wiley, 1997. Chapter 2, "The Myth of Technological Ease," and Chapter 8, "Corporate TechnoStress," are especially relevant to the stresses of system migration and training issues.

Zuboff, Shosana. *In the Age of the Smart Machine: The Future of Work and Power.* New York: Basic Books, 1988. Excellent background reading, it deals with the initial computerization of work, but these issues are relevant for migration as well.

Getting to the Summit:
How Do You Get There from Here?
A Climber's Guide to Consortium Formation

Margaret Hawthorn
Dean Frey
Virginia Roy

Workshop Leaders

Jill Emery

Recorder

SUMMARY. The presentation dealt with the formation and development of state-and province-wide, multitype library consortia in North America and its impact on major serial vendors. This workshop was divided into three areas: an overview survey of consortia formation, a look at the formation of a specific consortium (the Alberta Library), and finally a summary of views of major vendors on consortia and the services vendors can provide for consortia. *[Article copies available for a fee from The Haworth Document Delivery Service: 1-800-342-9678. E-mail address: getinfo@ haworthpressinc.com]*

Margaret Hawthorn is Serials Librarian, University of Toronto (Mississauga) Library.

Dean Frey is Network Coordinator, Alberta Public Library.

Virginia Roy is Marketing Manager, Faxon Canada.

Jill Emery is Serials Librarian, RJT Library, Texas Southern University.

[Haworth co-indexing entry note]: "Getting to the Summit: How Do You Get There from Here? A Climber's Guide to Consortium Formation." Emery, Jill. Co-published simultaneously in *The Serials Librarian* (The Haworth Press, Inc.) Vol. 36, No. 3/4, 1999, pp. 415-420; and: *Head in the Clouds, Feet on the Ground: Serials Vision and Common Sense* (ed: Jeffrey S. Bullington, Beatrice L. Caraway, and Beverley Geer) The Haworth Press, Inc., 1999, pp. 415-420. Single or multiple copies of this article are available for a fee from The Haworth Document Delivery Service [1-800-342-9678, 9:00 a.m. - 5:00 p.m. (EST). E-mail address: getinfo@haworthpressinc.com].

Margaret Hawthorn recently spent a research leave investigating "the incidence, formation process and governance of state and province-wide consortia." Once Hawthorn was able to identify sixty consortia through Web searches, she contacted their development officer or the state or provincial librarian to perform a telephone questionnaire. The questionnaire queried how and when the consortium was formed, how it was managed, what services were offered, and how it was funded. Hawthorn found that in the past three years there had been an explosion of consortium development throughout North America.

The two main reasons for the recent rapid development of consortia was found to be the advent of electronic serials databases and the Library Services and Technology Act (LSTA), which had been signed in September 1996 in the United States of America. The provisions of this act provided federal state-based funding for links among libraries and for the established consortia to acquire and share computer systems and communication technology. The goal was to provide library and information services to the underserved–the urban poor, rural populations and the disabled. Also required was the submission of a five-year plan by April 1, 1997, giving a major boost to statewide consortium formation.

From her survey, Hawthorn found a number of interesting trends. For the most part, consortial agreements that covered state- or province-wide, multitype libraries had been formed within the past two years, and the finalizing of structure and membership was still ongoing. Usually, these types of consortia had been initiated by a state/provincial library/commission and in conjunction with universities and/or educational departments.

These consortia were developed to serve all citizens either through libraries or through eligibility but not everyone was connected at this time. Members were defined as being universities, K-12, public libraries, government offices, community groups and businesses.

Some of the services that are being offered included database licensing, interlibrary loan coordination, union listing of serial holdings, technical set-up/troubleshooting, training, creative support (Web development, etc.) and management support (grant applications, statistics, etc.). Overall membership is voluntary and governance is performed by an advisory board or management group. State/province library staff or a separate consortium corporation/staff tend to manage the consortium. Communication about the consortium is disseminated primarily through Webpages and electronic mail.

The majority of the consortia have a disclaimer/collection policy/ mandate or content guidelines. Only three consortia stated that they did not have a collection management policy yet. The funding sources are made up of a mix of federal government funds, state/provincial government funds, participating institutions and municipal level funds. Thirty-two of the sixty consortia do have an evaluation process.

Hawthorn then gave the following Web addresses for consortia that she found interesting:

- Michigan: http://www.mel.lib.mi.us; http://www.accessmichigan. lib.mi.us; http://www.merit.edu/michnet/
- Maine: http://www.state.me.us/msl/mlo.htm#definition
- South Carolina: http://www.sciway.net/aboutsciway/html
- Missouri: http://www.more.net

Next, Dean Frey took us through the journey of the creation of the Alberta Library. The Alberta Library project began as a "province-wide multi-type library network aimed at providing Albertans with barrier-free access to the materials and information resources in all libraries and arose out of an evolving interdependence and connection among libraries in delivery service." The project started as a way to link four university libraries, thirteen college libraries, seven regional public library systems, eleven municipal libraries and various special libraries and library organizations that existed in the province of Alberta.

There were many planning stages that occurred over four years time from 1990 to 1993 throughout the province to help create the mission statement and basic principles for the Alberta Library.

Once a draft version of the vision statement and the key issues was synthesized from regional meetings, a document was presented in small group sessions at the Alberta Library Conference. Some of the key issues to be addressed were access to information, equity, lifelong learning, freedom of information, and accountability. From these sessions the following values were identified: universal access, freedom of information, lifelong learning, intellectual freedom, innovation and cooperation/working together. At the Red Deer Action Forum in February 1995, a representative group of Alberta's library community met with a group of individuals from a diverse range of occupations and activities to help crystallize the vision. Alberta's library community envisioned "a barrier free, universal access for all Albertans delivered in a dynamic model of cooperation, which extends beyond walls and beyond current levels of performance." This concept was then identified as "The Alberta Library." Next a vision for the Alberta Library was developed: "The Alberta Library will ensure access to the universe of information and ideas."

From here an implementation team was created and, due to access issues, the K-12 libraries had to drop out. It is hoped that in the near future, they can be added back into the project. In 1996, a business plan was created along with a constituent assembly and an interim board of directors. In January of 1997, the incorporation of the Alberta Library was finalized. Soon after, a business and service plan were drafted and the offices of the executive director and executive committee were filled. Work teams were then developed to oversee the following areas: advocacy, education and training, resource identification and optimization and resource sharing.

The work teams then set about initiating certain projects. A database licensing agreement was negotiated on behalf of the Alberta Library for the *Encyclopedia Britannica*. Netspeed technology summits were developed and presented at technical conferences and the Alberta Access Project was begun to provide access to resources for the visually impaired. For the future, the Alberta Library is furthering the technology and network planning. They hope to develop federal partnerships and institute some private sector initiatives as well as improve interlibrary loan and document delivery, and they are also working towards a reciprocal borrowing program. For further information on the Alberta Library contact: Lucy Pana, executive director at altalib@planet.eon.net or Gerry Meek, chair of the board at Gerry. Meek@public-library.calgary.ab.ca or their Website: http://www.library. ualberta.ca/altalib

Virginia Roy of Faxon Canada was the last presenter of the workshop. Roy gave an overview on the roles that vendors can play in relation to consortia and which services vendors may be able to supply to consortia in the future. Outlining some of the advantages for vendors when working with consortia, Roy listed the following: the ability to develop value-added services, a chance to improve marketshare, and a chance to enhance publisher relations and create industry partnerships. Some of the challenges that vendors are currently facing are threats to marketshare, creation of new business models, increased competition and consortia-driven cancellation of print subscriptions. Presently, Roy explained, vendors are in the process of consolidating their current services and offices, learning to manage new paradigms such as consortial agreements, providing reports and added-value services and building relationships across the publisher-library boundaries.

A number of issues that consortia are facing can possibly be addressed by vendors. These issues include developing the relationship between the publisher and the consortium, negotiating licensing agreements, developing aggregated content of material and resolving issues and questions about shared print material. Roy sees vendors as being able to play a vital role in broadening a consortium's access to publishers and their material as well as being able to provide a more cost effective way to access material. A vendor/aggregator in the future may be able to provide home-grown interfaces that access multiple publishers, authentication of services and sites, administrative services such as tracking Uniform Resource Locators (URLs) and aiding in the increasing demand for document delivery.

Another role that the vendors may play is in the negotiation of licensing agreements. At this point in time, the vendor's role is not great, but in the future there are plans to become more of a facilitator between the consortia and the publisher. In many cases, the vendors, as opposed to the consortia, would have legal expertise more readily available to them. Another issue is that generic cross-publisher agreements or national license agreements are not seen as profitable by the publishers. This may be a role where vendors can develop a standard for use. Vendors are also moving into the realm of becoming aggregators of content. Currently, vendors are committing a lot of research and development to this area of growth and are developing technology and investing in the needed software. While still in the developmental stages, vendors are looking at offering a "single point of access" to publishers and their material. Due to the nature of their businesses, vendors can offer a wide variety of value-added services to consortia.

Print is still 89 percent of a vendor's business, and some consortia are looking into sharing print materials. New business models need to be developed to examine how the cost-sharing of print materials can be created without there being a cost increase for print services.

In summation, Roy depicted the future of vendors as becoming integrators that offer a combination of the following services: licensing services, access services, print and electronic subscriptions along with other consortial management services such as reports management. Vendors must continue to consolidate, manage, report, add value and build relationships. We were left with the following questions to contemplate: "What about smaller publishers and orphan libraries? Are consortia transitional? Do consortia threaten the fulfillment of individual library requirements? Are agents expected to handle the leftovers?"

Audience participation was lacking following the presentation in part due to the various points that were left up to consideration. There was a short discussion concerning consortia contact people and many in the audience felt that this person needed to be made more readily known on Websites and literature distributed by the consortia. This was followed by another brief discussion concerning the net value of a consortium and how it would be configured. This plays an important role when trying to negotiate for network-shared electronic material. A concrete answer to this question was elusive due to the varying nature of the numerous consortia being currently developed.

Building an Electronic Journal Collection from the Ground Up

Susan H. Zappen
Jennifer Taxman

Workshop Leaders

Becky Schwartzkopf

Recorder

SUMMARY. Providing access to electronic journals is an important issue facing all libraries. Because of a strong commitment to electronic access at Skidmore College, the procurement of electronic journals is a critical issue for their library. The process of building an electronic journal collection at Skidmore is described from the standpoints of collection development, acquisitions, cataloging, instruction, evaluation and future needs. *[Article copies available for a fee from The Haworth Document Delivery Service: 1-800-342-9678. E-mail address: getinfo@haworthpressinc.com]*

Susan Zappen, head of technical services, and Jennifer Taxman, head of public services at Skidmore College, described their library's

Susan H. Zappen is Head of Technical Services, Lucy Scribner Library, Skidmore College.

Jennifer Taxman is Head of Public Services, Lucy Scribner Library, Skidmore College.

Becky Schwartzkopf is Serials Librarian at Mankato State University, Mankato, Minnesota.

[Haworth co-indexing entry note]: "Building an Electronic Journal Collection from the Ground Up." Schwartzkopf, Becky. Co-published simultaneously in *The Serials Librarian* (The Haworth Press, Inc.) Vol. 36, No. 3/4, 1999, pp. 421-428; and: *Head in the Clouds, Feet on the Ground: Serials Vision and Common Sense* (ed: Jeffrey S. Bullington, Beatrice L. Caraway, and Beverley Geer) The Haworth Press, Inc., 1999, pp. 421-428. Single or multiple copies of this article are available for a fee from The Haworth Document Delivery Service [1-800-342-9678, 9:00 a.m. - 5:00 p.m. (EST). E-mail address: getinfo@ haworthpressinc.com].

approach to providing access to electronic journals. Because of the high percentage of student computers, an external-degree program and a fully networked campus at Skidmore, the provision of electronic journals is a critical part of library services. The library staff at Skidmore College work closely together to develop a system to serve their patrons' needs.

Taxman and Zappen posed the following questions as a framework for their session:

- How do we know what we want?
- How do we get it?
- Now that we have it, what will we do?
- Was it worth it and what's next?

HOW DO WE KNOW WHAT WE WANT?

Zappen emphasized the importance of having a current collection development policy that takes into consideration electronic journals. Formulating a collection development policy at Skidmore involves working closely with faculty in each subject area, investigating classes taught in each discipline and being aware of student assignments. Based on their needs as a small liberal arts college, acquisition objectives were developed that serve the campus needs. Skidmore College chose to include electronic resources within their general collection development policy rather than develop a separate statement. Taxman and Zappen provided a sample collection development policy for history that is divided into the following sections: treatment, quality, format, and price. A sampling of collection development policies from other libraries that include information on electronic resources is available at http://www.ala.org/rusa/codes/codecd.html.

Taxman indicated that curriculum relevance, interdisciplinary nature and relevance to the current collection were important characteristics for the evaluation of subject matter needs as Skidmore's collection development policy was formulated. Significant considerations were the level of treatment, date of publication, language, geographic coverage, and currency. According to Taxman, a critical criterion for electronic journals is the quality of the product. Key considerations related to quality are presentation (ease of reading screens); literary quality; accuracy and reliability; searching capability; comprehensiveness; authority; and perspective. Concerning format issues, Taxman emphasized the need to compare print to electronic coverage before canceling journal subscriptions whether in print, CD-ROM, microform or AV. Price options must be scrutinized carefully when considering electronic journals. Each vendor or publisher approaches the licensing of their product in a unique way. Also critical to funding considerations for electronic journals is the high inflation rate for serials.

HOW DO WE GET IT?

Zappen addressed the significance of acquisition decisions related to the purchase of electronic journals. At Skidmore, with no additional budgeted funds available for electronic serials and a commitment to a 50/50 budget for serials/monographs, budgeting is an important factor to consider. Canceling print and microfilm subscriptions has been necessary to provide funds for electronic journals. Various consortial agreements have allowed the library to provide access to electronic journals at a lower cost. Without consortial agreements, Skidmore would not be able to offer electronic access to approximately 1,000 serial titles. These arrangements have increased the number of titles available to patrons at Skidmore College. (A listing of Websites with information about consortia is attached.)

According to Zappen, a critical part of the acquisition process is the licensing for electronic access to journals. The vendor license is a *legal document* that must be read, understood and adhered to. Zappen advises that individuals from several areas of the library and on campus–systems, technical services, public services and purchasing– should be involved when considering the terms of a license for electronic access. An excellent resource when reviewing license agreements are Websites dealing with licensing. A list of licensing Websites is attached.)

NOW THAT WE HAVE IT, WHAT DO WE DO WITH IT?

Taxman described the current situation at Skidmore that has created some complications for providing access to electronic journals. Because Skidmore's OPAC is not Web-based, direct connections from the catalog are not possible. Uniform Resource Locators (URLs) appearing in the catalog must be written down and then searched on the Web. The libraries' Webpage provides a listing of all electronic journals by title and subject. Julie McGinnis, catalog and database maintenance librarian at Skidmore College, provided information concerning the cataloging practices related to electronic journals. The following steps are taken when electronic journals are cataloged: test URL accuracy; locate OCLC bibliographic record; determine holdings; input holdings; input barcode; input location and status in 949 field; verify accuracy of all information; update and export OCLC record; load record into local system; change call number to "Available via WWW"; and modify 590 field as new holdings are added to the site. A complicating factor for cataloging electronic journals is the lack of information provided by some vendors about title changes. JSTOR was cited as an example of a vendor that is good about contacting libraries concerning updates and changes.

Skidmore has been very active in publicizing the availability of electronic journals throughout their campus. Such venues as department or campus newsletters are used to inform patrons of electronic resources. Zappen also uses fliers and posters available from many electronic journal publishers to post on campus. Subject librarians personally contact faculty about journals in their area.

Bibliographic instruction is a key resource to inform students about electronic journals according to Zappen. Open instruction sessions for students are also offered. Printed guides are available with instructions for accessing various electronic resources. All electronic journal titles are listed with access instructions in the periodical area.

WAS IT WORTH IT?

Assessing and evaluating electronic journals is a critical part of Skidmore's plan, according to Zappen and Taxman. Statistics from vendors are scrutinized regularly. Zappen warned that statistics must be studied carefully. Each vendor provides statistics in a different format and to evaluate them you need to know exactly what action is being tallied: each hit? each key stroke? each download? She warned that statistics from the various vendors and publishers cannot be easily compared. The following reasons were given for an increase in electronic journal use at Skidmore College: a young faculty who used electronic journals in their graduate programs; faculty who use information technology in the classroom; bibliographic instruction sessions; and the high percentage of faculty who read and respond to e-mail notices.

Another method used to evaluate electronic journals is surveying. Because statistics don't tell you who is using the material, Zappen and Taxman plan to survey faculty and students on campus to learn more about their use of electronic resources. Zappen asked the audience for advice on how to administer a survey on campus. A couple of surveying methods were suggested: administer the survey following a specific bibliographic instruction session, administer the survey online along with general class evaluations.

Taxman and Zappen contend that they must keep "their feet on the ground" when they are considering the tradeoffs of providing electronic access to journals. License agreements are not always clear about or do not address the ability to access information if a current subscription is not maintained. If paper or microfilm subscriptions for these titles have been canceled, the access to some information may be lost. Some significant historical data, such as front covers and advertisements, are not available in electronic versions of journals. In some cases free-lance writers for such journals as *Time* or *Newsweek* refuse to sign over the copyright to allow their articles to appear in the electronic version of their journals. It is important to consider the significance of these features for your institution as decisions about electronic journals are being made.

WHAT'S NEXT?

Skidmore College Library is exploring the possibilities related to their retention policies for periodicals. Because of the emphasis on electronic journals at Skidmore, their new building was planned with five years of growth space for bound periodicals. At this time, subject bibliographers are reviewing the periodicals in their subject areas to determine appropriate retention practices. Because JSTOR archives are guaranteed, some microfilm subscriptions have been dropped. The current year in paper is retained for titles subscribed to in paper and electronically. Five years of unbound paper copies of JSTOR titles are being kept at Skidmore. Decisions about JSTOR backfiles are awaiting assessments from subject bibliographers. Zappen related that cancellations for paper periodical subscriptions are continuing to provide funds for electronic journal subscriptions. During 1996-97, 14 percent of Skidmore's materials budget was for electronic journals.

An issue for future discussion at Skidmore College Library is increasing the access to electronic journals. A major step in this direction will occur when their Web-based catalog becomes available. Labels for the shelves and lists of journals are also provided in the periodical area. Because of increased usage of the library, student workers are being trained as information assistants to provide front line triage when reference assistance is available and to staff a help desk during late night hours.

At the end of their talk, Taxman and Zappen opened the floor to discussion, questions and comments from the audience. During the audience discussion several librarians and publishers provided input from their perspectives of electronic journal access. The major points of discussion centered on legal concerns, accuracy of information and evaluation.

The legal and ethical concerns surrounding the provision of electronic journal access was a major concern expressed. License agreements and password protection for electronic access is a difficult issue for all. Providing access must be weighed against rules and regulations set up in agreements. A proactive stance was suggested. Work with publishers and vendors to create contract language that will meet your library's needs. Consortial arrangements for electronic journal access were suggested to ease the burden of license negotiations for individual libraries.

Determining methods to guarantee the accuracy of information provided electronically was also discussed because checking individual URLs can be a time-consuming task. It was suggested that software is available that automatically checks URLs and reports problems. Maintaining holdings and title accuracy was also a concern. One step that can be taken is contacting vendors or publishers and stressing the importance of accurate information for your institution.

Statistics were a significant discussion issue related to evaluation of electronic journals. A suggestion from a publisher was to make sure statistical needs are addressed in the license agreement for service. Once specific statistics are available they must be interpreted within the framework of the local setting.

Taxman and Zappen provided an excellent overview of electronic journal management at Skidmore College. The thought-provoking questions and lively discussion reflected the interest in the management of electronic journals throughout the serials information chain. From the level of interest shown for the topic it is obvious that these issues will continue to be discussed in the future.

HELPFUL LISTSERVS AND URLS

Collection Development

- Library Collection Development Listserv: Colldv-l@usc.edu
- Collection Development of Electronic Resources Listserv: Ecoll@ unllib.unl.edu
- Policy Statements for Electronic Formats: http://www.ala.org/rusa/codes/codecd.html
- ARL Electronic Journal Issues Discussion List: http://www.cni.org/Hforums/arl-ejournal
- SERIALST Webpage: http://www.uvm.edu/~bmaclenn/serialst.html

Cataloging

- AUTOCAT Listserv: Autocat@listserv.acsu.buffalo.edu
- CONSER (Cooperative Online Serials): http://lcweb.loc.gov/acq/conser/
- Guidelines for the Use of Field 856: http://lcweb.loc.gov/marc/856guide.html
- MARC Standards: http://lcweb.loc.gov/marc
- Library of Congress Standards: http://lcweb.loc.gov/loc/standards
- OCLC Bibliographic Formats and Standards: http://www.oclc.org/oclc/bib

Licensing

- Liblicense: http://www.library.yale.edu/~Llicense/index.shtml
- ALA Principles for Licensing Electronic Resources: http://www.ala.org/washoff/ip/license.html
- Software and Database License Agreement Checklist: http://www.utsystem.edu/OGC/IntellectualProperty/dbckfrm1.htm

Consortia

- International Coalition on Library Consortia (ICOLC): http://www.library.yale.edu/consortia/
- Consortium of Consortia in New York State: http://www.lib.rpi.edu/dept/library/html/consortia/nyscoc/

The Development and Use of a Genre Statement for Electronic Journals

Jennifer Weintraub

Workshop Leader

Janet McKinney

Recorder

SUMMARY. The proliferation of electronic resources led the librarians of Cornell University's Mann Library to develop genre statements to aid in their selection decisions. Genre statements, one for each of five classes of electronic information, supplement the collection development policy and assist the genre specialists in selecting titles by outlining general and specific criteria. They also serve as summaries, updated annually, of the present state of the collection of the genre and of future issues to be addressed. *[Article copies available for a fee from The Haworth Document Delivery Service: 1-800-342-9678. E-mail address: getinfo@haworthpressinc.com]*

The Albert R. Mann Library of Cornell University serves the College of Agriculture and Life Sciences, the College of Human Ecology,

---

Jennifer Weintraub is Bibliographer and Full Text Genre Specialist, Mann Library, Cornell University.

Janet McKinney is Acquisitions/Serials Librarian, Leon E. Bloch Law Library, University of Missouri-Kansas City.

[Haworth co-indexing entry note]: "The Development and Use of a Genre Statement for Electronic Journals." McKinney, Janet. Co-published simultaneously in *The Serials Librarian* (The Haworth Press, Inc.) Vol. 36, No. 3/4, 1999, pp. 429-434; and: *Head in the Clouds, Feet on the Ground: Serials Vision and Common Sense* (ed: Jeffrey S. Bullington, Beatrice L. Caraway, and Beverley Geer) The Haworth Press, Inc., 1999, pp. 429-434. Single or multiple copies of this article are available for a fee from The Haworth Document Delivery Service [1-800-342-9678, 9:00 a.m. - 5:00 p.m. (EST). E-mail address: getinfo@haworthpressinc.com].

the Division of Biological Sciences, and the Division of Nutritional Sciences. Genre statements were implemented at Mann Library four to five years ago. A genre is a class of electronic information. Librarians at Mann identified five genres (software, multimedia, full-text, numeric, and bibliographic) and assigned a genre specialist to each. Jennifer Weintraub is bibliographer and full-text genre specialist. The genre specialists are to be experts in the issues surrounding their genres, advocates for their genres, resource persons, and liaisons with other departments. They are not subject specialists. Weintraub pointed out that Mann's Internet resources are cataloged and accessible through Cornell's network via Mann's gateway (http://campusgw.library.cornell.edu), a factor that enters into license negotiations. In this case, "Internet" resources are those available through the Internet by any means (telnet, ftp, World Wide Web, etc.).

When the librarians at Mann began to consider the selection of electronic resources some years ago, they examined the universe of full-text materials available through the Internet. Some concerns emerged from the exercise. They found that the quality of electronic journals varied, as did other quality factors revolving around document format, organization, and printing. It quickly became apparent to them that this universe was thus far nonstandardized. The genre statements partially address these issues by defining acceptable standards, identifying the optimal and the acceptable formats of electronic journals, and laying out selection criteria.

What is a genre statement? Genre statements complement the collection development policy but do not supplant or override it. They cross subject areas rather than specify subjects in which to collect (that is covered in the collection development policy). Genre statements provide selection criteria and serve to facilitate communication between selectors and library divisions as well as with publishers and patrons. They annually summarize the state of the library's program for a class of electronic publications. Weintraub expects that the genre statements will not be permanent additions to the library's collection development policy. They were developed to assist the selectors during what she termed a "transitional period" while electronic resources are still relatively new and unsettled. The selectors use the genre statements and department policy statements, in which the academic departments state their collection preferences, in conjunction with the basic collection development policy as the bases of their selection decisions. Figure 1 illustrates how Weintraub views these three documents coordinating in the selection process (adapted from her slide presentation).

Three components make up the genre statement for electronic journals. The first is the collection development policy for the genre itself, which includes general principles and selection criteria. The policy begins with a definition of electronic journals. This is a statement that could vary among libraries' statements rather than being a generally-accepted dictionary definition. In Mann's statement it also includes general examples of electronic journals, such as the novel electronic title (no print equivalent) and the electronic edition (alternate format of a title). The next section is a statement of the subject scope of the collection. General guidelines follow; for example, usefulness and demand for the resource should compensate for the work required to catalog and support it, resources should have a "scholarly" tone, resources should be well organized, dates of coverage should be relevant to the subject matter, and resources are to selected at the title level. On this last guideline Weintraub did point out that Mann is beginning to consider acquiring aggregated collections.

A number of the specific selection criteria stand out as specific to the genre. For example, when considering the quality and authority of an electronic journal, Weintraub examines its equivalency to the print version. The content of electronic journals is not always superior to that of the print. The text and image formats of electronic journals are particularly important to the patrons of Mann Library. Due to the

FIGURE 1. Collection Development Policy

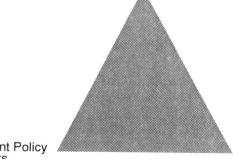

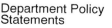
Department Policy Statements

Genre Statements

emphasis on the sciences, equations and other images must be shown and shown correctly. She will wait to select a title until it is well established, which can avoid dead links as well as a poor investment for the library. The electronic format allows for much greater flexibility in the organization of a journal, so for the patron's comfort, consistent organization from one issue to the next is an important factor. Another significant selection criterion is access. In this case, "access" refers to more than just whether the patron can "get to" and read the journal. The navigation through the journal or the issue by searching or browsing should be smooth and sufficient. The journal should be indexed, and journals that are linked through electronic indexes such as PubMed would be selected over those that are not. There should be links provided to referenced works throughout the journal. The other criteria are those that might be expected in a collection development policy: chronological guidelines, serial types, costs, and competing formats.

The next section of the genre statement describes the present state of the collection of the genre, updated annually. In this section the genre specialist profiles the current activity for selecting in the genre. It relates the titles or types of journals that were selected in the reporting year, the issues presently involved in selection for the genre, and statements concerning the implementation of the selection decisions. The specialist then examines the divisional workload throughout the library, examining the impact of selection decisions on the technical services and public services divisions and the wishes of those divisions relating to electronic journal selection. This helps to facilitate communication across the library's divisions. The final portion of this section of the genre statement lists the current selection strategy. The specialist enumerates a list of procedures and a series of selection sources. The selection strategy is personalized by the specialist and updated annually. Selection sources might include favorite and useful print resources, personal contacts, Websites, electronic discussion lists ("listservs"), and preferred search engines and specific search terms. The two reasons for including this section are to provide assistance for replacements when there is turnover in the specialist position and to serve as reminders for the specialists themselves.

The final section of the genre statement covers the future status or future plans for the electronic journal collection. It includes a discussion of issues that need to be addressed. For example, the infrastructure of selection might be an issue that requires attention. This would consider intra-library issues concerning the impact of selection decisions on other departments. The specialist identifies problems and trends in the universe of electronic journals to investigate in the coming year. Finally the goals for the next year are laid out. These would be action items requiring follow-up. For the Mann Library, Weintraub will be looking at weeding the electronic journals collection and reviewing large collections for selection consideration.

In conclusion, the characteristics of the genre statement are these: It complements the collection development policies by covering a specific class of electronic information across a range of subjects, it codifies selection criteria and standards for reference by the whole library, it facilitates communication between the library divisions, and it summarizes the state of the library's collection in the genre.

The workshop packed the room with thirty attendees. Weintraub left plenty of time for questions and discussion. The majority of the questions did not address the genre statement itself but rather the practices involved with selection and implementation of electronic journals as well as specific selection criteria at Mann Library. Two of the questions dealt with licensing. For Mann, the license must allow access across the Cornell campus due to campus policy and technology requirements. Since Cornell defines the campus network rather broadly, in terms of persons related to the university rather than the technology itself, even those that telnet in to the Cornell network must have access to electronic journals. Therefore, Weintraub will decide against selecting a journal that cannot meet this specification (although she may be willing to pay more for it for the access required). Factors in license negotiation that are "stop signs" are a license agreement that makes the library responsible for everything, especially the possible abuse by users, or that denies use of the title for interlibrary loan purposes. When asked about canceling print titles, she replied that they have cancelled only some general interest titles since the acquisition of UMI ProQuest. One attendee asked if she would select a title if there were no guarantee of access to archival issues. She may select it but would not cancel the print. She may also consult with interested faculty, take a look at the cost (free versus fee), or may even attempt to convince the vendor to archive it. All these factors include the issue of access to back issues after cancellation.

Mann Library currently provides approximately 400 electronic journal titles. Weintraub identified two strategies for weeding the collection. One will be to analyze use statistics, which would count the number of hits on a title through the library's gateway. The other would be to eliminate duplicates, such as titles available in both ASCII and World Wide Web formats.

Electronic Publishing:
The HighWire Experience

Vicky Reich

Workshop Leader

Cindy Hepfer

Recorder

SUMMARY. This report describes introductory remarks concerning Stanford University Libraries' HighWire Press and highlights of an "online tour" of the Website. Those attending the workshop then voted on several topics that presenter Vicky Reich was willing to address in the allotted time. In the session this recorder attended, those voting chose access/archiving, license agreements, and pricing/business models as their top priorities for discussion. *[Article copies available for a fee from The Haworth Document Delivery Service: 1-800-342-9678. E-mail address: getinfo@ haworthpressinc.com]*

Vicky Reich opened the workshop by presenting up-to-date information about Stanford University Libraries' HighWire Press (http://highwire.stanford.edu). As of the June 1998 NASIG presentation date, HighWire's publication list includes about seventy-five journal titles,

Vicky Reich is Assistant Director, HighWire Press and Digital Librarian, Stanford University Libraries.

Cindy Hepfer is Head, Collection Management Services, State University of New York at Buffalo Health Sciences Library.

[Haworth co-indexing entry note]: "Electronic Publishing: The HighWire Experience." Hepfer, Cindy. Co-published simultaneously in *The Serials Librarian* (The Haworth Press, Inc.) Vol. 36, No. 3/4, 1999, pp. 435-439; and: *Head in the Clouds, Feet on the Ground: Serials Vision and Common Sense* (ed: Jeffrey S. Bullington, Beatrice L. Caraway, and Beverley Geer) The Haworth Press, Inc., 1999, pp. 435-439. Single or multiple copies of this article are available for a fee from The Haworth Document Delivery Service [1-800-342-9678, 9:00 a.m. - 5:00 p.m. (EST). E-mail address: getinfo@haworthpressinc.com].

with new ones being added weekly. Each week about 30,000 pages per journal are processed for the Web. All of the journals have both Hypertext Markup Language (HTML) and Portable Document Format (PDF) pages. Images come in three sizes, a thumbnail GIF (Graphic Interchange Format), a full page GIF and a large JPEG (Joint Photographic Experts Groups) file. The images are of superior quality. Attendees were referred to the images of gels in *Journal of Cell Biology* (http://www.jbc.org).

While many of the HighWire titles are available free of charge, Reich noted that others require subscriptions. In her role as assistant director of the press, former serials and acquisitions librarian Reich advises publishers on subscription or business models–she said that some take her advice, but others do not. Most of the titles are owned by small associations who publish, on average, less than a handful of titles. HighWire's technological leverage allows these associations to compete with large publishers that are investing heavily in Web access.

Reich toured attendees through one of the HighWire titles, *Proceedings of the National Academy of Sciences* (http://www.pnas.org). She showed us the author and keyword search capabilities and the "toll free linking" among the HighWire titles. The key objective of this linking service is to disseminate research. When you are reading a full-text article from a HighWire Press journal, "toll free links" are citations linking to other HighWire journals that will allow you to access the full-text of the cited article at no charge. In other words, readers get access to the full text of articles even when they don't have a subscription. Interjournal links to full texts are provided for a long list of titles (for example, see http://ajpadvan.physiology.org/help/ijlinks. dtl). References are also linked to PubMed or other appropriate abstract and indexing databases. For an example, look at the references of a recent article in the *Journal of Clinical Investigation* (http://www. jci.org/cgi/content/full/102/2/283#References).

Reich explained that it is becoming more common for content available online not to also be available in the journal's print format. As an example, she cited *Pediatrics* (http://www.pediatrics.org), which is published by the American Academy of Pediatrics, and *Science* (http://www.sciencemag.org), which is published by the American Association for the Advancement of Science (AAAS). As this phenomenon increases, Reich believes that the electronic version–not the print version–will eventually become the "version of record."

Science, Reich explains, is experimenting with enhancing its research links. These hyperlinks–which are currently added by hand from articles in each issue that are carefully selected by the editors–allow users to access other Web material such as relevant courses, encyclopedias, and other materials. In essence, these are "refereed links" that HighWire is committed to maintaining. The enhanced research links service is very popular with high schools (HighWire and the AAAS get fan mail from students and teachers).

After the introductory remarks and tour, those attending the workshop voted on several topics that Reich was willing to address in the one-and-a-half-hour timeslot. In the session this recorder attended, those voting chose access/archiving, license agreements, and pricing/business models as their top priorities for discussion.

ACCESS/ARCHIVING

Reich explained that HighWire's Uniform Resource Locators (URLs) are predictable and have a consistent format. This is not because the content on the Web is captured and frozen, but rather because URLs are carefully kept up-to-date. The industry has been struggling hard to address the question of how to provide access to backfiles when a library cancels its ongoing subscription. Elsevier allows libraries to purchase files and store them locally; Academic Press provides access to those volumes to which a library formerly subscribed for a maintenance fee; OCLC will no longer store, but will distribute, its backfiles. However, some publishers of the titles that HighWire has mounted on the Web have decided not to collect ongoing revenue for back content; after a certain period of time, the content of their journals will be free to everyone. For a more complete list, see http://hwmg.stanford.edu/features.html#adv. What libraries are paying for, then, is very current access. *Journal of Biological Chemistry* will be free after twelve months; *Proceedings of the National Academy of Sciences* will be free after twenty-four. One audience member asked how long HighWire could maintain this: three years? five? ten? twenty? Can they truly commit to indefinite access? Reich said that to promise indefinite access would be foolhardy. However, the data tapes at Stanford are backed up by the computing center according to industry standards. In the past three years, HighWire has changed technological platforms three times. She notes that the technology is constantly changing and that the files are being migrated. An audience member from the Astronomical Society noted that migration is remarkably inexpensive.

LICENSE AGREEMENTS

Most of the journals published through HighWire do not use license agreements. Reich says that she tells publishers that license agreements are not needed and that, in fact, they entail high overhead costs. Some of the HighWire publishers such as Cell Press do, however, require license agreements. Instead of a formal license agreement, the titles have a simple terms and conditions statement and are based on fair use limitations of the United States Copyright Law (for example, http://hwmg.stanford.edu/apsterm.html). Definitions of "sites" are all the same or are negotiable (for example, http://hwmg.stanford.edu/jbcsite.html).

PRICING AND BUSINESS MODELS

The HighWire team has a list of questions for publishers who are thinking about how to price the online version. These questions include analyzing revenue from advertisements, the extent of individual subscriptions and of duplication at a single institution, and how the subscription base is geographically distributed worldwide. The answers they receive affect what makes sense in terms of recouping costs of producing the electronic version of the journal. Examples of the models are

- *Journal of Biological Chemistry*, which has an online price, a print price and no discount if a library subscribes to both,
- *Pediatrics*, which allows free online access because they know that their print revenue is not in jeopardy due to their print and the online products being different, and
- *Science*, which has a very large advertising base and a large proportion of individual subscribers. The American Association for

the Advancement of Science, the publisher, has serious concerns about institutional level IP access because they believe that they would lose a large number of the individual subscriptions. However, despite their concerns, they are allowing Stanford University trial unrestricted IP address access. Institutions can purchase baskets of specific IP addresses (for details see http://www.science-mag. org/subscriptions/libinfo.shtml).

Although librarians do not want to be forced to purchase bundles of print and online, this is the predominant product librarians are buying. A new model may develop where the online is the version of record and the print version is discounted.

Friedemann Weigel from Harrassowitz raised the issue of cost-based pricing versus what-the-market-will-bear for "added value" (the American Chemical Society approach). Weigel noted that, in time, librarians will not be able to compare the online with the print versions and their costs because the products will not be comparable. Reich noted that in all the HighWire examples, the online products differ from their print counterparts because of links and because brand new content appears only in the online version. With the online, it's easier for publishers to make derivative products. On the other hand, it is a challenge to explain all these different options to the marketplace.

Another audience member asked whether HighWire will ever become a content publisher instead of a "new wave printer." While there is interest in the idea and although they receive requests to become publishers, Reich says, HighWire is not competing with their publishers for content.

Access to Government Serial Information in a Digital Environment

Louise Treff-Gangler
Marit S. MacArthur

Workshop Leaders

Wayne Jones

Recorder

SUMMARY. Access to government information is a fundamental principle of American democracy. The federal depository program is one of the main ways in which government information is distributed to the public. Much of this information is now available in electronic form, and libraries must consider several major technical service and public service issues surrounding the provision of access to these electronic serial documents. *[Article copies available for a fee from The Haworth Document Delivery Service: 1-800-342-9678. E-mail address: getinfo@haworthpressinc.com]*

Access to government information is important in a democratic society. Two of the oldest legislative means of providing citizens with

---

Louise Treff-Gangler is Head of Government Publications at the Auraria Library, University of Colorado at Denver.

Marit S. MacArthur is Reference Librarian and Government Publications Serials Cataloger at the Auraria Library, University of Colorado at Denver.

Wayne Jones is Head of the Serials Cataloging Section at Massachusetts Institute of Technology.

[Haworth co-indexing entry note]: "Access to Government Serial Information in a Digital Environment." Jones, Wayne. Co-published simultaneously in *The Serials Librarian* (The Haworth Press, Inc.) Vol. 36, No. 3/4, 1999, pp. 441-447; and: *Head in the Clouds, Feet on the Ground: Serials Vision and Common Sense* (ed: Jeffrey S. Bullington, Beatrice L. Caraway, and Beverley Geer) The Haworth Press, Inc., 1999, pp. 441-447. Single or multiple copies of this article are available for a fee from The Haworth Document Delivery Service [1-800-342-9678, 9:00 a.m. - 5:00 p.m. (EST). E-mail address: getinfo@haworthpressinc.com].

government information are the Constitution of 1787, which requires that Congress "keep a journal of its proceedings" (i.e., the *Congressional Record*),[1] and the federal depository program, which was established in 1813 to send congressional reports, bills, and special documents to designated libraries.[2] Ensuing legislation in 1857, 1895, and 1962 expanded the program to include executive branch publications and mandated that all government publications delivered to designated depositories or to other libraries be available for public use without charge.[3]

Government information began to be distributed in electronic form with the CD-ROM version of the 1990 census. Online information began with the GPO's Federal Bulletin Board in 1990. Since then, information has been organized on gophers and is now widely available on the Web. The federal government disseminates more than 7,500 electronic databases each year and provides access to even more information through the Internet, gateways, and locator services. Some of the major sources of government information are

- serials available on CD-ROM;
- serials now available only on the Web;
- the GPO Access service, which provides the full text of the *Congressional Record* and the *Federal Register* as well as many other core documents. This is a heavily used service (thirteen million documents are downloaded each month)[4] which has become the cornerstone of GPO's provision of access to government information on the Internet; and
- the Federal Depository Library Program Electronic Collection, which consists of core legislative and regulatory GPO Access products; online products managed by GPO or by other institutions through agreements; links to online products under the control of the originating agencies; and CD-ROMs.

As of 1998, more than 35 percent of depository program information is available in electronic form.[5]

In 1996 five principles for federal government information were identified in the Study to Identify Measures Necessary for a Successful Transition to a More Electronic Federal Depository Library Program:

- The public has the right of access to government information.
- The government has the obligation to disseminate and provide broad public access to information.

- The government has the obligation to guarantee the authenticity and integrity of its information.
- The government has the obligation to preserve its information.
- Government information should remain in the public domain.[6]

However, current legislation (Title 44) stipulates that the only publications to be distributed to depository libraries are those that are tangible products; that is, not including online products. The Inter-Association Working Group on Government Information Policy, organized by the American Library Association, has developed a draft bill (the Federal Information Access Act of 1997) proposing a comprehensive revision of Title 44, which

- expands the definition of government information in all current or future formats from all three branches of government,
- reinforces the requirement that information should be provided without charge,
- requires that agencies not restrict information, and
- requires that information be archived.

Unfortunately, as of May 1998, the bill has yet to be introduced.

There are several services and products, both governmental and commercial, which compete with those offered by the depository program. Government agencies often allow one free password for depository libraries, but charge for individual users, site licenses, or additional passwords. On the commercial side, Bernan Press has published new editions of discontinued government serials, and the Congressional Information Service publishes several excellent statistical indexes. Furthermore, access to government information is being facilitated by partnerships between agencies and the GPO, and between agencies and universities.

How should libraries provide bibliographic access to online government information? Cataloging is the traditional method, but there are several other options, all of which have their own advantages and disadvantages:

- *Relying on general Web search engines:* These are familiar to users, but there are sometimes too many hits, often with poor-quality information.

- *Relying on specialized Websites maintained by others:* Good official and unofficial sites exist, but there is much duplication and the information is not tailored to your users or your collection.[7]
- *Creating your own Website:* This can be tailored to your users and your collection, but it is very labor intensive, requiring constant updating and Uniform Resource Locator (URL) checking, and it is not helpful to users of the catalog.
- *Providing printed lists of Websites:* These are inexpensive and may be a good option for low-tech libraries, but are also labor intensive and unhelpful to catalog users.

The cataloging of electronic government publications can be expensive for libraries, especially when budgets are shrinking and there are other options. URL checking is a constant necessity, and many catalog departments lack the time and expertise for cataloging electronic resources. However, there are also many reasons simply to catalog electronic government publications. Cataloging provides continuity and access in the catalog for all publications in all formats and promotes the use of government sources which users would otherwise miss. Many studies have shown that cataloged document collections get used more than uncataloged ones. Catalogs also provide superior access via controlled-vocabulary searching and authority control. All catalogs also provide the user with handy access to the location (URL) of electronic publications, and Web catalogs even provide direct access to the publications themselves. If electronic government serials are cataloged, then individual issues can be checked in so that users can easily know exactly what is available.

Many electronic government publications are serials, and the cataloging of e-serials can be generally problematic. The standards for cataloging e-serials are still being developed; even things as basic as the definition of a serial are considered inadequate for e-resources (e.g., databases, directories). Should separate cataloging records be created for titles in different formats (paper, fiche, CD-ROM, online, etc.), or should all be covered on a single record? Furthermore, an e-serial is ephemeral, and even after it is cataloged its content can change.

Government e-serials cataloging can be particularly problematic. Fifty percent of all government publications are never received by GPO, and so are not distributed and may not be cataloged. There can also be differences in content between electronic and paper or fiche versions of government serials. Special software is needed to read serials on some sites (e.g., many GPO sites require Adobe Acrobat), and many sites do not archive issues.

Help is available though. CONSER allows for a single-record option when cataloging e-serials, and a new definition of what constitutes a serial is being investigated. PURLs (Persistent URLs) are considered by some to be a good interim solution to the problem of URL links that become inactive. GPO is now using and maintaining PURLs. GPO is also cataloging depository electronic documents as well as other electronic government sites (using the CONSER single-record option), and its records and updates are available for batch loading from various vendors.[8] There are also various finding aids to direct you to the electronic versions of documents that you already have in print or on fiche,[9] as well as authoritative cataloging sites maintained by national and local institutions. And finally, libraries can avoid cataloging altogether by simply adding holdings for e-resources to already existing records for documents you have in nonelectronic form.

Cataloging of electronic government documents is still desirable and useful. The best approach to providing bibliographic access is probably a combination of those mentioned above, based on the needs and resources of the individual institution. Each institution should catalog what will most help its users, using batch loading if possible. At the very least, an institution could add electronic availability information and URLs selectively to already-existing records for nonelectronic documents.

The final part of the workshop dealt with the public services issues associated with providing access to electronic documents. Some of these issues are

- *selection:* Though a huge quantity of government information is available to even the smallest library, it must still be evaluated before it is put up on the library's Website;
- *multiple formats:* Some print serials have disappeared altogether, but many persist in print and/or CD-ROM and Web versions. Some are free, some require a password, some charge a fee;
- *the user:* In order to access electronic documents, the user now has to deal with printing and downloading problems, as well as various hardware and software issues and restrictions;

- *staff training:* There is a wide variety of software packages and a lack of standardization, and it is probably not practical to expect all staff to be experts in all products and software;
- *library instruction:* Hands-on instruction is necessary, with handouts detailing search strategies and examples.

GPO has drafted a list of guidelines for providing access to electronic documents:

- Provide no-fee access to workstations capable of accessing information on diskettes, CD-ROMs, and the Internet
- Provide access to electronic information for the general public
- Make tangible electronic products available in a timely manner
- Provide no-fee Internet access to the general public, including telnet and ftp capabilities to encourage downloading and/or transmission of electronic data
- Develop homepages for government information
- Provide fax and e-mail delivery of government information to distant users
- Provide public access to depository electronic documents, as well as the capability to download and print, with restrictions and costs consistent with those for other public services in the library
- Provide disk space on publicly available computers for temporary storage of electronic government information
- Provide appropriate reference service, help guides, and documentation for electronic products and the Internet
- Offer training for the general public in using electronic information

The emphasis these days is on enabling the user to access information directly. Librarians are necessary to assist users not only in finding information but also in evaluating it.

Questions and discussion after the workshop were excellent. The focus was on link checking, holdings, and cataloging. Who should be responsible for verifying that URLs on Websites are still active, public services or technical services staff? One possibility suggested was a committee to check the site. Some libraries are using Microsoft's FrontPage to check links, and others are using Tetranet Software's Linkbot.

When electronic documents are not cataloged but holdings are simply added to a record, how are individual issues checked in? Not many libraries are checking in individual issues; they are simply adding summary holdings statements. Those that are find that the results are useful but that the effort is very labor intensive. One library is indicating its holdings on its Website. Government agencies are often adding back issues of serials to their sites. Detailed holdings information would be a good service for vendors to provide.

When using the single-record approach in cataloging government e-serials, do the title and intellectual content of the print and electronic versions have to be the same? One library's policy is to follow the single-record approach even when the titles are different, but to create a separate record for the electronic version when the intellectual content differs. Why use the single-record approach at all? The main reasons are that it is cheaper to do so (saves times and money), and that users of the catalog prefer just one record (though at least one library's users actually prefer separate records).

NOTES

1. The Constitution of the United States of America, Art. 1, Sect. 5.

2. Katrina Stierholtz, "U.S. Government Documents in the Electronic Era: Problems and Promise," *Collection Management* 21 (1996): 43.

3. Ridley R. Kessler, Jr., "A Brief History of the Federal Depository Library Program: A Personal Perspective," *Journal of Government Information* 23 (1996): 371.

4. Andrew M. Sherman, "Statutory Reform of the U.S. Government Printing Office: A View from the GPO," *Journal of Government Information* 23 (1996): 267.

5. Gil Baldwin, "LPS Progress Report," *Administrative Notes* 19, no. 7 (May 15, 1998): 13.

6. Beth E. Clausen, "Federal Government Information: The Electronic Transition," *Mississippi Libraries* 60 (summer 1996): 36.

7. Selected useful sites are: GPO Access (http://www.access.gpo.gov/); Louisiana State University's U.S. Federal Government Agencies Directory (http://www. lib.lsu. edu/gov/fedgov.html); and several sites linked from ALA's Government Documents Round Table (GODORT) site (http://www.lib.berkeley.edu/GODORT/#GODORT).

8. Notable vendors of GPO records are: Auto-Graphics (http://www.auto-graphics. com/); LC Cataloging Distribution Service (http://lcweb.loc.gov/cds/mds.html); MAR-CIVE (http://www.marcive.com/); and OCLC GOVDOC Service (http://www. oclc.org/oclc/ promo/5858gvdc/5858gvdc.htm).

9. Some examples are: Pathway Services Browse Electronic Titles (http://www. access.gpo.gov/su_docs/dpos/btitles.html); Uncle Sam Migrating Government Publications (http://www.lib.memphis.edu/gpo/mig.htm); and Tom Tyler's GPO MARC Internet Resources (http://www.du.edu/~ttyler/mirintro.htm#gtr00).

Successful Web Journals:
The Wall Street Journal
and *The Chronicle of Higher Education*:
Two Live Case Studies

Neil F. Budde
Philip W. Semas

Workshop Leaders

Marla J. Schwartz

Recorder

SUMMARY. Two publishers of well-known print newspapers have launched successful Web versions. The editors described the evolution of their sites and discussed the advantages of Web editions: timeliness, depth of content, user-customized access to information, and community-building interactive forums. They detailed lessons learned, outlined future plans, and clarified similarities and differences between the two sites. Discussion centered on three main areas: library access and site

Neil F. Budde is Editor, *The Wall Street Journal Interactive Edition*, Dow Jones & Co. Inc.

Philip W. Semas is Associate Editor for New Media, *The Chronicle of Higher Education*.

Marla J. Schwartz is Chief, Acquisitions and Serials, Washington College of Law Library, American University.

[Haworth co-indexing entry note]: "Successful Web Journals: *The Wall Street Journal* and *The Chronicle of Higher Education:* Two Live Case Studies." Schwartz, Marla J. Co-published simultaneously in *The Serials Librarian* (The Haworth Press, Inc.) Vol. 36, No. 3/4, 1999, pp. 449-454; and: *Head in the Clouds, Feet on the Ground: Serials Vision and Common Sense* (ed: Jeffrey S. Bullington, Beatrice L. Caraway, and Beverley Geer) The Haworth Press, Inc., 1999, pp. 449-454. Single or multiple copies of this article are available for a fee from The Haworth Document Delivery Service [1-800-342-9678, 9:00 a.m. - 5:00 p.m. (EST). E-mail address: getinfo@haworthpressinc.com].

licenses, the nature of archives and article retrieval, and advertising. *[Article copies available for a fee from The Haworth Document Delivery Service: 1-800-342-9678. E-mail address: getinfo@haworthpressinc.com]*

This workshop brought together Neil F. Budde, editor, *The Wall Street Journal Interactive Edition* (http://interactive.wsj.com), and Philip W. Semas, associate editor for new media, *The Chronicle of Higher Education* (http://chronicle.com) to discuss how they launched successful Web versions of their respective publications.

Budde entitled his talk "Creating a Unique On-Line Publication," which sums up the goal of *The Wall Street Journal* to create an online publication that is significantly different from the print version and directed to a unique audience. The World Wide Web has allowed the developers to do all that they imagined in 1993 when the idea of an online edition first arose. They want to exploit the medium and make use of the qualities it offers: timeliness, global breadth, unique content, substantial depth of background information, personalization, and community. The *Interactive Edition* is updated twenty-four hours a day, seven days a week. For the editors, it is like printing the paper throughout the day. Response from users has run the gamut from "It's too much like a newspaper" to "It isn't enough like a newspaper," leading the editors to conclude that it is just right. It includes articles from all print editions of the newspaper and draws on the worldwide resources of Dow Jones. For the Internet readership, there is unique coverage of technologically oriented news and stories about the Internet, some of which eventually appear in print.

The full Interactive Edition was launched in April 1996, with paid subscriptions beginning in September 1996. Subscribers to the print publication, who comprise about one-third of the 200,000 Web subscribers, pay a reduced rate for the Web version. Most of them retain their subscriptions to the print newspaper as well. Budde later noted that not just young professionals are using the Website; the number of older users, including retired seniors, is increasing. The interactive nature of the Web allows subscribers to set up interest profiles so that they receive "my daily news" updates and personal portfolios to track investments. They can also engage in moderated discussions with other readers. The Web allows the paper to supplement articles with video and audio links, as well as access to stock prices while reading news about companies. These are intelligent links that let the reader decide where to go from a pull-down menu. Detailed company information is also linked to every article.

Included in the subscription price are *Wall Street Journal* and *Barron's* articles as published in the interactive *Journal,* including exclusive content and articles from the Asian and European editions, and Dow Jones Newswire articles. Readers may purchase articles for $2.95 each from the Dow Jones Publications Library, which includes *The Wall Street Journal, The Asian Wall Street Journal, The Wall Street Journal Europe,* and *Barron's* as they appeared in print, as well as Dow Jones News articles from the most recent fourteen days. It also includes about 5,000 other publications from around the world. Since the Web version is constantly being updated, the archive contains the paper as it existed at 2:00 A.M. each day.

Semas asserted that *The Chronicle of Higher Education* may have been the first newspaper on the Internet in 1993 when it began a free gopher service called *Academe This Week.* It consisted of job ads and limited editorial material from the paper. In April 1994, an *Academe This Week* Website was added and in July 1995, *Academe Today* started as a password-protected Website for *Chronicle* subscribers only. It contains the full text of *The Chronicle* updated every Monday, an archive back to 1989, daily news updates by e-mail and on the Web, and early access to job ads for subscribers. In May 1998 the two sites merged into a single site, part of which is free and part password-protected.

The subscription price of the newspaper includes access to the online service, and all classified ads go on the Web at no extra charge. E-mail is used to drive traffic to the Website and build ties with readers; it is sent five days a week to subscribers, and on Monday morning it lists the contents of that week's paper. Original content each day includes daily news, a moderated interactive discussion forum called "Colloquy," and technology coverage. Semas noted that while *The Wall Street Journal* is a daily paper that is updated every hour on the Web, *The Chronicle* is a weekly paper that is now updated daily. To draw traffic and promote the site, some of the articles are available without a password, particularly those that deal with technology issues. Most articles, the archives, and all statistical data require a password. Fifty-seven percent of the 93,000 subscribers to *The Chronicle of Higher Education* have registered as users of the Website. Web users tend to be younger, but more administrators than faculty members use the Website. The site records one million "page views" each week, and 75 percent of these are to access job ads. It has led to increased numbers of subscriptions, 100 of which are sold via the Web each week, and more classified advertising, up 12 percent in the last year and 40 percent since 1993.

Semas listed the lessons they have learned:

- E-mail is the Internet's "killer ap."
- Classified advertising is the No. 2 "killer ap."
- The things you worry about at the start will not be your real problems; e.g., indiscriminate sharing of passwords.
- Update more frequently online than in print.
- Engage your readers; try to create a "community."
- Don't think of your Website as a separate service. Take the view that you have one service with print and online components. (This is in contrast to the philosophy of *The Wall Street Journal* of creating a unique service on the Web.)
- Use print to promote the Website and vice versa.
- Keep it simple. Sit on your designers. Beware of Java, Shockwave and other "hot stuff."
- Content is more important than technology; technology should serve the content.
- But use the technology.
- Be patient.
- Experiment. As Wayne Gretzky said: "You miss 100 percent of the shots you don't take."

Next on the horizon for *The Chronicle* may be personalization of the online offerings, online-only subscriptions, and site licenses.

The animated discussion centered on three main areas, none surprising for an audience of mostly librarians: library access and site licenses, the nature of the archives and article retrieval, and advertising. Neither *The Wall Street Journal* nor *The Chronicle of Higher Education* has figured out how to offer a site license without losing paper subscribers. *The Chronicle* offers only one user identification and password per paper subscription but allows libraries to provide access at a single terminal at the reference desk. They provide free access to the job ads and other selected portions of the Website and in the future may launch an enhanced "career center" in order to reach graduate students and new PhDs. *The Wall Street Journal* also requires each individual subscriber to register for the online service. Both are concerned about libraries and corporations offering access through their networks and about the number of people sharing passwords. Budde noted that fees currently charged do not cover operating costs of the Website; he hopes to make a profit for the first time next year. Semas said that *The Chronicle*'s online efforts support its overall profitability.

Questions were raised about the ease of article retrieval, fees charged, and the longevity of the archives. Both sites archive material in searchable databases. *The Wall Street Journal Interactive Edition* charges $2.95 per article, a price determined by the pre-existing Dow Jones News Retrieval Service. Budde said that he would like to lower the cost and sell more articles. *The Chronicle of Higher Education* archives editorial material since 1989; job ads are available for the current and previous week. There is no extra charge for subscribers. Neither site has a permanent archive of the Website as it has evolved over time. Budde commented that while there is a tape archive and the most recent fourteen days are readily available, there may not be a "picture" of the front page. Semas remarked that while they have archived the most recent designs of the Website, the earlier ones are not available.

In response to a question about advertisers, Budde noted that they were asking for more prominent display on the Website, the Web equivalent of "above the fold," or visible on the screen without having to scroll down. He remarked that while it is difficult to balance their requests with what is best for the readers, when ads were first placed near the top of the front page there were only two objections. *The Chronicle*, on the other hand, groups all ads at the bottom of the home page. While all advertisers want to know as much as they can about the readers, both publications have a privacy statement that assures readers that no information about individuals is revealed. An outside service handles advertising for *The Wall Street Journal,* and the ads are targeted by domain.

In conclusion, both Budde and Semas felt that discontinuance of their respective print publications was a very remote possibility. While the tripling cost of newsprint could force more changes, for now the speed of access, clarity of display, and portability of computers would all have to improve before *The Wall Street Journal* would discontinue print, and in fact they are adding ten-year capacity to the printing presses. At this time many readers of the print newspaper are using the Web version to save and print articles. For *The Chronicle*, some items might go online and not be in the printed paper, e.g., long lists of names or job ads, while the function of the printed paper could evolve to include more analysis and longer pieces.

The Real World
of Integrating Electronic Resources
into a Web OPAC

Christina E. Carter
Sever Bordeianu
Nancy Dennis

Workshop Leaders

Peter C. Whiting

Recorder

SUMMARY. For the researcher, there has been an increase in the availability of electronic resources that includes electronic journals, databases and full-text resources. A Web OPAC is a powerful tool that links all of these electronic resources for easy access. Workshop presenters described their experience with establishing a Web OPAC and how systems, serials cataloging and reference dealt with it. *[Article copies available for a fee from The Haworth Document Delivery Service: 1-800-342-9678. E-mail address: getinfo@haworthpressinc.com]*

Christina E. Carter is Head, Reference Department, General Library, University of New Mexico.

Sever Bordeianu is Head, Serials Cataloging Section, General Library, University of New Mexico.

Nancy Dennis is Director, Library Technology Development, General Library, University of New Mexico.

Peter C. Whiting is Cataloging Librarian at Prairie View A&M University.

[Haworth co-indexing entry note]: "The Real World of Integrating Electronic Resources into a Web OPAC." Whiting, Peter C. Co-published simultaneously in *The Serials Librarian* (The Haworth Press, Inc.) Vol. 36, No. 3/4, 1999, pp. 455-460; and: *Head in the Clouds, Feet on the Ground: Serials Vision and Common Sense* (ed: Jeffrey S. Bullington, Beatrice L. Caraway, and Beverley Geer) The Haworth Press, Inc., 1999, pp. 455-460. Single or multiple copies of this article are available for a fee from The Haworth Document Delivery Service [1-800-342-9678, 9:00 a.m. - 5:00 p.m. (EST). E-mail address: getinfo@haworthpressinc.com].

Sharing experiences encountered in the process of establishing a Web OPAC at the University of New Mexico General Library was the goal of Nancy Dennis (director, Library Technology Development, General Library), Sever Bordeianu (head, Serials Cataloging Section, General Library), and Christina Carter (head, Reference Department, Zimmerman Library). As Dennis put it in her introduction of the workshop to the serial librarians in the audience, she and her two other colleagues are not experts in implementing Web-based OPACs. Their experience could be summed up by the title of an upcoming ALA session called "Playing the Game While Writing the Rules."

The University of New Mexico General Library is an Innovative Interfaces site and host to the LIBROS consortium with more than four million records. In 1995, the library planned for a hardware upgrade that would include a Web OPAC. At the same time, the library was acquiring more and more Web resources such as electronic journals, databases, and full-text resources. To find a solution for handling electronic items, management teams of the library staff were formed to discuss issues and problems of implementation. Their results can be found in *Library Hi-Tech*, volume 15, number 3-4 (1997). In 1997, the library began the transition from a command driven, text-based catalog to the GUI-based Innovative Interfaces WebPAC.

The question is no longer "Why have a Web-based OPAC?" but "How will it be done?" and "What type features should the OPAC have?" There are many advantages to the Web OPAC. It can support protocols such as telnet, http, ftp and gopher. It can also support files and document formats like Portable Document Format (PDF), HTML (Hypertext Markup Language) and Standard Generalized Markup Language (SGML). Even library resources, such as user guides and help guides, can be hypertext-linked to and from a Web OPAC. For the PC user, a graphical browser such as Netscape or Internet Explorer is required to access a Web OPAC.

There has been a phenomenal growth in Web-based information technology applications. By embracing these standard applications, libraries are no longer in a smaller niche market or isolated from mainstream consumer and business markets. Because libraries share resources with consumers and businesses, the cost of technology has gone down. Dennis gave an example of a powerful feature called the embedded search statement that uses an HTML reference to produce a link that has the capability to retrieve information that can be limited by subject and/or date. As a result, it can produce for patrons a search that has current up-to-date information.

In the world at large, Web technology is changing rapidly and new standards are needed to accommodate all of these changes. However, the Web OPAC and the classic text catalog will have to co-exist for the foreseeable future because patrons will still be accessing the catalog from dumb terminals. Dennis concluded the introduction of the workshop by emphasizing that electronic resources behave differently and feel different in a Web catalog because the display is so unlike a text-based catalog.

SYSTEM ISSUES

Dennis talked about the systems infrastructure requirements for the Web OPAC: server, desktop and network. The server capacity may require an upgrade to handle the increased number of users. Data will be served simultaneously to telnet devices (dumb terminals) or to Web browsers. The system should support retrieval and display of bibliographic data, graphical logos and images. The system network is mounted on a TCP/IP network, the protocol of the Internet. To facilitate Web OPAC site management, HTML editing programs that allow for the creation of HTML documents, log files, and Web access management programs should be considered.

The basic desktop hardware configuration for access to a Web-based catalog should include a PC with a Pentium II processor, 32 MB RAM, a video card and a sound card. The public PCs are equipped with fifteen-inch color monitors while the staff has seventeen-inch color monitors. Printing is a local option (from shared network laser printers or stand-alone ink jet printers).

Basic software configuration should include a GUI (graphical user interface) operating system (i.e., Windows or NT). The graphical browsers such as Netscape or Internet Explorer with the capability to support applications like Acrobat scripts, graphical or AV file formats, JSTOR/PRINT, and telnet are also required. Local library issues might include patron access to word processing and e-mail. The Web OPAC needs a basic infrastructure to display simple graphical files; the rich multimedia files that the Web OPAC connects to require a more robust computing and networking environment, however.

System administration issues include the expense of logins, IP authentication and computer security to prevent hackers. To validate Uniform Resource Locators (URLs) in the bibliographic records, the library uses LINKBOT. The library staff will have to be trained on new programs, while the systems staff will have to learn new operating systems. Cost consideration should be given to upgrading computer software and computer hardware.

CATALOGING AND MAINTENANCE

Sever Bordeianu discussed the issues that cataloging encountered with the Web OPAC. The first problem was the lack of notification of the receipt and/or purchase of electronic resources. No workflow procedures had been established between the acquisitions and cataloging departments. Specifically, what the catalogers needed to know was the proper URL and the type of authorization, passwords, or restrictions that were required to access a particular resource. A new processing form was designed, and one of its main features was that it had contact people to track the electronic resource during its processing within the library.

Today, all catalogers have PCs on their desks that are hooked to the Internet, but, as the transition to more Web-based resources developed, it was realized that the catalogers needed to be trained on using Web browsers. They need to know how to get to their resources and how to evaluate and identify the pertinent information for the cataloging record. In time, the catalogers acquired the knowledge and were more comfortable with the Web. While not a CONSER library, the catalogers followed module 31 of the *CONSER Cataloging Manual*, "Remote Access Computer File Serials." Bordeianu explained that CONSER allows for either one record or two records. He researched the issue by examining other library catalogs, calling cataloging colleagues and talking to public services. The overwhelming decision was to go with the one-record approach for both electronic resources and print material. The fewer records, the less confusion for the patrons and the library staff.

Bordeianu gave an example of an OCLC record to show how simple the one-record method is. To indicate an electronic resource in OCLC, the two MARC fields that point the user to the electronic resource are the 538 (additional physical form available) and 856 (URL location). The cataloging department had to create local codes for the Innovative Interfaces catalog for electronic resources to indicate location, status, type and call number. Call numbers were put in the initial electronic resource records, but this created confusion when patrons were looking for the item on the shelves. Instead of a call number, the record has either a "password required" or "see URL above" statement. The classic text OPAC is more cumbersome for the user because the patron has to write down the URL, while the Web OPAC user can click on the URL and go directly to the item.

There are two check-in records in the staff mode for the print version and the electronic version. The identity field indicates if the record is online or print. For the print version, the check-in information is put in the box version, while the online version check-in does not use the box version but instead has a message telling where to get access to the Web version. The classic text OPAC has the electronic version listed second, after the print version. In the Web OPAC, the location of the electronic resource is listed first, before the print version. This makes it more accessible for the user since they can easily click on the electronic version.

REFERENCE POINT OF VIEW

Christina Carter then talked about the interaction of the patron and the reference staff with the Web in general and the Web OPAC. Patrons want more direct links from the Web OPAC to periodicals, databases, full-text articles, and other Internet resources. The Web is not a traditional source, so the user has to be trained on how to evaluate the Web resources. A patron might be confused both by the overwhelming amount of information on the Web OPAC and the differences between items held locally and those on the Web.

The scope of periodical research has changed from a traditional search method of finding a citation to the article from print or electronic indexes, determining if the library has the periodical title and issue, locating the physical article and making a copy of the article or using document delivery. With the Web OPAC, there is just one site where the patron can find a full text of the article that he/she wants. For example, the patron can go to JSTOR, FirstSearch, Project Muse and from one record in the Web OPAC to access this information. There are many search options with a Web OPAC that will help the patron in doing research. The reference staff plans on redesigning the initial screen the patron sees, with the aim of making the full-text material more obvious to the researcher.

Policy issues are also important for each of the libraries at the University of New Mexico. There have to be library policies to serve the university students and faculty who use the library. Additionally, since the university is a public institution, policies are necessary for situations where the public and university patrons need equal access to information. Issues that have to be resolved include who can access which database and who gets passwords for database access. There also has to be a priority at the reference desk for whom to assist, since patrons can use on-site or e-mail or phone reference services. Phone references have jumped dramatically because so many patrons are doing research remotely. Policies for acceptable use have been written for Internet use and e-mail use within the libraries.

Carter then discussed end-user policies, which have to be developed for sufficient access to the local catalog. Priorities have to be set up for patron access by establishing time limits for access to the PC. The library also wants to provide productivity software.

The Web OPAC has driven instructional change for the reference librarians. Search protocols and types of resources have changed for both the reference librarian and the library user. The reference staff have had to teach patrons how to locate and cite information; they have also had to keep current of changes in software and hardware. Carter emphasized that staff training has become a part of the reference staff duties. The staff have to be knowledgeable about how resources have been cataloged and how to access PDF files and other Internet formats. Without training, the reference staff will feel overwhelmed not only by the technology but also by the growing electronic collections and content. A good training program will help decrease the stress on library personnel.

In conclusion, Carter took this quote from their University of New Mexico colleague Paul Weiss who, in turn, had borrowed it from First Lady Hillary Clinton: "It takes a village . . . to successfully plan, implement and support a Web-based OPAC." All the units of the library, along with the campus computing center and patrons, utilize technology to successfully deliver electronic resources via a Web OPAC.

Digital Information:
The Library Director
as Collection Development Officer
and Head of Technical Services

Kit Kennedy

Workshop Coordinator

Jane Hedberg
George Lupone

Workshop Leaders

Diane Grover

Recorder

SUMMARY. "Sometimes the perfect solution is not an option" was the opening attention-grabber for this workshop. From different perspectives, a library director, a serials librarian, and a serials vendor each

---

Kit Kennedy is Director of Academic Sales, Blackwell's Information Services.

Jane Hedberg is Serials Librarian and Preservation Administrator, Clapp Library, Wellesley College.

George Lupone is Deputy Director, University Library, Cleveland State University.

Diane Grover is Head, Periodicals and Binding, Suzzallo Library, University of Washington.

[Haworth co-indexing entry note]: "Digital Information: The Library Director as Collection Development Officer and Head of Technical Services." Grover, Diane. Co-published simultaneously in *The Serials Librarian* (The Haworth Press, Inc.) Vol. 36, No. 3/4, 1999, pp. 461-466; and: *Head in the Clouds, Feet on the Ground: Serials Vision and Common Sense* (ed: Jeffrey S. Bullington, Beatrice L. Caraway, and Beverley Geer) The Haworth Press, Inc., 1999, pp. 461-466. Single or multiple copies of this article are available for a fee from The Haworth Document Delivery Service [1-800-342-9678, 9:00 a.m. - 5:00 p.m. (EST). E-mail address: getinfo@haworthpressinc.com].

recognized a trend towards library directors becoming more directly involved in collection development and technical services decision-making. The presenters believe a number of factors are creating this trend, including tighter budgets but higher service expectations, increasing availability and importance of library materials in electronic formats, and their accompanying complexity, costs, and related issues. This interactive workshop explored several scenarios related to the changing roles of library directors, serials librarians and vendors. *[Article copies available for a fee from The Haworth Document Delivery Service: 1-800-342-9678. E-mail address: getinfo@haworthpressinc.com]*

In Kit Kennedy's introduction, she described the vendor's increasing contact with library directors. She also characterized a new role for the vendor as "carrier pigeon," which she described as an informal communication link between library staff and their directors. Directors are getting more involved in serials services and decision-making because of the greater expense of electronic formats and all the infrastructure, consortial, long-term commitments, and public relations implications they bring.

Jane Hedberg is a serials librarian at a college library, reporting to the director. In recent years, her director has assumed responsibilities at the vice-presidential level, dealing with telecommunications, computing, and information services as well as the library. Demands on the director and the library are significant enough that the library is looking at its first major organizational review.

George Lupone, a library director, described several reasons that directors are getting more involved in technical services. He described the need to think broadly and articulate the library's vision, building a consensus in the community about the vision. Because the vision now involves radically different ways to carry on the same business–selecting, acquiring, organizing, making available information and teaching its use–the library director is called upon within the organization to help "bridge the gap" between present-day reality and the vision. Library directors are getting involved in changes to electronic formats because of the significant financial decisions, long-term commitments, and consortial agreements. With such profound changes in libraries, staff resources need to be reallocated, sometimes including reductions. When major changes in staff occur and there are new patterns of staffing, it is the role of the director to set the tone and lay out the parameters. As a director, he sees his role as delivering and integrating information technology into the students' learning experience. In his own institution, he is very aware of trade-offs, citing the reduction in print journals but the increase in electronic formats, new services such as tables of contents, and more comprehensive databases.

SCENARIOS

The two sessions of the workshop each explored two scenarios, with workshop participants randomly chosen to participate in groups. For each scenario, participants were asked to consider the following questions:

- What's your reaction?
- What do you do and how do you communicate it?

At the end of a twenty-minute discussion, participants wrote key points on a board, followed by discussion including all workshop participants.

WORKSHOP SESSION #1

- *Scenario #1 ("New Director")*
  Your library has a new director with a reputation for reorganizing and a keen interest in digital information. You have been in your present position for the past seven years. Your library has recently formed a committee to decide what to access. You are not a member of that committee. Your director has called a meeting of department heads to review strategies and digital initiatives to place your library in the forefront of the profession.
- *Scenario #2 ("Licensing")*
  You have been handling licensing for CD-ROMs and databases. Your library is moving rapidly into access of electronic information. It is assumed that these licenses will be part of your routine work. Your director does not understand why you cannot take on special projects and why you are asking for an additional full-time staff person to free you up to work through licenses and access issues.

DISCUSSION

- *Scenario #1 ("New Director")*
  Participants in this group emphasized the importance of advocating a continuing role for the serials librarian in selection and purchasing decisions, including making a case for serving on the newly forming committee charged to make decisions. The group recommended that the serials/technical services/collection development librarian seek to understand the director's motivations for high profile purchases and reorganizing. They also discussed the emerging need for the library to maintain an active and continuing public relations effort on campus, in partial response to political pressures from administration and faculty.
- *Scenario #2 ("Licensing")*
  The group's primary coping strategies were to educate the director as to the ramifications, difficulties and trade-offs; to work on developing standards for licenses, including an evaluative process; and to look to consortia in order to gain economies of scale. This group suggested the possibility of working as a team to handle license agreements, rather than having the responsibility fall to one person. There were a number of comments about working in the new arena of licensing, which often involves legal counsel. One participant described the current situation as "having an entrepreneurial task with little money to leverage."

The scenarios from the first workshop session had some common themes and conclusions. A primary one was the call for serials librarians to communicate assertively with their directors, educating directors in the difficulties and trade-offs of licensing issues. Working on committees or task groups was emphasized, with the ability to bring more knowledge and ideas to the planning, and the ability to spread the work among more people. Both groups discussed the potential role of vendors to create marketing and publicity opportunities which libraries could use with their constituencies. There was also significant discussion regarding the need to standardize licenses, working with publishers on criteria that work, and taking advantage of consortial agreements where possible. Several positive comments were made regarding consortial agreements, due to their potential for pooling resources, cutting costs, and delivering more services because of the economy of scale. However, it was also mentioned how complex consortial agreements can be, both for the individual library and for the staff working directly with the consortium.

WORKSHOP SESSION #2

- *Scenario #3 ("Statewide Consortium")*
  Your director, who has been at the library for five years, has recently been appointed chair of a state-wide consortium to cancel print and replace with digital information in three years. Your library has not delved heavily into e-journals. Your director is very keen and wants your input and recommendations.
- *Scenario #4 ("Millennium Deadline")*
  Your library has been given a mandate to provide full digital access by the millennium. Your director needs to show that a minimum of 50 percent of the collection is e-journals and/or digital information. At present you offer access to a select number of electronic journals (no publisher packages). Your director has named you chair of the Electronic Resources Committee.

DISCUSSION

- *Scenario #3 ("Statewide Consortium")*
  This group discussed a number of strategies and concerns. Their primary approaches were to work with the director to discover his or her motivations and to understand the political reasons and pressures from the consortium for such a three-year mandate. Secondly, they would develop a cross-functional group that included members from within the institution and from among the other consortial members. Last, they would develop a plan, including the many issues and steps involved in such an implementation. The plan would begin with an environmental scan, perhaps with an outside consultant. It would include working directly with users to gather information on how they do research. There would be emphasis on evaluating infrastructure needs and reviewing the implications for staffing and organizational structure. They planned to be very clear about trade-offs.

Some issues that would have to be addressed during implementation included consortial/site license issues, public relations and educational issues, a phased implementation approach, perhaps by language or discipline, or a mixed approach that might include article purchase along with licensing.

- *Scenario #4 ("Millennium Deadline")*
  After an immediate response from one participant ("kill yourself") the group quickly moved to discussing solutions and strategies. The action steps for this group were quite similar to the report of the Scenario #3 group, and focused on "educating" the director, evaluating the current state of electronic materials access available in their library, consulting with their serials vendor for assistance, creating multiple layers of plans, and forming a committee with similar make-up. They also added ongoing assessment and evaluation as key to a process that would likely last beyond the millennium.

General discussion within the combined groups at this workshop focused on the serials/technical services/collection development librarian's evolving role, including becoming the voice of reality. Both groups in this workshop suggested first evaluating the collection to see how much access the library was already providing to electronic materials. This background information could be leveraged to show the library was on its way to meeting the digital challenge.

This group did not believe that availability of electronic formats would necessarily meet the requirements of this deadline, and that the plan would likely have to be adjusted for availability, feasibility and practicality. Further, many staff will still be maintaining the existing print collections, and they will need support through periods of change. General conclusions closely followed the theme of the 13th NASIG conference, "Head in the Clouds, Feet on the Ground."

Eeee!-Serials:
Providing Access to Online Serials

Jennifer Edwards
Amanda Xu

Workshop Leaders

David R. Rodgers

Recorder

SUMMARY. Two serials catalogers, Jennifer Edwards of MIT and Amanda Xu, formerly of MIT, presented their experiences working with electronic serials. Edwards discussed concrete experiences and issues such as MIT's pilot project for cataloging e-serials, current policies and work-flow, and problems of catalog maintenance. Xu presented a broader perspective on what is happening beyond MIT and how e-serials may develop in the near future. Her topics included definitions of electronic serials, access features provided by publishers, aggregators and libraries, and challenges presented by e-serials. *[Article copies available for a fee from The Haworth Document Delivery Service: 1-800-342-9678. E-mail address: getinfo@haworthpressinc.com]*

Jennifer Edwards is Serials Cataloger, Massachusetts Institute of Technology Libraries.

Amanda Xu is Product Designer, KnowedgeCite, Inc.

David R. Rodgers is Assistant Acquisitions and Collection Development Librarian, Baylor University.

[Haworth co-indexing entry note]: "Eeee!-Serials: Providing Access to Online Serials." Rodgers, David R. Co-published simultaneously in *The Serials Librarian* (The Haworth Press, Inc.) Vol. 36, No. 3/4, 1999, pp. 467-473; and: *Head in the Clouds, Feet on the Ground: Serials Vision and Common Sense* (ed: Jeffrey S. Bullington, Beatrice L. Caraway, and Beverley Geer) The Haworth Press, Inc., 1999, pp. 467-473. Single or multiple copies of this article are available for a fee from The Haworth Document Delivery Service [1-800-342-9678, 9:00 a.m. - 5:00 p.m. (EST). E-mail address: getinfo@haworthpressinc.com].

INTRODUCTION

Jennifer Edwards and Amanda Xu presented their ideas about and experiences with electronic serials. Following the theme of the 13th Annual NASIG Conference, they divided their presentation into two parts. Jennifer Edwards presented a "feet on the ground" section focusing on concrete work flow and policy issues involved in e-serials at MIT. Amanda Xu presented the "head in the clouds" section dealing with a broader, more theoretical perspective.

PART I: E-SERIALS AT MIT

Edwards began with an overview of the staffing and organization at MIT. There are eleven library branches and divisions. While each branch checks in and claims its own serials, a central serials cataloging unit services the entire campus. There are from one to four staff members at each of the branch or division locations who do check-in and claiming. MIT has recently added a professional position in the acquisitions department with responsibility for digital resources. This person negotiates licenses, sets up demonstrations and maintains the online list of full-text e-journals. One unit head, three original catalogers and four copy catalogers constitute the serials cataloging section. Original cataloging is done at the MIT core level, a standard just below the CONSER core.

Two groups play central roles in setting policies for electronic resources at MIT. The Electronic Resources Cataloging Policy Group (ERESCAT) met weekly for over a year to set cataloging criteria and policies. The Networked Electronic Resources Discussion Group (NERD) was also established to review products and resources proposed by subject specialists/selectors. Policies are made available on their Webpage.

In beginning to work systematically with electronic serials the first basic question to answer was, What would be cataloged? The group decided to catalog only full-text resources. MIT catalogs all paid-subscription resources and catalogs "free" titles only when requested by subject selectors. Electronic serials may be cataloged at the individual title level or the package level. MIT wants to minimize the number of records in the catalog and thus prefers to annotate the original record (usually the print-version record) to show the existence of the electronic journal. If, however, the print title has been cancelled, or the e-title is significantly different from the original, MIT will enter a separate record for the e-journal.

Catalogers often discover the existence of electronic resources while cataloging the print version of a serial. Catalogers investigate these URLs and either edit the URL in cataloging copy, delete URLs that are not relevant or accessible, or add URL annotations as appropriate. Holdings statements are not created for electronic serials.

Edwards then described the workflow for the e-journals pilot project and compared it to current practice. During the pilot project they cataloged several electronic collections such as those available through JSTOR, AIP and IOP, as well as fourteen individual titles, for a total of seventy-six titles. They then analyzed work flow and results and weighed the merits of using separate records for e-serials versus simply annotating the print-version record. All seventy-six titles were cataloged at CONSER level. Fifty-seven were done by annotating the print record and nineteen were cataloged on separate records. The first efforts in cataloging these resources required thirty-one minutes for annotating the original (print) record and thirty-three minutes for creating a separate record. Cataloging times improved significantly as they gained more experience.

In current practice the serials cataloging section relies heavily on the digital resources librarian for information on new titles that need to be cataloged. All serials catalogers participate in cataloging electronic serials. Serials cataloging does maintain the catalog to reflect changes in Uniform Resource Locator (URL), title or format and to indicate ceased titles. However, the unit usually relies on public services for notification of these changes. Serials cataloging has determined that automatic URL checking is the responsibility of the systems office and is not in the purview of cataloging or acquisitions.

The library maintains an alphabetically arranged list of e-serials on its Website. The library's subject resource pages also provide access to these titles. Currently, the MIT public catalog does not have direct links to URLs, so patrons must cut and paste the URL from the catalog into a Web browser. However, there is hope for a Web-based public catalog sometime in the summer of 1998.

Edwards provided a handout that included a summary of MIT's electronic resources cataloging policies, examples of notes and holding statements displaying in the OPAC, and a list of URLs for serials cataloging and electronic resources at MIT. These policies were summarized above. The serials cataloging section homepage is currently found at http://macfadden.mit.edu:9500/colserv/sercat/, with links there to electronic resources, cataloging polices, serials cataloging procedures, and standards for core-level cataloging.

The first half of the presentation prompted several questions. Following are some of the questions and answers. Question: Are the URLs in the catalog records title specific or vendor specific, for example, would there be one record for the Academic Press collection IDEAL or would there be records for individual titles? Answer: The records are title specific. Question: Are electronic journals arranged on the homepage alphabetically or by subject? Answer: Both. Question: What about maintenance issues for holdings? Answer: They depend mostly "on the kindness of strangers," and do the best they can with what is known at the time. Question: Does MIT keep statistics on usage of the electronic serials home page? Answer: No. Question: Does it cost more to add an e-journal to the collection than a print journal? Answer: They have no hard data, but adding and processing e-journals does involve a lot more people, including the NERD group, public services and systems librarians. Question: How accurate are the URLs that are initially found listed in the print serial or on cataloging copy? Answer: Only nine URLs required revision. Servers do change and people make typos, but MIT has not had major problems with URL accuracy. Question: Who handles licenses and usage restrictions? Answer: The digital resources librarian. Question: When the choice is made to annotate the original record to show the existence of an e-serial, is the original record always a print-version record? Answer: Not necessarily. Question: Does MIT add online resource annotations to both a CD-ROM and a print record? Answer: No, only the print record. Question: How does MIT handle the issue of multiple versions of journals, for example, a print journal, its electronic equivalent, and another electronic version available in LEXIS/NEXIS? Answer: LEXIS/NEXIS is considered a database and is treated at the collection level. There is nothing in the public catalog to indicate that an individual title is in the LEXIS/NEXIS database. Patrons must know that the resource they want is there. Question: Is MIT working with fellow consortium members to develop cataloging standards? Answer: MIT is a member of the Boston Library Consortium. The consortium is discussing how individual catalog practices affect the other members, but as yet they have set no binding group policies.

PART II: E-SERIALS BEYOND MIT

Amanda Xu began the second part of the presentation by polling the audience to determine which groups were represented. There were from five to eight each of publishers, vendors, and reference librarians. The majority of attendees were catalogers (more than forty) and people working in acquisitions (approximately twenty-five).

Xu then gave an overview of topics she would cover in her presentation. Topics included definitions (what are e-serials?), typical access features offered by publishers or aggregators, models of access provided by libraries, barriers to access, technical challenges to access, emerging Web standards and technology, and future directions for e-serials.

During the definitions section, Xu discussed the Library of Congress interim guidelines for cataloging electronic serials and the "model C" proposed by Jean Hirons and Crystal Graham.[1] Xu listed the proposed model C categories, which include

- Journals (articles, single issues or packages)
- Databases (direct local access, remote access)
- Online services such as AOL, Dialog, or LEXIS/NEXIS
- Online discussion groups
- Websites

Next, Xu discussed access features provided by publishers and aggregators. Publishers typically offer the full-text of individual articles, single issues, or packages for journals as well as scanned images using SGML, HTML, PDF, and PostScript. Some also offer "linking of internals and externals," which means linking abstracting and indexing services to OPAC holdings. Publishers are also engaged in parallel publishing of print and electronic formats and expansion of the non-print content by adding such features as pictures, chemical structures, and graphics not made available in print format. Some publishers are beginning to provide online access to recent back issues of journals. E-mail alerting services are also becoming popular.

A recent development in electronic serials is aggregators who provide, in one package, a collection of several journals from different publishers accessible through one search system. Many are adding indexing and abstracting services, tables of contents, document delivery, and links to library holdings to these packages of full-text electronic journals. Aggregators provide a wide variety of gateway technologies including local and remote hosting, Web-based, and Web-to-Z39.50 gateways.

More and more library consortia are being formed around the country and illustrate both a centralized purchasing and centralized access services model. In the centralized purchasing model members of a consortium collaborate in identifying, selecting and purchasing electronic resources. Access to these resources is provided and supported locally by individual libraries. Two important features of the centralized access model are access to all consortium resources via a common gateway and centralized technical support and training. One particularly interesting consortium is OhioLINK. Noteworthy aspects of this consortium include the Electronic Journals Center, availability of 1200 full-text journals from Elsevier and Academic Press, electronic resources fully cataloged by OCLC Techpro, access to e-serials through a single search engine, and archiving of back issues.

Suggestions for individual libraries include an e-journal's homepage organized by subject, a trials page to highlight new resources being considered for purchase, and on-site search engines that allow librarywide and campuswide searching of all resources through a single gateway.

Xu moved next to a discussion of problems and barriers. These include pricing and site licensing, copyright, speed and reliability of retrieval and delivery channels, content quality, management reports, and usage analysis. There are still many problems related to browsing, displaying search results, downloading and printing as well as problems finding technical support for equipment and software. Xu divided the technical challenges for e-serials access into two parts: (1) navigation (layout, linking content, structure and maintenance), and (2) retrieval (search engines, online catalogs, Web to Z39.50 gateways and object-oriented technologies). There are also formidable challenges involved in describing these resources and making the records available in the public catalog.

The presentation concluded with Xu mentioning briefly the list of suggested readings she had compiled and discussing a wish list for the future. She expressed her hope to soon be able to search a whole range of years and journals in full text through a seamless process. She also described the need for easier identification of the most relevant materials in the expanding sea of information and for large-scale hypertext Web search engines.

While there are still many barriers and obstacles to overcome in the area of e-serials, technology will continue to proliferate, bringing new choices and products as well as new means to overcome the problems and barriers.

NOTES

1. The following URLs may be helpful in understanding the issues involved in the proposed model C: <http://www.nlc-bnc.ca/jsc/confpap.htm> contains the text of the original proposal for model C in "Issues Related to Seriality," by Jean Hirons and Crystal Graham, presented at the International Conference on the Principles and Future Development of AACR, Toronto, Canada, October 23-25, 1997; and <http://lcweb.loc.gov/acq/conser/serialty.html> is a CONSER page that contains two proposals for a modified model C.

Turning Our World Upside Down:
Will Technology Change Pricing?

Susan B. Hillson
Nancy H. Knight

Workshop Leaders

Nancy Newsome

Recorder

SUMMARY. Technological advances are changing the way information is being distributed, not only regarding the channels that are being used but also the manner in which information is acquired. Subscription pricing models are currently undergoing tremendous change as publishers and vendors search for appropriate ways to see a return for their investment in this new technology. At the same time, libraries are searching for answers to their own dilemma of paying for the dramatic increase in the cost of subscriptions with shrinking budgets. Sixteen pricing models are presented, along with the pros and cons of each. *[Article copies available for a fee from The Haworth Document Delivery Service: 1-800-342-9678. E-mail address: getinfo@haworthpressinc.com]*

Information consultants Susan Hillson and Nancy Knight presented their findings regarding new pricing models that have come about as a

---

Susan B. Hillson is Director, Business Partnerships, Imark Technologies, Inc.
Nancy H. Knight is Vice President, Client Relations, Imark Technologies, Inc.
Nancy Newsome is Head of Serials, Hunter Library, Western Carolina University.

[Haworth co-indexing entry note]: "Turning Our World Upside Down: Will Technology Change Pricing?" Newsome, Nancy. Co-published simultaneously in *The Serials Librarian* (The Haworth Press, Inc.) Vol. 36, No. 3/4, 1999, pp. 475-482; and: *Head in the Clouds, Feet on the Ground: Serials Vision and Common Sense* (ed: Jeffrey S. Bullington, Beatrice L. Caraway, and Beverley Geer) The Haworth Press, Inc., 1999, pp. 475-482. Single or multiple copies of this article are available for a fee from The Haworth Document Delivery Service [1-800-342-9678, 9:00 a.m. - 5:00 p.m. (EST). E-mail address: getinfo@haworthpressinc.com].

result of technology. As background to presenting the models, they discussed the historical context of how technology has affected pricing. Historically most pricing models were based on a per unit subscription. Then as print began to evolve to electronic delivery, there were online media priced per use based on time, CD-ROM priced as a subscription, and now the Web, with various pricing models involving subscription, per unit, per use, or a combination. The dilemma entails the dramatic increase in the cost of subscriptions, which has been calculated at more than 140 percent over the last ten years. To a large degree, technology is the cause of the dilemma, but it is possibly also the solution.

The Internet has created one of the greatest distribution delivery options available to publishing. The Web offers a variety of unique features not previously available. These features include hyperlinks to unique sites, sources, bibliographies, chemical formulas, graphics, anatomical drawings, 3-D models, and a host of references and indexed Internet sites; and interactive elements such as making selections, answering questions, or contributing to a living article. Technical makeup of the Web enables repackaging of existing print products and suites of information that can be accessed via search session, subscription, or article. The Web also enables usage to be identified, quantified, and analyzed. All of this technology comes at a cost. Most publishers look for a return on their investment in twenty-four to thirty-six months. Their investments include maintenance of all formats (print, CD-ROM, diskette, magnetic tape, Web), additional production and distribution costs for each format, the search engine, value-added features, and the cost of running an online publishing program twenty-four hours a day, seven days a week.

From the libraries' perspective there are also costs and infrastructure issues to consider. There must be the appropriate mix of PC's and dumb terminals. There are interface issues. Are available platforms compatible with the publisher's delivery systems? The role of the information technology people on campus has changed to that of a collaborative partner. This is a change within the library from the last five years.

The acquisition of information has become more complex, with many more choices available. Ordering channels include direct from the publisher, via a subscription agent, through consortia or a union group, or through a gateway or aggregator. The number of available distribution channels makes decision-making more difficult, but this will sort itself out over the next year to eighteen months. The ordering maze also includes licensing issues such as distribution, access, archiving, printing, storage, etc. The library must also consider the best-published source considering the discipline, interface, price points, and whether the product is compatible with campus hardware infrastructure.

Historically, pricing models have gone from pay, to own versus pay, to access of one database at a time, to access based on simultaneous usage, remote access, search across multiple journals, databases and linked sources, etc. The added-value components enabled by the Web that have changed pricing models include

- ASAP (As Soon As Publishable) availability versus waiting for an issue's worth of articles to be assembled
- links to other articles published in the same journal
- links to articles published in other journals
- links to corrections
- links to more recent articles that cite it
- access to more detailed data or multimedia information
- link to reader comments or discussion forum
- dual publishing in electronic journals in separate fields, e.g., chemistry and biology with appropriate attribution
- "living article," where the user can see an ongoing research project or experiment
- embedded software programs that allow users to mirror the author's work by running simulations of their own
- "modular" articles, e.g., describing an experimental technique referenced via links to other sources

We are in the midst of a paradigm shift regarding pricing that is forcing us to analyze our present and past holdings as they relate to the new definition of "holdings." Some publishers are looking at a "total spend" by libraries on all formats of their products in developing pricing models.

The new models are based on a variety of parameters including usage, the universe of journals subscribed to, format, site licenses, etc. Publishers are developing pricing that enables them to offer customized products, consistent interfaces, charges for data or access, and charges for the added-value features listed above.

Hillson and Knight presented sixteen pricing models based on recent interviews with selected publishers and vendors, several articles, and discussion on the Liblicense listserv regarding e-content pricing models, held during January and February 1997.

The audience was randomly divided into sixteen small groups, each assigned one of the pricing models, and was given ten to fifteen minutes to discuss and identify the pros and cons of each model. A spokesperson from each group shared the highlights of the discussion. Following is a list of those models and a summary of each group's comments regarding the pros and cons.

1. Print + Add-on Surcharge for the E-Version
- *Pros:* This model has more added value to the patron, who is then given a choice of media–print or electronic. The users benefit from accessing a "virtual" library and the library benefits from having an archive.
- *Cons:* There were a number of issues related to information delivery, including having to pay more for the same data, equipment issues, and related personnel costs. There was also a question regarding the level of comfort users will have on accessing information from multiple platforms without standards. The audience also wondered if the electronic version would be faithful to the print version of the same journal.

2. Total Dollars Spent for All Media + %
- *Pros:* This is an advantage for large research libraries; it minimizes processing costs and offers a predictable formula for acquiring a wide range of information.
- *Cons:* It's complex; libraries can't guarantee a total budgetary amount from year to year. There is also a question of fairness for small libraries.

3. Electronic + Add-on Surcharge for the Print
- *Pros:* Small academic libraries can meet general needs; it's also good for special libraries with an emphasis on electronic access.
- *Cons:* Maintaining both electronic and print is costly in terms of staff and equipment resources; libraries feel compelled to do so in order to build an archive.

4. Electronic Is Free with Print Subscription
- *Pros:* It's straightforward; it's a good test of the electronic version; it expands the availability of the journal; libraries can get use patterns more easily.

- *Cons:* Libraries feel pushed into doing something they're not necessarily ready to deal with; libraries may be forced to hold on to the print whether they want it or not; the mindset that it's free may be misleading.

5. Based on Ports or Seats
- *Pros:* Will have as much access as ports or seats; this is a good choice for special libraries for selective use products; it enables libraries to cancel the print subscription; it's a convenience for the public in general.
- *Cons:* There are hidden costs of technical support and maintenance of hardware; difficulty in tracking; resources are wasted when ports are not in use.

6. Size of Library Acquisition Budget
- *Pros:* This equalizes libraries' ability to pay for information and is based on a predictable formula.
- *Cons:* There is potential for unequal treatment in subject areas; cost of living increases could have a negative effect, forcing a library to pay more for a journal in a subsequent year.

7. Number of Simultaneous Users
- *Pros:* This can be advantageous if a library can determine the appropriate number of users; a publisher in the group felt it was a good model.
- *Cons:* It's difficult to measure appropriate number of users; the patron can't be assured of access; publishers differ in how to group the number of users.

8. Document Delivery (per article, per chapter, etc.)
- *Pros:* Supply is usually immediate; it offers access to journals not in the library's holdings; it has the potential to reduce material costs; it encourages more cooperative collection development.
- *Cons:* There are additional equipment costs; limiting to IP address can limit users outside the institution; relying on document delivery too heavily reduces the integrity of the collection and may contribute to an overall increase in future subscription prices; difficult to budget.

9. Prior Usage + Added Percentage
- *Pros:* If statistics are accurate, then the library theoretically pays only for what is used.

- *Cons:* It's difficult to budget; have to rely on accuracy of the usage statistics; degree, program or enrollment changes at the institution can cause dramatic change in usage.

10. No Relation to Any Print Product Whatsoever
- *Pros:* Provides access to enhanced information; processing costs may be less.
- *Cons:* Pricing may be totally ad hoc; archiving questions need to be addressed; the integrity of content may be in question.

11. Sliding Scale of Various Sorts, Including Fte's, Department Size, etc. (the more users, the higher the price)
- *Pros:* This is advantageous for smaller institutions; makes a fair model for consortia; provides guaranteed revenue for the publisher; works well with budgeting.
- *Cons:* This can be a problem for distance learning and reciprocal borrowing; question regarding administration of the numbers on which price is based; there is a potential for paying for non-use.

12. Group Purchasing
- *Pros:* Provides more leverage; provides the possibility of buying more of a package; everyone benefits from more content; for the publisher, visible to a wider audience.
- *Cons:* The ordering process is more complex; it's difficult to comparison shop; libraries become locked into a more complex arrangement; lost independence and flexibility for those in the group; smaller institutions may not have the hardware necessary; the publisher may be reluctant to make concessions unless it's a large group.

13. Certain Categories of Users Get a Cheaper Price (institution versus individual)
- *Pros:* The options are firm; it's clear what the options are and how they apply. Good for individuals.
- *Cons:* This model migrates with difficulty into the electronic environment; it's difficult to budget. Bad for institutions.

14. Subscription plus Transaction (subscribe to X number of journals and have access to others on a transactional basis)
- *Pros:* This is attractive alternative for low use or expensive journals; it offers the ability to track usage.
- *Cons:* There needs to be a cap on the transaction cost and a clear understanding of what the cost is; there is a possibility of being

locked into specific titles for a period of time; the definition of a transaction needs to be clear.

15. Account Setup, plus Transaction
- *Pros:* This probably follows more truly the cost of publishing; the transaction costs may be lower because there is an account setup fee; usually good statistics on usage.
- *Cons:* The product may not be useful and therefore the account setup cost is a waste of resources; difficult to budget; difficult to administer.

16. Free Access
- *Pros:* The price is right.
- *Cons:* There is no free lunch, always hidden costs; the quality of content may be questionable; level of customer support available is probably minimal or nonexistent; use statistics are probably not available; it feeds the public misconception that everything on the Web is free.

The question and answer period following the small group sessions, though brief, had excellent audience participation and brought up further points not covered thoroughly in the small groups. One of these was the issue of archiving, which the audience felt deserved tremendous consideration in acquiring electronic journals. Double paying for both print and electronic as a way of archiving was mentioned numerous times. Links were also mentioned as an important added-value consideration. Other issues included training and classroom needs and the space-saving potential. An interesting question came up for publishers regarding whether it is still important to measure circulation, and if it can be measured accurately electronically. A publisher in the audience answered that most of those taking the electronic version have not yet dropped the print, and that there is also the question of advertisements to consider. He stated that we have far more usage information electronically since technology can measure hits at the article level.

AUTHORS' NOTE

Interviews were conducted with the following publishers and vendors: Academic Press, Chemical Abstracts Service, Blackwell's Information Services, The Dialog Corporation, EBSCO Information Services, Elsevier Science, The Faxon Company, Information Access Company, Institute for Scientific Information, Northern Lights

Technology, OCLC, Oxford Analytica, Inc., and Springer-Verlag New York. Material was also drawn from discussions held in January and February 1997 on the subject, "E-Content: Pricing Models" on LIBLICENSE-L (electronic bulletin board). Available from listproc@pantheon.yale.edu.

SELECTED BIBLIOGRAPHY

Chuang, John Chung-I and Marvin A. Sirbu. "Network Delivery of Information Goods: Optimal Pricing of Articles and Subscriptions." In *The Bundling and Unbundling of Information Goods*. Available: http://ksgwww.harvard.edu/iip/econ/chuang.html. September 18, 1998.

MacKie-Mason, Jeffrey K. "PEAK: Pricing Electronic Access to Knowledge." Available: http://www-personal.umich.edu/ ~ jmm/presentations/peak-harvard97. September 29, 1998.

_____ and Juan F. Riveros. "Economics and Electronic Access to Scholarly Information." First version January 1997, current version February 2, 1997. Available: http://www-personal.umich.edu/~jmm/papers/peak-harvard97. September 29, 1998.

Wilkinson, Sophie L. "Electronic Publishing Takes Journals into a New Realm." *Chemical & Engineering News*, May 18, 1998. Available: http://pubs.acs.org/hotartcl/cenear/980518/elec.html. September 18, 1998.

The Latest on Latest (Entry) and Other Hot News on Seriality

Jean Hirons

Workshop Leader

Kevin M. Randall

Recorder

SUMMARY. Jean Hirons presented the latest developments regarding the definition of serial and the bibliographic description of serialesque works. In particular she discussed the modified model C, a conceptual model for separating the bibliographic world into monographic and ongoing entities (as opposed to the current separation into monographic and serial); and incorporating entry, a proposed method for handling title changes for electronic journals that impose the new title on all of the older issues. *[Article copies available for a fee from The Haworth Document Delivery Service: 1-800-342-9678. E-mail address: getinfo@haworthpressinc.com]*

In her workshop, Jean Hirons presented the latest developments regarding the definition of serial and the bibliographic description of serialesque works. Her presentation was divided into two parts, modified model C, and incorporating entry. Each part was followed by a question and comment period.

Jean Hirons is CONSER Coordinator, Library of Congress.
Kevin M. Randall is Head of Serials Cataloging, Northwestern University.

[Haworth co-indexing entry note]: "The Latest on Latest (Entry) and Other Hot News on Seriality." Randall, Kevin M. Co-published simultaneously in *The Serials Librarian* (The Haworth Press, Inc.) Vol. 36, No. 3/4, 1999, pp. 483-490; and: *Head in the Clouds, Feet on the Ground: Serials Vision and Common Sense* (ed: Jeffrey S. Bullington, Beatrice L. Caraway, and Beverley Geer) The Haworth Press, Inc., 1999, pp. 483-490. Single or multiple copies of this article are available for a fee from The Haworth Document Delivery Service [1-800-342-9678, 9:00 a.m. - 5:00 p.m. (EST). E-mail address: getinfo@haworthpressinc.com].

MODIFIED MODEL C

In October 1997, Jean Hirons and Crystal Graham presented a paper called "Issues Related to Seriality" at the International Conference on the Principles and Future Development of AACR in Toronto. At that time they argued that serials be redefined to remove the requirements for separate parts and numbering, as proposed in the second of three models presented in the paper–model B. After the paper received an enthusiastic response, the Joint Steering Committee for the Revision of AACR (JSC) charged Hirons and CONSER with the preparation of rule revision proposals in support of the recommendations. After ALA Midwinter 1998, four working groups were set up to work on various aspects of the charge via e-mail, Hirons' group being charged with redefining "serial."

In further discussions regarding model B, Hirons said, people began commenting that it would not work for various kinds of materials. A major problem was the reliance on a distinction between publications that are intended to continue indefinitely and those that are not, and this may not always be a reasonable, or even possible, distinction to make. And aside from difficulty in applying the model to new media, there would be difficulty in distinguishing between different print publications, especially if the requirements for separate parts and numbering were to be removed.

The most popular aspect of the Hirons/Graham paper was the broader concept of "ongoing publications," which Hirons said was not really appropriated by model B. Hirons and her colleague Regina Reynolds decided to go back to that concept and worked out a revised model C approach that would not define everything strictly in terms of monographs and serials, but would instead emphasize the "ongoing" aspect.

The proposed new approach, dubbed "modified model C," would see a "bibliographic universe" consisting of "monographic entities" and "ongoing entities" (see Figure 1).

"Monographic entities" are those that are complete as issued, regardless of physical format, and those that are irregularly revised, for example issued in infrequent/irregular editions.

"Ongoing entities" are those that are not complete as first issued and are intended to continue, though not necessarily indefinitely. These would include serials (as currently defined), numbered and

FIGURE 1. Modified Model C

The Bibliographic Universe

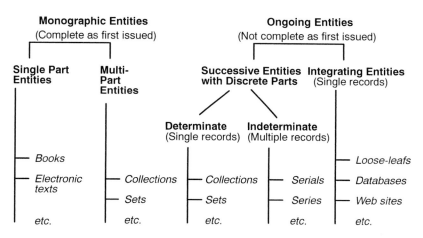

unnumbered series, multiparts that are not complete as first issued, and looseleaf services and electronic resources intended to be added to or updated (such as databases, Websites, etc.).

The primary advantage of the new model is that, under ongoing entities, it distinguishes between

- "successive entities" with discrete parts that can be divided between those intended to continue indefinitely (e.g., serials) and those that are finite (e.g., multiparts) and
- "integrating entities" that need no such division but are distinguished by having a single source of title that can change over time (e.g., the old title page is thrown out when a new one is issued); these can be in the form of looseleaf services, databases, Websites, etc.)

At one time, Graham had proposed establishing a new category of "bibliographic hermaphrodites," materials that are not truly monograph and not truly serial, but have features of both. However, in the Toronto paper she reversed her stance, and Hirons stated some theoretical and practical reasons for keeping to two categories, with the "hermaphrodites" under the new concept of the "ongoing umbrella." For example, while different manifestations of the same work (such as print, CD-ROM, microform, Website) may act differently and may be cataloged differently, it would be desirable to be able to tie them together in the catalog, so the searcher can retrieve them together. The ongoing umbrella recognizes more broadly the potential for change; it recognizes seriality without making everything a "serial" (the concept of serial would not actually be changed, but the traditional serial would now be a subset of the broader concept of ongoing entity); it accommodates "integrating entities" (a newer term for what have more commonly been called "updating entities"); and it does not require a new bibliographic level code in USMARC–a change that the Machine-Readable Bibliographic Information Committee (MARBI), OCLC, and local systems might be reluctant to implement.

Hirons mentioned some specific things that the new model would and would not do. It *would* separate ongoing entities into categories for purposes of considering how many records will represent the bibliographic entity, what cataloging techniques are most effective, and where there are gaps in AACR2. It would *not* specify where in AACR2 each category should be covered, indicate who should catalog what, or call for major changes in everything we are doing. In fact, she said, it would maintain the status quo in more areas than model B might have.

In concluding her presentation of modified model C, Hirons discussed the potential impact of the model on AACR2, USMARC, and cooperative cataloging programs such as CONSER, acknowledging that there are serious concerns to be addressed.

DISCUSSION

The general response to modified model C appeared to be favorable. Some comments were that the solution seems "elegant," more intuitive, and moves us closer to dealing more effectively with the reality of how things are published. One attendee remarked that it better matches the mindset of academic users when it comes to allowing some things such as e-mail discussion lists to be categorized under the same general umbrella as journals.

Questions and concerns in specific areas were raised. Some of these pertained to fitting monographic entities into the model, treatment of monographs with serial supplements, and the problem of reprints of serials. In response to one question, Hirons said that there are still open questions about multiparts, but she does not envision the use of successive entry for title changes in multiparts, nor does she see identical treatment for serials and multiparts as necessary or likely.

A significant amount of discussion revolved around the role of the bibliographic level in the MARC record. It was pointed out that the bibliographic level does have important consequences in some systems, and users (as well as staff) have difficulty making a distinction between serials and monographs. Should there be a third level covering ambiguous publications? Regarding the MARC format in general, Hirons reassured the audience that while the charges to the AACR review groups concern the rules, not the format, the groups do want to come up with something that will both fit into the current MARC structure and not be tailored to any specific system.

INCORPORATING ENTRY

Hirons began the section on incorporating entry by asking, Where do electronic journals fit? Should they be thought of as successive or as integrating? Electronic journals pose particular difficulties because they have discrete parts in the form of articles and are thought of as "serials," but they often have a single source of title and act more like integrating entities. The problems arise when trying to determine how changes of title should be handled. Should they be cataloged by successive entry, latest entry, or a combination of both?

She then discussed a new concept–incorporating entry–first introduced by Sara Shatford Layne of UCLA at the CONSER Operations Committee meeting in May. The problem addressed by the proposal is that of the electronic journal that changes title and imposes that new title on all of the earlier issues. For instance, if Title A changes to Title B, then changes to Title C, and if the publisher puts the current title on all issues of the journal in the database, someone looking at the journal for the first time during one of the later titles might think it has carried only that title.

Under the incorporating entry concept, as envisioned by Layne, a new record would be created for a title change, but each record would begin with the first issue of the entire publication, and a note would explain that the new title incorporates the former title. Hirons gave an example for a real life situation, *BMMR*, as it might be described under incorporating entry (see Figure 2).

FIGURE 2. Incorporating Entry Records

```
022      0070-3616
245 00 BMMR $h [computer file].
362 0   93.8.1-97.05.02.
580      Incorporated into: Medieval review.
7?? 10 $t Medieval review $x 1096-746X


022      1096-746X
245 04 The medieval review $h [computer file].
362 0   93.8.1-
580      Incorporates: BMMR.
7?? 10 $t BMMR $x 1070-3616 $g Aug. 1993-May 1997
730 02 BMMR.
```

Among the advantages of incorporating entry put forth by Hirons are that it would maintain the identity of earlier titles (which is important for archived copies, ISSN, and abstracting and indexing services) and that it permits flexibility on the part of individual cataloging agencies, which may retain all of the records or only the latest, as they prefer. Incorporating entry would allow us to describe in the national database what happens to the publication over time, but would not need to result in latest entry's problem of having a single record that lives on in the local catalog even when a subscription is discontinued. Also, incorporating entry would work well in the cooperative environment, imparting more validity to new records created for new titles when the cataloger is unaware of earlier titles. As is now the case with looseleaf publications, new records will be created, sometimes inadvertently, for different titles; a cataloging agency may not have all of the information, or it may not have the authority to change existing records on the database. Under incorporating entry, the new record will still be valid and can be added to by authorized agencies as information is found.

Hirons stressed that while latest entry was being discussed as a mechanism for handling title/entry changes for at least some electronic publications, it was not being considered for print publications. While applying latest entry to electronic publications and successive entry to print would cause problems in matching up records for corresponding titles and formats, incorporating entry (since it retains the idea of separate records for successive titles) would make it much easier to do this matching up.

She admitted that the idea is not a maintenance-free solution: for example, upon receiving a new title change, a library retaining only the latest record would need to get the new record from OCLC, remove its holdings from the old record, etc. Other questions include, How many previous titles, and how much information pertaining to them, should be included in each record? Would this work for integrating entities, or only for entities with discrete parts?

As to the next steps for modified model C and incorporating entry, Hirons mentioned several presentations during the upcoming meeting of the American Library Association, including a presentation to JSC. Subsequent work being planned includes reports and recommendations from the four AACR Review groups, a MARBI discussion paper, rules prepared for the Committee on Cataloging: Description and Access, and review by JSC.

For more information, Hirons directed the audience to the CONSER Website at http://lcweb.loc.gov/acq/conser/serialty.html.[1]

DISCUSSION

The material on incorporating entry received mixed response, with the afternoon session being generally more favorable than the one in the morning. A good deal of discussion revolved around latest entry. Some attendees saw little difference between a latest entry record and the most current in a series of incorporating entry records, or wondered about the need for incorporating entry records for the earlier titles that are no longer in existence. Citing the possibility of large maintenance burdens with multiple records in an incorporating entry approach, an attendee suggested as an alternative a latest entry record with a note explaining the incorporating relationships and with some kind of control of the multiple ISSN. Another attendee expressed ambivalence over incorporating entry and preferred successive records for management purposes, but found latest entry to be "intellectually appealing" because it keeps the "intellectual integrity" of a journal's run in one location on one holdings record.

Some comments regarded user response to the records. It was mentioned that some CONSER participants are currently being asked by their constituents to break out latest entry records because patrons aren't understanding them. One attendee said that whatever approach is taken, the real problem is getting non-catalogers to read catalog records successfully. Another attendee observed that users just want the material–they want to find what they want, no matter how they search for it; they don't want to work at interpreting the records; and they don't want to have to look in multiple places.

Other concerns and questions raised: Would incorporating entry be used *only* when old issues are retitled, or in other cases as well? Will record length become a problem? Are we moving into actually cataloging the Website (or URL) instead of issues? How will we be able to teach such a sophisticated approach to our staff? Are we perhaps addressing problem situations that are only a small minority? Hirons herself asked the legal catalogers in the audience how they felt about using incorporating entry for looseleaf publications and received mixed response.

Near the end of the workshop, one attendee noted that "we live in a more and more bibliographically complicated world and we have to find new solutions to reflect that." Hirons commented that at the same time things are getting more complex, the experience level of the catalogers is going down. The challenge is to figure out how to balance all of this, and the other part of what she is working on in this area concerns developing a training program.

NOTES

1. At the time of the preparation of this manuscript (July 27, 1998), the modified model C appearing on the Website was a revised version prepared shortly after Hirons' presentation at the NASIG conference.

E-Journals, Kansas Style

Charlene N. Simser

Workshop Leader

Mike Beier

Recorder

SUMMARY. The presentation, "E-Journals, Kansas Style," looks at the traditional roles that researchers, publishers, and libraries have had in the production, distribution, cataloging, and archiving of peer-reviewed journals. This discussion then went on to talk about a few of the factors in today's academic society that have seen these roles begin to change: spiraling cost, the technology boom, and WWW ease in publishing, to name a few. The focus of the presentation then turned to the cooperative undertaking between the Great Plains/Rocky Mountain Hazardous Substance Research Center (HSRC), Kansas State University, and the KSU Libraries, and their joint venture to produce a peer-reviewed electronic journal. *[Article copies available for a fee from The Haworth Document Delivery Service: 1-800-342-9678. E-mail address: getinfo@haworthpressinc.com]*

INTRODUCTION

As she began the presentation, Charlene Simser commented that she probably should have chosen a more descriptive title than "E-

---

Charlene N. Simser is Serials Cataloger, Kansas State University Libraries.
Mike Beier is Library Director, Southern Virginia College.

[Haworth co-indexing entry note]: "E-Journals, Kansas Style." Beier, Mike. Co-published simultaneously in *The Serials Librarian* (The Haworth Press, Inc.) Vol. 36, No. 3/4, 1999, pp. 491-495; and: *Head in the Clouds, Feet on the Ground: Serials Vision and Common Sense* (ed: Jeffrey S. Bullington, Beatrice L. Caraway, and Beverley Geer) The Haworth Press, Inc., 1999, pp. 491-495. Single or multiple copies of this article are available for a fee from The Haworth Document Delivery Service [1-800-342-9678, 9:00 a.m. - 5:00 p.m. (EST). E-mail address: getinfo@haworthpressinc.com].

Journals, Kansas Style," and indeed her slide presentation included the phrase, "Adventures in Partnering," but when she submitted the abstract originally she thought it sounded catchy enough. I would have to agree that the title did not do justice to the importance of the subject. The content of this particular workshop is much more significant than the casual title indicates, and strikes at the very core of a major topic concerning libraries today: the role of the modern library in publishing. Should libraries seek an expanded role in partnering to develop, publish, catalog, distribute, and archive journals? A more accurate title for the presentation perhaps could have been "The Process of Cooperation in Developing a Peer-Reviewed Journal."

OVERVIEW

This presentation began with a look at the traditional roles of researchers, publishers and libraries in the production of a peer-reviewed journal and discussed a number of projects in which these roles are expanding or changing. It then looked in detail at the project involving the Great Plains/Rocky Mountain Hazardous Substance Research Center (HSRC), Kansas State University, and the KSU Libraries, who became involved in a cooperative venture to produce a peer-reviewed electronic journal.

TRADITION

Librarians, publishers, and aggregators are familiar with the traditional roles each has played in the production, distribution, and storage of journals over the last century. Traditional publishing in academia has involved a researcher, often associated with and financially supported by a host university. The researcher submits an article to a publisher for possible inclusion in a journal. The publisher distributes the potential article among respected authors and researchers in the field for peer review. Once reviewed and accepted, the researcher transfers copyright to the publisher, who makes the article available in print and perhaps electronically, often through an aggregator. The library would then purchase the journal and/or access to the material in electronic format.

NEW DIRECTIONS

Libraries and consortia are taking steps to expand their traditional role with projects such as university-based digitization projects. Examples of this include Project MUSE, JSTOR, the Humanities Text Initiative, and the Scholarly Communications Project. Libraries are also producing information in the research areas they support. At KSU the materials being digitized for increased access strongly support the university's agricultural strengths and include historical and current materials. At first, KSU, as with other libraries, found that digitization projects took a back seat to the pressing problems of day-to-day operations, balancing the budget, and major projects such as remodeling.

What has helped get the project at Kansas State University off the ground is the development of a policy that defined the collection development role toward digital/electronic materials and mandated the cataloging and linking to e-format material that had been acquired by legitimate means. Having a policy that specified what material must be cataloged helped stimulate action but also opened up discussion on many aspects of digital access that had never been considered. The number of exceptions and exemptions that need personal attention continues to grow and includes display problems caused by the subfields in the 856 field range, particularly on those records that had come in as depository items. Many of the problems and how they are handled were discussed, and a number of public and technical services screens for these resources were displayed and explained.

PARTNERING

In 1997 the Great Plains/Rocky Mountain Hazardous Substance Research Center (HSRC) obtained a grant to develop a peer-reviewed electronic-only journal. Kansas State University is headquarters for a 14-institution consortium, which was established in 1989. The center is part of a national organization that carries out programs of research, technology transfer, and training.

Those initially involved were Pat McDonald (extension assistant at HSRC and an engineer), Mike Somers (head of technical services, KSU), Dr. Larry Erickson (director of HSRC), Ruth Ellis (chemistry librarian, KSU, working on hazardous substance grants), Karen Cole (library's associate dean, KSU), and Charleen Simser (serials cataloger, KSU).

Initial discussions revolved around five areas:

- the origin of the project and publishing concepts
- the role of the libraries in the electronic journal project
- how to archive the material
- cataloging the journal
- marketing and sales
  Some goals for the project:
- to create the first electronic-only journal in that subject area
- improve delivery time for the HSRC research
- provide an inexpensive alternative to expensive journal subscriptions
- evaluate the Internet as a vehicle for the delivery of refereed research results

The project earned about \$42,000 in grants the first year. The initial discussions went smoothly, with the library representatives and the HSRC personnel both getting a better understanding of the contributions and expectations of each in the venture. But when the first issue was brought up online, it was discovered that there was still a lot of work to be accomplished and many points to polish. The journal's homepage is located at: http://www.engg.ksu.edu/HSRC/JHSR/.

As an example of initial oversights, when the first articles came up in January 1998, the Hypertext Markup Language (HTML) files that were displayed had no bibliographic citation information on the page. Someone who may have linked to the article from a keyword Web search would have no idea that it was part of an electronic journal and that there was no link back to the journal's home Webpage. Other problems include funding, marketing, archiving, technical support, and personnel changes. Each new concern is being addressed as it comes up, but there is still a long way to go. One of the most important lessons learned is that the library needs to be fully involved from the beginning, perhaps even as the initiator of the idea, so that it has a stronger voice in all aspects of the project. Progress details of the project were discussed at length.

DISCUSSION

The discussion ranged through a number of areas. Part dealt with clarifying some of the technical details that had been briefly introduced, including taking some suggestions as to how some of the cataloging and archiving problems might be solved. It was an active discussion with many good ideas expressed. One archiving concern comes from the decision of the HSRC to keep only the current volume of the journal on its Website. The library has volunteered to archive the older volumes, but then links would need to be rewritten and set for the new server, along with a few other technical fixes. Format is another ongoing concern. The articles have been mounted in both HTML and Acrobat formats, but many machines in accessing libraries might not be able to handle Acrobat, which may be confusing to the user. One thing that came out in the discussion was that it takes time to work through the problems that always seem to materialize out of the blue. Even though it has taken several months longer than anticipated, those involved with the HSRC/KSU joint project feel it is a success and are working toward its continuation. During the discussion, quite a bit of enthusiasm was exhibited for the project by the academic faculty, but there is still a hesitance for many to stretch outside their historical roles and venture into such an electronic/technical area. With the strengths that libraries have these days in technical processes, it seems like these partnerships would be a natural outgrowth, especially in the areas where the sponsoring university has its own academic strengths. More and more, these ideas are coming to the forefront in the digital library discussions within the academic library setting and among the administration and faculty on the full university level. One session attendee from the University of Arizona spoke of how their library has become involved in a very pro-active way in electronic publishing projects. What it took for them was to go beyond the "this-could-be-our-role" stage, and actually say, "This *will be* our role." As a result, they were able to get some money to take on two projects, and the successful completion and marketing of these two projects has led them into two more opportunities. It takes that positive, proactive attitude and time, but it can be done.

Dear Abby, Dear Abbot:
Practical Advice for the Serials World

Christa Easton
Tina Feick
Laura Parker

Workshop Leaders

Jill Emery

Recorder

SUMMARY. This workshop was designed to be an open forum to discuss concerns and give practical advice to the serials librarian. As it turned out, the main issue that was discussed was the claiming of non-receipt material. A better understanding of how claimed issues are dealt with was achieved across the spectrum of attendees. *[Article copies available for a fee from The Haworth Document Delivery Service: 1-800-342-9678. E-mail address: getinfo@haworthpressinc.com]*

Steve Murden from Virginia Commonwealth University introduced the three panelists: Christa Easton, Tina Feick, and Laura Parker.

Christa Easton is Coordinator, Serials Group and Government Document Serials, Stanford University Libraries.

Tina Feick is Vice President, Blackwell's Information Services.

Laura Parker is Sales Representative, Electronic Publishing, Academic Press.

Jill Emery is Serials Librarian, Texas Southern University.

[Haworth co-indexing entry note]: "Dear Abby, Dear Abbot: Practical Advice for the Serials World." Emery, Jill. Co-published simultaneously in *The Serials Librarian* (The Haworth Press, Inc.) Vol. 36, No. 3/4, 1999, pp. 497-501; and: *Head in the Clouds, Feet on the Ground: Serials Vision and Common Sense* (ed: Jeffrey S. Bullington, Beatrice L. Caraway, and Beverley Geer) The Haworth Press, Inc., 1999, pp. 497-501. Single or multiple copies of this article are available for a fee from The Haworth Document Delivery Service [1-800-342-9678, 9:00 a.m. - 5:00 p.m. (EST). E-mail address: getinfo@haworthpressinc.com].

Murden then read the workshop description that explained that this would be an open forum for the exchange of concerns and practical advice for the serials librarian. Next, Easton took a show of hands to demonstrate that the audience comprised half librarians, half vendor or service provider representatives, a few publisher representatives, but no integrated library systems (ILS) vendor representatives. It was then determined that a third of the audience was there for the format of the workshop, a third for the speakers, and a third for both the format and discussion. The most consistent thread of the discussion was about the claiming of non-receipt material.

The first question was, "Is the four-to-six-week claim response time really needed by the vendor/publisher? Couldn't they respond more quickly?" Tina Feick responded that the four-to-six-week claim response interval was an industry standard and that was the amount of time it took to verify whether the issue was available or not. Laura Parker seconded this response. This led to other vendor and publisher representatives from the audience agreeing and stating further reasons for this standard, namely, number of staff allotted to claiming, response time from foreign publishers, even for faxed material, and availability of extra issues.

One librarian asked how automated claiming systems, now in wide use by most libraries, impacted the vendors/publishers. Feick stated that because more claims were coming in, more people were being designated by the vendors to deal with the increase. A vendor representative in the audience seconded these statements and further stated that with automated claiming, the vendors have become a "dumping ground." They must sort and sift through the claims that are being automatically generated. It did not appear to this representative that any checking of the claiming was being done before the claims were sent electronically to the vendor or publisher. Librarians in the audience said the claims were being checked before they were sent out and that the librarians went to extreme measures trying to ensure that they were not "dumping" electronic claims on the vendors or publishers.

Someone asked how premature claims were handled. Feick responded that some were sent back to the libraries and some were sent on to the publisher. Someone wondered why so many first issues of a volume had been delayed this year. The answer from Parker was that the advent of electronic production at a number of publishers had resulted in the delay. The shift from one production method to another had been more labor intensive than expected, but now that the shift had been made, Parker did not foresee a future delay in issues. Parker then answered the previous question, stating that publication delay notices were often not mailed by the publishers because the notice would arrive at the same time as the issue.

The next question was, "Why can't there be electronic responses to electronic claims?" All three panelists stated that there is no current electronic data interchange (EDI) system that allows for electronic claim responses. This was furthered by audience comments to the same effect. The lack of ILS representation at this forum was mentioned as part of the problem, the people designing the systems are not always aware of the needs of the systems users.

One vendor representative stated that on-site mail delivery services at many libraries are factors in the non-receipt of material. Librarians in the audience agreed that this was sometimes a contributing factor. The changes to the United States mail protocols were also seen to cause problems in delivery and receipt of material due to the street address being required on an address label. One person suggested talking to the area or local post office to see how label adjustments could be made to be more in line with the current protocol.

Another vendor representative then said, "The way predictive check-in is designed, claims will always be a problem." A vendor representative further asked if claim checkers or claim response mechanisms were being used by the librarians. A number of librarians responded that they did indeed use the claim checkers and claim response mechanisms to insure that duplicate claims were not sent out. The majority of the audience in attendance agreed that predictive check-in systems needed to be made more flexible to change claiming limits and to make allowances for standing orders and subscriptions that were not published on a specific timetable. Another problem that was noted is the inability for some integrated library systems to show the non-receipt of some material.

A librarian pointed out that it is valid to ask where issues are, since we are paying for the service of claiming when using vendors. A vendor representative responded by saying the most important relationship for the vendor is with the publishers, not with the libraries. He further stated that the lines of communication had to be left more open with the publishers so that publication information from the publishers could be more forthcoming and passed along to the libraries. Problems with fulfillment services were mentioned. Susan Davis gave a short overview of the concurrent session, "How I Learned to Love Neodata," which had been presented by Marcia Tuttle the day before. She encouraged those in the audience to attend this meeting if they hadn't already done so. One vendor representative stated, "The best way to claim weeklies is to go to the newsstand and buy them." This comment was met with a few gasps from the audience. The vendor representative went on to explain that frequently there were not enough extra issues available to supply multiple libraries after subscription disturbances of weekly publications. Backserv and Alfred Jaeger were mentioned as sources to help fill in missing issue gaps.

The concern over multiple subscriptions and how they were handled by fulfillment centers was addressed. The problem occurs when a library has more than one subscription to a weekly and the fulfillment service does not recognize the multiple subscriptions. Instead, it compacts the subscriptions into one. As an example, an order for three copies of *Newsweek* results in a single copy of *Newsweek* that has been paid for for the next three years. Davis said that Centrobe (the new name of Neodata) is in the process of working closely with the vendors to ensure that this sort of subscription problem is cleared up.

One librarian stated that some larger libraries with multiple subscriptions to fulfillment magazines had started using the same suppliers that supply publications to bookstores and that this alternative appeared to be working well for the libraries.

A vendor representative addressed the issues of extended subscriptions and supplemental payments from fulfillment houses and publishers. She proposed that both these ways of doing business were basically illegal. Wasn't money that had been accepted for goods the same as a contract? It was pointed out that with supplemental invoicing, the checks were returned asking for more payment; therefore, money had not been accepted. The vendor representative still asserted though this practice was unethical. Members of the audience agreed. This whole discussion was labeled "provocative."

Someone asked if claims had an impact on pricing. The vendor/publisher community replied that claiming had not impacted on the cost structure of material at this time. However, more staff were being moved over to work on the claiming of non-receipt material.

There was a discussion concerning the inconsistent issue numbering and irregular publishing of certain publishers. Parker responded that frequently this occurs because of last minute editorial changes to publishing schedules that had been set up months in advance. One vendor representative complained about a specific publisher. It was stated that this publisher would be publishing in consecutive order this upcoming year.

Someone asked about how title changes of electronic journals are handled. Parker responded that in the case of Academic Press e-journals, the title change notifications were sent to the vendors just as any other title changes would be. The other publisher representatives on hand stated that this was their practice as well.

The discussion began to wind down at this point. The audience seemed pleased with both the discussion and the format of the workshop. Both the audience and the panel found the discussion to be helpful and stated a need to continue these "open-forum" workshops at future NASIG conferences.

Law Libraries, Hospitals, Museums, Colleges, and Government Offices All Sharing One Automation Project

Annamarie Erickson

Workshop Leader

Leanne B. Hillery

Recorder

SUMMARY. In 1994, the Chicago Library System (CLS), a state-funded inputting agent for 918 multitype libraries within the city of Chicago, contracted with Ameritech Library Services to automate its member libraries. The server is contracted from Ameritech while the libraries lease the integrated system from CLS. During the automation process, CLS worked closely with member libraries to set automation goals, plan for retrospective cataloging, and train library personnel. The unique plan and support provided by CLS and Ameritech made automation a reality for many of the small collections within the partnership. *[Article copies available for a fee from The Haworth Document Delivery Service: 1-800-342-9678. E-mail address: getinfo@haworthpressinc.com]*

This workshop was presented by Annamarie Erickson, formerly automation librarian for the Chicago Library System, who now works

Annamarie Erickson is Membership Liaison/Automation Technology, Chicago Library System.

Leanne B. Hillery is Serials Librarian, University of Miami School of Law Library.

[Haworth co-indexing entry note]: "Law Libraries, Hospitals, Musuems, Colleges, and Government Offices All Sharing One Automation Project." Hillery, Leanne B. Co-published simultaneously in *The Serials Librarian* (The Haworth Press, Inc.) Vol. 36, No. 3/4, 1999, pp. 503-508; and: *Head in the Clouds, Feet on the Ground: Serials Vision and Common Sense* (ed: Jeffrey S. Bullington, Beatrice L. Caraway, and Beverley Geer) The Haworth Press, Inc., 1999, pp. 503-508. Single or multiple copies of this article are available for a fee from The Haworth Document Delivery Service [1-800-342-9678, 9:00 a.m. - 5:00 p.m. (EST). E-mail address: getinfo@haworthpressinc.com].

for Ameritech Library Services as sales representative for the Midwest. The purpose of this workshop was to discuss methods of building consortiums and working within already existing partnerships. Erickson began by describing her experience in working on large-scale automation projects for the Illinois State Library. During the past four years, she worked on establishing the Virtual Illinois Catalog that replaced Illinet Online in May 1998. The new system is a fiber optic network that contains the catalogs of fifteen hundred Illinois libraries including all of the major universities in the state. Erickson also worked on a project called SILO, which is the most inclusive multi-type online serial union list state program in the United States. The database contains over 500,000 copy-specific holdings statements for over fourteen hundred libraries.

The bulk of the presentation covered Erickson's work with automating the Chicago Library System (CLS). The Chicago Library System is one of twelve library systems within the state of Illinois. It is the smallest geographically, covering only the addresses within the city of Chicago, but it is the largest demographically. CLS is a funded agency of the Illinois State Library and is the inputting agent for 918 multi-type member libraries including the Chicago Public Library with 81 branches, 550 public school libraries, 12 private school libraries, 51 academic libraries, and 224 special libraries.

As automation librarian, it was Erickson's responsibility to oversee interlibrary loan, delivery, reference backup, bibliographic access, and consulting for automation within the city. She worked intensively on communicating with member libraries about these services and their benefits. Under the title automation, CLS was mandated by the state to offer a central library automation project. The State of Illinois would provide CLS with a large server on which the databases of member libraries would be loaded. The only stipulation set by the Illinois State Library was that it be a shared automation project with Z39.50 standards. The search for an integrated library system that could accommodate the vast numbers and varied degree of automation and vendors employed by member libraries was a difficult undertaking.

The Center for Library Automation began on June 30, 1994, with a contract between Ameritech Library Services and the Chicago Library System. The Center for Library Automation is based on a dual outsourced automation scheme. CLS contracted the server from Ameritech, while member libraries lease the integrated system from CLS. It is Ameritech's responsibility to maintain the server, do load testing and increase capabilities, keep database consistency records, and do daily backups. All system upgrades are also covered in the contract. All of these arrangements were negotiated in order to provide the most reasonable cost for member libraries.

The system is not hardware specific. Either IBM compatibles or Macintosh computers will connect to the server. Ameritech designed the system to operate on any type of LAN or WAN, to connect to other library systems, access the Internet, vendors, suppliers, local or remote databases or departments within a member's organization. The system uses a TCP/IP protocol and is Z39.50 compliant. The client operating systems are Windows95 or NT. Erickson recommended that when choosing a Windows-based operating system, NT is preferable because it is faster and does better multitasking.

Security was built into the system internally by passwords and file systems. Firewalls between the client router and Ameritech router maintain the protection needed by special libraries (corporate and law). The system is closed using 56K frame relay lines between the library and the server to further protect the integrity of member databases. Although the system is closed, members have the option to make their records public. As a result, CLS maintains two servers. One server is provided for members who wish to have closed databases and the other is for those who prefer to have public catalogs.

Erickson stated that a variety of software choices are offered in order to meet the diverse functionality demands of CLS members. The system supports Horizon, Scholar, and Dynix software. All options are fully integrated with public and staff access, authority control, circulation, acquisitions and fund accounting, serial control, cataloging, reserves, and advanced booking. Specifically, the Horizon software is highly customizable, allowing each member library to define how they want their systems to run. To preserve the integrity of the indexes, a standard MARC map was used. The MARC map was created with member input and direction from CLS. A very liberal interpretation of USMARC was employed and as new fields are added, the standard MARC map and indexes are updated.

Erickson presented the Center for Library Automation to CLS members and assisted in guiding them through the preinstallation process. CLS helped members establish overall program goals and project objectives with a long-range strategy for automation. It was then possible to determine if what was implemented in the short term had growth potential to address longer-term goals and requirements. Erickson stressed that it is always important to understand the distinction between requirements and specifications. Requirements are local library-based aims, while specifications are the technical blueprints of the computer system design. Many member libraries were not yet automated, so at this stage, Erickson helped them plan to inventory, weed and perform retrospective conversion of their collections. She stated that consortial environments are not the place for creative cataloging. Too much customization does the patron a disservice. The current trend is toward interfaces that are standardized. The more standardized the systems are, the easier they are for patrons to use and interpret. The standardization process must be performed on all library files that will be indexed, including bibliographic records, serials check-in, vertical file, and borrower, collection and overdue records. Erickson added that it is also necessary for retrospective conversion records purchased from vendors to be compatible with the system and the records of other consortium members.

The Chicago Library System is also responsible for the training of library staff in newly automated member libraries. Training begins with two-day self-paced modules covering the operating system and an overview of searching, cataloging, and circulation. Next, intensive module training begins with two days of PAC and CIRC for all library staff members. This is followed by group training of staff from several libraries in specific areas such as cataloging, serials, and acquisitions. These sessions are held on a rotating basis, with schedules sent to all CLS libraries so that new or transferred staff can be trained at that time. Erickson feels that this method provides an even and consistent degree of training.

Erickson turned the focus of the presentation to the CLS Website. A discussion of the consortium members ensued, with a focus on the various types of libraries in the system and the special concerns of each. She stressed that the attractive aspect of such a consortium is that the libraries could receive state-of-the-art automation capabilities for less money than doing it on their own. Also, this was the first opportunity that many of the smaller libraries had to automate. The assistance provided by CLS was invaluable.

Erickson continued by discussing several new consortia that are in the process of being formed using Ameritech Library Services. In her current position, she is working with groups including the State of Iowa Libraries Online, the Indiana University Campuses, the Utah Academic Library Council, the California State University Unified Information Access System and DALNET, a multitype consortium of Detroit area libraries. Erickson stated that forming consortiums is an option that more libraries will need to consider in the future. In order for libraries to recoup costs from declining budgets, especially for serials, resource sharing will become a viable and necessary option. At this point, Erickson took a short break to set up the next part of her presentation. During the break, she fielded questions from a small but enthusiastic audience.

One workshop participant asked who generally initiates consortial agreements. Erickson said that in the case of the Chicago Library System, CLS acted on the state mandate to seek out vendors. In another example, the Detroit Public Library and Ameritech were already in discussions to work together. They actively sought out other libraries to join them to form DALNET.

A second question concerned the architecture of such automated systems. Erickson explained that this could vary. For example, in DALNET, each library has its own server and user client. The Utah Academic Library Council has a central server at the University of Utah that the other members link to. In the case of CLS, the central server was given to the system by the state of Illinois.

Another participant asked about the cost of Ameritech services. Erickson replied that Ameritech sets its prices by the number of simultaneous users, not by the number of workstations. As a result, the price is determined by how busy you are. Data can be manipulated through the client server on an unlimited basis. Charges for simultaneous users are only incurred when records are imported or exported. Erickson added that automation is always an expensive undertaking. If you are automating, she recommended that you go to your state library for grant money. State libraries will also give money for setting up consortial agreements. She added that law libraries with historically significant collections could also get funding.

Erickson concluded her presentation with a demonstration of Ameritech's resource-sharing system software. She led the group through the task navigator functions, including demonstrations of the ILL status and lending screens and the historical tracking of loans and lends in the system. In a consortial environment, it is possible to set up local library units for each library in the system and maintain a list of ILL/document delivery partners for each member. It is also possible to establish lending sequences for up to twenty-five pre-selected lenders. The system automatically sends requests to libraries in this group.

A participant asked if these searches were in ranked order. Erickson responded that the requests would be sent in a sequence from one lender to another. The request is not sent to all of them at once. She feels that this feature is an asset of the system. The list of lenders is already set up. There is no need to do any searches on lenders to set up the list. The automated search process makes the system very fast.

The final question from the audience asked if Ameritech does retrospective conversion. Erickson stated that Ameritech can help facilitate retrospective conversion for their customers. Also, in her experience with CLS, the state gave money for participants to automate and purchase records from vendors. In some cases, CLS gave grants to nonprofit institutions for retrospective conversion.

EDIFACT Implementation:
One Goal, Three Partners:
Library, ILS Vendor
and Subscription Agent

Friedemann Weigel
Cindy Miller
Michael A. Somers

Workshop Leaders

Joan M. Stephens

Recorder

SUMMARY. The full economic benefit of EDI can only be realized with the use of EDI for the complete cycle of business transactions. Kansas State University Library, Endeavor Information Systems, and Harrassowitz are working in partnership to implement the full cycle of UN/EDIFACT transactions. In this workshop, speakers representing the partners in this project discussed the implementation process, including interface problems, workflow changes, critical elements, and other les-

---

Friedemann Weigel is Managing Partner, Information Systems Director, Harrassowitz, Booksellers and Subscription Agents.

Cindy Miller is Director, Product Management and Strategic Planning, Endeavor Information Systems, Inc.

Michael A. Somers is Chair, Technical Services Department, Kansas State University.

Joan M. Stephens is Head, Acquisitions and Serials, Georgia State University.

[Haworth co-indexing entry note]: "EDIFACT Implementation: One Goal, Three Partners: Library, ILS Vendor and Subscription Agent." Stephens, Joan M. Co-published simultaneously in *The Serials Librarian* (The Haworth Press, Inc.) Vol. 36, No. 3/4, 1999, pp. 509-513; and: *Head in the Clouds, Feet on the Ground: Serials Vision and Common Sense* (ed: Jeffrey S. Bullington, Beatrice L. Caraway, and Beverley Geer) The Haworth Press, Inc., 1999, pp. 509-513. Single or multiple copies of this article are available for a fee from The Haworth Document Delivery Service [1-800-342-9678, 9:00 a.m. - 5:00 p.m. (EST). E-mail address: getinfo@haworthpressinc.com].

sons learned in the process. *[Article copies available for a fee from The Haworth Document Delivery Service: 1-800-342-9678. E-mail address: getinfo@haworthpressinc.com]*

Three representatives of different links in the serials chain teamed up for a workshop on electronic data interchange (EDI) in serials processes. The presenters were: Friedemann Weigel, managing partner, information systems director, Harrassowitz; Cindy Miller, director of product strategy, Endeavor Information Systems, Inc.; and Michael A. Somers, chair, Technical Services Department, Kansas State University (KSU) Libraries. The presenters provided a general background of EDI using invoicing as a specific example to illustrate its implementation.

Weigel opened the workshop by defining EDI as "the transfer of structured data, by agreed message standards, from one computer application to another by electronic means with a minimum of human intervention." Thus EDI allows a library to conduct business functions more efficiently. Time and financial costs are offset by savings in processing costs and a faster trading cycle. For example, one study estimates that 80 percent of libraries' claims could be resolved if the libraries had access to publisher dispatch data, which can be transmitted as an EDI transaction.

While EDI has been a mainstay in many business areas for a long time, it is relatively new to the library field because of the complex product description (the bibliographic description), a relatively low price per item, and the very large number of transactions. Now, eleven standardized message types or transaction sets are available to cover the entire trading cycle for libraries. They include quotes, orders, claims, invoices, and others. Although two standards are currently available, ANSI ASC X12 and EDIFACT (EDI for Administration, Commerce and Transport), all new transactions are being developed to be compatible with EDIFACT.

After presenting his overview, Weigel gave some specific information about the process. First he talked about the three components involved in the exchange of data. The first part is a message standard such as EDIFACT or ANSI ASC X12. The second is EDI-enabling software that translates information from the subscription vendor's format to the ILS system's format and vice versa. Some estimates indicate that this part of the process is responsible for 40-50 percent of the effort involved in implementation. The third part is a method of transmission that is usually a value-added network (VAN) or ftp.

Weigel next described the EDIFACT invoice structure, which is also made up of three sections: header, detail, and summary. He used an example of EDIFACT raw data to illustrate the sections. For each EDIFACT message one header section is present that notes the message type, provides unique identifying information, and gives other general information applicable to the entire invoice, such as vendor and library. Each message can have many detail sections, each comprising thirteen segments that constitute a single invoice line and including information specific to each title represented on the invoice. The summary section is included only once on each invoice and carries totals and some checking and security information.

After Weigel's presentation, Cindy Miller of Endeavor talked about EDI development from the perspective of an integrated library system (ILS) vendor. Endeavor entered the UN/EDIFACT field in 1996, which was about the time SISAC and BISAC announced movement toward X12/UN/EDIFACT compatibility. Endeavor's newly developed acquisitions and serials module was designed for electronic commerce. Endeavor was pleased to find that Kansas State University, their first client to go into production, wanted to use EDI, and that Harrassowitz wanted a development partner for UN/EDIFACT.

With the partnership in place, Endeavor joined EDItEUR, the Pan-European Book Sector EDI Group, formed to coordinate the development, promotion and implementation of EDI in the books and serials sectors. Once Endeavor secured the group's guidelines, they expected to proceed quickly with implementation. However, KSU needed to implement invoice processing first. Normally invoicing is implemented near the end of the implementation process because it is the most complicated step. Moreover, the guidelines for invoices were not completed. However, these potential setbacks put Endeavor in a position to participate in and influence standard development.

Endeavor initially planned to develop its system to be compatible with a standard format and to use a third-party converter package to translate the data between the subscription vendor and the ILS. Eventually this plan was dropped when it became apparent it would be costly to libraries and that KSU preferred that the translator be built into the ILS. Instead Endeavor developed its own parser to translate vendor transmissions to a format Endeavor's Voyager system can use.

The EDIFACT messages are integrated directly into the acquisitions and serials module.

Finally, on September 24, 1997, Kansas State University became the first library in the world to load UN/EDIFACT invoices for serials. Miller pointed out that this project was truly a worldwide effort involving several sites in the United States as well as Germany and England.

Endeavor expects serials claims and responses to be operational by the summer of 1998. Purchase orders and quotations will follow. Because invoices are the hardest to implement, Endeavor does not expect to experience as many problems with the additional functions. Endeavor also expects to extend UN/EDIFACT into other parts of the Voyager system, such as for billing end users for services such as document delivery.

Somers then talked about the project from the library viewpoint. He first described some of the decisions KSU had to make. One major decision had to do with translation software. This issue was resolved when KSU's preference to have a converter built into the Voyager software was adopted by Endeavor. KSU made another decision when they chose to use ftp for file transmission after learning that the cost of using a VAN was prohibitive. Efforts to find another university department to share VAN expenses proved fruitless. In fact, Somers had to explain to the KSU bursar's office what a VAN is.

Somers also had to resolve some workflow issues. He had to determine who would or could handle the new work. He had to look at existing workflow to determine how it would change and what procedures needed to be developed or revised. He also had to set up an ftp account for delivery and pick-up of files between KSU and Harrassowitz. He expected all of this work to result in improved financial management, including shortening their six-week payment cycle.

KSU's first beta test with a Harrassowitz invoice included 397 line items. It loaded in three minutes. He has since loaded an invoice with 3,000 line items in twenty-four minutes. His hope to discontinue paper invoices soon indicates the success of the project.

Using copies of Voyager screens as illustrations, Somers walked the group through the EDI driver function of Endeavor. He remarked that the library has complete control over the workflow once a file has been picked up from the vendor. He also noted that although EDI is an electronic process, human intervention is important and necessary.

Somers observed that an invoice rarely processes error-free, and he outlined some potential problems. One problem is that memberships do not process well. Service charges can also be problematic since subscription vendors handle them differently. Fund coding is another area of concern for Somers since Voyager can assign fund codes only on a percent basis rather than on a dollar amount. He stressed the importance of communication among all parties to work out problems. Somers concluded by outlining some of the benefits KSU enjoys, including saved staff time and secured functions.

The three speakers did an excellent job of presenting their topics, including a clear explanation of what EDI is and how it can benefit all links of the serials chain. The format of examining the same project from three viewpoints gave the audience a broader understanding of the topic than would have been possible with one speaker.

They also showed how hard it is to implement new technology. The project encountered many problems and involved much work. This aspect was illustrated by Miller's comment that she has an archive of over seventeen hundred e-mail messages about the project.

Because each partner in the project had much to gain from a successful implementation, cooperation was at a high level. All three emphasized the importance of communication and compromise.

The illustrations and comprehensive handouts were also useful, and seeing how the raw data, which can look like gibberish, get mapped into the system helped make the process clearer for the audience.

To those of us who have done EDI work and have found it somewhat frustrating, it was reassuring to hear that things did not go smoothly for this group either, but that ultimately they succeeded.

"Barbarism Is the Absence of Standards": Applying Standards to Untangle the Electronic Jumble

Betty Landesman
Beth Weston

Workshop Leaders

Lucy Duhon

Recorder

SUMMARY. Many standards have been developed over the years to manage serial information. From the familiar ISSN, to the Serial Item and Contribution Identifier (SICI), which tracks serial information down to the article level, to the new Digital Object Identifier (DOI), which locates discrete components of information in the electronic world, methods for searching, retrieving, and performing transactions on serial publications and their contents continue to expand, particularly in the electronic environment. The serials professional needs to be involved in the development and approval of relevant emerging standards, or risk losing authority in the way serial information is stored and disseminated. *[Article copies available for a fee from The Haworth Document Delivery Service: 1-800-342-9678. E-mail address: getinfo@haworthpressinc.com]*

Betty Landesman is Systems Training Librarian, Gelman Library, George Washington University.
Beth Weston is Serials Librarian, Gelman Library, George Washington University.
Lucy Duhon is Assistant Serials Librarian, Carlson Library, University of Toledo.

[Haworth co-indexing entry note]: "'Barbarism Is the Absence of Standards': Applying Standards to Untangle the Electronic Jumble." Duhon, Lucy. Co-published simultaneously in *The Serials Librarian* (The Haworth Press, Inc.) Vol. 36, No. 3/4, 1999, pp. 515-522; and: *Head in the Clouds, Feet on the Ground: Serials Vision and Common Sense* (ed: Jeffrey S. Bullington, Beatrice L. Caraway, and Beverley Geer) The Haworth Press, Inc., 1999, pp. 515-522. Single or multiple copies of this article are available for a fee from The Haworth Document Delivery Service [1-800-342-9678, 9:00 a.m. - 5:00 p.m. (EST). E-mail address: getinfo@haworthpressinc.com].

The purpose of this workshop was to familiarize the audience with the standards that affect work with serials today, particularly in the electronic environment, and to bring the audience up-to-date on the latest developments. Beth Weston and Betty Landesman opened the workshop by listing eight serials functions affected by standards: ordering and claiming, check-in, payment, identification, location, searching, retrieval, and rights management. The workshop leaders then presented, in detail, eight types of standards that have applications in these functions.

ISSNs

Weston explained the origin and purpose of the International Standard Serial Number (ISSN) and the eligibility requirements for a publication to be assigned an ISSN. With the exception of reproduction microforms, different physical formats of a serial title require different ISSNs. Different file formats (e.g., ASCII, PostScript) of an online journal, however, do not require different ISSNs. Evolving guidelines on what defines a serial in the electronic environment are making the assignment of ISSNs even more complex.[1]

In print, as well as in the electronic environment, the ISSN provides for accurate identification of titles at ordering and claiming time, foolproof check-in, verification of correct billing on vendor invoices, and a hook-to-holdings link between abstracting and indexing services and a library's holdings of a particular journal title.

SICIs

The Serial Item and Contribution Identifier (SICI), prescribed by ANSI/NISO standard Z39.56-1996 (Version 2), "defines a variable length code that will provide unique identifications of serial items (e.g., issues) and the contributions (e.g., articles) contained in a serial title."[2] Weston displayed a diagram of the three required segments of the SICI and explained how the segments identify aspects of a serial publication. The SICI, which builds upon the ISSN and other standards, positively identifies a serial publication and its components, as well as its format (e.g., paper, microform, or electronic).

The SICI may be used as an element within an electronic data interchange (EDI) transaction to provide dispatch data from vendors and publishers. It facilitates the entry of check-in data to a library's automated system, and identifies issues to be claimed. Online serial issues, and even articles, may be received automatically using this technology. Payment may be linked to discrete parts of a serial publication; this has implications for the traditional subscription model of access to journal literature. The SICI acts as a location identifier by allowing links to other articles and serial components. It does not, however, contain elements relating to ownership.

EDI

Landesman continued with a discussion about EDI, or the automatic exchange of business information in electronic format between computer systems. The Serials Industry Systems Advisory Committee (SISAC), CSISAC (in Canada), and the International Committee on EDI for Serials (ICEDIS) have approved "X12" standards (named for the committee that created them), or transaction sets, for use in the serials industry. Landesman explained the steps necessary for the approval and adoption of these standards.

Transaction sets contain identifying information (such as the ISSN and SICI) about serial items being ordered, claimed, and paid for. Some transaction sets approved for serials use are purchase order, invoice, ship notice/manifest or dispatch, order status report, price list, and product list. As an example, during check-in, the 856 Ship Notice/ Manifest transaction set gives the shipment date of a serial issue; this obviously prevents premature claiming.

EDI for Administration, Commerce and Transport (EDIFACT) was developed by the United Nations and is used widely in Europe. Eventually the UN/EDIFACT format will become the standard, as "any new work will be done as UN/EDIFACT messages, rather than ANSI X12 transaction sets."[3]

HOLDINGS

Another area of standards to affect serials control is holdings. The workshop leaders summarized the three ANSI/NISO standards for serial holdings display developed since 1980. ANSI Z39.42-1980, *Serial Holdings Statements at the Summary Level*, standardized only the display of summary holdings. A few years later, ANSI Z39.44-1986, *Serial Holdings Statements*, was developed. Originally intended to focus on the display of detailed issue-specific holdings and to act as a companion to the previous standard, its scope was changed to include both detailed and summary holdings after discrepancies between the two standards appeared. Z39.42 was eventually withdrawn; however, its use is still widespread, as Landesman demonstrated by displaying a screen shot of George Washington University's holdings for a title in OCLC's Union List. Some library online catalogs still use this display standard, based on the original derivation of their holdings from OCLC's Union List.

A new standard, NISO Z39.71-199X, *Holding Statements for Bibliographic Items*, was approved in January 1998 and will replace both Z39.44-1986 and Z39.57-1989 (non-serial holdings), so that serial and non-serial material can be handled in one integrated standard.[4]

Holdings standards affect the way issues are checked in, they mark the ownership of particular issues within a library, and they may one day be able to respond to a search statement requesting a particular issue.

METADATA

Weston continued by discussing "metadata," or data about data. Also referred to as "a document surrogate" or as "representational data," metadata is essentially the documentation of electronic files in the online environment. There are two basic metadata models: the database paradigm, and the markup paradigm. In the first, metadata serve as attributes with values and are stored in a record separate from the information object. In the second, metadata are embedded in the information object, usually by tagging the data, using Standard Generalized Markup Language (SGML). Marking an object automatically indexes it and facilitates its direct retrieval. This tagging can also create catalog records automatically.

Weston described the Dublin Core, "a 15-element metadata element set intended to facilitate discovery of electronic resources," as filling the niche between the unstructured full-text Web indexes and more structured, complex frameworks such as MARC.[5] She described the three categories of elements that make up the Dublin Core, a markup type of metadata model.

In terms of retrieval, metadata can directly access another resource via a hotlink, much as the 856 field in a MARC bibliographic record does. Rights metadata may be used to determine the terms and conditions (i.e., price and limitations on use) of a digital object. Descriptive data elements embedded in electronic resources greatly simplify the searching and retrieval of objects. These data elements may either be author-generated, created by search engines "on the fly," or created by information professionals.

DOIs

Weston displayed a diagram of a Digital Object Identifier (DOI) and explained its origin and purpose. Developed by publishers, the DOI is both an identifier and a specific implementation of that identifier.[6] It routes people to information objects on the Internet. Built upon existing schemes (such as the SICI), the DOI contains a dumb identification number that is persistent for the life of the object, regardless of ownership.

Publishers are responsible for depositing DOIs and associated Uniform Resource Locators (URLs) into a directory system. A sort of resolution service, the DOI directory records changes so that users will automatically be routed to the current URL.

The DOI identifies articles, order forms, etc., during ordering and claiming functions. It supports purchasing at the article level. Eventually, the DOI may become a point of payment between the object and the end user. The DOI system is being widely accepted by publishers, while the National Information Standards Organization (NISO) is considering the approval of the DOI as an identification standard.

Neither searching nor retrieval is yet a possibility within the DOI system, nor is there currently a link between it and a library's catalog. The DOI currently acts as a direct link between the publisher, or rights-owner, and the end user; in the future there may be a standardized model that would allow rights transactions to be automated. At this time, DOIs only identify resources; they do not contain any copyright enforcement mechanisms.

LOCATORS

Landesman discussed locators for electronic resources, including URLs, Uniform Resource Names (URNs), and Uniform Resource Identifiers (URIs). The Internet Engineering Task Force (IETF) is working on standardizing the way resources are named so that they may be more easily located and retrieved by end users.

The URL indicates the computer address of a document. As most users know, this method of naming a resource is unreliable, as file-names frequently change and sometimes move to different computers. The URN is meant to provide a unique, persistent, location-independent identification for a resource.[7] The URI is a general term that includes URLs, URNs, and the still evolving concept of a Uniform Resource Characteristic (URC), a form of metadata. OCLC's Persistent URL (PURL) system registers resources and their addresses in its PURL server, where it maintains a constant "address," regardless of host file changes. It is the responsibility of the file owner, however, to submit filename or location changes to the PURL service. Another system recently proposed for the mnemonic naming of resources is Universal Serial Item Names (USINs).[8]

With regard to serials in the electronic environment, locator services may or may not identify the content of the resource, depending on the specificity of the naming service. Locators link end users to resources; when URLs change, all links need to be updated to reflect that change. Locators help users search and retrieve documents only insofar as the file information is kept current. In terms of rights management, locators must be accurate in order to correctly identify a resource and make it available to authorized users.

Z39.50

Finally, Landesman presented the NISO standard for information retrieval between different systems, Z39.50. Landesman demonstrated a search, using the Library of Congress (LC) Website and entering the Z39.50 gateway to other library catalogs. She conducted an author search on an Innovative Interfaces, Inc. catalog and then demonstrated the same search on a DRA catalog at another site on the gateway. The query results looked similar despite differences in library systems. The Z39.50 standard, now in its third version (1995), while helping to make the differences in individual library systems transparent, does not provide a standard way to retrieve serial holdings data, only bibliographic data. This means that when a user connects to another system the holdings often are not retrieved. Another quirk, perhaps the responsibility of the LC Website, is that from within each individual library catalog in the gateway, there is no indication to the searcher which catalog is currently being viewed.

How does Z39.50 affect various serials functions? It assists at ordering and claiming time by allowing simplified searching of other library catalogs. There is no standard method, however, for providing location, holdings, and circulation information to the user. In terms of rights management, the standard enables the physical and fiscal control of access to databases and resources.

CONCLUSION

Discussion and questions from the audience followed the workshop. Someone asked whether, with all the different standards being developed, one would eventually come to be the main standard. The workshop leaders replied that although resolution services compete heavily, often different standards serve slightly different purposes. Each constituent of the serials world has its own perception of needs, while NISO has its own structure to follow.

Another person asked why URLs change so often. Locations may change because the file creator moves. A change in the file name within a site often creates difficulties in accessing the site. Personal homepages are some of the most fickle sites on the Web, with regard to filenames and addresses. An audience member from OCLC commented that the PURL server is merely a stopgap measure to address this problem.

Other participants wanted clarification on the differences among the various identifiers. Someone finally commented that the idea of standards competing with one another was a "barbarism on its own." Asked whether they could foresee a standardization of all of the standards mentioned, the workshop leaders replied "No," and that relevant standards are being developed in many areas outside the serials chain.

Landesman added that it behooves serials professionals to know what is on the horizon, and to become involved in standards development by sending comments to the working group, IETF. Beth Weston urged everyone to read *SISAC News*. Librarians need to decide which standards to support, and to do this, they need to be involved in the creation and development of standards and systems.

NOTES

1. Jean Hirons and Crystal Graham, "Issues Related to Seriality," in *International Conference on the Principles and Future Development of AACR.* (Oct. 23-25, 1997). Available: http://www.nlc-bnc.ca/jsc/r-serial.pdf. 24 July 1998.

2. Forward to *Serial Item and Contribution Identifier*, par. 1. Available: http://sunsite.berkeley.edu/SICI/version2.html#agency. 24 July 1998.

3. *Serials Industry Systems Advisory Committee*, par. 7. Available: http://www.bookwire.com/bisg/sisac.html. 24 July 1998.

4. NISO, *Holding Statements for Bibliographic Items*, par. 1. Available: http://www.niso.org/commital.html. 24 July 1998.

5. Stuart Weibel and Eric Miller, *Dublin Core Metadata*, par. 1. Available: http://purl.oclc.org/metadata/dublin_core/. 24 July 1998.

6. The International DOI Foundation, Digital Object Identifier System. Available: http://www.doi.org. 24 July 1998.

7. William Arms, Leslie Daigle, Ron Daniel, Dan LaLiberte, Michael Mealling, Keith Moore, and Stuart Weibel, "Uniform Resource Names: A Progress Report," *D-Lib Magazine*, February 1996. Available: http://www.dlib.org/dlib/february96/02arms.html. 24 July 1998.

8. Robert D. Cameron, "Towards Universal Serial Item Names," *CMPT TR 97-16* (Dec. 3, 1997). Available: http://www.cs.sfu.ca/pub/cs/TR/1997/CMPT97-16.html. 24 July 1998.

Build It So They Will Come: Blueprints for Successful Webpage Development

William Terry
Ellen Greenblatt
Cynthia Hashert

Workshop Leaders

Lucien R. Rossignol

Recorder

SUMMARY. As librarians become more familiar with the World Wide Web and its potential as a resource tool, it is increasingly important that they are able provide Web access suited to their and their users' needs. This workshop provided general guidelines as well as guidelines geared to technical services departments for the design, creation and maintenance of Webpages. *[Article copies available for a fee from The Haworth Document Delivery Service: 1-800-342-9678. E-mail address: getinfo@haworthpressinc.com]*

The ubiquitousness of Websites on the World Wide Web was quickly demonstrated at the beginning of this workshop when William Terry (director of technology at NetPubs International) asked audience mem-

William Terry is Director of Technology, NetPubs International.
Ellen Greenblatt is Assistant Director for Technical Services, Auraria Library.
Cynthia Hashert is Serials Acquisitions Librarian, Auraria Library.
Lucien R. Rossignol is Head, Acquisitions Services, Smithsonian Institution Libraries.

[Haworth co-indexing entry note]: "Build It So They Will Come: Blueprints for Successful Webpage Development." Rossignol, Lucien R. Co-published simultaneously in *The Serials Librarian* (The Haworth Press, Inc.) Vol. 36, No. 3/4, 1999, pp. 523-528; and: *Head in the Clouds, Feet on the Ground: Serials Vision and Common Sense* (ed: Jeffrey S. Bullington, Beatrice L. Caraway, and Beverley Geer) The Haworth Press, Inc., 1999, pp. 523-528. Single or multiple copies of this article are available for a fee from The Haworth Document Delivery Service [1-800-342-9678, 9:00 a.m. - 5:00 p.m. (EST). E-mail address: getinfo@haworthpressinc.com].

bers to indicate how many had Websites. Terry then began by providing a generic look at what someone might go through when contemplating establishing a Website. He presented components for a generic Website. This was followed by a review of the current technology. Terry concluded with a glimpse into the future, mentioning possible developments which will require the attention of those contemplating a Website.

Prior to planning for a new Website, one must ask why it is advantageous have a Website in the first place. Terry pointed out that in the early 1990s Web technology began receiving a great deal of media exposure with predictions of great things to come. As a result, many corporations boarded the Website bandwagon without fully understanding the inherent implications of such a premature move. They expended incredible amounts of money on these projects. The following year it was estimated that three out of five of these corporations had actually shut down their Websites. A major flaw in their approach, Terry pointed out, was that the corporations had not spent enough time, if any at all, on determining in advance what they were trying to accomplish, what their goals were, and how to best contact their potential audiences. In the last four years corporations have learned how people use online capabilities, and they have incorporated Web outreach into their public relations missions.

Audience members should profit from corporate America's learning exercise, Terry advised. Anyone contemplating the creation of a Website should ask several questions, theoretical and pragmatic: Why create a Website? What will make the site useful? Who is the primary audience? Who is the secondary audience? What are their online capabilities? How much time do they spend online? Questions of a more pragmatic nature include: What resources are available locally (in-house)? Who is going to create the site? Who is going to maintain it? Is outsourcing an option and to what extent? Most important of all: is there or is there not institutional buy-in, i.e., will there be support from the local organization, be it corporate, academic, or governmental?

Websites are not static. They comprise programs that evolve. However, the model of an edifice can nevertheless still serve as a mechanism for explaining the process of building a Website.

LAY OF THE LAND

Collegial support is mandatory. From the very beginning of a Website creation project it is necessary to garner support and expertise from all the people who may be in any way connected with the creation project or in some way have significant contributions to make to it. It is also important to note that traditionally, the technology has been designed by IETFs (Internet Engineering Task Forces), composed of nonpartisan individuals. However, Web technology is now designed by the WWW Consortium (W3C), whose principle members are companies with vested proprietary technology. They possess the expertise and interests in specific areas. They are on the forefront of technological development and as a result are able to develop protocols and standards. This means, however, that the hot new feature on the Microsoft browser may not be worth designing into your Website because it may not make it into the protocol standard.

TENANTS AND GUESTS

Who comprises the primary audience (tenants)? Who comprises the secondary audience (guests)? The primary audience should be the focus of any Website creation project, though it is unlikely that all audience members will be reached. Project leaders should strive to select suites of tools, capabilities, and basic designs to reach the greatest number of potential users. Surveys of potential users are invaluable tools to gain knowledge of the user community. Using surveys, one can find out about browsers used by potential clients, comfort levels surrounding issues of new capabilities, connections to the Internet, the kind of information which will likely be sought at the Website, and hardware issues.

BLUEPRINTS

Here the key is planning ahead. It is important to know what one's options are and to know how to use them before users do. Once options have been identified, it must be determined whether they already exist or will have to be created. Can something that already exists be converted to meet a new need? Are the design elements consistent? Is navigation through the site obvious and repeatable? Will e-mail discussion groups be included? Images? How many? Will counters and guest books be included to provide statistical usage information? These and similar questions must be asked at the beginning of the project. Though this process may be more labor-intensive at the beginning of the design phase, it will ultimately result in a better designed and, therefore, more useful product.

RAISING THE WALLS

Whether data will appear as one continuous stream or be separated by discrete page markers is yet another item to consider. Moving away from hardcopy model is crucial because the model of a printed piece of paper is not necessarily as important in an electronic environment. Which of the two approaches is more efficient in terms of searching will likely be determined by user needs and experience. This underscores, once again, the need to know one's audience. Navigating through the Website is yet another key consideration as the purpose of any Website is to provide access to both information and services. How well or poorly the navigation scheme is planned can make or break a site in terms of its utility to users.

ACCESS

Restrictions placed on who has access to what electronic documents are probably the last but nevertheless one of the most important items to be evaluated in the process of planning a Website. Terry illustrated this point by comparing subscriber vs. membership models for electronic serials subscriptions. The subscriber model is the more complex of the two. With the subscriber model, individual users have limited access to the defined universe of electronic serials, i.e., specific issues within specific volumes and years, etc. The membership model provides much broader access, i.e., several titles for a given time frame.

Cynthia Hashert (serials acquisitions librarian) and Ellen Greenblatt (assistant director for technical services) both at Auraria Library, next discussed Webpage creation from a library technical services perspective. Hashert addressed the reasons and benefits associated with a technical services Webpage, and Greenblatt the more mechanical aspects including design and structure.

Hashert began her portion of the program by underscoring a point made earlier by Terry, that of knowing one's audience. In addition to technical services staff, other audiences for a technical services Webpage may exist as well. Perhaps other library staff may need to look at the technical services Webpage in order to answer a question for a library user. Librarians from other institutions may want to peruse other library, more specifically technical services, Webpages to obtain ideas on how to design their own Webpages. Vendors may also be interested in viewing a technical services Webpage. Other reasons for creating a technical services Webpage include centralization, currency, customization, efficiency, and communication.

A technical services Webpage allows for centralizing information that is needed by technical services staff. The distribution of policies that and procedures is facilitated by a well-maintained page. Changes to documentation that occur frequently can be made globally with one quick change to the Web version as apposed to a hardcopy version with its attendant considerations of word processing, printing, photo-copying, etc. A technical services Webpage will allow a librarian to organize information that is important to departmental staff and com-bine it with departmental information such as policies and procedures, statistics, contact information, and holdings of potentially helpful Websites from the hundred that are available on the Internet. Three of these sites include Acqweb, Cataloger's Reference Shelf, and Internet Library for Librarians. Sites that are accessed frequently can be high-lighted and displayed prominently to minimize the amount of search-ing (navigating) required. Efficiency is achieved by allowing staff to gain access to information quickly via electronic media vs. locating the same information more slowly in hardcopy format.

A technical services Webpage can offer better communication with-in and outside the department. A page that lists staff, their e-mail addresses, and their telephone numbers is very useful. A page that lists that information, plus subject specialities, responsibilities, and job descriptions is even better. Forms for ordering materials, suggestions for ordering, cataloging errors, transfers, rush cataloging, and sugges-tions for cataloging electronic resources can be more beneficial if they are available on a technical services Webpage. Depending on local circumstances, it might be possible to develop a mailing list for the technical services department. This would provide an easy line of communication to all departmental staff.

The first consideration is who is to build the Webpage. There are three options: a commercial firm such as NetPubs International, a Webmaster, or a team/committee. If a staff member is selected, a good way for him or her to start is by looking at other technical services Webpages. Another useful resource is Barbara Stewart's book *The Neal-Schuman Directory of Library Technical Services Home Pages.* Stewart also maintains a Website at http://tpot.ucsd.edu/Cataloging/ Misc/tech_services.html. Web development resources include individual institution computer centers, Yahoo, CNET's Builder.com and other library-specific resources.

Hashert and Greenblatt reiterated Terry's emphasis on ease of navigation as an important design consideration. A homepage button that returns users to the main Webpage is important. Pull-down menus can be useful. Frames that allow users to view multiple pages at once are loved by some, hated by others. Search (keyword or phrase) and site (pages, documents, procedures) indices are good navigation aids. Other design considerations include: consistency (endow the site with its own identity); simplicity (limit pages to one basic concept); graphics (aesthetics vs. functionality and thumbnails to provide access to large images); and ADA issues (avoid blinking or scrolling text and titles for horizontal rules and abbreviations).

Whether to include specific kinds of information on the Internet, an intranet, or both is an important content consideration. Financial information, internal reports, and internal forms lend themselves to inclusion on an intranet while non-proprietary information is better suited to the Internet.

Greenblatt concluded her remarks by emphasizing the importance of a maintenance plan for one's Website. She stressed a centralized maintenance responsibility to avoid confusion once the site is up and running as well as the need to develop a plan to preclude haphazard maintenance. Equally important, she noted, is the need to keep a master file of all pages. This file should contain a Webpage profile of each separate page and give specific information about each page and specify subordinate and related pages. Finally, one should use a link checker during regular maintenance sessions to assure that all links appearing on the Webpage are valid. LibraryLand includes a list of such checkers.

Do Holdings Have a Future?

Frieda B. Rosenberg

Workshop Leader

Cathy Kellum

Recorder

Rather than a summary, this is an edited version of the author's paper, which is available at http://www.lib.unc.edu/cat/mfh. The site contains the paper, the manual, and the models of related serial record structure that the author outlined in her presentation.

SUMMARY. Holdings are multipurpose data which libraries use to acquire and control publications, display information to users, and manage physical and sometimes virtual items. This workshop focused on how the various functions interact, what further services librarians will demand from automation of their holdings, and what they can do in the meantime to make their holdings more useful. The workshop gave special attention to the USMARC Format for Holdings Data (MHFD), its features, advantages and difficulties, and its particular role in convey-

Frieda B. Rosenberg is Head, Serials Cataloging, University of North Carolina at Chapel Hill.

Cathy Kellum is OCLC Services Training Supervisor, SOLINET.

[Haworth co-indexing entry note]: "Do Holdings Have a Future?" Kellum, Cathy. Co-published simultaneously in *The Serials Librarian* (The Haworth Press, Inc.) Vol. 36, No. 3/4, 1999, pp. 529-539; and: *Head in the Clouds, Feet on the Ground: Serials Vision and Common Sense* (ed: Jeffrey S. Bullington, Beatrice L. Caraway, and Beverley Geer) The Haworth Press, Inc., 1999, pp. 529-539. Single or multiple copies of this article are available for a fee from The Haworth Document Delivery Service [1-800-342-9678, 9:00 a.m. - 5:00 p.m. (EST). E-mail address: getinfo@haworthpressinc.com].

ing serials information. It explored possibilities for adapting the format to solve the special problems associated with multiple versions and title changes. *[Article copies available for a fee from The Haworth Document Delivery Service: 1-800-342-9678. E-mail address: getinfo@haworthpressinc.com]*

A large group of NASIG attendees were welcomed to the workshop by the presenter who, happy to see so many people interested in the topic, stated that holdings, if they don't have a future, must have a very lively present: one on which, perhaps, we can build. She mentioned that some of the audience may have attended because holdings in automated systems can be a problem area for staff, precisely because they are at the hub of so many activities and are met with in so many forms. Staff responsible for them want to know whether there is a way to reduce duplication of work, to steer between rigid rules and utter permissiveness, and whether each person who works with holdings is obliged to go it alone in finding this balance. Some of these conditions may apply:

- Holdings work is little understood by and little supported by library administrators.
- Reference staff and users have very high expectations but often don't understand what. they're viewing–or don't look at holdings when they should.
- Staff has very little guidance available in working with holdings.
- Changing online systems causes concern about how it will affect the holdings.
- You wonder why you and your colleagues have to input holdings for the same material into different files in different ways with little coordination among you.
- Your online system does not implement certain standards.
- There are real practical problems for your library in following certain standards.

The standards issue was stressed throughout the workshop, because of the vicious circle that is established when standards are not available or not regarded. Data that are inconsistently formed or that use a standard in conflicting ways may be a real stumbling block when a library wishes to upgrade or add features to the system. A library might be forced to say, "Don't implement the standard for us; it wouldn't work for the way we have done our data." On the other hand, if you are consistent in the way you don't follow standards, and you can distinguish the parts of your record–at a minimum, the holdings from the notes–you probably will be able, with the aid of extra programming, to migrate your nonstandard holdings into a standard MARC holdings format, perhaps making use of the free-text options in that format.

Many libraries start out with serials systems that do not completely support standards. Even if we can't code completely for the standard and aren't able to use all of its functionality, we have a responsibility to have our holdings at least in conformance, not in contradiction, to the demands of this standard. The speaker expressed a desire to see a consensus to come out of the workshop; that there be a sense that we might use our common interest and strength and skill in a quest for five things:

- More consistency in holdings data
- Cooperative development of a better and more workable model to use, a better standard itself (developed cooperatively like the bibliographic record)
- Cooperative and competitive urging of better implementations in our systems (suggesting that the serials system be put at the top of the list of desired features, rather than last)
- Better guidance in the form of interpretation and documentation
- Archives of content, such as publication patterns and the publication data itself, that we can draw upon

Since the workshop topic was proposed to NASIG, the picture has continued to change. Initially, as more and more holdings were visible online from all over the globe, things seemed very hopeful for holdings. Then starting about 1994 or 1995, there were many less favorable signs, such as emphasis on those new virtual items in the public catalog that are not "held" by the library and talk of de-emphasizing local collections and turning our catalogs into finding aids for global information; frequently hearing a somewhat over-exaggerated report that the MARC format for holdings was little spread and little supported; the MARC Holdings Format Interest Group at LITA disbanded and simply became the MARC Formats Interest Group; and a consultant at the Library of Congress wrote an article about how LC was designing a non-MARC holdings serials system and made the claim that "no library uses the MFHD for check-in and claiming," which would be news to many libraries that do.

However, over the past couple of years Web catalogs spread. New looks for the OPAC and new ways of navigating give us the chance again to assess how we allow search and display of information to users. New emphasis is put on making the holdings screen informative, and this is true even for electronic resources even when we do not give holdings per se for those items. Not one but several vendors have announced new implementations of the holdings format. As always, these vary in completeness. The Library of Congress gave up its separate system and bought a system, Endeavor's Voyager, which does utilize the MFHD. The interest in remote searching of holdings has revived discussion of standards for holdings structure and content. The newest NISO holdings display standards (Z39.71) have been reballotted and approved, and should be published in fall 1998. All of these trends have induced people to take a look at what holdings are and do, and what libraries want from them.

Holdings are at the hub of library serials use and serials management, just as central as the bibliographic record. A holdings record can do all of the following: serve as a basis for check-in and claiming, record bound units, with barcodes for circulation, generate a spine label, display a summary holdings statement to users, become part of a Z39.50 retrieval from a remote site, serve as a report to a union list, or answer a reference question. The portion of reference questions dealing with serial holdings is in some surveys reported to be over 40 percent. It hasn't been easy for the holdings format to do all that, for vendors to program it, or for us to code it.

HISTORY OF THE STANDARDS

Timing has been unfortunate in a number of ways. Holdings are among our newest bibliographic standards, all arising during the 1980s. First came the display standards. These were developed for a paper and microfiche environment, including union lists, starting with one now-superseded summary display standard, Z39.42. It allows open entries, does not include captions, and records only at the highest level, for example, the volume, which was counted as held if the library held 50 percent or more of it. There is no provision for recording of supplements and indexes. There is data conforming to this standard being loaded even today. This summary standard, Z39.42, conflicted with the next detailed holdings display standard, Z39.44, and how they had to be resolved. In the end, a combined summary and detailed standard was published. Its summary holdings level defined "holding" a volume differently. The volume is now counted if the library has any of it. There are captions in Z39.44. There are even display options, mindful of all those libraries with older data: enumeration and chronology could be reported together or separately; at the new fourth level of holdings, every gap in holdings now had to be recorded fully; the presence of a volume is a guarantee that the library owns the entire volume (or at least did so at the time of the report).

Meanwhile, another set of standards had to be reconciled, and these were the monographic standards–Z39.57. The new combined standards are being put together as Z39.71. The news was that the balloting that took place early this year was successful, but there were some comments raising questions that need to be worked out before the final version can be published.

Z39.71

The new standard is impressive. It has flexibility where the former standard was extremely rigid. It gives more space to instructions for itemization, that is, the presentation of holdings in terms of individual items, which is the way many libraries want to present them today, because that way we can present, as well, the special status, notes, etc., that apply to the individual volumes as volumes. It has eliminated some of the excessive detail and repetition that occurred in the old standard whenever there was a gap in holdings. Captions, for example, can be omitted in the part of the holding that comes after the hyphen. There can be an open holding at level 4, the most detailed level. The presentation at either level can include a "separate" presentation of enumeration and chronology, rather than adjacent presentation, that is, v.1-2 (1991-1992) as well as v.1 (1991)-v.2 (1992). In the earlier standard, the first presentation was an option only at Level 3.

THE USMARC FORMAT

The standards for holdings display, which fit in a modestly sized, slender book, should be distinguished from the holdings format, which is in a big binder. A concise version of it is available on the MARC Website at the Library of Congress; the whole is available at the Library Corporation's Website. However, for the purposes of this workshop, the speaker developed a special version with a more explanatory approach, the *USMARC Format for Holdings Data Handbook*.

The *USMARC Format for Holdings and Locations* was in its final form just about the same time as the publication of Z39.44. The publication date is 1986. With the second edition in 1994 it became the *USMARC Format for Holdings Data*.

The MARC holdings format was developed by libraries in the field, members of the Association of Southeastern Research Libraries (ASERL) who wished to have a means of communicating holdings to each other for purposes of resource sharing. It was created by serialists for serials. The Southeastern Library Network (SOLINET) played a leading role in its development. You often hear about how serials were kind of shoehorned into the bibliographic format, which was made for monographs–but the MFHD was made with serials in mind.

Did the aforementioned display standards come into the picture? Yes, they did; that is, the two groups consulted, but the format is kept deliberately out of the business of prescribing a display. Those who wish to display holdings in terms of physical pieces are perfectly capable of doing so using the MARC holdings format. It is capable of generating many types of displays, but the success is dependent on the programmers who implement the format in a particular system.

Several things characterize the holdings format. It is very complex. It contains various pieces of data that have to work together. If a piece is missing, not only that piece of information but perhaps the entire display or the entire functionality is lost. The unique feature of the format is the "paired fields" construction of the actual holdings data, with the captions in one field which is then linked by means of a shared number in a subfield to a series of data fields containing the corresponding enumeration and chronology. The contents of both the caption fields and the enumeration-chronology fields are then displayed together.

It uses a fairly small range of fields in comparison to the bibliographic standards, using only those beginning with "0," "5," and "8." Access fields such as the 856 were originally designed for the holdings format. Like the bibliographic standards, the MFHD has been extended by some vendors with proprietary fields and subfields which might begin with "9" or some other number or letter.

Some difficulties exist for workers with the format. As noted, it has been subject to neglect, with few revisions and even fewer interpretations, because it is thought of as a carrier for local data. Standards have not been enforced, and incomplete, nonstandard implementations lead to nonstandard data that later cannot be accommodated correctly. To gain ground, we must once again focus our attention on the holdings format and make a case for the functionality that we need.

Despite the significance of local information, it has a strong and very stubborn bias toward those aspects of local data that are important in the national and global arena for interlibrary loan, union lists, and the like. It does not allow for a lot of management data. But even on the global front it is somewhat behind the times, because it leaves out some crucial data such as availability of individual volumes, requiring that to be accommodated elsewhere in the system to be sought out and combined with holdings data by remote search engines. Also, very little of the essential, complex coding can be done on an automated basis.

The format has some ambiguities, notably the concept of expansion of a compressed holding. You can explode it once it is compressed, but can you do it accurately, by automated computer algorithm? Even knowing how many issues were supposed to be published in a volume doesn't tell you how many issues actually appeared, what their designations looked like, and how many were combined issues. Also, though physical pieces can be coded, it is not easy to show unambiguously to users, staff, and interlibrary loan which of your data represent physical pieces unless you code them all that way and are able to make a blanket statement to that effect.

Another problem is that there is often a divided responsibility, divided workflow, and distinct procedures for different flows of holdings work. In some institutions, the check-in staff are responsible for coding in new annuals and irregulars, which often get barcoded on receipt, while the periodicals get their final coding when received back by binding staff or by branch librarians. In contrast to the level four coding of the annuals, the periodicals often get an open-entry summary holding. In some cases, the latter can be considered level 4 (as permitted in the newest standard), because the staff is conscientious about noting gaps. But in others, periodical information is not kept up to date. This is something each library has to work out.

The programmer's job in making the format work may be fairly characterized as difficult. A vendor-librarian discussion on the MFHD held at ALA in 1995 brought this out very clearly. Even the basic premise of the paired fields is complex. NISO standards prescribe a display whose elements are in what we know as 362 order, "enumeration-chronology, enumeration-chronology": v.1:no.2(1996: Feb.)-v.3:no.5 (1998: May). Even option B–the other optional order–does not have the data in the same order as the MFHD: v.1:no.2-v.3:no.5(1996: Feb.-1998:May).

The MFHD also prescribes input in the form enumeration-enumeration, chronology-chronology, as option B does, but it also requires data at one level to be expressed in one segment; it cannot be repeated. A statement with incomplete ranges and levels as above is not possible in coded form unless manipulated programmatically, since the first level of enumeration (a) and the second level of enumeration (b) are not repeatable. Data would have to be input in the form. At this point, very few vendors seem to be manipulating the data so that the data of the second level ($b and $j) can display interspersed with the first level as it is in the option B example above, let alone the option A display above that. Some enumeration, in particular, has internal hyphens. It would be dangerous to interpret a hyphen as always representing a connector between the first element and the last element of a range. If holdings communication were at the same level of sophistication as bibliographic standards, we would need to reserve all of those elements of holdings punctuation, as we do for internal punctuation in the bibliographic standards. Until these matters are settled, it is best to accommodate complex data by using the free-text field options in the format.

BENEFITS OF AUTOMATED HOLDINGS

If you have a good implementation of the format, it provides for some things you are *supposed* to have and other things you really need, such as

- A way to make a copy- and location-specific report or combined report at your volition easy ways to navigate or jump among screens of related data

- Easy copying of information from one place to another with automatic resequencing
- Minimal need to recode when you have to move data or insert data
- Ample space for notes and the means to enter commonly used ones via codes or shorthand
- Clear, easy-to-interpret interface
- Automatic compression of holdings if you have the publication pattern data (automatic compression of holdings should be possible at the volume level even without that data!)
- Correct linkage with other modules; access to information and editing capability for all related data from inside your MFHD program without having to back out
- Provision for ordinal numbers, which appear before their captions rather than after
- The ability to use free-text holdings and/or notes and coded holdings together with proper display and ability to suppress the former in favor of the latter

You should be able to express almost any kind of enumeration or chronology in coded form, or if not, in free-text form. Programming can be created to transfer the data into almost any display. Someone should test the capability by inputting test data. This sounds elementary but is crucial. Buy a system on the basis of what exists, not what is promised–another time-honored maxim.

You should have enough space, at long last, to give any amount of detail you need about the copy at a particular location, the individual piece, or the relationships between one holdings record and another, one bibliographic record and another. You should be able to display all the data that exists to the public if you want to. There is no excuse for giving you the option to show only check-in data or only summary data, so don't accept that. It should be as easy for the public to navigate and identify what information is being shown as it is for you. In short, you need the ability to display what you have in the optimal way to help your users interpret the information.

HOLDINGS PITFALLS

It is our responsibility to avoid some of the possible sins against data consistency, such as mixing caption data and enumeration-chronology data in the coded fields, even if you end up with something that looks right. Be careful with indicators and with link and sequence numbers. It is better to leave indicators blank than to code them with the wrong information. Provide a training program and make sure that if you have various units doing the coding in several different work-flows, they are all using the same guidelines and methods. Make notes in a standard wording. If you use macros or codes, you have a better chance of having consistent wording, something that can be globally changed when you need to do that.

THE FUTURE OF HOLDINGS

There are so many frontiers in holdings. One of them is the World Wide Web. Web linking between citations on remote databases and individual local holdings records is already being offered by some commercial companies, just as they offered "hooks-to-holdings" in the non-Web catalogs of the past. This kind of linking is possible in-house as well. If there is a separate MARC holdings record that can be accessed over the Web, we may be able to use its control number in a Web address that could be accessed via library-created finding aids for such materials as newspapers or serials in special collections or subject areas. In terms of public service, we need to make sure that we add value to the greatest extent possible to the information we give the public about holdings. The new standard should have provision for multiple versions (i.e., print, microform, and electronic publications).

The last part of the presentation dealt with the structure of relation-ships between bibliographic records, especially those expressed by 776 fields (multiple versions) and 780/785 fields (title changes). The audience viewed models of the present structure contrasted with several alternative structures, which relied upon either consolidating or linking among holdings records. The audience was encouraged to consider and comment on these and other topics raised in the paper even after leaving the conference.

The speaker entertained questions from the audience on such topics as vendor design and barcoding problems. She then concluded with a discussion concerning the problem that no party seems to be taking responsibility for holdings and the development of standards, and proposed that we unite to look for support within existing organiza-tions or form a new organization for this purpose.

SELECTED RESOURCES
ON THE USMARC HOLDINGS FORMAT

Anderson, Greg. "A Shared Publication Pattern Database: Patience, Planning, and Priority." *Serials Review* 21, no. 4 (fall 1991): 70-72.

Barry B. Baker, ed. *USMARC Format for Holdings and Locations: Development, Implementation, and Use.* New York: The Haworth Press, Inc., 1988.

Bernhardt, Melissa (Melissa Beck). "Dealing with Serial Title Changes: Some Theoretical and Practical Considerations." *Cataloging and Classification Quarterly* 9, no. 2 (1988): 25-39.

Goldberg, Tyler, and Eric Neagle. "Serials Information in the OPAC: A Model for Shared Responsibility." *Serials Review* 21, no. 4 (winter 1996): 55-63.

McNellis, Claudia Houk. "A Serial Pattern Scheme for a Value-Based Predictive Check-In System." *Serials Review* 21, no. 4 (winter 1996): 1-11.

Rosenberg, Frieda. "Managing Serial Holdings." In *Managing Serials.* Edited by Marcia Tuttle, 237-256. Greenwich, Conn.: JAI Press, 1996.

Van Cura, Mary Ann. "A Step Beyond Shared Patterns: A Shared Holdings Record Database." *Serials Review* 17, no. 3 (fall 1991): 72-76.

Wallace, Patricia M. "Serial Holdings Statements: A Necessity or a Nuisance?" *Technical Services Quarterly* 14, no. 3 (1997): 11-24.

For holdings documentation, see http://lcweb.loc.gov/marc.

For information on the use of holdings in remote retrieval, see http://lcweb.loc.gov/ z3950/agency.

13th Annual NASIG Conference Registrants, University of Colorado-Boulder, June 18-21, 1998

Conference Registrants	*Organization/Institution*
Aaron, Amira	Faxon Company
Abaid, Teresa	Florida Atlantic University
Acton, Deena	National Library of Medicine
Adams, Agnes	University of Nebraska
Aiello, Helen	Wesleyan University
Aitchison, Jada	UALR Palaski County Law Library
Albano, Christine	Cleveland Public Library
Albee, Barbara	Faxon Company
Alexander, Whitney	Innovative Interfaces
Algier, Aimee	Santa Clara University
Allen, Dianne	Faxon Canada
Allgood, Everett	New York University
Andrews, Susan	Texas A&M University–Commerce
Anemaet, Jos	Oregon State University
Arcand, Janet	Iowa State University
Arenales, Duane	National Library of Medicine
Arnesen, Sandra	University of Denver Health Sciences Center
Arnold, Teresa	Swets & Zeitlinger, Inc.
Ashman, Allen	Kentucky Union List of Serials
Attree, Mary	Arnold
Aufdemberge, Karen	University of Toledo
Axtell, Maureen	Saint Martin's College

Badics, Joe	Eastern Michigan University
Baia, Wendy	University of Colorado at Boulder
Bailey, Clare	Bureau of National Affairs, Inc.
Baker, Mary Ellen	California State Polytechnic University
Baker, Jeanne	University of Maryland
Baker, Carol	University of Calgary
Ballard, Karon	University of Kansas
Barash, Mariya	University of Detroit Mercy
Basch, Buzzy	Basch Subscriptions
Baxter, Michelle	UnCover Company
Beach, Regina	Mississippi State University
Becker, Louis	New York Public Library
Bedford, Tracey	UnCover Company
Bedor, Donna	Fort Lewis College
Beier, Mike	Brigham Young University
Belcher, Dana	East Central University
Bell, Carole	Northwestern University
Bender, Mary	University of Wyoming
Bendig, Deborah	OCLC
Bennett, Marsha	Boston Public Library
Bergin, Edward	Rice University
Bernards, Dennis	Brigham Young University
Bianchi, Marcia	Reed College
Birch, Tom	Baker College
Blessey, Tamalane	Xaviar University of Louisiana
Blixrud, Julia	Association of Research Libraries
Blosser, John	Northwestern University
Bobich, Marianne	Texas Christian University
Boissy, Robert	Faxon Company
Bordeianu, Sever	University of New Mexico
Born, Kathleen	EBSCO Information Services
Boyce, Peter	American Astronomical Society
Brackbill, Isabel	Los Alamos National Laboratory
Bradley, Melissa	Denver Public Library
Branham, Janie	Southeastern Louisiana University
Brass, Evelyn	University of Houston
Breed, Luellen	University of Wisconsin-Parkside
Brennan, Molly	Virginia Tech
Briscoe, Georgia	University of Colorado Law Library

Broadway, Rita	University of Memphis
Bross, Valerie	California State University, Stanislaus
Brown, Michael	University of New Mexico
Brown, Ladd	Virginia Tech
Brown, Elizabeth	Johns Hopkins University
Brown, David	BIDS
Bruce, Beverly	MCB University Press
Budde, Neil	Wall Street Journal
Bull, David	Routledge Publishers
Bull, Greg	University of St. Thomas
Bullington, Jeff	Trinity University
Burk, Martha	Babson College
Burke, David	Villanova University
Burks, Suzan	Ball State University
Burleson, Robert	American Chemical Society Publications
Buskirk, Colleen	San Diego County Public Law Library
Butler, Joan	University of Michigan
Byunn, Kit	University of Memphis
Calk, Jo	Blackwell's Book Services
Callaghan, Jean	Wheaton College
Campbell, Cameron	University of Chicago
Cap, Maria	Los Angeles County Law Library
Caraway, Beatrice	Trinity University
Cargille, Karen	University of California, San Diego
Carlson, Melvin	University of Massachusetts, Amherst
Carter, Trina	University of New Mexico
Casetta, Prima	Getty Research Institute
Castellani, Maggie	Cleveland Museum of Art
Chaffin, Nancy	Arizona State University
Champagne, Tom	University of Michigan
Chan, Karen	Eastern Washington University
Chang, Ling-Li	Loyola University of Chicago
Chang, Hui-Yee	University of California, Santa Cruz
Chesler, Adam	Kluwer Academic Publishers
Chou, Charlene	Columbia University
Chressanthis, June	Mississippi State University
Christ, Ruth	University of Iowa
Christensen, John	Brigham Young University

Clarkson, Jane	Florida State University
Cleary, Robert	University of Missouri, Kansas City
Cochenour, Donnice	Colorado State University
Cohen, Joan	Bergen Community College
Collins, Jill	Boise State University
Conger, Mary Jane	University of North Carolina at Greensboro
Congleton, Robert	Temple University
Connelly, Barb	University of Notre Dame
Conway, Cheryl	University of Arkansas Fayetteville
Cook, Eleanor	Appalachian State University
Cook, Karen	Bowdoin College
Copeland, Nora	Colorado State University
Corbett, Sue	Blackwell Publishers
Corbett, Lauren	Old Dominion University
Corrsin, Steve	Columbia University
Costales, Glada	UnCover Company
Council, Evelyn	Fayetteville State University
Courtney, Keith	Taylor & Francis Ltd.
Cousineau, Marie	University of Ottawa
Cowhig, Jerry	Institute of Physics Publishing
Cox, Brian	Elsevier Science
Cox, John	Carfax Publishing Ltd.
Cracknell, Linda	Wilfrid Laurier University
Crowell, Loretta	Detroit College of Law
Curtis, Jerry	Springer Verlag
Czech, Isabel	Institute for Scientific Information
Dalton, Bobbie Lou	Davidson College
Dane, Steve	Kluwer Academic Publishers
Darling, Karen	University of Oregon
Davis, Julianne	University of Wyoming
Davis, Trisha	Ohio State University
Davis, Eve	EBSCO Information Services
Davis, Susan	State University of New York at Buffalo
Davis, Carroll	Columbia University
Dawson, Julie Eng	Princeton Seminary
Day, Nancy	Linda Hall Library
Dean, Jo Janet	Clark County Library District
DeBlois, Lillian	Arizona Health Sciences Library

DeBuse, Judy	Washington State Library
Deeken, JoAnne	Clemson University
Degener, Christie	University of North Carolina, Chapel Hill, Health Sciences
Dennis, Nancy	University of New Mexico
Deyoe, Nancy	Wichita State University
Diedrichs, Carol Pitts	Ohio State University
Doerr, Tom	CARL Corporation
Dolan, Anne	Fort Hayes State University
Dougherty, Kathleen	National Agricultural Library
Douglass, Janet	Texas Christian University
Downey, Kay	Cleveland Museum of Art
Draper, Anne	National Library of Canada
Dresia, David	American Society of Civil Engineers
Druesdow, Elaine	Duke University
Drum, Carol	University of Florida Science Library
Duckenfield, C. J.	Clemson University
Duhon, Lucy	University of Toledo
Dygert, Claire	American University
Dykas, Ann	University of Missouri, Kansas City
Early, Steve	Center for Research Libraries
Easton, Christa	Stanford University
Edwards, Jennifer	Massachusetts Institute of Technology
Elie, Carolle	New York Public Library
Ellis, K. D.	University of Tennessee
Ellison, Suzanne	Memorial University of Newfoundland
Emery, Jill	Texas Southern University
Endres, Ellen	Martinus Nijhoff
Ercelawn, Ann	Vanderbilt University
Erickson, Annamarie	Chicago Library system
Ernst, Gordon	West Virginia University
Essency, Janet	Minot State University
Fales, Susan	Brigham Young University
Farwell, Anne	CANEBSCO
Faust, Dror	Puvill Libros
Feick, Tina	Blackwell's Information Services
Ferley, Margaret	Concordia University
Ficken, Carol	University of Akron

Fields, Cheryl   National Library of Medicine
Fiske, Melanie   Moravian College
Fitzgerald, Sharon Quinn University of Maine
Fletcher, Marilyn   University of New Mexico
Flores, Yolanda   Las Vegas-Clark County Library District
Fogler, Patricia   Air University
Folsom, Sandy   Central Michigan University
Foroutan, Mitra   RoweCom
Foster, Connie   Western Kentucky University
Fowler, David   Texas A&M University, Corpus Christi
Frade, Pat   Brigham Young University
French, Pat   University of California, Davis
Frey, Dean   Alberta Library
Frick, Rachel   Faxon Company
Fried, Jonathan   R. R. Bowker
Frohlich, Anne   McNeese State University
Fry, Joy   University of Kansas

Gallina, Thomas   Dawson/Faxon
Gammon, Julia   University of Akron
Gans, Alf   ISA Australia
Gao, Vera   University of Colorado Auraria Library
Garralda, John   UnCover Company
Gasser, Sharon   James Madison University
Gedye, Richard   Oxford University Press
Geer, Beverley   Trinity University
Germain, J. Charles   PCG, Inc.
Getz, Malcolm   Vanderbilt University
Gibbs, Nancy   North Carolina State University
Gienger, Katherine   University of New Mexico
Gifford Fenton, Eileen   JSTOR
Gill, Carol   Trinity University
Gillespie, E. Gaele   University of Kansas
Gimmi, Bob   Shippensburg University
Gisonny, Karen   New York Public Library
Glazier, Mary   EBSCO Information Services
Glenn, Christine   American Phytopathological Society/APS
         Press
Gobin, Kip   University of Virginia Law Library

Goldsmith, David	Florida International University
Gonzales-Small, Grace	New Mexico State University
Gordon, Marty	Franklin & Marshall College
Gordon-Gilmore, Anita	Fort Hays State University
Gormley, Alice	Marquette University
Graber, Marla	University of Colorado Health Sciences Center
Graf, George	Trinity College
Graves, Shirley	Loma Linda University
Grawemeyer, Jane	SIRSI
Gray, Gayl	National Center for Atmospheric Research
Green, Carol	University of Southern Mississippi
Greenblatt, Ellen	University of Colorado Auraria Library
Greene, Phil	EBSCO Information Services
Grenci, Mary	University of Oregon
Grenier, Gerry	John Wiley & Sons
Grieme, Fariha	University of Minnesota
Griffin, JoAnne	Tufts Health Sciences Library
Griffith, Joan	Harrassowitz
Grima, Sunee	Weber State University
Groth, Mike	Kluwer Academic Publishers
Grover, Diane	University of Washington
Guay, Beth	University of Maryland
Gurshman, Sandra	Information Quest
Guzi, Gloria	Cleveland Public Library
Haas, Ruth	Harvard University
Haest, Ruth	University of New Mexico
Hagen, Tim	Northwestern University
Hall, Susan	Delaware State University
Hamaker, Charles	University of North Carolina at Charlotte
Hamilton, Fred	Louisiana Tech University
Hanus, Norine	University of Prince Edward Island
Hardy, Burmma	University of Wyoming
Harmon, Amanda	University of North Carolina at Charlotte
Harris, Sandy	Linda Hall Library
Harris, Jay	University of Alabama, Birmingham, Lister Hill Library
Harrison, John	Bates College
Harrison, Colin	Everetts

Hartman, Steven   Swets & Zeitlinger, Inc.
Harwell, Rolly   East Tennessee State University
Hashert, Cynthia   University of Colorado Auraria Library
Hawrychik, Shelley   University of Toronto
Hawthorn, Margaret   University of Toronto
Heckman, Steve   Heckman Bindery, Inc.
Hedberg, Jane   Wellesley College
Heitman, Herrick   Washington State Library
Helinsky, Zuzana   BTJ/Library Service
Helmetsie, Carolyn   NASA–Langley Research Center
Henderson, Kittie   EBSCO
Henderson, Charlotte   Southern University
Hendren, Carol   CCLA
Hepfer, Cindy   State University of New York at Buffalo
Heterick, Bruce   Blackwell's Information Service
Hill, Janet Swan   University of Colorado at Boulder
Hillery, Leanne   University of Miami Law Library
Hillson, Susan   Consultant
Hinger, Joseph   St. John's University Law Library
Hirning, Lorraine   Athabasca University
Hirons, Jean   Library of Congress
Hodge, Stan   Ball State University
Hodson, Richard   Blackwell's Information Services
Hoey, Peter   Royal Society of Chemistry
Holland, Jeff   Portland State University
Holley, Sandra   University of Texas Health Center at Tyler
Holley, Beth   University of Alabama at Tuscaloosa
Holt, Tom   California State University, Hayward
Hopkins, Randall   EBSCO Information Services
Horiuchi, Linda   Idaho State University
Horn, Maggie   State University of New York at Albany
Howard, Robert   Information Express
Howarter, David   University of California, Santa Barbara
Hoyer, Craig   Swets & Zeitlinger, Inc.
Hoyle, Mary Sue   EBSCO Information Services
Hughes, Charles
Hulbert, Linda   St. Louis University Heath Sciences Center
Hurd, Sandra   EBSCO Information Services
Hurst, Michele   Kent State University
Huynh, Valorie   Johns Hopkins University

Inger, Simon	CatchWord
Irvin, Judy	Louisiana Tech University
Ivins, October	Publist Company
Jaeger, Don	Alfred Jaeger, Inc.
Janes, Joseph	Internet Public Library
Janes, Jodith	Cleveland Clinic Foundation
Jedlicka, Beth	University of Georgia
Jenne, Bonita	Minnesota Historical Society
Jiang, Yumin	Cornell University
Jizba, Richard	Creighton University
Jo, Julitta	State University of New York at Stony Brook
Johnson, Judy	University of Nebraska–Lincoln
Johnson, Kay	University of Tennessee
Johnson, Sharon	Austin Peay State University
Johnston, Judy	University of North Texas
Jones, Wayne	Massachusetts Institute of Technology
Jones, Florence	Colorado State Library
Jurries, Elaine	University of Colorado Auraria Library
Kara, William	Cornell University
Katz, Stephen	Colorado School of Mines
Katz, Toni	Colby College
Kawecki, Barbara	EBSCO Information Services
Keates, Gwenda	John Wiley & Sons, Ltd.
Keller, Mike	Faxon Canada
Kellog, Martha	University of Rhode Island
Kellum, Cathy	SOLINET
Kelly, Karon	Natinal Center for Atmospheric Research
Kennedy, Kit	Blackwell's Information Services
Kern, Kristen	Portland State University
Keyhani, Andrea	OCLC
Khosh-Khui, Sam	Southwest Texas State University
Kimball, Merle	College of William and Mary
King, Shawn	North Central College
Kingery, Kathy	UnCover Company
Kirkland, Kenneth	DePaul University
Knapp, Leslie	EBSCO Information Services
Knight, Nancy	Consultant
Kobyljanec, Kathy	Case Western Reserve Law Library

Kolodzey, Ann	Widener Law Library
Krieger, Lee	University of Miami
Kropf, Blythe	New York Public Library
Kunkel, Marita	Oregon Institute of Technology
Kusma, Taissa	Academic Press
LaFrenier, Douglas	American Institute of Physics
LaGrange, Johanne	Columbia University Health Sciences Library
Lai, Sheila	California State University, Sacramento
Lamborn, Joan	University of Northern Colorado
Landesman, Betty	George Washington University
Lanphear, Shawn	EBSCO Information Services
Larocque, Sue	CISTI
Lathrom, Kathy	University of Kansas
Leadem, Ellen	National Institute of Environmental Health Sciences
Leathem, Cecilia	University of Miami
Lee, Janet	Regis University
Leiding, Reba	James Madison University
LeJeune, Lorrie	O'Reilly & Associates
Lempart, Mimi	Smith College
Lentz, Janet	University of Pennsylvania
Lenville, Jean	University of Richmond
Lenzini, Rebecca	CARL Corporation
Lewis, Linda	University of New Mexico
Lin, Selina	University of Iowa
Lindquist, Janice	Rice University
Loffredo, Bob	Faxon Company
Loghry, Pat	University of Nevada, Reno
Loughner, William	University of Georgia
Lowe, Chrysanne	Academic Press
Lucas, Ann	Thomas Cooley Law School Library
Lucas, John	University of Mississippi Medical Center
Lunde, Diane	Colorado State University
Lupone, George	Cleveland State University
Luther, Judy	Market Development Services
MacArthur, Marit	University of Colorado Auraria Library
MacArthur, Susan	Bates College
MacLennan, Birdie	University of Vermont

MacWithey, Mary	Prairie View A&M University
Madison, Susan	UnCover Company
Maher, Diane	University of San Diego
Majors, Mary Ellen	University of North Carolina at Pembroke
Malinowski, Teresa	California State University, Fullerton
Mallett, Bobbie	University of Maryland
Malone, Debbie	Ursinus College
Mann, Marjorie	WLN
Mantor-Ramirez, Cathy	University of Texas at Austin
Manzella, Paula Lynch	Thomas Jefferson University
Marill, Jennifer	Washington Research Library Consortium
Markley, Susan	Villanova University
Markwith, Michael	Swets & Zeitlinger, Inc.
Marsh, Corrie	Gale Research Inc.
Martinez, Dolores	University of Wyoming
Martinez, Joanne	University of Arizona
Matthews, Priscilla	Illinois State University
Matthews, Pam	Gettysburg College
Matthews, Karen	Emporia State University
Maxwell, Kimberly	Massachusetts Institute of Technology
May, Bill	Faxon Company
McCafferty, Pat	Case Western Reserve University
McCaslin, Pam	Faxon Company
McClary, Maryon	University of Alberta
McClure, Wanda	University of Kentucky
McCutcheon, Dianne	National Library of Medicine
McDermand, Bob	San Jose State University
McDonald, Lynn	FLICC/FEDLINK
McDonald, Margaret	University of San Diego Law Library
McDougal, Barbara	US Patent & Trademark Office
McGrath, Kat	University of British Columbia
McGrath, Ellen	State University of New York at Buffalo Law Library
McHugh, Terri	Elsevier Science, Inc
McHugo, Ann	Dartmouth College
McKay, Sharon Cline	Blackwell's Information Services
McKee, Amy	University of North Carolina at Greensboro
McKee, Anne	Blackwell's Information Services

McKinney, Janet	University of Missouri, Kansas City Law Library
McLean, Carrie	North Carolina Central University
McNair, Alison	Dalhousie University
McNair, Richard	Canadian Armed Forces
McReynolds, Rosalee	Loyola University–New Orleans
McShane, Kevin	National Library of Medicine
Melnychuk, Dianne	Cedar Crest College
Meneely, Kathleen	Cleveland Health Sciences Library
Menzel, Johannes	Academic Press
Mering, Meg	University of Nebraska–Lincoln
Merriman, Faith	Central Connecticut State University
Metz, Karen	University of Colorado Health Sciences Center
Middeldorp-Crispijn, Ineke	Martinus Nijhoff International
Milam, Barbara	Kennesaw State University
Miller, Cindy	Endeavor Information Services
Miller, Heather	State University of New York at Albany
Miller, Jim	University of Maryland
Miller, Judy	Valparaiso University
Mills, Pam	University of Minnesota
Mills, T. F.	University of Denver
Mills, Vicki	University of Arizona
Moles, Jean Ann	University of Arkansas for Medical Sciences
Moody, Marilyn	State University of New York at Buffalo
Moore, Wendy	Furman University
Moran, Sheila	Massachusetts General Hospital
Morse, Carol	Walla Walla College
Mouw, James	University of Chicago
Mullins, James	Villanova University
Mullins, Teresa	OCLC
Murden, Steve	Virginia Commonwealth University
Murphy, Lynne F.	McGill University
Murphy, Sean	Fairmont State College
Myers, Mary	International Monetary Fund, Joint Bank-Fund
Nalepa, Laurie	John Carroll University
Neilson, Susan	American University
Nelson, Carol	Ball State University
Nelson, Catherine	University of California, Santa Barbara

Nesto, Mary Ann	Westfield State College
Neufeld, Sue	US Air Force Academy
Neville, Shelley	Ameritech Library Services
Newsome, Nancy	Western Carolina University
Nguyen, Hein	National Library of Medicine
Nichols, Patty	Fort Hays State University
Nolan, Elizabeth	Williams & Wilkins
Norton, Nancy	VTLS, Inc.
Novak, Denise	Carnegie Mellon University
Novak, Linda	Lehigh University
Nowosielski, Maryna	National Library of Canada
Oberg, Steve	University of Chicago
O'Connell, Jennifer	EBSCO Information Services
Ogburn, Joyce	Old Dominion University
O'Leary, Susan	EBSCO Information Services
O'Loughlin, Patricia	Casalini Libri
Olsen, Renate	Regis College
O'Neill, Jill	Institute for Scientific Information
Oparanozie, Teri	Sam Houston State University
Ouderkirk, Jane	Harvard University
Page, Julie	University of California, San Diego
Page, Mary	Rutgers University
Pang, Amy	University of California, Santa Barbara
Paradis, Olga	Baylor University
Parang, Elizabeth	Pepperdine University
Pardue, Beverly	Lawrence Public Library
Pardue, David	University of Kansas
Parker, Laura	Academic Press
Peale, Barbara	New Mexico State University
Perry, Beth	Carson-Newman College
Perry, Sara	CISTI
Persing, Bob	University of Pennsylvania
Phillips, Patricia	University of Texas at El Paso
Pierce, Louise	York College of Pennsylvania
Pitts, Linda	University of Washington
Pollock, Carlene	Waverly, Inc.
Pope, Liz	Community of Science
Powell, Allen	EBSCO Information Services

Powers, Susanna	Tulane University
Prabha, Chandra	OCLC
Pribyl, Althea	Blackwell's Book Services
Pritchard, Eileen	California Polytechnic State University
Qualls, Jane	University of Memphis
Radbourne, Margaret	John Wiley & Sons, Ltd.
Rafter, William	West Virginia University
Rake, Nancy	University of Kansas
Raley, Sarah	EBSCO Information Services
Ralston, Joan	Villanova University
Ralston, Rick	Indiana University
Randall, Kevin	Northwestern University
Randall, Mike	University of California, Los Angeles
Rankin, Juliann	California State University, Chico
Ray, Tom	Library of Virginia
Reich, Vicky	HighWire Press
Reinalda, Roy	Faxon Company
Renfro, Illene	University of New Mexico
Reynolds, Regina	Library of Congress
Rieley, Sarah	Wellesley College
Riley, Cheryl	Central Missouri State University
Rioux, Maggie	MBL/WHOI Library
Risser, Irene	Millersville University of Pennsylvania
Roach, Dani	Macalester College
Robischon, Rose	United States Military Academy
Rodgers, David	Baylor University
Rodriguez, Adolfo	Universidad Nacional Autónoma de México
Rogers, Marilyn	University of Arkansas
Rose, Jim	Blackwell's Information Services
Rosenberg, Frieda	University of North Carolina at Chapel Hill
Rossignol, Lu	Smithsonian Institution
Roth, Alison	Blackwell's Information Services
Rothaug, Caroline	John Wiley & Sons Inc.
Rowlison, Lisa	Lewis & Clark College
Roy, Virginia	Faxon Canada
Rozum, Betty	Utah State University
Rubenstein, Nancy	Southern Methodist University
Ruelle, Barbara	Emory University

Rumph, Virginia	Butler University
Ruthenberg, Donnell	Data Research Associates, Inc.
Salk, Judy	R. R. Bowker
Sanford, Deborah	Bridgewater State College
Savage, Steve	Wayne State University
Saxe, Minna	City University of New York Graduate School Library
Scherlen, Allan	Applachian State University
Schmitt, Stephanie	Texas Tech University
Schneider, Kit	IPD
Scholl, Miki	Hamline University Law Library
Schreiner, Suzanne	University of Puget Sound
Schroeder, Patricia	Association of American Publishers
Schwartz, Marla	American University Law Library
Schwartzkopf, Becky	Mankato State University
Scott, JoAnne	University of Chicago
Scott, Sharon	Texas Tech School of Law
Sehgal, Gail	University of Wyoming
Seikel, Michele	Stanford University
Semancik, Frank	Faxon Company
Semas, Phil	Chronicle of Higher Education
Sercan, Cecilia	Cornell University
Severt, Lois	University of Louisville
Shaffer, Barbara	University of Toledo
Shannon, John	Schreiber Shannon Assoc.
Shea, Marsha	San Diego State University
Sheffield, Becky	Ball State University
Shelton, Judith	Georgia State University
Shelton, Melinda	Birmingham Public Library
Shipman, Jean	University of Washington, Health Sciences Library
Sibley, Debbie	University of Massachusetts
Sievers, Arlene Moore	Case Western Reserve University
Signori, Donna	University of Victoria
Simmons, Emma	Texas A&M University–Kingsville
Simser, Charlene	Kansas State University
Sinha, Reeta	Emory University Health Science Center Library

Slater, Alex	University of Kansas
Sleeman, Allison	University of Virginia
Sleep, Esther	Brock University
Slough, Marlene	Eastern Illinois University
Smets, Kristine	Johns Hopkins University
Smith, Angel	University of Evansville
Smith, Merrill	EBSCO Information Services
Smith, Patricia	Colorado State University
Smith, Tommy	EBSCO Information Services
Smith-Griffin, Linda	Louisiana State University
Somers, Michael	Kansas State University
Sonberg, Paul	Blackwell's Information Services
Souliere, Sherry	Simmons College
Spence, Duncan	Publishers Services Ltd.
Spina, Marie	New York University
Sprague, Nancy	University of Colorado at Boulder
Springer, Fran	American Graduation School of International Management
St. Germain, Joan	NOAA/NIST Library
Stamison, Christine	Blackwell's Information Services
Steele, Patrick	Cuyahoga County Public Library
Steely, Jeff	Baylor University
Stephens, Joan	Georgia State University
Stern, David	Yale University
Stewart, Wendy	Portland State University
Stickman, Jim	University of Washington
Stokes, Charity	University of Nebraska–Lincoln
Stone, Evalyn	Metropolitan Museum of Art
Su, Julie	Virginia Henderson International Nursing Library
Sullenger, Paula	Auburn University
Sullivan, Kathy	Winona State University
Sullivan, Sherry	Swets & Zeitlinger, Inc.
Sutherland, Laurie	University of Washington
Sweet, Kathy	Phoenix College Library
Taffurelli, Virginia	State University of New York at Brooklyn
Tagler, John	Elsevier Science
Taxman, Jennifer	Skidmore College

Teaster, Gale	Winthrop University
Temos, Rodney	American Chemical Society
Templeton, Carol	University of California, Santa Barbara
Tenney, Joyce	University of Maryland, Baltimore County
Terry, Stan	EBSCO Information Services
Terry, William	NetPubs International
Tetro, Cathleen	Westview Press
Thompson, Elizabeth	Swets & Zeitlinger, Inc.
Thornton, Chris	Case Western Reserve University
Thorrat, Lori	University of Rochester
Tian, Jie	California State University, Fullerton
Todd, Cindy	University of Maryland
Tolenano, Kathryn	MCB University Press
Tong, Dieu Van	University of Alabama at Birmingham
Tonkery, Dan	Faxon Company
Toren, Beth Jane	West Virginia University
Toussaint, Jo Ann	University of St. Thomas
Treff-Gangler, Louise	University of Colorado Auraria Library
Tumlin, Markel	University of San Diego
Turitz, Mitch	San Francisco State University
Turkel, Susan	Bryn Mawr College
Turner, Laura	University of Texas at Austin
Tusa, Sarah	Lamar University
Tuttle, Marcia	University of North Carolina at Chapel Hill
Tytko, Debbie	University of Waterloo
Uppgard, Jeannine	University of Connecticut School of Law Library
Urdahl, Alicia	UnCover Company
Valino, Nenita	Anne Arundel Community College
Van Auken, Gayle	Linda Hall Library
Vent, Marilyn	University of Nevada, Las Vegas
Vernon, Carol Ann	University of Kansas
Villiere, Lisa	University of Denver
Vockel, Barbara	Michigan Technological University
Vukas, Rachel	EBSCO Information Services
Waite, Carolyn	Tufts Health Science Library
Waite-Franzen, Ellen	University of Richmond

Walker, Dana	Harvard University
Wallace, Pat	University of Colorado at Boulder
Wallas, Philip	EBSCO Publishing
Walsh, Terry	Faxon Company
Walter, Mark	Seybold Publications
Waltner, Robb	University of Colorado at Denver
Wang, Margaret	University of Delaware
Ward, Colleen	Oklahoma City University
Watson, Virginia	Brigham Young University
Watts, Dee	Sage Publications, Inc.
Weaver, Christine	Swets & Zeitlinger, Inc.
Weigel, Friedemann	Harrassowitz
Weintraub, Jennifer	Cornell University
Weislogel, Judy	Elsevier Science
Weiss, Paul	University of New Mexico
Welch, Mary	University of Kentucky
Wendland, Melody	Emporia State University
Wesley, Kathryn	Clemson University
Westall, Sandra	Innovative Interfaces
Weston, Beth	George Washington University
Whipple, Marcia	SPAWAR Systems Center
Whisler, Karen	Eastern Illinois University
Whiting, Peter	Prairie View A&M University
Whitney, Marla	Faxon Company
Whittaker, Martha	Academic Book Center
Wiles-Young, Sharon	Lehigh University
Wilhelme, Judy	University of Michigan
Wilhite, Marjorie	University of Iowa
Wilke, Mary	Center for Research Libraries
Wilkerson, Judith	University of Oklahoma Health Sciences Center
Wilkes, Helen	University of Georgia
Wilkinson, Fran	University of New Mexico
Willey, Kayla	Brigham Young University
Williams, Gerry	Northern Kentucky University
Williams, Mary	Tarleton State University
Williams, Sheryl	University of Nebraska Medical Center
Williams, Sue	University of Colorado at Boulder
Williams-Jackson, Crystal	Saint Louis University

Willis, Barbara	University of Colorado at Boulder
Willmering, Bill	National Library of Medicine
Wilson, Betsy	University of Washington
Wilson, Jenni	Blackwell's Information Services
Wilson, Kit	University of Alberta
Wilson, Margaret	University of Kansas
Winant, Joshua	Yankee Book Peddler
Winchester, David	Washburn University
Winjum, Roberta	University of Hawaii at Monao
Winkler, Jean	Colorado State University
Wishnetsky, Susan	Northwestern University Medical School
Woell, Yvette	Argonne National Laboratory
Woods, Janet	University of Wyoming
Xu, Amanda	Massachusetts Institute of Technology
Yanney, Donna	Georgia College & State University
Young, Naomi Kietzke	Southern Methodist University
Zappen, Susan	Skidmore College
Zhang, Yvonne	California State Polytechnic University, Pomona
Zhou, Yan	Columbia University
Zilper, Nadia	University of North Carolina at Chapel Hill
Zuidema, Karen	University of Illinois Chicago
Zupko, Laura	Chicago Public Library
Zuriff, Sue	University of Minnesota

Index